265
POW

THE
EUCHARISTIC
MYSTERY

THE EUCHARISTIC MYSTERY

Revitalizing the Tradition

DAVID N. POWER, O.M.I.

CROSSROAD • NEW YORK

1992

The Crossroad Publishing Company
370 Lexington Avenue, New York, NY 10017

Printed in the United States of America

Library of Congress Cataloging-in-Publication Data

Power, David Noel.
    The eucharistic ministry : revitalizing the tradition / David N.
Power.
        p. cm.
    Includes bibliographical references.
    ISBN 0-8245-1220-0
    1. Lord's Supper—Catholic Church. 2. Mass. 3. Catholic Church—
Doctrines. 4. Catholic Church—Liturgy. 5. Lord's Supper—
Catholic Church—History 6. Mass—History. Catholic Church—
Doctrines—History. I. Title
BX2230.5.P69 1992
234'.163—dc20   92-29777
                                                                          CIP

Contents

PREFACE

The memorial of Christ's death and resurrection is today celebrated amid the ruins. There are first the ruins of a Catholic piety that for four centuries seemed to hold eucharistic devotion at the center of church life. When faulted for its inadequate basis in scriptural origins and early church tradition, it seemed to fall asunder. It remains in ruins, whatever nostalgic efforts are at times made to recapture it. Though liturgical rites have been reformed and there is a much greater confluence at the communion table than had been the case for centuries, no coherent ritual edifice has taken the place of the old piety or of the doctrinal explanation that supported it. Elements of the old still vie uneasily with the new, and congregations compete with each other in the effort to forge a public symbol that brings persons together in one faith and one hope. Charity and affection are not enough to keep unity and communion.

The collapse of late medieval and post-Tridentine piety was bound to occur, even had the Second Vatican Council not been convened. It collapsed along with the nineteenth-century Catholicism that had attempted to protect people against modernity and the rise of a post-Christian society. It was necessary for it to give way to a faith and a ritual that would enable people to find their communion in Christ within the commerce of the world, whether in dialogue with it or in the endeavor to keep alive a counterwitness. To remain functional a public symbol of this sort needs much liturgical change and a theology and catechesis that go with it.

The ruins of the ecclesiastical edifice are found amid the ruins of an idyllic age of civilization marked by the conviction of progress in things human. Ironically, when the Christian churches became alert to modernity this latter was itself at the point of collapse. The coherence of states and societies within themselves began to dissolve as people contended over the values that must prevail for the human good. The coherence of a world order collapses as political, cultural, and economic empires crumble and the interaction between populaces is endangered. Horrific and inhuman events, such as the Nazi attempt to exterminate the Jewish people or Pol Pot's slaughter of millions in Cambodia, or the capacity of a bomb to destroy the Japanese cities of Hiroshima and Nagasaki, or the political exploitation of peoples reduced to famine have drawn attention to the sufferings imposed by ideological conquests and by the extreme employment of the tools of progress.

In themselves, these are gruesome realities. When recorded, they are heard as tales that tell of the collapse of the human in the midst of advancement. In remembering them, we attempt vainly to count the victims and at the same time give them some face and a name. On Flanders fields, in the keeping of extermination camps as places of pilgrimage, in the memorial to the dead of the Vietnam war, visitors face absurd death and the absurdity of the aspirations that cause it.

A contemporary history is impossible without the history of victims. The histories of conquest and achievement have collapsed with the order of things to which they aspired. Humanity needs a whole new way to speak of itself in the memory of suffering, even at a time when it often hides the suffering, the dying, and the dead from view.

The Eucharist makes the church. It makes it as God's covenant people. It makes it in the memory of Christ's suffering, into which the memory of all human suffering is to be gathered. It makes it as a witness, in the midst of the collapse of the human, to God's fidelity and love. Paradoxically, the sacrament can take on new shape as a coherent church action to the extent that eucharistic memorial is alert to the human, to the ruins in the midst of which it is celebrated, to the victims of human history and the sufferings that show forth when the edifice of the human collapses.

Does tradition still have the power to allow such a celebration of Christ's pasch and God's advent in Christ? Such is the faltering question of this book. To answer it requires a careful examination of tradition, with due attention to the relation of ritual and thought to culture and society. Conversation with this tradition elicits some orientation for our own time.

To do the study as well as possible, with proper attention to prayer, practice, and thought, not every period of history is given the same attention. It is better to probe some chosen periods more fully than others. The method of inquiry proposed stands out more clearly than would be possible in an effort to attend equally to every particular age and tradition. At the same time, enough attention is given by way of survey to the full extent of tradition to allow the work to serve as an introduction to the range of eucharistic thought across the centuries and to its appropriation within present-day circumstances. In the final chapter, the work risks some suggestions for a practical agenda. They will be no doubt much criticized. That is in a way their point. They are a reminder that together communities and churches must pass from reflection to practice, but that this has to be done in a communion of hope, with a faith bred by attention to tradition and to humanity's suffering, and with a ready self-criticism.

I would like to acknowledge assistance from several persons in writing the book. At an early stage of the work, the response of William Loewe was very helpful in guiding me to chart a course. Donald Dietz assisted me with important insights into the theology of Thomas Aquinas. Michael Downey, Richard Fragomeni, David Dawson, Luis Tagle, and William Antonio read all or part of the manuscript at various stages of its production, asked helpful questions, and made helpful suggestions. William also helped me to correct the proofs and to prepare the index. The faculty of the Oblate School of Theology in San Antonio gave me homely hospitality for part of a term while I was at work on the text. Frank Oveis of Crossroad maintained an interest in the task throughout, despite its slow progress. To all of these persons, my gratitude.

ACKNOWLEDGMENTS

Acknowledgment is hereby made to the following publishers:

to Alba House Publishers for excerpts from *The Paschal Mystery*, edited by Adalbert Hamman and Thomas Halton (copyright by the Society of St. Paul);

to Augsburg Fortress Publishers for excerpts from *The Supper of the Lord*, by John Reumann, and from *Condemnations of the Reformation Era: Do They Still Hold?* edited by Wolfhart Pannenberg and Karl Lehmann;

to The Liturgical Press for excerpts from *Prayers of the Eucharist: Early and Reformed*, by R. C. D. Jasper and G. J. Cuming, *Eucharist*, edited by Daniel Sheerin, and *Eucharistic Prayers of the Roman Rite*, by Enrico Mazza;

to *The Pastoral Press* for the quotation from Mary Collins in *Women in the Church*;

to Paulist Press for excerpts from *Sharing the Eucharistic Bread*, by Xavier Léon-Dufour (copyright by the Missionary Society of St. Paul), and *Francis and Clare: The Complete Works* (copyright by Colm Luibheid);

to Princeton University Press for excerpts from Erwin Panofsky, *Abbot Suger on the Abbey Church of Saint-Denis;*

to the University of Notre Dame Press for excerpts from *The Eucharist: Theology and Spirituality of the Eucharistic Prayer*, by Louis Bouyer, and *The Ancrene Riwle*, rendered in modern English by M. Salu;

to Westminster/John Knox Press for excerpts from *New Testament Apocrypha*, edited by W. Schneemelcher and R. Wilson.

ABBREVIATIONS

CCSL	Corpus christianorum, series latina
CSEL	Corpus scriptorum ecclesiasticorum latinorum
DS	Denziger-Schönmetzer, *Enchiridion symbolorum*
PG	J. Migne, *Patrologia graeca*
PL	J. Migne, *Patrologia latina*

Part I

STATING THE QUESTION

Chapter 1

THE EUCHARIST TODAY: PROBLEMS IN A POSTMODERN WORLD

The manner of celebrating the Eucharist has changed so much in recent years that it is necessary to reconsider the ways in which the church understands and receives its eucharistic tradition. Many studies have been done on various parts of the tradition, but what is needed is a systematic reflection that is attuned to the present situation and opens up fresh possibilities for eucharistic celebration.

The manual for a computer program opens with a section on "Getting Started." This chapter is about getting started in doing eucharistic theology today. It opens with some specific examples that raise questions and moves on to describe the situation that needs to be addressed. Then it sets the program for reviewing and appropriating the data of tradition in ensuing chapters.

EXEMPLIFYING THE ISSUES

A few years ago, the Congregation for Worship of the Roman Curia approved a text of the Mass for use in the dioceses of Zaire.[1] A eucharistic liturgy adapted to the people's culture had been worked out over a number of years under the jurisdiction of the episcopal conference of that country. Commonly referred to as "le rite Zairois," it had in time been proposed to Rome for approval. Roman authorities approved the text with some modifications but could not bring themselves to allow an African liturgy outside the confines of the Roman rite. Hence they insisted that the approved text should bear the title of "Roman Missal

---

1. For the text, see Congregatio pro Cultu Divino, "Le Missel Romain pour les diocèses du Zaire," *Notitiae* 24 (1988): 455–72.

for Use in the Dioceses of Zaire." This bypassed the fact that the rite was not merely a matter of fresh texts and ritual actions, but resulted from a conscious effort to find an African model of assembly. One of the more notable innovations in the liturgy is the remembrance of ancestors. Exemplifying the problem in accepting elements from non-European cultures, the congregation asked that this commemoration be in some way accommodated to the Roman canon's remembrance of personages from the Old Testament. This in fact seems to do justice neither to the relation of Old Testament history to Christian faith nor to the relation of African peoples to the ancestors whom they venerate.

This example of problems attendant on liturgical development in Zaire illustrates much about eucharistic practice at the end of this millennium. Specifically, it shows how difficult it is to sponsor "an organic development" of liturgical forms and texts, as suggested by the Constitution on the Liturgy of the Second Vatican Council.[2] How do the demands of the living context relate to the attention that needs to be given to tradition? How much must new liturgies be kept within the boundaries of ancient liturgical families? In particular, is it right that churches founded from churches of the Roman rite be kept within that rite, despite vast cultural differences?

In practice, it is a living church, not desk work, that generates new forms of liturgical celebration, be these later considered as liturgical renewal or as deviations from authentic tradition. The history of the Roman rite itself illustrates the difficulty found in wedding cultural adaptation with respect for traditional forms. The *libelli,* or booklets, gathered together in the collection entitled the *Verona* or *Leonine Sacramentary* provide texts that belong for the most part to the Roman liturgy of the fifth and sixth centuries.[3] Looking back on these prayers, authors speak of the genius of the Roman rite, remarking on how well the texts reflect the culture and ecclesial sense appropriate to persons living in the city of Rome, conscious of its cultural inheritance and of the need to withstand barbarian intrusions.

In the Carolingian epoch, the same rite, at a somewhat later stage of development, was adapted to the temperament of the barbarian populace of the northern land mass. In this adaptation, new prayers and

---

2. Second Vatican Council, *Constitution on the Sacred Liturgy,* no. 23: "There must be no innovations unless the good of the church genuinely and certainly requires them, and care must be taken that any new forms adopted should in some way grow organically from forms already existing." The English translation is taken from *Vatican Council II: The Conciliar and Post Conciliar Documents,* edited by Austin Flannery (New York: Costello Publishing Company, 1977), 10. This norm is complemented by those for adapting the liturgy to the temperament and traditions of peoples, nos. 37–40.

3. On the nature and provenance of this book, see Cyrille Vogel, *Medieval Liturgy: An Introduction to the Sources,* translated and revised by William G. Storey and Niels Krogh Rasmussen (Washington, D.C.: Pastoral Press, 1986), 38–46.

rites were allowed to express the more exuberant temperament of non-Roman cultures. Though many different liturgical books resulted from the adaptation, they all have an affinity to each other in ritual structure and in style.[4]

The unification of the liturgy for the entire empire met certain political and cultural purposes, but two historical factors raise questions about its success as an organic cultural development. On the one hand, scholars are wont to refer to the new stress on exorcisms, consecrations, blessings, anointings, sacred objects, multiplication of prayers, and the like, as *accretions* to the Roman rite. This hardly suggests a successful organic development.

On the other hand, there is the fact of the growing estrangement of the people, who had to resort to nonliturgical forms of devotion. The attempt to adapt to the culture by these so-called accretions was not in fact efficacious in fostering participation or in generating an organically coherent liturgy. The retention of the Latin language during a period when vernacular languages were developing made liturgy increasingly the work of clerics and monks. While Latin continued to be used in liturgy, other forms of religious devotion were formulated in vernacular languages, so that there was no integration of the two. It was as much cultural conservatism as religious principle that caused the retention of Latin, but it did contribute to the sense of awe surrounding priestly activity.[5]

In recent years the use of spoken languages in celebration has been an impetus to larger change, even while causing problems in finding an appropriate idiom for worship. Once people began to use traditional texts in rather wooden vernacular translations, they sensed how unsuited they were. With the effort to write new texts, new questions arise about liturgical posture, ritual act, visual representation, and forms of chant. How the new relates to traditional forms, while still being culturally appropriate, is an issue not readily resolved. The cultural issues that come to sharp relief in a country like Zaire are seen to have their place in all churches, including those of a Eurocentric culture.

These examples illustrate what is asked of a theology that is intended to serve celebration. It has to address the issue of developing creative forms of worship that are both genuinely new cultural creations and in continuity with an ancient tradition. It has to be able to address the

---

4. See ibid., 61–102.

5. On the vicissitudes of language evolution in relation to religious life, see, for example, Michael Richter, "Latina lingua — sacra seu vulgaris?" in *The Bible and Medieval Culture*, edited by W. Lourdaux and D. Verhelst (Leuven: Leuven University Press, 1979), 16–34. On the cultural impact of both Latin and emerging vernacular languages, see the survey with bibliography in B. B. Price, *Medieval Thought: An Introduction* (Oxford and Cambridge, Mass.: Blackwell, 1992), 93–118.

need for organic development within a living church. To use a somewhat current phrase, it has to exemplify the genuine nature of the day's
conversation with tradition. In the act of tradition or handing on, what
counts is not just the content of past teaching or knowledge of ancient
forms. The ways in which these are now received, and in the process
interpreted, demand attention.

Before proceeding further therefore, a word needs to be said about
the present situation of eucharistic worship and about a way of analyzing the elements that constitute the tradition of worship.

WHERE WE NOW STAND

Diversity in Celebration

There is at present a great diversity in the way in which communities
celebrate the Eucharist, a diversity that is related to cultural change.
Culture is a system of symbols, rites, images, beliefs, values, ideas, and
ethical norms that a people holds in common and that gives a populace a way of living in the world. Ideally, it expresses a coherent and
public way in which its adherents, individually and collectively, can appropriate things, events and relationships, so that the world in which
they live retains its coherence and unity. At critical moments of history,
events and the emergence of new data disturb this coherence and people begin to look for ways in which to reconstruct their cultural outlook
and world-view. Not everyone moves at the same pace, and different
persons and different groups integrate the old and the new in different ways. From this there results a certain cultural dissonance. Nowhere
does this show more powerfully than in attitudes to traditional rituals
and on public occasions requiring ritual celebration.

As we well know, in the Eurocentric world today the very notion of a
common culture is in flux. Different cultures are coming together within
nations and on continents, so that cultural patterns in effect express a
certain pluralism in outlook and value, a pluralism within which not all
live with the same ease. As we also well know, the need for a religious
referent in cultural ideals that in the past was often taken for granted is
put to question. Among those who continue to profess religious belief, it
is related to the newly emerging culture in different ways, with greater
or less openness to pluralism. Those of a Christian faith, or even those
within the same church, experience some dissonance among themselves
in cultural and religious perspective.

It is not in the least surprising, given the central place accorded
the Eucharist in Christian ritual and in Christian life, that in this situation of cultural flux churches now experience a ritual dissonance and

a ritual pluriformity in its celebration that renders its role as a center of unity problematic.[6] There is a range of divergent celebrations going from the retrieval of the Latin Mass to feminist liturgies, from large-scale papal rites to small-group gatherings that foster a more ready face-to-face interaction among the participants, from highly stylized ceremonial to services that within a certain structure allow for more ready improvisation.

It is to this situation that theological research and inquiry is addressed. None of the elements in the situation can be neglected, none of the ritually expressed aspirations rejected out of hand as inappropriate or inauthentic. The question whether the process of liturgical change ought to be called accommodation, adaptation, inculturation, or even fresh incarnation, most often raised in regard to the cultures of the African and Asian continents, appears to have pertinence for older Christianities as well.[7]

The proliferation of types of assembly and of types of liturgy is an expression of the decentering of church life. The result of this can be either an end of communion, a church more splintered than through any previous historical schism, or a pluricentric communion of one church. At present, along with such symbols as the power of the papacy and the power of hierarchy, the place of the Eucharist as a public symbol of unity is dysfunctional. Public symbols inasmuch as they are public need to command a common response. When they are interpreted in opposing ways, command divergent responses, or promote contrasting ethical positions, they no longer serve the purpose of common bonding. All of those who take part in a Eucharist may do so in faith and piety, but if they hold to very different ideas about its meaning and its relation to the church its celebration divides rather than unites. This comes out very clearly in the ways in which celebrations clash with each other.

Looking to the Eucharist as a public symbol does not of course in and of itself offer a eucharistic theology. It simply turns attention to one of the roles that it plays in Christian life and allows us to ask in what ways its celebration either impedes or fosters a sense of communion and common Christian identity.

While it has fulfilled this role in the past, it has in fact been celebrated in a diversity of ways in different periods of history. It has been

---

6. For descriptions of different types of eucharistic gatherings in the postconciliar church, see Gerard Defois, "Typologie du rassemblement chrétien aujourd'hui," in *Sacrements de Jésus Christ*, edited by Joseph Doré (Paris: Desclée, 1983), 161–82; Henri Denis, "La communauté eucharistique aujourd'hui," *La Maison-Dieu* 141 (1980): 37–67.

7. For a recent discussion of cultural issues as they affect liturgical renewal, see Anscar Chupungco, "A Definition of Liturgical Inculturation," *Ecclesia Orans* 5 (1988): 11–23. See also the same author's books, *Liturgies of the Future: The Process and Methods of Inculturation* (New York: Paulist Press, 1989), and *Liturgical Inculturation: Sacramentals, Religiosity, and Catechesis* (Collegeville, Minn.: Liturgical Press, 1992).

celebrated with great care for the proclamation of the word, as it has been celebrated with a purely ritual reading of the scriptural texts. It has been celebrated as the action of an active assembled community, as it has been celebrated as a priest-centered offering, with the attention of the faithful focused on this. The texts in sacramentaries and lectionaries and missals often appear the same across a period of time, with but minor modifications. The ritual setting and performance however meant that they did not always have the same resonance in the life of the congregation or church. While the Eucharist functioned as a public symbol, what it expressed about communion with and in Christ and about church identity differed from one situation to another, or from one epoch to another. It is important to grasp the meaning and significance of this diversity in the way that we now read tradition, faced as we are with a new cultural challenge, in a much more culturally pluralistic world.

In addition, it is helpful to note that one does not understand how Christian faith has been and is expressed through the sacrament of the Eucharist by simply analyzing its liturgical celebration through the ages and in the present. Any manual of liturgical history finds it necessary to include accounts of the devotional practices that were part of Christian life but do not fit strict definitions of liturgy.[8] Such are self-ministered communion of the faithful in their homes, the reservation of the sacrament in private or public places, either for communion to the sick or for purposes of adoration, exposition and procession of the Blessed Sacrament, and the prayer texts offered to the people for private recitation during Mass. At first some of these devotions give the impression that they run counter to the liturgy or that they are very personal or private. Nonetheless, they belong to the ways in which the Eucharist has acted as a public symbol and as a central point of Christian identity and belief.

In all the different modes of celebration noted in postconciliar years, communities want to give the sacrament a public role and to find in it a core expression of what it means to be a Christian in today's cultural settings. There is a deep-seated persuasion that it is the faith-community's central confession of faith and the key moment of the presence of Christ and of the Spirit in the church. What have broken down are its links with other public symbols, its relationship to the supposed given of church structure, and its power to offer an overarching vision of the world.

---

8. The most complete and up-to-date history is Hans Bernhard Meyer, *Eucharistie: Geschichte, Theologie, Pastoral*, vol. 4 of *Gottesdienst der Kirche: Handbuch der Liturgiewissenschaft* (Regensburg: Pustet, 1989). See also the variety of articles indexed under "Eucharist" in *The New Dictionary of Sacramental Worship*, edited by Peter E. Fink (Collegeville, Minn.: Liturgical Press, 1992), 1340.

The Modern World in Dissolution

That is the Eucharist's position within the church, but its position has much to do with the problems affecting culture in society as a whole. Though it kept in place a strong hierarchical principle, in some respects the Second Vatican Council showed a belated and incomplete attention to the concerns of the modern world.[9] The liturgical renewal which it espoused and reinvigorated, and for which it set theological and canonical norms, absorbed the much-discussed attention to the human person that is noted in modern philosophies. In asking for the active, comprehending, and conscious participation of assemblies, it accepted modern ideals of intersubjective action and communication, as well as a rather rational confidence that it would be possible to engender rites and symbols comprehensible to all. It was also in some of its actions privy to the modern world's overwhelming trust in historical evolution and its hope for a better humanity, a trust almost amounting to a myth of progress.

Little attention was given in the reform of liturgical books to the disillusionment that many had begun to feel with the world that emerged from recent centuries. Liturgical reforms failed to note trends already at work among the faithful who saw the disintegration of the social and ecological fabric attendant on the failures of the age to live up to its humanistic ideals. To be alert to this disintegration does not in fact require the deep analysis, necessary for a fuller understanding.

In the 1960s one might have expected that church leaders would have attended to what the Holocaust of the Jewish people had done to a modern sense of the human subject and of human history. True, there was some attempt to establish a foundation for better relations between Jews and Christians, but what this wanton destruction meant for humanity and for Christian faith was not explored very deeply. Indeed, where does the fate of the Jewish people get attention in liturgy, even today? Other factors that have been inadequately considered in liturgical reform are impending ecological travail, the emerging role of women in society, and ethnic and cultural pluralism in civic societies and in churches.

It is first and foremost the tragic events of our era that put their questions to what Eucharist confesses and celebrates. When Christians proclaim the hope of resurrection, new creation, and light in the very proclamation of Christ's death, what does this say to massive and meaningless death, not only of individuals but of peoples and cultures? Putting the question conversely, what does senseless suffering

---

9. The concepts of modern and postmodern are hard to define and to date, since they are quite disputed. However, the modern is more particularly associated with the interest in the human subject of the eighteenth and nineteenth centuries, and the confidence in its power to know itself and control its universe.

and death do to the images of pasch furbished by eucharistic traditions? Proclaiming in Christ redemption from evil and death, the memory of victims cannot be left out of the picture.

In the wake of disillusionment, it has become common to talk of living in a postmodern world. There are many descriptions of what is referred to as postmodernity, and like any cultural phenomenon it is a milieu in which people live without always being able to analyze its components. Some of its aspects may however be pertinently named. To begin with, it is a marked and nagging disillusionment with what the Eurocentered world thought it had achieved in the wake of the Enlightenment. Despite the great attention given in modern times to the human subject, it is being slowly realized that modern society has not achieved a deep understanding of the human person or of the social order. Its technological advances have not brought progress and prosperity to the world, and indeed have caused much environmental damage. History has escaped the control of reason and is broken apart by the appalling advent of evil, the Holocaust in particular disrupting all myths either of human progress or of divine providence. There is then no comprehensive myth by which people can live today, either of human progress or of sacral pervasiveness. Neither is there a philosophy that succeeds in offering a coherent explanation of the whole of human reality.

Some respond to this situation by confessional fundamentalism, but this is hardly a formula for survival or for evangelization, and least of all for hope. Others react with a complete disavowal of the accomplishments of recent centuries, but this puts at risk some of the modern world's genuine achievements.

Philosophers and students of human thought and culture probe the roots of the present cultural situation with their critique of what they call the modern and the premodern. The battle is waged over whether we ought to keep alive the metaphysical tradition of Western thought, or discard it as the ultimate cause of the deviations of the modern world. Much of the critique of a philosophical and cultural tradition is accounted for under the name of deconstructionism. At times those classed as deconstructionists, whether they admit the term or not, are accused of dilettantism and obscurantism, and of course every movement has its excesses. The importance of the critique, however, cannot be ignored. It has implications for theology and its reading of tradition, with definite consequences for the church's eucharistic confession and celebration of faith.

To begin with, the critique questions the capacity of modern philosophy and psychology to understand the human self and the world. The modern mind developed considerable confidence in its power to represent reality, allowing a ready access to knowledge of the self, to a knowledge of past reality, and to a vision of the world. Any form of representation however, be it imaginary, visual, literary, conceptual, or even juridical, is but a projection and an interpretation, not a form of immediacy to the reality represented. To have access either to human consciousness or to a knowledge of the past, one must take the long detour of reflecting on a plurality of interpretations. In interpreting a tradition, wherever a people or an authority is tied inexorably to one meaning, there is a suppression of others that deserve to be heard.

In conjunction with this critique, there is a new attention to the way in which language itself is held captive to certain standard usages, ideals, and ideologies. In secular studies, there has been the attempt among structuralists of different sorts to work out the clear rules of language and ritual use, so that a knowledge of the language or ritual system is a key to all possible meanings. In the religious arena, there is the claim of authorities to be able to formulate truths in terms that have held firm for centuries. What is fundamentally questioned in all of this by the postmodern critique is the assumed relation between thought and language, in which clear priority is given to thought. Western philosophies, both ancient and modern, appear to share the persuasion that thought has priority over language, or that language's function is to express clear meanings. This leads in many cases to a resultant instrumentalization of language, where it is made to serve clearly defined purposes.

In writings of what is called the postmodern critique, more is made of the awareness of the poetic, of the play of language in search for meaning. A certain way of using language, of using a play of words and forms, is in fact a way of opening up perception, of offering fresh possibilities of meaning not yet thought. There are more possibilities of meaning in a text, in a symbol, or in a ritual than have in fact as yet emerged. There is a sense in which it has to be said that language speaks to us more than we speak it.

There are some important negative implications in this critique of the instrumentalization of language. One is to note that where there are official or prevailing interpretations of a past tradition, of a text, or of a rite, other possible interpretations, perhaps allowed by the text or the rite, have been suppressed. Such interpretations have voices, potential interpretations. The reading of tradition looks for ways therefore of retrieving those voices, of allowing them to speak, as it looks to texts and practices that belonged to social and cultural minorities.

The desire to hear these voices goes hand in hand with a critique of power and its uses, and indeed of the illusions of the role of power in ordering church or society and in interpreting tradition. This means not only juridical power or political power, but also such power as the power of intellectuals and the power of movements, whether elitist or popular. If all persons are to be allowed to participate more fully in social and cultural life, better ways of intersubjective action that allow for a more broadly based part in interpretation and the choice of expression have to be discovered.

Furthermore, in attending to the postmodern we have to be alert to the way in which the use of language and the use of power affect the understanding of history. When language is engaged to express clear thoughts and power is used to control order, history can be given the appearance of a well-ordered progression. The meaning and succession of events and epochs are thought to be subject to some prevailing and intelligible order. This may be seen as intrinsic to nature, or the result of human invention, or as due to divine providence. Such a sense of order is not verified by the data. In fact, the past is always represented to us in its interpretations or in what remains of its artifacts. Rather than capturing the sense of all of this in one ordered whole, we are faced with a plurality of interpretations and meanings, or at times with incomprehensibility. Postmodern critique asks us to be attentive to the discontinuities of history, to its lack of logic and comprehensible pattern. It invites us to refrain from imposing preconceived notions of order on events, or from forcing what cannot be explained into some ideal explanation.

As this postmodern critique affects eucharistic theology, basic questions have to do with the use of the notion of causality in sacramental theology, the models of representation employed, the role afforded language in celebration, and the exercise of power, both within sacramental usage and in defining its meaning.[10] Though it has served well in recent ecumenical dialogue, even the image of memorial as representation of a past event is affected by a critique of our understanding of the historical.

Openness to tragedy and critique does not mean discarding all that is still to be learned from metaphysical tradition and from modernity, but it invites us to attend to them in a critical way. From metaphysical tradition, the contemporary world needs to keep alive the questions of the deep structures of human being in time and in the world, and of its relation to the transcendent. While, in face of critique, more restraint may be demanded in what is said of a prevailing order and in what is said of God, the questions themselves cannot be discarded.

From modernity, this postmodern time needs to keep most of all the respect for the human subject and the effort to allow human persons responsibility for their own lives and participation in the common enterprise. Much of the appreciation of how symbols and traditions affect our lives would not have come about without the gains of the centuries

---

10. In sacramental theology, the most consistent attention to postmodern critique is to be found in Louis-Marie Chauvet, *Symbole et sacrement: Une relecture sacramentelle de l'existence chrétienne* (Paris: Ed. du Cerf, 1988).

after the Enlightenment. While there is a necessary reserve in face of claims to understand the human person, the effort to grasp the desires, rights, cognitional structures, and actions of the individual and collective person cannot be relinquished, even if this requires a difficult and often tentative procedure of interpretation.

This is not to reestablish the claims to permanency of either the medieval or the modern past, but to raise the question of how it is possible to engage in a conversation with the past amid the ruins of a culture and a civilization. The past contains more than has been given classical or canonical status. Whatever the criticisms of the prevailing order of things, there is never indeed a purely new beginning. It may well be the retrieval of submerged factors in tradition that can offer unattended possibilities for the present.

In attempting to go beyond the limitations and failures of modernity, without retreating to the classical order of the premodern, religious faith has to undertake several tasks in order to become a viable force. While not discarding the role of doctrine, it recognizes how much interpretation is already involved in its formulation and so returns to its own roots in memory and story. It recognizes the plurality of traditions within its own history and develops a new interest in traditions and voices that have been marginal in the past, but that may have more to say to the present. In looking to the centrality of story, symbol, and confession of faith, it attends to the possible distortions in interpretation as well as to the unexplored vitality of other configurations and interpretations. There is thus both a critical and a constructive role to the interpretation of tradition.

CONVERSING WITH EUCHARISTIC TRADITION

In light of the foregoing, what can be said about reading eucharistic tradition in a way that speaks to the present emergency? Since the Eucharist is of its nature a confession of faith and belongs within a faith tradition, it is always celebrated and understood in reference to the event of Christ's death and the witness to that death that comes to the church through the Gospels. It is integral to that faith that the Eucharist, or Lord's Supper, is essential to the mediation of Christ's death and that it belongs to the origins and foundation of the church as a communion of faith in Christ. There is therefore a common referent amid the diversity of eucharistic traditions, interpretations, and appropriations.

This common referent is in fact threefold. In the first place, every age looks back to the starting-point, which is the New Testament narrative of the Last Supper. Though this is already a diversified account, it is the witness given to the church of all ages about the origins of the

Lord's Supper, or Eucharist, and about its central role in the church's communion in the death and resurrection of Christ. A further point of reference is the celebration or ritual that the early church practiced. Though it can be known only through the gospel narrative, which is already an interpretation of the rite, there is always some concern with this original ritual in the developments of eucharistic tradition. As well as to the gospel narrative and the ritual, there is the reference to the salvific death of Christ, whose meaning is expressed in the Eucharist. In every age, the church takes account of these beginnings and what they mean. On the other hand, this early tradition has been subject to constant interpretation, both theoretical and practical.

With the need for eucharistic renewal in mind, our own time has to find a way for reading or conversing with eucharistic tradition that is attentive to all the factors that constitute a tradition. It has to take account of the interplay between practice on the one hand and thought about the mystery on the other. It also has to look at the cultural influences at work and the questions faced by each generation. The *lex orandi* has no precedence over the *lex credendi,* nor vice versa, but in any age the two intersect in ways that need to be considered.

After some preliminary observations about what is implied in reading texts from the past, four particular factors to which we will attend in eucharistic tradition will be noted. These are: (a) the canon of remembrance; (b) ritual performance; (c) the relation of Eucharist to ethics; (d) the appropriation of thought-forms into the explanation and ordering of the sacrament. More succinctly, the attempt is to see the link between remembrance, ritual enactment, Christian practice, and eucharistic doctrine. It is not possible to divide up chapters under these precise headings, but one needs to keep in mind that it is the elucidation of this relation that constitutes true liturgical theology.

Reading Texts from the Past

Many are the attempts at historical reconstructions of the past and many the histories of liturgy that utilize them. A certain amount is known in this way, both about practice and about influential ideas. We need however to keep in mind that there is no direct access to the past, either to its practice or to its thought. The written word, the cultural masterpiece, the archeological remains of places of worship, the things known to have been used in celebration, are all a stage removed from the historical situation in which they emerged and from the mind or the devotion of their authors. They suggest meanings and attitudes and open up speculative and practical possibilities more readily than they let us know what exactly went on, however good the reconstructions may appear. The interpretation of these possibilities is moreover affected by our own religious and cultural perceptions, as well as by our commitments. In this sense, we are two steps removed from the actual events and ideas of the past. The first removal occurs in writing or setting down in material production. The second occurs in the act of interpreting, which is done from a particular optic, divergent from the optic of the past.

All reading of past traditions is influenced by commitments and by the outlook that such commitments engender. The outlook becomes more conscious and differentiated in the process of reading and interpreting. Those who are conscious of this tend to speak of philosophical and theological, rather than of historical, reconstruction and are more attentive to its implications. In other words, they are aware that the way in which evidence of the past is read is affected by a particular theological interest, or that one may in fact deliberately bring this interest to the reading of tradition.

This being the case, we have to be critical of our own biases and ideologies when we put forward the evidence of tradition. While commitments are brought to interpretation, they can also be clarified or even changed in examining tradition. For example, the commitment to an ideal of love, perhaps expressed in the word *agapē* taken from the New Testament, means that we bring the will to find freedom for all and reconciliation between all to our investigations. At the same time, these investigations serve to make us aware that we do not have a definition of love ready to hand, but that we look for its realization in the midst of bias and prejudice, sometimes learning about the conditions of its free expression from what we see to have been impediments to its exercise.

Like any human body, the church at any given time and in any given place constructs for itself operative models of human and ecclesial reality. These feature in the way in which it regulates its liturgical life, which is always the locus of core and primary symbols. An understanding of the models, insofar as these can be discovered, offers insight into the construction and meaning of the world in which the church and its members live, the stance from which all else is seen, and the part that liturgical action plays in shaping that world. The models adopted are in part an appropriation of what is found in ecclesial sources and traditions, and in part an appropriation of insights offered by human wisdom and philosophy at the time. There is no alternative to this effort to express the gospel in language and rites that come from the interface between gospel and culture. It is the necessary mode in which God is present to a people.

It is from seeing the constant effort to let the gospel find as it were fresh incarnation in a culture, while challenging this culture to faith in Christ's memory, that we are informed and disciplined in a like task. Current models of the world are evoked, challenged, modified in the process of entering into conversation with these past models. At the same time, we endeavor to make out what is necessary to the gospel and what may have been a less fortunate accommodation to culture, not so much for the sake of judging the past as for the sake of being judged and converted ourselves.

The Canon of Remembrance

With these preliminary observations in mind, the first factor or element in tradition that captures our attention is what is dubbed here the canon of remembrance.

The word *canon* is used to refer to what is taken as normative in the celebration of the Eucharist, in order that it be a faithful proclamation and commemoration of Christ's death and resurrection. Normativity is not understood here in a juridical sense. It covers whatever is the constant and accepted mode of celebration in any age, whether determined by church authority or by custom. It has to do with the texts, prayers, and rituals that are considered suitable. It has to do not only with content but also with forms and with the manner in which texts are proclaimed or rituals performed. It extends to include what was not strictly liturgical but gained a large place in church practice, such as processions, various devotions, and commonly used private prayers.

The normative in fact differs from age to age or from church to church. Even such a central element as the eucharistic prayer has varied in both content and form, an emphasis sometimes being given to narrative thanksgiving, sometimes to intercession. Not only does the internal form change, but the manner of proclaiming an identical text may differ considerably, as in the audible or silent recitation of the canon of the Roman Mass.

Other variable elements in the canon of remembrance have to do with the reading of the scriptures, the relation between the action of the people and the action of the presiding minister, the kinds of chant considered suitable or unsuitable, or the form of the bread and wine prescribed. These things cannot be looked upon simply as matters of style for they have profound theological and spiritual implications.

In discussing how we may learn today from the way in which different traditions have formulated a canon of remembrance, some priority is given to the adequacy of language. Since language has been for so long instrumentalized, even in the celebration of the Eucharist, its expressivity and its power to transform reality have to be recovered. This means attention to images, forms of expression, symbols, and metaphors on the one hand, and the violence done to them in their suppression, manipulation, or silencing on the other.

Ritual Performance

The influence on eucharistic development of ritual studies, coming from the fields of anthropology and sociology, has been enormous. These risk being reductionistic if attention is limited to behavioral and social patterning and not extended to how rites express meaning. While to immediate perception ritual is quite simply a formalized repetition of patterned behavior, to understand its origins, its meanings, and its impact on personal and social action is not a simple matter. Any ritual belongs within a complex of conventions, beliefs, symbols, and institutions. It places the participants within a larger world of value and meaning, while presuming to offer them a common identity and bonding. It is prescriptive inasmuch as its patterns are set, however rigidly or loosely.

Rituals of any sort, when they function well, allow participants to find their place in the world that they inhabit and to relate their felt experience to a greater whole. Even in an alien society the ritual group finds a way to secure its own identity by way of contrast with prevailing culture. The history of the Eucharist clearly shows how it functioned in this way for Christians of old. They did, for example, express their place in a pagan society as witnesses to Christ and because of this counteridentity worked out a way of living and of viewing reality that precluded such things as military enlistment, acting in the theater or amphitheater, and taking on some civic duties such as that of a magistrate. This is in marked contrast with a ritual that expressed a close relation between church and society, as well as with the attempts to develop an alternate ritual when this cohesion was challenged. Each of these kinds of ritual performance involved a view of the world and of the world's relation to God.

How boundaries are set by ritual is important to a people's sense of identity. While finding their place in society through ritual enactment, they define the boundaries of their world. Ritual enactment expresses who may be included and who must be excluded from the community and how roles are assigned internally. The relative places of women and men, of ordained and baptized, are expressed in the way in which the place of worship is disposed and in the way in which the rites are performed. Rules about participation are important in setting the relations of the community to other groups and persons in society, since they signify a greater or less openness to relations with others, as they also define the areas of possible interaction with them. In conjunction with this, how other groups are spoken of in ritual is important. Here the example of Christian ways of naming the Jews is of great historical and current moment. After all, when a rite is not shared with others there can be a variety of reasons why this is so.

In learning from the nature of ritual performance in the past, attention has to be given to the use of power and ideology in the internal ordering of communities and in the drawing of boundaries. If this restricts participation or the full inclusion of persons or groups in the act of communion or impedes eucharistic developments that would seem more consonant with the Eucharist's gospel origins, the adequacy of the ritual performance concerned is open to question.

Relation to Ethics

The proclamation of Christ's death and resurrection in the Eucharist is complemented by the living witness of believers and disciples. Even the development of the image of sacrifice in early Christianity testifies to the close relation between the two. As will be seen, the application of this cultic terminology to the Christian life and to the sacrament of the Eucharist develops in a way that shows the two to intersect. Furthermore, excommunication was imposed from the start on account of conduct inappropriate in participants at the Lord's table. In other words, not only deviations in faith but certain kinds of ethical misconduct excluded people from the Lord's table.

The relation between ethics and Eucharist can be looked at from two angles, each approach complementing the other. On the one hand, Eucharist embodies an ethical ideal that Christians are in turn expected to embody in their lives. This is a common homiletic theme, exemplified in Augustine's invitation to neophytes to receive in the body of Christ that which they have become in baptism, or in the Roman Pontifical's admonition to those about to be ordained presbyters to imitate that which they are appointed to celebrate. How the ethical ideal is drawn from the sacrament says much to how the sacrament itself is understood to represent Christ and the church.

On the other hand, the ethics or praxis of a community bespeaks how well it has appropriated what is eucharistically expressed. Thus it may serve to offer a critique of the manner in which the church celebrates and understands what is celebrated in the sacrament. In the course of church history, the intersection of the order of justice and of the order of charity has been envisaged and acted out in different ways. At any given time it is of interest to eucharistic theology to look for a relation between the ethical paradigm relating these two and the approaches taken to the celebration and explanation of the Eucharist.

In asking how Eucharist affects Christian ethics today, and so in asking what is garnered from the conversation with tradition, the praxis option of the reader looms large. In this respect, a concern of our own time has to do with how well past eucharistic practice kept alive the desire for the transcendent and how well it evoked the practice of love. Another important ethical consideration has to do with the inclusion of the socially, personally, and religiously marginalized, and with the ways in which Eucharist fosters the appropriation of suffering into an ethical vision of the world.

Use of Thought-Forms

In adopting the kind of historical approach that allows for the possibility of reconstructing past events, some look to the New Testament and early church history for an ideal celebration and doctrine of the Eucharist. The postconciliar liturgical reform of the texts and rites was somewhat affected by this approach. It was thought, at least in part, that if it were possible to get behind accretions to a pristine form of celebration, it would be possible to restore this to good effect. The kind of historical investigation thus espoused is not without validity, but it must include the perception that from the beginning the proclamation of the gospel and the memorial of Christ in sacrament were affected by a variety of cultural patterns of thought. Thus it is that in more recent study the matter of cultural adaptation throughout the ages has been taken up as a point of historical inquiry. This inquiry cannot be left at a superficial level. It has to consider the influence on the Eucharist of mythical and metaphysical ideas that express fundamental perceptions of reality.

Commemoration is always a key word in eucharistic theology. The forms that it has been given and the ways in which it is interpreted are much influenced by the ideas that people in a culture have of cosmos and history and by how they distinguish between or relate the order of creation, the general flow of human history, and the history of salvation. Both the contemporary situation and the retrieval of the notion of sacramental memorial ask for keener attention to how understandings of history affect Eucharist.

With regard to the thought patterns used to explain the Eucharist, it is particularly important to note how they influence notions and forms of representation. Christian faith claims that Eucharist represents both the power and the pasch of Christ in an efficacious way. Furthermore, it represents both Christ himself and the church. However, the nature and the power of representation have been quite diversely conceived, and this has had strong impact on theology and practice.

Christian theology has not been free of some naive realism in evoking Christ's presence and in attributing the sanctifying power of the passion to sacramental action. However, there have always been more critical theologies that eschewed simplistic explanations and were more aware of cultural patterns.

If there is a particular question that current theology has to put very seriously to earlier ages, it has to do with the way in which the workings of grace and sacrament are related to concepts of history, as this affects notions of commemoration and representation. In an age keenly conscious of the discontinuities of history, how the memory of Christ is related to the vagaries of time is of vital importance.

CONCLUSIONS FOR THE PROGRAM

In light of the foregoing considerations about the contemporary situation and about the style of conversing with eucharistic tradition, it is clear why one has to go beyond a broad survey of eucharistic history and why the study is too complex to allow consideration of every period of history in equal depth. Some key periods have therefore been chosen for fuller consideration. These are that of the New Testament beginnings, that of the pre-Nicene church, and that part of the Middle Ages to which the theology of Thomas Aquinas relates. For each age, account is taken of liturgical texts, liturgical practices, related spiritualities, and prevailing theologies. Connecting chapters offer a more cursory look at other periods and at doctrinal formulations.

It will be asked of each period how its consideration affects the current ecclesial scene. As much care as possible has been taken with historical and textual accuracy, but the primary purpose of the work is systematic and practical reflection, so that much information is accepted from scholars in other fields. In other words, what is sought is the understanding and challenge that eucharistic tradition opens up to us in our own ecclesial and social context. All of this is followed by a final section of the book in which the critical look at tradition is allowed to open up an approach to eucharistic theology and practice that may serve the church in our day.

Part II

EUCHARIST
IN THE NEW TESTAMENT

Chapter 2

THE NEW TESTAMENT
TEXTS EXAMINED

Two contemporary approaches to the scriptures affect the investigation
of eucharistic texts in the New Testament. On the one side, there is the
attempt to offer a historical reconstruction of events and sayings. On the
other, there is the reading of the scriptures as literary texts, not simply
in the sense in which works of fiction are literature but in the sense that
the texts are read as imaginative renderings of events and sayings, with
meaning rather than chronicle as the purpose.

For those who consider that the eucharistic tradition of the church is
founded on fidelity to what Jesus said and did at the Last Supper and
to the practice of New Testament times, historical reconstruction is vital.
This reconstruction, however, proves difficult. What Jesus did, what he
said, whether this was the paschal night or a paschal supper, are among
the unresolved questions of New Testament exegesis.

Without relying on the possibilities of reconstruing the events of the
night preceding Jesus' death, the New Testament texts may be read for
the meaning that they give to eucharistic practice. Such a reading takes
account of the fact that the church, its ministries, and its practices, grew
out of faith in the risen Christ more than out of obedience to his specific
dictates. What emerges is an awareness of the pluralism in eucharistic
thought and practice reflected in a diversity of texts coming from different communities. Access to the events of the Last Supper and to early
Christian commemorations of the pasch is had only through the diverse
interpretations of the New Testament books.

Presenting the trends and results of New Testament studies on the
Eucharist in a work of systematic theology is a formidable task, given
their abundance and diversity and the need for the systematic theologian to avoid the mistake of an incompetent duplication of the biblical
scholar's task.[1] The questions of historical reconstruction cannot be ig-

---

1. Detailed exegesis of texts is not usually given in this work, but the footnotes are
intended to refer to readily available bibliography in scriptural studies.

nored, for they have left their mark on theology and always keep us mindful of the reality of events behind the texts. However, more attention is given here to how the texts express the meaning of the Eucharist by their use of expressive forms and images.

Two chapters are required to consider the material. While theological rather than exegetical questions are kept to the fore, the procedure is somewhat different in each chapter. In this one, the major purpose is to present the texts normally considered pertinent to the origins of the Lord's Supper, or Eucharist. In the next, more attention is given to theological considerations rooted in a reading of the texts.

Five points are treated in this chapter: (a) the issues of historical reconstruction; (b) the evidence about meal sharing in the early church communities; (c) the distinction made between two supper traditions; (d) the actions and words of Jesus at the supper; (e) the distinctive approaches of the four supper accounts.

THE PROBLEMATIC
OF HISTORICAL RECONSTRUCTION

Some of the theories that seem less current or less pertinent today have to do precisely with historical reconstruction. As John Reumann has remarked, "Scholarship in recent years has loosened our hold on the Upper Room as *the* origin for the Lord's Supper in Christianity, at least as a single direct-line cause."[2] Much the same can be said of the hold on the community setting of New Testament supper accounts or on the chronology of the last days of Jesus, or of the hold on early Christian practices. With that in mind, something may be noted of interpretations that have not been confirmed and hence cannot be allowed to play a great part in eucharistic theology.

One might begin by recalling the theories that spoke of two types of meal in early Christian churches. At one time, this was suggested as the principal reason for the differences in the texts that refer to the meals kept in early communities, as well as for the differences in accounts of the supper in the upper room.

Hans Lietzmann favored the idea that there were two kinds of meal, one that he identified with Jerusalem and the other with the Pauline churches.[3] He located the origins of the first type in the meals that Jesus took with his disciples during the time of his ministry, believing that

---

2. John Reumann, *The Supper of the Lord: The New Testament, Ecumenical Dialogue, and Faith and Order on Eucharist* (Philadelphia: Fortress Press, 1985), 49.

3. For different two-meal theories, see I. Howard Marshall, *Last Supper and Lord's Supper* (Grand Rapids: William B. Eerdmans, 1980), 130–33. Marshall gives references to the literature on the topic.

these resembled the meals of other religious *haburoth*, or fellowships. In continuing this kind of meal the Jerusalem church blessed and broke bread and drank a cup of wine in expectation of the Lord's coming. The second kind of meal was modelled on the Last Supper, a passover meal, and it was then celebrated as a solemn memorial of Jesus' death.

Ernst Lohmeyer modified this hypothesis. He distinguished between a Galilean type of meal and a Jerusalem type. The former he identified with Lietzmann's Jerusalem meal and the latter with the Pauline. Another modification given to the theory was that of Oscar Cullmann, who attributed a connection between the postresurrection meals of Jesus and the Pauline supper.

The theory of the two kinds of meal, in whatever form it is presented, originates in the problem of harmonizing New Testament texts on Christian gatherings. Does the Book of the Acts of the Apostles on the breaking of the bread have the same referent as the Pauline texts on the Corinthian community's communion? Do the three Synoptic accounts of the Last Supper have the same or similar community settings, with the same or different liturgical practices? Does the Emmaus story in Luke's Gospel deserve distinctive attention in reconstructing early Christian practices? In the theories there is both an attempt to account for textual difference and an attempt to allow for diversity in church practice. This seems legitimate, but the historical reconstructions are fragile and strain too much to establish a factual diversity, both in the practice and in the meaning of the community gatherings. What remains of this attempt is the need to consider the import for the future of the church of different ways of holding Jesus and his death in memory.

Other theories that can be usefully recalled at this juncture are ones that concentrate on the Last Supper itself as originating point of the Eucharist, or Lord's Supper. Joachim Jeremias is well remembered for his discussion of the passover character of the Last Supper, as well as for the reactions that his argumentation evoked.[4] After reviewing arguments for and against the holding of a paschal seder by Jesus and his disciples, he opted in favor of the pasch. Many have continued to argue against this.[5] There is a fairly common opinion abroad now that one cannot be certain that the meal was a celebration of the passover feast but that it is nonetheless possible to speak of the paschal setting or paschal atmosphere in which the meal was eaten and the blessings invoked. Very recently, however, Cesare Giraudo, on the basis of a comparison with the passover seder, has supported the thesis that the meal was a passover

---

4. See Joachim Jeremias, *The Eucharistic Words of Jesus*, translated by Norman Perrin (Philadelphia: Fortress Press, 1977), 15–88.

5. Marshall adduces these arguments from different sources, *Last Supper and Lord's Supper*, 62–66.

one.[6] This involves the possibility of a historical reconstruction of the seder at the time of Jesus, which is important to him because it is in this context that he interprets the actions and words of Jesus and determines the significance of the Eucharist as a commemorative action. Despite such impressive efforts, it may be more straightforward to note the intentional paschal references in the accounts without feeling it necessary to decide the factual question.

In similar vein, exegetes have given much attention to reconstructing the actual words of Jesus over the bread and over the cup. This is not a purely sacramental issue but one that has more importance for christology since it has to do with Jesus' own intention and understanding in face of impending death.[7] While in some circles there is considerable reluctance to give up this quest, it seems to be no easier to resolve than it is to resolve other quests for the Jesus of history deemed important for christology and soteriology.

One of the answers to the problem of eucharistic origins has been to appeal to the liturgical setting in which the supper accounts originated.[8] In other words, it is suggested that these accounts are not directly from an oral or written tradition but that they were formulated as they now stand within the celebration of liturgy. Since the supper texts belong clearly within a greater narrative, it is probably incorrect to think that they were taken directly from liturgies. Nonetheless, it is useful to note that they may reflect diverse liturgical formulations. To note that the death of Jesus was remembered from early times in ways that reflect some pluralism in its salvific interpretation relativizes the question about the chronology or dating of the accounts and the attempt to decide which is oldest.[9] This would be important only if one were looking for evidence of an early institution that set the order and form of the celebration for future times.

---

6. Cesare Giraudo, *Eucaristia per la Chiesa: Prospettive teologiche sull'eucaristia a partire dalla "lex orandi"* (Brescia: Morcelliana Editrice; Rome: Editrice Pontificia Università Gregoriana, 1989), 162–86.

7. See, for example, Rudolph Pesch, *Das Abendmahl und Jesu Todesverständnis* (Freiburg im Breisgau: Herder, 1978); Heinz Schürmann, *Jesu ureigener Tod: Exegetische Besinnungen und Ausblick* (Freiburg im Breisgau: Herder, 1975), 66–96; id., "Jesus' Words in the Light of His Actions at the Last Supper," *Concilium* 40 (1969/2): 119–31. For a specific connection between this and the institution of the Lord's Supper, see Willi Marxsen, *The Beginnings of Christology together with the Lord's Supper as a Christological Problem*, translated by Paul J. Achtmeier and Lorenz Nieting (Philadelphia: Fortress Press, 1979), 92–117.

8. This was much favored by Gregory Dix, with surprising results for liturgical scholarship. See *The Shape of the Liturgy*, with additional notes by Paul Marshall (New York: Seabury Press, 1983), 50–70. For a concise presentation by a scriptural scholar, see Xavier Léon-Dufour, *Sharing the Eucharistic Bread: The Witness of the New Testament*, translated by Matthew O'Connell (New York: Paulist Press, 1987), 82–84, with notes on the literature, 337.

9. On this, see Marshall, *Last Supper and Lord's Supper*, 35–40, as well as Table 3 in the Appendix.

In summary, historical reconstruction has been used as a way of settling certain questions about the Eucharist. First, it has been used to establish different meal practices, each with its own distinctive meaning, in New Testament times. Second, it has been used to settle argument about the paschal character of the Last Supper. Third, it was used to give the exact words and actions of Jesus at this meal, thus reflecting the supposed intentions of Jesus regarding his own death and his memorial. Fourth, it has been used to establish the chronology of the supper accounts in relation to each other.

In none of these instances are there definitive answers. What has come to the fore is that in the effort to discuss historical facts, much attention was actually given to literary forms and meanings. It is at least partly as a result of this that there are now biblical and theological readings of the texts that attend to the primacy of theological questions, even when the matters raised by reconstruction cannot be resolved. With this in mind, the issues noted at the beginning of the chapter can be addressed.

COMMUNITY MEAL SHARING

The historical reconstruction of the Last Supper is spiked with exegetical difficulties relative to what actually took place. Even were it beyond doubt, this in itself would not put the sacrament in its proper setting. The supper narratives come down to us as an integral part of an ecclesial tradition. For this reason, to set a context for the supper narratives recent scholarship has looked at the commemorative action of early churches as it belongs to the common life of these communities. The starting-point for a study of the Eucharist in New Testament texts is then the account of church life, not the account of the supper.

Rite and Meal in Early Christian Communities

The common meal is presented as an essential element of the life of the early disciples. Its exact significance and the relation to it of the sacramental action in bread and wine is not as clear. The two most prominent texts concerning common meals are Acts 2:42ff. and 1 Corinthians 10 and 11. Whether or not these texts indicate the existence of a ritual action distinct from the meal, they show that in two different settings the Lord's memorial belonged within the setting of a common meal and of other forms of community bonding.

Much has been written about the breaking of the bread mentioned

several times in the Acts of the Apostles.[10] There appear to be good arguments for finding that the term refers to the specific ritual that expresses
the nature and unity of the church community rather than to the meal
taken in common, even if the former is joined with the latter. Putting
it quite simply, meals taken in common in the church of Jerusalem or
in house-churches founded by the apostles (e.g., Acts 20:7–11) are not
generally designated by this term. Hence where it is used, something
special must be intended.

Since the ritual of the breaking of the bread was practiced on the
occasion of gatherings that included the common meal, it is likely that
the term refers to a blessing and breaking of bread that in Jewish fashion preceded the meal. In a Jewish household the meal did not begin
until the father of the family had said a blessing, broken bread, and
distributed the pieces to those around the table. We do not have direct evidence for texts of such Jewish blessings at the beginning of the
common era, any more than we have Christian texts, with the possible
exception of the *Didache*. Some reconstruction is attempted and Lucien
Deiss draws on later sources for this text of a usual blessing:

> You are blessed, Lord our God, King of the universe, you who have
> brought bread forth from the earth.[11]

The blessing was said over the bread but it prefaced the meal, rec-
ognizing that all earth's goods come from God. Christian scholars of the
early eucharistic tradition give most of their attention to the blessing
over the cup at the end of the meal when looking for Jewish precedents
or parallels, but this breaking of bread at meal's beginning cannot be
ignored. It is a rite that is essentially related to the meal, yet in a ritual
sense it is distinct from the rest of the meal. The reference to the action
of Jesus in breaking bread at the Last Supper could have given this first
blessing a special meaning for his disciples, distinguishing it even more
clearly from the rest of what took place at the meals shared in common.

In examining the texts about the breaking of the bread in the Acts of
the Apostles, Léon-Dufour says:

---

10. See Jeremias, *The Eucharistic Words of Jesus*, 119–22; Léon-Dufour, *Sharing the Eucharistic Bread*, 21–29; Marshall, *Last Supper and Lord's Supper*, 126–30.

11. Lucien Deiss, *Springtime of the Liturgy: Liturgical Texts of the First Four Centuries*, translated by Matthew O'Connell (Collegeville, Minn.: Liturgical Press, 1979), 6. Note what
Louis Bouyer has to say about this blessing: "But the meal did not officially begin until
the father of the family or the presiding member of the community had broken the bread
which was to be given to the participants, with this blessing: Blessed by thou, JHWH, our
God, King of the universe, who bringest forth bread from the earth." In *Eucharist: Theology and Spirituality of the Eucharistic Prayer*, translated by Charles Underhill Quinn (Notre
Dame: University of Notre Dame Press, 1968), 80.

While referring to the sacramental rite as a whole, the term "breaking of bread" emphasizes the element of sharing, within unity, that characterizes the Christian celebration, an emphasis all the more justified since according to Luke the community's daily life reflected that unity and sharing. There is no doubt that Christians applied an idea inherited from Judaism and saw the breaking of the bread as a symbol of the unity Christ had in mind in bringing the faithful together.[12]

If we examine the texts in Luke's writings, we see that he shows that this ritual is there connected with the unity, or *koinonia*, that includes assembly, word (the teaching of the apostles), and that internal charity which involved some sharing together of common goods and mutual care. The extent to which Christians at Jerusalem or elsewhere actually shared common meals is not clear, so that all Léon-Dufour says is that it was "likely" that the rite was celebrated on the occasion of a full meal.[13] At the very least it has to be said that the rite mentioned in Acts was performed by people accustomed to the practice of a common meal, and so in this sense at any rate its significance is related to such a meal, even were it to be separated from it on occasion. At any rate, the rite of breaking bread cannot be fully understood except in relation to all the elements of the common life.

It seems to be rarely mentioned by exegetes, yet one of the questions that could be asked in light of what is said about the breaking of the bread is whether the Eucharist was ever celebrated in bread alone, without the cup ritual whose Jewish parallel was the blessing of the cup at the end of the meal. Now that more is known of the rites of Judeo-Christian churches in postapostolic times, the possibility of a rite in bread alone seems more likely.[14] A daily repast would not necessarily have included wine or the blessing of wine at the close of the meal, and a rite in bread alone could have preceded and then survived the eventual fusion of the two blessings.

In the Letter to the Corinthians, the precise relation of bread rite to wine rite is not fully clarified, though it is clear that Paul writes of bread and cup.[15] That the Corinthian Christians ate together as a sign of their unity is indubitable, as it is also indubitable that ideal and reality were in conflict. Social distinctions marred the appearance of common bond-

---

12. Léon-Dufour, *Sharing the Eucharistic Bread*, 23f.
13. Ibid., 25.
14. This is discussed in the fourth chapter of this book, p. 72f.
15. On the relation of the Lord's Supper to the common meal at Corinth, see Léon-Dufour, *Sharing the Eucharistic Bread*, 21; Gerhard Theissen, "Social Integration and Sacramental Activity: An Analysis of 1 Cor 11: 17–34," in Gerhard Theissen, *The Social Setting of Pauline Christianity: Essays on Corinth*, translated by J. H. Schutz (Philadelphia: Fortress Press, 1982), 145–74.

ing. Paul addresses this in the light of the communion signified in the blessing and sharing of the loaf and the cup.

The implication of Paul's words is that when he wrote the blessing and sharing of bread took place at the beginning of the meal, while the blessing and sharing of the cup took place at the end. However, this did not imply that other victuals were shared in common, so that between the two rites there was a marked absence of sharing, a kind of practice of separate tables where social distinctions were much in evidence. Paul deals with this in two ways. First he exhorts the people to greater charity, less snobbery, and greater *diakonia*, or mutual service. Then to support his exhortation he puts great emphasis on the unity signified by the bread and cup rites. He may have favored, as is sometimes suggested, a complete separation of the sacramental ritual from the meal. This would have been one way of avoiding the abuses that marred the celebration. It would also have underlined the distinctive character of these rites as a commemoration of the Lord's death. It would not have solved the lack of practical communion among the disciples of Corinth and may have weakened the relation of the sharing of Christ's body and blood to the ideal of the common table.

In brief, within the New Testament context the rites of shared bread and shared cup, with their respective blessings, cannot be fully understood except in relation to that unity where shared word, mutual service, crossing of social barriers, shared goods, and shared meals are of the essence. To look for the commemorative and eucharistic significance of the ritual without this multiple reference is vain.

Religious Significance of Meal Sharing

It has been pointed out many times that the religious meal was not in their time peculiar to the disciples of Jesus. In the first decades of the common era, among Jews and other peoples alike, the common meal was an important way of expressing and cementing unity among the members and of bonding with the holy.[16] In noting this, however, commentators find that the specific thing about Christian gatherings was that they did not share a common table because they were already one for some other reason, but found their center and source of unity at the table itself. For Jewish groups for whom the religious meal outweighed even the Temple cult as an expression of bonding, the primary focus was on the Torah. Deriving their unity from the gift of the Torah, they shared common meals in praise of Yahweh. For the Qumran sect, to take

---

16. For a good overview, see Charles Perrot, "L'eucharistie comme fondement de l'identité de l'Eglise dans le Nouveau Testament," *La Maison-Dieu* 137 (1979): 109–25. See also Marshall, *Last Supper and Lord's Supper,* 13–29.

another important example, the meal with its ritual observances was the gathering place of the pure. Presence at the table required religious purity and marked off the participants from the impure.

As distinguished from the meals of the pure, Christian gatherings were such that ideally they did away with discrimination and signified that new eschatological oneness in which there was neither pure nor impure, male nor female, Jew nor gentile, slave nor free. As compared with the meals of devout Jews, the Christian table-sharing was itself the source of the communion of all in Christ, because of what was proclaimed and shared there. It was because they shared their food and drink in the name of Christ that Christians were one. Though of course this involved the profession of the one faith, the communion in eating and drinking was the central and most significant act. The Synoptic accounts of the Last Supper and Paul's admonitions to the Corinthians show that the focus was brought to center on the bread and wine, with their clear interpretation as the gift of Christ's body and blood. This meant that a ritual of eating and drinking took over from a meal as such, but the religious meal remained as background to the peculiarities of what this signified for believers.

Given the importance that the shared table had for early communities, commentators note further the reference to meals in the ministry of Jesus as narrated in the Gospels.[17] Not only did Jesus share a common purse and a common table with the small band of intimate disciples, but he integrated a certain kind of table practice into the preaching of the coming of God's rule. That he took meals with tax-collectors and public sinners was a scandal to the pious, but for Jesus himself this was tied up with the forgiveness of sins that he proclaimed (Luke 5:29f.). In the feeding of the crowds recounted in Mark's Gospel (Mark 6 and Mark 8) there may well be a deliberate redactional intention of paralleling this action from the public ministry with the practice of Christian assembly. The action of Jesus in blessing God and in then breaking and distributing the bread there and at the Last Supper is identical in both cases.[18]

Postresurrection stories also include occasions on which Jesus ate and drank with the disciples. In particular, the encounter with the two disciples on the way to Emmaus has been taken as a way of combining a resurrection story with a catechesis on the assembly.[19] This narrative links the recall and explanation of the scriptures with the recognition of Jesus in the breaking of the bread. Thus it points to the new manner of the presence of the risen Christ among believers.

In short, what is known about the gatherings of early Christians is

---

17. See Reumann, *The Supper of the Lord*, 4f.

18. See Marshall, *Last Supper and Lord's Supper*, 95f.

19. See Louis-Marie Chauvet, *Symbole et sacrement: Une relecture sacramentelle de l'existence chrétienne* (Paris: Ed. du Cerf, 1988), 167–76.

complemented in the New Testament by stories of meals in accounts of the ministry of Jesus and by postresurrection narratives. All of these texts thus serve as elements in eucharistic catechesis and understanding, even if some of the finer points of exegesis remain open to discussion.

TWO SUPPER TRADITIONS

Two problems have dogged exegetical studies of the supper narratives. First of all, there is the need to relate the four accounts of the three Synoptics and First Corinthians to each other. Are there in reality four accounts, or are the four reducible to three or even two? Second is the problem of relating the story of Jesus' gathering with his disciples on the eve of his passion in John's Gospel with the supper narratives of the eucharistic tradition. While John's Gospel tells of the washing of the feet preceding a meal and of the love command, it does not include the table ritual or any words of Jesus over bread and wine.

Xavier Léon-Dufour offers a way of reading the texts that to some extent cuts across the exegetical problems and presents rich insight for eucharistic theology. To distinguish between the Johannine account and the other texts he notes two kinds of tradition about the final meal of Jesus.[20] The first he calls a cultic tradition and the second a testamentary. He places the four texts that speak of the table actions and words of Jesus in the cultic tradition because they serve to give a foundation to the church's ritual or cult and may well have taken elements in their formulation from the cult itself. He takes the Johannine account as principal evidence for the testamentary tradition, so called from the practice of leaving a testament to those who outlive one. In the Johannine Gospel, the story of Jesus' final evening with his disciples, where his mind is clearly on his impending departure, has the characteristics of a farewell meal. Jesus speaks of how he is to be remembered and bequeaths counsels and an example of service and love to his companions and followers. The testament is graphically embodied in the washing of the disciples' feet by the master himself in preparation for their meal together. It provides a way in which he is to be remembered that complements the table ritual.

As will be seen, Léon-Dufour shows where at points the two traditions interlock in the gospel texts. When they are taken together, they offer a foundation that allows us to place the church's continued eucharistic practice within the context of its discipleship and its obedience to Christ's command that his followers should serve one another.

---

20. Léon-Dufour, *Sharing the Eucharistic Bread*, 82–95.

The Cultic Tradition

The interest in the cultic tradition lies in what it says of the words and actions of Jesus that are considered the basis for the church's ritual action. It gives an authoritative basis to the liturgical practice of the church which is then assumed to use the same rites. While in the manner of the Jews Jesus shared a full meal with the disciples, the liturgical tradition gives sacramental status to the blessing and breaking of bread at meal's beginning and to the blessing and sharing of wine at meal's end.

Léon-Dufour, as is quite common, distinguishes two principal forms of the narrative, calling one the Markan and the other the Antiochene account. He notes the differences between them.

As far as the blessing is concerned, the Greek verbs describing the prayers over the elements are not symmetrical in the accounts. The Greek apparently had two options for translating what was probably the one Aramaic word, this corresponding to one Hebrew term, *brk*. While controversies surrounding the nature of the Jewish blessing prayer cannot be considered here, one has to ask whether a difference of prayer form is intended by the two Greek verbs, *eulogesas* and *eucharistesas*. The English translation of Léon-Dufour renders the first as "pronounced the blessing" and the second as "gave thanks." In the original French text, so as to establish some symmetry, the author even substitutes *eulogesas* for *eucharistesas* in the account given by Paul and Luke of the blessing over the bread. This has Jesus pronounce a blessing over the bread and give thanks over the cup of wine. In this way, Léon-Dufour seems to make an intentional distinction between two kinds of prayer. Yet elsewhere, like some other exegetes, he finds that there is no essential difference between the two Greek verbs insofar as they are chosen to translate the Aramaic.[21] It may in fact have been hard to find a Greek term which would render the complexity of the *berakoth* or blessings, since Jewish blessing includes elements of praising, sanctifying and giving thanks, without clear formal or conceptual distinction between them.[22]

If there is not then much difference to be made between blessing and giving thanks, the cultic tradition shows the following elements: a blessing, a breaking and distribution of bread, and a blessing and sharing of a cup. To the blessing and the action are added the words of Jesus about

---

21. Ibid., 99.

22. See Cesare Giraudo, *La struttura letteraria della preghiera eucaristica: Saggio sulla genesi letteraria di una forma* (Rome: Biblical Institute Press, 1981), 260–69. Noting the Hebrew roots *brk* and *ydh* of Jewish blessing, Giraudo places them both in the context of a tradition of confession of praise, within which the people acknowledged the sovereignty of God in the alliance. He finds that the prevalence of *brk* in later prayer is a liturgical standardization of a richer tradition. For him, the Greek verbs in the New Testament simply show the problem of finding good translation and precede any Christian liturgical standardization of terms and formulas for prayer.

both bread and cup, but the texts do not clearly indicate whether these were said within the two blessings or after them. The actions and words will be more fully considered further on.

The Testamentary Tradition

In referring to the story of this final evening in the Johannine Gospel as a testamentary tradition, Léon-Dufour places the meal in the genre of farewell meal and the words of Jesus to his disciples in the genre of farewell discourse. It is not new to talk of this section of the Gospel as a farewell discourse and to compare it with other such biblical discourses, especially with Genesis 49 (Jacob to his sons), Deuteronomy 33 (Moses to the Israelite people), and Acts 20:17–38 (Paul to the elders of Miletus). What Léon-Dufour adds to this reading of the text is his stress on the washing of the feet as an exemplary action of service that is integral to the testament left by Jesus. It is an action in which he symbolically shows the meaning of his own life and ministry, just as he does with the gift of the bread and wine in the ritual tradition. The command to do to others as he himself has done is primarily an ethical admonition. This would mean that along with the memorial of Jesus in the ritual, there is a practical remembrance of him in the mutual service that his followers render to each other.

Thus far, Léon-Dufour points to the conjunction between liturgical remembrance and community ethic. This is important since it underlines the fact that as a memorial action the supper functions only in conjunction with practical discipleship. However, the author relates the washing of the feet even more closely to liturgical memorial. He points out that as an interpretative action the washing of the feet shows that Jesus wished to be remembered in his role of servant. As part of the supper tradition this complements the words over bread and cup that point to the shedding of his blood and to the sealing of the covenant.

To support this point of view, he indicates how elements of the testamentary tradition show up in the cultic. The first echo is heard in the eschatological saying about the "fruit of the vine" in all three Synoptic accounts of the final meal with the disciples (Matt. 26:29; Mark 14:25; Luke 22:18). These are not directly related to either blessing but look like part of a larger discourse in which Jesus talks to the disciples of his impending departure, explaining the meaning of his ministry and of his imminent death.

The more important echo of the testamentary tradition in the cultic comes in the words about service in Luke 22:19–38, following the blessing and sharing of the ritual cup of wine. Within the very context of the table ritual Jesus presents himself as a model of service to his followers, a model that is to be kept in the ritual and that qualifies the role of presiding at table as well as exemplifying relations in the community. Just as Jesus showed himself to be a servant, so the one who presides at the ritual meal in the community of followers is to be as the one who serves. The impact of these words is stronger when they are set alongside the washing of the feet and the command to render such service to each other as a way of keeping the memory of Jesus alive.

In noting the importance of placing the ritual of bread and wine in the fuller context of shared meals, the relation of this to mutual service in the community was already mentioned. In allowing the testamentary tradition of the supper to complement the cultic, the relation of Eucharist to service is corroborated. The way in which memory of Jesus Christ is to be kept is also enlarged. The remembrance of Jesus in the sacrament has to cull elements from the farewell actions and discourse of the Lord, both for the understanding of his death and for the sake of a faithful discipleship.

ACTIONS AND WORDS OF JESUS

The Accounts

Without going into the textual arguments, it is helpful to note how the actions and words of Jesus in the two basic cultic accounts are summarized by Léon-Dufour:[23]

> *Antiochene:* And having taken the bread, having pronounced the blessing, he broke it and gave it to them, and he said: THIS IS MY BODY WHICH [is] FOR YOU. DO THIS IN MEMORY OF ME. Likewise, after the meal, the cup, saying: THIS CUP [is] THE NEW COVENANT IN MY BLOOD.

> *Markan:* And as they were eating, having taken bread, having pronounced the blessing, he broke it and gave it to them and he said: THIS IS MY BODY. And, taking the cup, having given thanks, he gave it to them and he said to them: THIS IS MY BLOOD OF THE COVENANT, WHICH IS SHED FOR THE MULTITUDE.

In relation to the bread, the words of the Markan account are minimal: This is my body. The Antiochene account adds: which [is] for you, or given for you. In relation to the wine, the words "the new covenant in my blood" of the Antiochene account contrast with "my blood of the covenant" in the Markan, words to which the latter adds "which is shed for the multitude."

---

23. Ibid., 99–101. In the Antiochene account, he combines Paul and Luke. To the Markan account, he assimilates that of Matthew.

What is placed directly in evidence in the Antiochene version is the cup that is to be shared, and this goes with the innovative action of Jesus at this point of the meal. After the final blessing of a Jewish meal, all normally drank from their individual cups. The New Testament text implies that Jesus shared one common cup with all those at table with him. It would seem that this carried over into the church's ritual, for it is the action that Paul highlights in pointing to the celebration as sign of *koinonia*.

The Markan account on the other hand underlines the forecast of the shedding of Jesus' blood for the sealing of the covenant, a deed that enables those who partake of the table to share in the covenant. There is no good warrant for finding an emphasis on the elements in the Markan tradition that is absent in the Antiochene, however much Catholic and Protestant traditions have appealed to either one or other of the two texts in support of contrasting opinions about the Eucharist. Jesus' identification of the bread and wine as his body and blood is essential to both forms of the cultic tradition. So also is the connection between the table action and his forthcoming death. Rather than finding contradictory accounts, one might point to two somewhat different interpretations or theologies, each stressing a particular aspect of what is remembered and recounted.[24]

A final point of difference between the two forms of the tradition has to do with the memorial command. It is found in the Antiochene tradition but not in the Markan. It is difficult enough to account for this absence in the latter, just as it is difficult to know why the words occur at the bread-breaking in the original Antiochene form and are then added to the cup by Paul. It is possible that this is further evidence of a ritual in bread alone and can be connected with the breaking of the bread mentioned in Acts.

Interpretation

Interpretation of the texts cannot be based on a historical reconstruction that would retrieve the exact order and words of the supper. Though the texts relate to a specific event, each author fits the account into the purpose and structure of the total work. The texts come out of communities that profess faith in the risen Christ and that are versed in their respective liturgical celebration of Christ's memory and presence. The composition is rooted in a common soteriological and eucharistic faith and is then given the particular twist of each writer.

Biblical scholars give considerable importance to the setting in which

---

24. A discussion of the meaning of this identification of bread and cup with Jesus' body and blood belongs to the discussion of symbolism offered below.

the Gospels place the supper. It is part of the passion narrative and hence is linked to the meaning of Jesus' trial, suffering, and death. It is further related to the passover, even if it is not clear that a passover meal is described. The evangelists clearly want the final days of Jesus to be seen in the context of the passover feast. The account in Mark 14:12–16 refers to the preparation of the upper room as a preparation for a passover meal and makes the meal shared by Jesus and his disciples on the occasion of the feast a way of marking the passover of Jesus himself. In Luke 22:15 the desire of Jesus to eat the passover with his followers is presented as one with the anticipation of his suffering. It is as the passover of Jesus himself that the rites take on a memorial character, so that some authors speak of the account of the meal as of a charter account for the church's own actions after Christ's death and resurrection.[25]

Turning first to the actions, it is to be asked what significance is attached to the action of breaking the bread, and to those of giving first bread and then cup to the disciples. Most of the actions might be seen as nothing other than the gestures of the head of the household if it were not for the interpretative words that draw attention to them. It is as in a painting when a usually ordinary gesture is put into high relief: the very fact of drawing attention to it gives it significance. The action of sharing only one cup is however quite unique in itself, since that would not have been the usual procedure at a table gathering.

Some scholars suggest that these *gestures* of Jesus belong in the genre of prophetic action.[26] They are read as a kind of parable in deed, intended to attract attention and beg for interpretation. Like Jeremiah breaking the potter's earthen flask (Jer 19:10) or Ezekiel shaving off his hair, burning part of it, and scattering some around the city, while binding the rest into the skirt of his robe (Ezek 5:1–4), Jesus acts in a way that compels one to ask what he is about. Not only are these actions descriptive of some action to be taken by God, but they carry in themselves all the force of divine intention. In what he does with the bread and wine Jesus portrays actions to be done to his own person. There is an inevitability and a divine force to what is thus prophesied.

In turning to the *words* over bread and cup, one has to reckon with the peculiarities of each narrative. In including the invitation found in "Take" or "Take, eat," Mark and Matthew accentuate the fact that what is said of the bread and of the cup is one with the action of giving them to be consumed. On no account can it be said that the elements are divorced from the table sharing.[27] In either version of the cultic tradition it is clear that in offering the elements Jesus highlights the fact that in

---

25. See G. D. Kilpatrick, *The Eucharist in Bible and Liturgy* (Cambridge: Cambridge University Press, 1983).

26. See Schürmann, "Jesus' Words in the Light of His Actions at the Last Supper."

27. See Marxsen, *The Beginnings of Christology*, 99–102.

this passover celebration he is completely dedicated to the service of his followers. The table-gift that he extends is the sign of his communion with them in self-gift.

Luke and Paul make a closer connection between the gift of bread and the forthcoming death by adding the words: "which is [given] for you." In the past, attempts have been made to find a sacrificial meaning in these words. There might be more justification for this in a Pauline than in a gospel context, and it is certainly hard to relate the sacrificial meaning to Jesus' own intention. In reading the Synoptic accounts of the supper it is well to remember that these Gospels, while certainly seeing its importance, do not have a highly developed salvific interpretation of the death of Jesus.[28] It is something that he undergoes in consequence of his proclamation of God's rule and in the loving service of his followers, but beyond these points one cannot decipher a strong theology of salvific death.

Much has been written on the meaning of the word *body*, sometimes contrasting the *soma* of the cultic tradition with the use of the word *sarx* in the discourse on the bread of life found in John 6, more properly translated in English as "flesh."[29] Between the Scylla and Charibdis of fleshly identification with the bread and of the adoption of a theory of pure sign, there lies a better appreciation of the symbolic, to be applied either to *soma* or to *sarx,* as of course also to *aima* (blood). The *body* in Semitic language refers to the person as one who expresses self, acting and communicating with others. The *blood* is the life-principle and its use highlights the fact that life is a gift, sacred in such a way that it belongs to God and can be taken away only by God.

Both words take a more specific meaning from the context in which they occur. In this instance, since Jesus is present at the head of the table it is clear that there is no material identification between his material flesh and blood and the things given to eat and drink. However, that does not reduce the meaning of their gift to a pure allegory of Jesus' death. Jesus genuinely identifies himself as a living person with the gift, in ways brought out by the use of the two images in tandem with the reference to his death. He genuinely gives his own self to the disciples in a communion of life, covenant, and eschatological hope that springs from his self-surrender.

When these words were recited as a memorial in a community that

---

28. The exegetical studies on this point are handsomely reviewed by Edward Schillebeeckx, *Jesus: An Experiment in Christology,* translated by Hubert Hoskins (New York: Seabury Press, A Crossroad Book, 1979), 273–329.

29. These discussions often have to do with Roman Catholic and Protestant controversies over real presence. These show up even today, for example in the more Protestant concerns of Marshall, *Last Supper and Lord's Supper,* and in the more Catholic ones of Léon-Dufour, *Sharing the Eucharistic Bread.* These controversies are considered in chapter 12.

had received the witness of Jesus' resurrection, they would have readily signified a real gift of himself even then in that ritual action, though this had to carry with it the consequence of resurrection faith. In the Eucharist the risen Christ continues to give himself in the bread and wine. As at the supper, he takes body among the faithful in bread that is broken, shared, and eaten. As at the supper, he shares blood, the principle of life, in a common cup. The covenant blood is given in wine poured out, in a cup passed from hand to hand and drunk. The full import of this form of bodiliness is found in the belief of the risen Lord's continued presence among the disciples in the power of the Spirit that binds them together in eschatological hope.

CHARACTERISTICS OF THE FOUR ACCOUNTS

Something has to be said, however briefly, about the special meaning given to the supper and to the Eucharist by each of the four accounts within the two traditions.

Throughout the course of his Gospel, the writer of Mark includes the meals of Jesus in the proclamation of the coming of God's rule. The work is also punctuated with predictions of the passion, building these into its literary structure. In this way the puzzle of the two titles, Son of Man and Son of God, is kept in focus, looking to a resolution that will be found only in the final appearance at the end of time of this mysterious personage, though it is anticipated in the passover setting of supper and passion. Jesus' anticipation of his death at the supper, as well as his anticipation of the kingdom, is expressed in the words: "Truly I say to you, I shall not drink again of the fruit of the vine until that day when I drink it anew in the kingdom of God." Given the highly apocalyptic expectation of the Markan community, this points forward to the ultimate revelation of the Son of Man that could not be long delayed. Memorial in such a setting would have all the characteristics of this expectation.

The Matthean story of the supper does not differ significantly from the Markan. The Gospel, however, is much less apocalyptic and does more to anticipate and corroborate community structures of some durability. The same ritual performance would have a different resonance since it would locate memorial in a time for building the kingdom.

The most distinctive characteristic of the Lukan account has already been mentioned, for it is this which combines elements from the testamentary tradition with the cultic. The farewell character of the meal is brought out in what precedes and in what follows the blessings. It is as they sit down to table that Jesus says to those whom this Gospel calls apostles: "I have earnestly desired to eat this passover with you before I suffer; for I tell you I shall not eat it until it is fulfilled in the kingdom of God" (Luke 22:15f.). This is immediately followed by the drinking of an initial cup, to which similar words are attached (vv. 17f.). Only then does the account proceed to the ritual actions taken up by the church, so that they are given an eschatological character that harmonizes with Jesus' farewell testament. That this includes remembrance of him as servant emerges from what follows at the end of the meal, namely, his admonition to the apostles who set to arguing about precedence among themselves. Only those who serve as Jesus served (Luke 22:24–27) will be fit to judge with him at the final advent of the kingdom (vv. 28–30).

Paul's supper narrative occurs in a context where he is teaching about community *koinonia* and keen to root it, with its correlative *diakonia*, in the celebration of the Lord's Supper. This prompts him to give a very full meaning to the image of *soma*, or body. Not only does it refer to Christ's gift to the community in the ritual but it includes reference to the church or body of the faithful. In allowing the one image and signified reality to include both Christ and the church, Paul teaches the intimate communion of all in Christ that is celebrated and nourished in the supper ritual.

The Pauline text is more readily related than the Synoptic story to the sacramental communion of the living church with the risen Christ, whose death it remembers and proclaims. Whereas in the Gospels Jesus himself is shown to be eager to see the coming of God's rule, Paul locates eschatological expectation in the church's sacramental proclamation: "For as often as you eat this bread and drink this cup, you proclaim the Lord's death until he comes" (1 Cor. 11:26). Thus the eschatological expectation of the Lord's coming that emerges from his death is carried over into the church's worship and therewith into its life, lived in the wisdom of the cross and in the hope of the resurrection, as the rest of the letter so abundantly teaches.

This is in keeping with Paul's general tendency to concentrate more on the death and resurrection of Jesus in his preaching of the gospel than on the historical person and his actions. It is he who writes of Christ as the pasch, or as the fulfillment of the type of the Passover Lamb (1 Cor. 5:7). It is he too who points more to the presence of Christ among the faithful through the Spirit than to the record of his earthly ministry. In keeping with this Pauline trend, the hymn in Philippians 2:6–11 extols the image of Christ's self-emptying and exaltation. It is more mythic and condensed in style than the commemoration of the passion narrative.

CONCLUSION

In this chapter, attention has been given to the key New Testament texts on the Eucharist. Note was taken of the importance of the meal setting

of the rite in early communities and consequently of the appropriation of meal symbolism into eucharistic celebration and its explanatory
tradition. Attention was given to the insight gained from the relation
between two supper traditions, one cultic, the other testamentary. The
ways in which the actions and words of Jesus are recorded in the cultic
tradition were noted, and a word was added about the specific perspective of each of the four supper narratives. The next chapter will explore
a theological reading of New Testament evidence.

Chapter 3

CONTEMPORARY READING OF THE NEW TESTAMENT TEXTS

A theological reading of New Testament texts takes its point of departure in the ways in which the texts themselves interpret the events narrated. Within the horizon thus opened up, it asks what issues are raised by this interpretation for the continued role of the Eucharist in the life of the church.

There are thus three major divisions to the chapter: (a) the meaning of the memorial command in the supper narrative; (b) the use of historical master images in interpreting the significance of what is remembered; (c) the relation of the Eucharist to Christian life and to Christian identity.

THE MEMORIAL COMMAND

The command to keep memorial belongs to the Antiochene tradition. In Luke it is found after the words over the bread, and in Paul it is attached to both bread and cup rites. There is the expected debate over whether Jesus actually spoke these or similar words, with a more common tendency among scholars to say that he would at least have indicated the desire to be remembered through this ritual. In translating the Greek word into English, sometimes *memorial* is chosen, sometimes *remembrance,* and sometimes *memory.* This depends on whether one wants to accentuate the ritual character of the action or the community's remembrance.

Studies on the biblical foundations of eucharistic memorial are many and intricate.[1] Some attention is given to the possibility of Hellenic influences because the command is found in Paul and not in the Markan tradition, but by and large studies on this point concentrate on the background of Jewish memorial practices and ideas. In offering a survey of explanations, Fritz Chenderlin points out that theories owe as much to the philosophical or commonsense presuppositions of their authors as they do to the biblical text. This is a caution to keep in mind in entering the discussion and to it one may add that whether in Hebrew times or in Christian, it is doubtful whether at any given moment a single or univocal meaning was attached to memorial action.

In the history of Israel, many things constituted a memorial (*zikkaron*) of God's salvific actions among the people, inclusive of places, monuments, commandments, feasts, and rites. Here the interest is in the memorial character of acts of worship, which include narrative, prayer, and symbolic rites.

When the passover seder is taken as the Hebrew exemplar for Christian remembrance, what are noted are its recall of a divine ordinance, the narrative of the events remembered, the hymns and prayers of blessing, the ritual actions, and the dialogical exchange between the table participants. This model can be helpful if three cautions are kept in mind. First, the passover seder of the early common era is itself subject to historical reconstruction since there are no contemporary documents of the seder available. Second, it is wrong to think of a direct transition from the seder to Christian memorial rites. Third, neither the passover seder nor any table ritual is the sole Jewish influence on Christian remembrance. The synagogue services, the Temple cult, and psalmody all included remembrance and all have to be considered for their possible relevance to Christian eucharistic memorial.

Key Elements in Keeping Memory

A descriptive rather than explanatory account of Jewish memorial includes six features.

First, worship is based on ordinances received from God. Any such service has to be authenticated by appeal to ordinance. However, dif-

---

1. In this study orientation is drawn principally from the following: Fritz Chenderlin, *"Do This as My Memorial": The Semantic and Conceptual Background and Value of Anamnesis in 1 Corinthians 11:24–25* (Rome: Biblical Institute Press, 1982); Brevard S. Childs, *Memory and Tradition in Israel* (London: SCM Press, 1962); Nils Dahl, "Anamnesis: Memory and Commemoration in Early Christianity," in *Jesus in the Memory of the Early Church* (Minneapolis: Augsburg Press, 1976), 11–29; Max Thurian, *The Eucharistic Memorial*, 2 vols., translated from the French by W. G. Davies (London: Lutterworth Press, 1960/61); Claus Westermann, "The 'Re-presentation' of History in the Psalms," in *Praise and Lament in the Psalms*, translated by Keith R. Crim and Richard N. Soulen (Atlanta: John Knox Press, 1981), 214–49. To these add the works of Giraudo, Jeremias, Kilpatrick, Léon-Dufour, and Marshall cited in the preceding chapter.

ferent forms of the same ritual celebration, affecting both the manner
of its celebration and its meaning, are given such a basis. This may be
exemplified in the ordering of the feast of the pasch in texts taken from
the Pentateuch. In one case of the command to keep the paschal feast
what is highlighted is the prophetic action performed with the blood of
the paschal lamb (Exod. 12), while in another what is to be chiefly remembered is the crossing of the Red Sea (Exod. 14). In one case there
is a marked preference for a domestic ritual (Exod. 12), in another for
a priestly (Deut. 16). This shows that for all the importance of staking
a claim to divine ordinance, the Israelite people had different ways of
interpreting these ordinances and their meaning.[2]

The second feature of memorial follows from the first, namely, the
idea that worship is a reciprocal or covenantal relationship in which the
initiative stands with Yahweh.

Third, the continuance of worship, its feasts, and its rituals is a sign
that God remembers the people and past salvific deeds. In the prayer
itself there is the plea that God continue to remember. God's promise is
invoked, in the expectation of divine fidelity, not only to the people but
to God's own trustworthiness.

Fourth, Israel's remembrance is integral to this covenant, an enactment of a vow never to forget. Thus worship is a proclamation of God's
marvelous deeds and an act of praise.

Fifth, certain elements recur in the different kinds of memorial service, whether in feast, in table seder, in synagogue service, or in Temple
cult. Such are the narrative of the deeds remembered, the recital of the
divine command to keep memory, prayers of blessing, and ritual actions
that have covenantal significance.

Sixth, the anticipation of God's kingdom is inherent to memorial. As
they keep memorial, the people of Israel look forward to the eschatological fulfilment of the covenant. According to the different moments
of their history, this may mean different things, but they always expect
to see the promises of the covenant fulfilled in the advent of God's reign.

Further Considerations

In taking these six elements as basis for Christian eucharistic memorial, there is already a good grounding for eucharistic catechesis and for
the regulation of worship. Beyond these elements, authors tend to vary
somewhat in their explanations. Some have commented on the mimetic

---

2. It cannot go unremarked that similar differences show up in Christian celebrations
of the pasch. In earliest times, as we know from homiletic traditions, Exodus 12 was the
core reading for the paschal celebration. Later Exodus 14 took over in importance and
Exodus 12 was sent back first to Friday and then to Thursday, where it is today in the
Roman rite.

nature of the rites of the Temple cult in order to suggest the mimetic nature of eucharistic ritual. That the Temple cult ever served as a mythic reenactment of divine actions is however now highly disputed. In any case to look for a mimetic or figurative representation of the passion in ritual is to obscure the fact that the event is brought to celebration in a service that does not offer this kind of imitation.

Others have pointed to the relation between praise and sacrifice, whether in the Temple cult or in the sacred meals that took on increasing importance in some fellowships. Naturally, many underline the role of *haggadah*, or narration of God's deeds, that recurs in various kinds of service, but this raises questions as to the fixity and the quality of such narrative. By looking upon it as a ritual recital, the factor of tradition is underlined. It would be mistaken however to think that the recital is without some variation. Indeed, even the two examples of the paschal remembrance noted above offer two different ways of remembering the same event.

In his recent work Cesare Giraudo has revived interest in the paschal seder as the immediate background to the Last Supper.[3] He hopes thereby to bring out key characteristics of the Eucharist, both in its forms and in its meaning. He talks of the nature of *haggadah* and more especially of the recall of the memorial command as recital. On this basis, he institutes a parallel between the institution of the paschal meal for the Israelites and the institution of the Eucharist for Christians.

He notes that the eating of the paschal lamb marked the end of the people's sojourn in slavery and the prophetic beginning of their new story as a people of Yahweh. The seder is the repetition of the original meal, as commanded at the time of the Exodus. The original meal celebrated the people's deliverance by the blood of the lamb, but as a prophetic sign it pointed both to the immediate future of the crossing of the Red Sea and the long-term future of the generations who would continue to profit from God's action. It signified God's intervention in freeing them from the slavery that they were leaving behind and promised a future in which they and their descendants would exist as a people. The seder is the continuation of this original meal, now however recalling rather than pointing to the future crossing of the Red Sea, while continuing to point to the eschatological future. From there Giraudo goes on to say that the seder does not make the past events present but makes its participants present to the past events, when covenant was struck and promises given.

On the basis principally of the memorial command Giraudo explains

3. For the way in which he relates seder, supper, and Eucharist, see *Eucaristia per la Chiesa: Prospettive teologiche sull'eucaristia a partire dalla "lex orandi"* (Brescia: Morcelliana Editrice; Rome: Editrice Pontificia Università Gregoriana, 1989), 162–243.

the Eucharist by way of parallel with the origins of the paschal seder. For him, if anything is reenacted in the Eucharist, it is not the death and resurrection of Christ but the Last Supper. In this meal, Jesus marked the term of his preaching of the coming reign of God, indicated the meaning of the passion and death as a salvific and prophetic divine intervention assuring salvation to future generations, and laid down the way in which this death was to be remembered. As a continuation of the supper, the Eucharist now recalls rather than foretells the death and resurrection, while still expressing the promise for the future. The effect of the rite thus instituted is not to make the past events present again, but to make ensuing generations of Christians present to the past event of Christ's pasch and hopeful of its promises.

The theory can in some way cast light on the meaning of the Eucharist, but it embodies some uncertainties. Among these are the reconstitution of the seder, the reconstitution of the supper, and more deeply the notion of the relation between past and present implied. Given the state of the question in biblical scholarship, one is more inclined to agree with John Reumann's conclusion to his survey of studies on *anamnesis*:

> The meaning of anamnesis thus remains unsettled in biblical studies, in spite of considerable advances beyond notions of mere human recollection. It hovers between the two senses exhibited in Psalm 111:
> (a) God "has caused his wonderful works to be remembered" *in his congregation* where thanks and praise are given, and
> (b) "*He* is ever mindful of his covenant" (Psalm 111:4–5).[4]

Given this state of things, Reumann suggests that covenant has to be taken seriously as an important key to the meaning of memorial. It denotes a continued relationship between Yahweh and Israel in which both are active, God in fidelity and the people in obedience.

Kinds of Remembrance

As a living relationship, the idea of covenant provides a context within which changing approaches to keeping memorial may be understandable. In all of the literature, there is some distinction made between cultic reenactment, approaches giving priority to spiritual reality over ritual, and prophetic remembrance. It seems impossible to say that any one of these viewpoints determines the meaning of memorial. It may be more correct to see them as three distinct tendencies in Israel, just indeed as they continue to be three distinct tendencies in the church.

---

4. John Reumann, *The Supper of the Lord: The New Testament, Ecumenical Dialogue, and Faith and Order on Eucharist* (Philadelphia: Fortress Press, 1985), 33.

The cultic or priestly approach has been seen to involve some reen-actment of salvific deeds through mimetic rites. However, research points to the foundation of the cultic in narrative or recital, and to the accompaniment of Temple worship by proclamatory psalms. The dis-tinctive characteristic of the cultic may be less mimesis than its capacity to bolster existing institutions and laws.

Spiritual commemoration gives more importance to prayer and com-munity than to ritual. The accent is placed on purity of life and obedi-ence to the Law. With the concentration on the spiritual rather than on the Temple, the principal forms of worship are the blessing and praise of shared meals among the devout followers of the Law. By the second century of the common era, the *Mishnah* shows how this spiritualization of worship worked for the people at large in the importance given to the study of Torah after the disappearance of the Temple cult.

Prophetic Remembrance

The nature of prophetic remembrance seems worthy of more attention. It both helps us to understand what Jesus did at the supper and of-fers a possible example for developments in eucharistic memorial. It is the kind of remembrance that reinforces fidelity to the covenant, while opening up new perspectives on the future that are not narrowly tied to existing religious and political institutions. In the history of Israel it is prominent in times of upheaval and change.

Some recent scholarship opts for use of the term *recital* to describe the nature of memorial narrative, especially in relation to public or cov-enant worship.[5] There is however a risk that *recital* be understood as rote, suggesting a fixed, unchangeable format to the story. In the forms of narrative employed in prophetic remembrance there is room for in-sertion of new perspectives into the narrative, though the foundational story remains the same. At the supper Jesus clearly recalled the covenant and God's promises to the people, as he may well also have recalled the creation story. However, his reported words show that he introduced new features in the way that he interpreted the promises, relating them both to himself and to a changed eschatological expectation. This seems to fit into a form of prophetic remembrance.

The biblical paradigms for the relationship of this kind of remem-brance to worship are found in Nehemiah 9 in the praise of Ezra, priest and scribe, and in the laments of the Book of Psalms. It is interesting to note that the Book of Nehemiah has to do with the restoration of the

---

5. This is the term preferred by Giraudo, *Eucaristia per la Chiesa.* For varieties within the forms of recital, see Walter Brueggemann, *Abiding Astonishment: Psalms, Modernity, and the Making of History* (Louisville, Ky.: Westminster/John Knox Press, 1991).

Law and is a priestly text. That the priests and scribes may embody the form of this remembrance, and that it can be linked with the restoration of obedience to the Law and of Temple worship, indicates clearly enough that there is no inherent split between the spirit of the Law, priesthood, and prophecy.[6] What draws attention, however, is the way in which recent past events and the new circumstances of the people call for a recasting of the story of the covenant and a new perspective on its promises.

The historical remembrance here envisaged is no mere recital of a known *haggadah*. Quite often the more or less set recital of a story may have been adequate to liturgical memorial. It could also have been a way to prevent extravagant expression by persons not well versed in God's word. It is not however set recital as such that constitutes memorial but narrative, narrative that links the future of the present with its past. Prophetic remembrance is needed when the link has disappeared for the people who hear the story. It takes the form of a reconsideration and even a recasting of the narrative in face of struggle, catastrophe, and sin. It is totally rooted in the collective memory and speaks of the activity of God for the people. However, it gets inside the experience of catastrophe to discern and proclaim the new ways in which God, in fidelity, is now acting and how the future looks in light of this. It provides reassurance and hope for the future because it finds the ways of evoking and narrating salvific events that instill faith despite what appears in the present to be contrary to divine promises. It was in times of distress that Israel's most vivid memories were conjured up and new ways of appealing to God's promises constructed.[7] While one finds this approach more than anywhere in the prophetic books, the psalms and the text quoted from Nehemiah recalled above show how this outlook could be integrated into the public cult.

History is not concentrated in one single event that is then unfolded or repeated through time, with subsequent events as it were patterned on it. Nor do the people expect to be present at, or relive, the Exodus in any literal sense. History provides continuity from one event to the next, from one era to the next, by way of an imaginative recall that reveals potential for the future, even when an apparent discontinuity emerges. The events remembered, Exodus and covenant, serve as a memory and a

---

6. For the place of the Book of Nehemiah in the restoration of the Temple and the renewal of covenant, see Jacob Neusner, *From Testament to Torah: An Introduction to Judaism* (Englewood Cliffs, N.J.: Prentice-Hall, 1988), 9–14.

7. See Walter Brueggemann, *The Creative Word: Canon as a Model for Biblical Education* (Philadelphia: Fortress Press, 1986), 40–66; Id., *The Prophetic Imagination* (Philadelphia: Fortress Press, 1983). That such remembrance is still prized by Jewish people today is evident from the reformulation of the Passover Haggadah after their victimization under the Nazi regime. On this, see Lawrence A. Hoffman, *Beyond the Text: A Holistic Approach to Liturgy* (Bloomington and Indianapolis: Indiana University Press, 1987), 126–44.

metaphor that shapes the people's identity and self-understanding, but the metaphor takes on new life in face of tragedy and surprise. The people had their beginning in the patriarchal covenants and in the Exodus redemption and find promise in their recall, since they hold a guarantee of divine election. Disaster or some surprising new event, such as the good done for Israel by Cyrus the Persian, puts this promise into question and shows the uncertainty of its shape. At that point, prophecy calls forth a renewed way of remembering the event that faces it with the calamities that have befallen the people or events that recall it to the justice of the Torah, so that in light of these very calamities future expectations are reformulated. Simultaneously it puts their worship and institutions at issue and asks for their revitalization, maybe even for change in their form and structure.

Where this prophetic strain dominates, Israelite worship, in its Temple ritual, its domestic assemblies, and its revivalist gatherings (as recounted for example in Nehemiah), is not a repetition of, nor a being present to, past events. It is a representation of the past events in the form of historical narrative and blessing. By appealing to the psalms, Claus Westermann shows that such narrative is at the core of representation and that it is completed by the vow of praise and becomes one with songs of praise and blessing, capable of incorporating both repentance and lament.[8] Pointing to the psalms of lament and to other biblical and extrabiblical laments, he shows how in times of distress the narrative and praise are reshaped. The very contrast between the present calamity and the promise included in salvific events recalled, postulates a new look at these events and at continuity between them and the present. Not all of Israel's woes can be laid at the door of their sinfulness or infidelity to the covenant. Where they are due to external forces, Yahweh's own fidelity seems to be in question. The vow of praise stands up in face of this, but remembrance must consider anew what God did and how God presently walks with the people. In such a situation, there is an inevitable reevaluation of those religious and civic institutions such as the priesthood and the kingship that Israel had thought to be the bearers and guarantors of divine presence and divine protection. Some destructuring and restructuring of institutions may be necessitated by narrative remembrance and the renewal of fidelity.[9]

If we take this prophetic remembrance as a key to the understanding of Jesus' memorial command at the supper, it is possible to get insight

---

8. Westermann, "The 'Re-presentation' of History in the Psalms." In *La struttura letteraria*, Giraudo also treats Nehemiah 9, indicating how it includes repentance as well as praise in face of remembrance. He does not address the inclusion of a lament in face of what not even the people's sin can explain.

9. On this, see Walter Brueggemann, "The Hopeful Truth of the Assembly," in *David's Truth in Israel's Imagination and Memory* (Philadelphia: Fortress Press, 1985), 87–109.

into what is recounted of his words and actions, as also into the nature
of the Eucharist as a memorial action. In the accounts of the passion and
of the supper, Jesus is seen to grapple with the certainty of his betrayal
and death. This is contrary to the trust that he placed in God in proclaiming the coming of the kingdom. Throughout his ministry, it had been
necessary for him to reconcile the promise of messianic fulfillment with
rejection of his preaching and his person. Facing death at the supper,
obedience and prophetic narration coincide with a recasting of eschatological expectation when Jesus is said to look forward to the kingdom,
to drinking the fruit of the vine in the kingdom. This indicates that he
anticipates what lies beyond his betrayal and death and that he sees in
that future the fulfilment of the covenant promises regarding the final
establishment of God's reign.

Starting with these pointers, the whole meal may be seen as a prophetic moment, when Jesus reshapes the memory and the promise of
passover and covenant in face of the tragedy of his own death and his
abandonment by God. In fidelity to the covenant of Israel and in evoking
its deepest meaning in the twin commandment of love, he had preached
the advent of God's kingdom. His word had been rejected and he was
to be judged a blasphemer, given over to death by the one whom he
addressed as *Abba*. Instead of leading to despair, in face of this rejection his words and actions reinterpret the meaning and the promise of
salvation and locate them in the death itself. It is thus that it is to be remembered and it is in the act of this prophetic service that he himself
is to be remembered. When the early Christians were filled with faith
in his resurrection and celebrated the remembrance of his death, they
could see the promise of the resurrection in the words about his forthcoming death. They could also see the anticipation of his coming anew,
as this is evoked in Paul's version of the supper. Their own remembrance
therefore would not only look back to the death and receive the self-gift
of the risen Lord, but it would continue to interpret present history in
the light of the eschatological expectation opened up by Jesus' passover.

Event to Word

In understanding memorial in this fashion, a good starting point is to see
how an event is brought to word, or to narrative, and how it is given its
meaning in this process. It is this that gives it its power to act as a force
within history, shaping and transforming human reality. The event in
the case of the supper memorial is the passion of Christ, to which the
supper itself is integral. The supper obviously takes its meaning from
the passion, but on the other hand the passion as an act of Christ is given
succinct expression in the actions, blessings, and gift-words of Jesus at
the meal.

In memorial celebration, once brought to narrative the event then enters the word of the blessing that flows from the story and expresses the God/people relation that ensues from the event remembered. It is in the power of this blessing that the table elements of bread and wine are transformed into the body and blood of Christ and are received as the gift of Christ himself. The reception of this gift is thus a communion both in his passion, which is remembered as a turning-point in history and as an expression of a new eschatological expectation, and in the new life of Christ himself, raised up from the dead. The repeated ritual action brings this memory and this gift to successive generations and diverse peoples and enables them to be part of the eschatological hope that was forged in the pasch of Christ.

Schematically this can be expressed as follows:

The event is brought to narrative.

The narrative is brought to blessing.

The blessing transforms the bread and wine into the body and blood.

The body and blood is received as a gift from Christ, communion in Christ's life and a communion in the presence of the passover event in history.

The entire action, based as it is on narrative remembrance, looks forward to the fulfilment of the covenantal promises and puts all historical experiences into this horizon.

USE OF HISTORICAL MASTER IMAGES

As a succinct narrative expressing not only the meaning of the supper but that of the Christ event itself, the supper accounts serve as a model of how story formulates historical continuity and meaning. It is their art of storytelling that allows the accounts to place the events surrounding Jesus of Nazareth into the history of the covenant and to show the link of the church's memorial action with this history and with the anticipation of God's reign. Much of the accounts' power lies in their use of the historical master images of covenant, pasch, suffering servant, and sacrifice. These images give the words and actions of Jesus at the supper their density and their eschatological value.

Historical master images are those that continue to be used throughout a tradition in connection with an ongoing series of events. They serve both to interpret each event and to establish a link between it and those that come before and after it. They are future-oriented for they suggest expectations about what is yet to come by the very reason of their constant deployment in interpreting history. They do not have a rigid or inflexible meaning, but they are enriched in meaning by reason of the events of which they are predicated. Since their predication of events is often unexpected and expresses new insight, they may be called the root metaphors of a tradition.

The advantage of referring to them as metaphors lies in that this brings their predication to the fore. Rather than suggesting that the images have fixed and stable meanings, it becomes clear that it is in their predication that they offer meaning, not simply in themselves, and that this meaning is determined by the predication rather than brought to it ready made.

Thus, for example, in secular history the word *right*, though already having a certain weight takes on fresh meaning from being predicated of a bill passed in assembly, from being applied to what is adjudicated in a court of law, from being seen as that which when denied cheapens human life, and from being fought for in the streets.

From the Hebrew scriptures, one could take the example of the images of covenant, exile, and kingdom. They are constantly used to speak of historical events, from the call of Abraham, through the Exodus and the entry to the promised land, and into the periods of Israel's vicissitudes. They are repeated in face of disasters and deliverance from disaster and open up the expectation of the coming Messiah. Each event is given significance through these potent images and is woven into the ongoing and future-oriented historical tradition.

Within this practiced use of master images, through the images of pasch, covenant, suffering servant, and sacrifice, the simple actions and words of Jesus at the supper offer a key to his place in God's work of human salvation. It is to be expected that they continue to play a role in the eucharistic tradition of the church.

Pasch/Passover

As already mentioned, various inconclusive attempts have been made to show that the last meal of Jesus with his disciples was a paschal seder. Such historical reconstruction is not necessary to the paschal significance given to it by the Synoptic Gospels. By using the image, the Gospels place the final events of Jesus' earthly sojourn into the chronology of the festive year and thus into the history of the Jewish people. The death of Jesus and the ritual of the evening take their significance from the fact that they are built into this story.[10]

---

10. The Johannine Gospel is even more insistent on relating the events of Jesus' ministry to the feasts of the year and on the fact that this farewell meal relates to the pasch.

The Poem of the Four Nights recited on the feast is quite well known.[11] It picks out the key nights of creation, of the sacrifice of Isaac, of the deliverance from the slavery of Egypt, and of the future night when the Messiah will come. Each of these nights is in continuity with the others but it has itself a transformative effect on history. Within this setting, evoked by mention of the feast, Mark gives a passover significance to the death of Jesus and relates it to the expectation of the coming of the Son of Man. According to the account, key to this meaning is the celebration of the passover with the disciples in the upper room.[12]

Covenant

It is in the words of Jesus over the wine that reference is made to the covenant, or more specifically to the blood of the covenant, or the covenant in the blood. As the words are related, this blood is shed "for you/for the multitude."

Reumann's discussion of the use of this image shows two things. First, it is difficult to determine exact references in the Hebrew scriptures. Second, the covenant is an image that opens up vistas of interpretation beyond a link with any specific text. With most scholars he opts for the translation of *diatheke* as *covenant* rather than *testament*, but points out that it is unclear which model of covenant is intended. One possibility is the covenant promised in Jeremiah 31:31. Another is the Mosaic covenant, suggested by the parallel with the shedding of blood in the sacrificial rite described in Exodus 24. A third is the covenant made by Yahweh with Abraham. He concludes:

> The Lord's Supper as covenant is a matter of grace whether it is based on the Abraham model or reflects something of Sinai. And like the Exodus experience or David's divine prerogative, it could

---

11. On this, see R. Le Déaut, *La nuit pascale* (Rome: Biblical Institute Press, 1963). For convenience, one can find the text of the Targum on Exodus 12:42 in Léon-Dufour, *Sharing the Eucharistic Bread: The Witness of the New Testament*, translated by Matthew O'Connell (New York: Paulist Press, 1987), 190–91. See also I. Howard Marshall, *Last Supper and Lord's Supper* (Grand Rapids: William B. Eerdmans, 1980), 78.

12. Since they are concerned with historical reconstruction, both Jeremias and Giraudo suggest that in the course of the meal Jesus would have referred the meaning of the paschal lamb to himself. See Joachim Jeremias, *The Eucharistic Words of Jesus*, translated by Norman Perrin (Philadelphia: Fortress Press, 1977), 220–25; Giraudo, *Eucaristia per la Chiesa*, 256–64. The gospel texts, however, do not make this connection and they give paschal significance to the actions of Jesus in a broader way. The connection of course is quite legitimately made by Paul but it does not belong to the story of the eucharistic institution.

be abused (cf. Exod. 32:4, 6; Num. 25:1–18; 21:5–6; 16:41–49; in light of 1 Cor. 10:1–11).[13]

The very flexibility of the image and its reference shows how it relates the death of Jesus and its commemoration to a history that unfolds through many episodes and will continue to an eschatological time of final consummation. Though when coupled with the image of blood-shedding it recalls the Sinai sacrifice narrated in Exodus 24, giving sacrificial meaning to the death of Jesus or to the ritual of commemoration is not the sole purpose of its usage. Any sacrificial predication that is insinuated has to be allied with the renewal of the covenant and the promises of the covenant, as well as with the reality of covenant relationship forged between God and the disciples of Jesus in the sharing of the cup.

Suffering Servant

In the image of the shedding of blood "for the multitude" the Markan text probably makes reference to Isaiah 53:12, collating Isaiah 42:6 and 49:8. These texts belong to the songs of the Servant of Yahweh, in which a person or persons are there remembered for the willingness to endure suffering and contradiction for the sake of Yahweh. Through this suffering, a way of mediation is opened up between sinners and Yahweh. The servant is even said to have offered himself for the people, thus suggesting some kind of vicarious suffering.

The poems of the Suffering Servant bring out the way in which he exhausts himself in the service of others, submitting to contempt and abuse in so doing, even to the point of handing over his soul to death. To bring out the mediatory efficacy of this behavior the prophet sings of the servant handed over as a ransom or made a covenant for the transgressions of the people. He is even called "an offering for sin" (53:10), but this is metaphoric language to describe the worth of his voluntary suffering. Beyond the cultic images is the suggestion that cult itself does not suffice. There emerges a human figure who acts as mediator between God and sinful humanity because of his suffering "for the multitude." Appropriate language has to be found to express the extent and power of this dedication and self-gift.

When this reference is introduced into the story and words of Jesus, a vicarious action undertaken for the sake of others is intimated. Though

---

13. Reumann, *The Supper of the Lord,* 40. He adds: "The covenant aspect of the Christian Sacrament is a topic not yet exhausted in modern analysis." See 34–41 for the full discussion.

the meaning is clearly broader, some authors find a corroboration of a sacrificial reading of Jesus' death in the image of the Suffering Servant.[14]

Sacrifice

This brings us then to the use of the imagery of sacrifice to speak both of Christ's death and of the Eucharist. The comments on the other images show that in the supper accounts the introduction of cultic language to designate either Christ's death or the memorial rite is oblique rather than direct. Nonetheless in Christian history the use of sacrificial language has often occurred in expressing the link between the death remembered and the memorial rite. While this was a hot point of debate at the time of the Reformation, ecumenical discussions have tempered the issue by stressing the sacramental and memorial relation of the eucharistic sacrifice to Christ's death. This still does not explain how this sacrificial emphasis may be rooted in New Testament texts.

Not very long ago Henri Cazelles offered a solution to this problem by suggesting that the connection is indirect, rather than one that comes directly from the supper texts. He appealed to the practice of *todah*.[15] This is a Hebrew noun derived from a verb meaning "to make known." It is used of a type of prayer that proclaims the deeds and the power of Yahweh. Cazelles noted that in Leviticus 7:11–15 this prayer of praise is associated with the peace-offering, considered the most perfect of Jewish sacrifices. As he saw it, this happy coincidence of blessing and sacrifice is warrant for speaking of the Eucharist as sacrifice and for associating it with the proclamation of the atoning death of Christ.

Since then a much fuller study of *todah* has been made by Cesare Giraudo.[16] He finds it an even more fundamental form of prayer than *berakah* and agrees on its importance in Jewish worship. However, he is hesitant to accept its association with Leviticus 7 as sufficient warrant to call the eucharistic proclamation a sacrifice.[17] Such praise did indeed accompany some Temple sacrifices, and Psalms 50, 56, 106, and 107 are good examples of proclamatory prayers intended for use in Temple wor-

---

14. Thus Marshall, *Last Supper and Lord's Supper*, 91–93; Rudolph Pesch, *Das Abendmahl und Jesu Todesverständnis* (Freiburg im Breisgau: Herder, 1978), 95f. Giraudo speaks in more generic terms of "vicarious redemption," *Eucaristia per la Chiesa*, 256–64, and Léon-Dufour stresses the metaphorical sense of the cultic language, *Sharing the Eucharistic Bread*, 151–54.

15. Henri Cazelles, "L'anaphore et l'Ancien Testament," in *Eucharisties d'Orient et d'Occident*, vol. 1 (Paris: Ed. du Cerf, 1970), 11–21. The discussions about *todah* are excellently summarized in Léon-Dufour, *Sharing the Eucharistic Bread*, 41–44.

16. Cesare Giraudo, *La struttura letteraria della preghiera eucaristica: Saggio sulla genesi letteraria di una forma* (Rome: Biblical Institute Press, 1981).

17. Ibid., 266f.

ship. On the other hand, proclamatory praise was not confined to use in Temple worship and when separated from it became one of the primary means in developing a notion of spiritual worship. As a spiritual offering, the "sacrifice of praise" could be seen as the most perfect form of sacrifice. It may well be therefore in this sense that the Christian Eucharist came to be called a sacrifice of thanksgiving. How in the course of Christian centuries this was associated with a more priestly and cultic understanding of sacrifice will be seen in later chapters of this work.

The New Testament origins of the language leave us with the understanding that the Eucharist is sacrifice in a metaphorical sense rather than in the cultic sense of Old Testament sacrifices, though it has its origins in the cult and depends on it for its meaning. To speak here of metaphor does not reduce the Eucharist's efficaciousness in representing the death that it proclaims. The metaphoric use intended is a long way from the notion of "mere metaphor" or of metaphor as an adornment of language. It is rooted rather in the power of language to transform reality. It appeals to the polysemy of the word *sacrifice* and incorporates the various ways in which it is applied, first to the Christian life, then to the memorial liturgy, and finally to Christ's death. This is not a case of giving a univocal meaning to sacrifice. It is rather a matter of metaphorical usage that shows how these three realities belong together in constituting the right worship of God.

Passages in the First Letter to the Corinthians are of course brought to bear in supporting the sacrificial nature of the Lord's Supper. In 1 Corinthians 10, Paul compares the eating of the flesh of idols with the communion table of Christians. He does not seem, however, to be comparing sacrifice with sacrifice, but food with food and scandal with true *koinonia*. Christians might on principle eat of the flesh offered to idols and sold in the marketplace or placed before them on social occasions. There is no cultic involvement implied as they attach no importance to such offering and signify no intention of taking part in false worship. Their actions might all the same cause scandal to weaker members of the community, and if so they would offend against the table of the Lord where fellowship in Christ's body is expressed. Though they have no communion with the idols to whom the flesh they eat has been offered, they do have communion with Christ whose body and blood they share, and they ought to act accordingly in their relations with the others with whom they share at this table.

As a further matter of interest, there is a roundabout connection in the Pauline writings between Eucharist and the sacrifice of *todah*. This comes from the place that Romans 12:1ff. has in this letter. The structure of the letter is an adaptation of the structure of the Jewish prayer of praise and remembrance. In chapter 12 Paul argues that this kind of praise is actually given by Christ's disciples in a life lived according to the gospel, by which they present their bodies as an acceptable sacrifice and true worship.

Reflection on these four historical images shows how Christ's death is proclaimed and interpreted in the context of the Eucharist and how the Eucharist relates to it. They serve to fill out the idea of prophetic remembrance, for their use shows the imagery that can be put to use in a variety of ways to express what it means to keep memorial of Christ in the life of the church.

THE EUCHARIST AND CHRISTIAN LIFE

With this it is possible to pass on to how New Testament texts give insight into ways in which the eucharistic memorial relates to the life setting of communities. Three points will be considered: (a) the supper in its social setting; (b) the symbolism of bread and wine; (c) the Eucharist and human suffering.

The Lord's Supper in Its Social Setting

The distinction has been made between the cultic and testamentary traditions, noting the importance of service to the keeping of Christ's memory. Since in writing to the Corinthians Paul related service, or *diakonia,* with communion, or *koinonia,* one can turn to him to see how the Lord's Supper belongs in the life of the community.[18]

A Domestic Church. From both Paul and the Acts of the Apostles we are familiar with the domestic nature of Christian gathering and ritual celebration. The spread of churches in the diaspora meant the existence of communities, made up largely of gentiles, that had no relation to the Temple cult. The house-church was the center of their existence, where their bonding and communion were forged. Paul's insistence is that the communion in the one loaf and the one cup of the Lord's Supper is at the heart of this reality, making of Christians one body in Jesus Christ. All ministries relate to this in one form or another, whether they have to do with mutual care, with administration, or with edifying the faithful by word and with praising God.

There is no specific information about presidency of the Eucharist either in the Pauline letters or elsewhere in the New Testament. From

---

18. See Gerhard Theissen, "Social Integration and Sacramental Activity: An Analysis of 1 Cor 11: 17–34," in Gerhard Theissen, *The Social Setting of Pauline Christianity: Essays on Corinth,* translated by J. H. Schutz (Philadelphia: Fortress Press, 1982); Robert Banks, *Paul's Idea of Community: The Early House Churches in their Historical Setting* (Grand Rapids: William B. Eerdmans, 1980).

Luke's supper account we know that it was considered a service rather than a holding of rank, and since it had to involve teaching and blessing it is classifiable as a word ministry requiring the appropriate charisms. With what other ministries it was joined there is little way of telling. When the community received the visits of apostles, such as Paul, the table-blessing may well have been pronounced by him.[19] Otherwise one might suspect that it followed the model of a domestic gathering with the head of the house presiding at table. This could have left place for women as well as men to preside at the ritual, since some of the house-churches met where women members presided over community organization. At any rate, since the model of worship was at first deliberately nonpriestly there was no parallel with levitical cult to exclude them from the sacrifice of praise. This is an important point for current developments in eucharistic practice, when there are so many ideas abroad that corroborate the restriction of orders to male members of the church. The evidence of an age when women participated in church structuring does not simply constitute an argument for admission to ministry and order. It raises the question of the reshaping of order that takes place when women participate in this action.

The Vocabulary of Worship. Since the Eucharist in its domestic and familial setting became the center of Christian worship, there was a reworking of liturgical vocabulary to fit this reality.[20] It is found not only in Paul but also in 1 Peter, in Hebrews, and in the Book of Revelation. The adaptation of such a vocabulary seems to have started not with the Eucharist but with Christian life. It is the people for whom Christ gave his blood who are the temple of the Spirit, the living sacrifice, and the royal priesthood (1 Peter 2:4–10). It is the obedience to the gospel that is holy and pleasing to God, what Paul calls the offering of bodies as an acceptable sacrifice (Rom. 12:1). The preaching of the gospel is the priestly ministry of the apostle, since through it he brings the people to this acceptable offering (Rom. 15:16). The Eucharist itself is not spoken of in priestly terms. Since it is both the proclamation of the Lord's death and the communion of the people in the redeemed reality of the body of Christ, the later transfer of such vocabulary to it from people and from preaching is understandable.

---

19. Though there are problems about dating the *Didache,* it is to be noted that it sees bishops and deacons taking over from the apostles and prophets in the service of the Eucharist (*Didache 15, 1*). For a reconstruction of the original text and a French translation, see *La doctrine des douzes apôtres (Didaché),* translated by Willy Rordorf and André Tuilier, Sources Chrétiennes 248 (Paris: Ed. du Cerf, 1978).

20. For this, see Robert J. Daly, *Christian Sacrifice: The Judeo-Christian Background before Origen* (Washington, D.C.: Catholic University of America Press, 1978), 208–307.

Eucharist and Social Status. Since the house-gatherings brought together people of different social standing and status, the nature of their fellowship was an issue, one that we know most about in the church of Corinth. Building on the imagery of the one loaf, the one cup, and the one body, Paul pleaded for gatherings of a nondiscriminatory nature.[21] Participation in the Lord's Supper and discrimination could not go together.

In connection with this ideal of communion, certain questions arose within the Corinthian community that Paul felt obliged to address. They had to do with the use and appreciation of charismatic gifts, the meal that accompanied the ritual, the place of the poor in the assembly, and the public use of their gifts by women members. From the letter to Philemon, one may surmise that the place of slaves in the household church was also an issue in Paul's time.

Some of Paul's solutions do not seem to measure up to the basic principle of nondiscrimination. He seems to have seen the problems but to have been satisfied with what look like compromise solutions. Inasmuch as this reflects the tensions of life together, to see him tackling problems in this way may be salutary rather than disconcerting. At any rate, it means that his answers are not to be taken as the last word on the subject. It means that he may have succumbed to existing models of social relations and thus hindered the full participation in the life of the church of people of lower status and of women. This does not simply mean that such persons did not attain to full and equal membership in the church as established, but also that their contribution to the form of this establishment was neglected. This has to be integral to any critique of contemporary approaches to ministry, community ordering, and ritual.

It is likely that the eschatological outlook of the Christian people, brought to the fore in eucharistic celebration where the Lord's death is proclaimed "until he comes," tempered the need to resolve such practical matters. Limits were also imposed by attempts to avoid scandal, inside and outside the church. The ultimate liberating force of Christ's memory, divine judgment on all things human, and the hope of God-given freedom seem to have been tamed by the readiness to adopt existing social models, even while advocating greater charity among community members.

---

21. See Elisabeth Schüssler Fiorenza, "Tablesharing and the Celebration of the Eucharist," *Concilium* 152 (1982): 3–12. On Paul's attitude to the role of women in worship, see the same author's *In Memory of Her: A Feminist Theological Reconstruction of Christian Origins* (New York: Crossroad, 1986), 226–33.

The Symbolism of the Bread and Wine[22]

The Ritual. Though the Eucharist related to the common meal and to a sharing of goods in the church, it was tied to the specific rites of sharing bread and wine. It was in blessing, transforming and sharing these with them that Christ gave himself to his disciples, thus bequeathing them a memorial in which the risen Christ is ever present in the church. It was in the symbolism of the one loaf and the one cup that Paul found the meaning of eating and drinking the body and blood of the Lord. This was in essence to relate the commemoration of Christ's death and his abiding gift and presence to the most elemental nourishment of the people and to their sharing together in it.

The Biblical Imagery. The biblical imagery of feeding and nourishing is derived from its relation to God's covenant action. In the sixth chapter of the Johannine Gospel, the feeding of a crowd and the discourse on the bread of life are related.[23] The background to this is the story of the manna given to the people in the desert and the messianic expectation of the One Who is to Come. With the feeding of the thousands narrated at the beginning of the chapter the crowds thought to find such expectation fulfilled in Jesus. This touches on the profound but difficult connection between the need for life's sustenance and the desire for God.

Prophets such as Amos and Jeremiah made it clear that injustice and the neglect of the needy were gross transgressions of the covenant. Rightly therefore the people connected their vague desires for justice with their hope for the Coming One. In their attitude, however, Jesus finds a lack of any true awareness of how God's reign is to come and a failure to grasp the nature of his own mission. He then introduces the story of the manna into his instruction on faith. Though the manna (Exod. 16:1–36) was intended indeed to feed the people in the desert, it was also a sign that asked for faith, a faith of which many of the people freed from Egypt were incapable. In meeting the day's need, and only the day's need (for it was not to be stored against the morrow), it pointed to an eschatological future. Neither the people in the Old Testament story nor the people whom Jesus addressed could quite grasp what this meant about relations to the present time and the hope of the kingdom.

---

22. See Rouillard, "From Human Meal to Christian Eucharist," *Worship* 52 (1978): 425–39; 53 (1979): 40–56.

23. There is little exegetical agreement on how much of this chapter relates to faith in Christ and how much to the Eucharist. This does not need to be resolved to see how it illumines eucharistic symbolism.

Covenant Justice. The symbolism of blessing the bread and wine and receiving Christ's body and blood under this sign stands out well against this background. The people's hunger and needs, even their need for a justice that satisfies, is indeed expressed in the bread and wine brought to table. Their blessing in memorial of Christ is a promise of eschatological fulfilment. This points first to a fulfilment that is given ultimately through life in God, in the end time when God's rule prevails. It also promises however some anticipation of this rule in a world wherein people live by a covenant justice. Faith in Jesus as the One sent by God and the nourishment of the Eucharist come together to express hope.

Suffering and Sacrifice

Since Eucharist is the memorial of the suffering and death of Jesus Christ, seen in the light of the resurrection, it is of interest to see how relating suffering to eschatological hope helped to shape the vocabulary of sacrifice, and priesthood. The texts concerned do not speak of the Eucharist. What is of interest to eucharistic theology is their treatment of suffering, sacrifice and priestliness in the forging of a liturgical vocabulary and in relating the suffering of Christians to the memory of Christ's suffering.

The principal texts are found in 1 Peter and in Hebrews.[24] It was mentioned earlier that in prophetic remembrance Israel retold its story of salvific events in light of the apparent contradiction between reality and God's promises. Something of this sort happens in these two letters in response to the recipients' anguish and disappointment, which is looked at in the light of Christ's suffering and its outcome. Whatever the exact nature of the suffering and indignity endured by the intended readers of these letters, they apparently felt it to be a contradiction of their hope and expectation.

1 Peter. First Peter responds to this dilemma by the account of the suffering of Christ and by inviting the readers to an imitation of Christ. Because of the expiatory value of his innocent suffering, they who feel themselves to be held of little human estimation have the high calling of suffering innocently for the good of others. Their suffering, however unjustly imposed, is transformed into a proclamation of the good news of how Christ's suffering, descent into hell, and resurrection brought about human redemption. Not an exhortation to seek out suffering, such consideration offers a way of meeting it when it comes.

---

24. Help here is taken from Edward Schillebeeckx, *Christ: The Experience of Jesus as Lord,* translated by John Bowden (New York: Crossroad Publishing Company, 1980), 251–93.

This Petrine letter makes abundant usage of the image of the Suffering Servant, whose importance in the supper accounts has been noted (see 2:21–25; 3:17; 4:15). Much is made of the fact that the suffering of Christ, as of Christians, is innocent. This is what gives the blood of Christ its price value in redemption, for it is that of a lamb without blemish (1:20). The soteriological significance of this suffering is expressed in the descent into hell or the place of the dead (3:19) where Christ announces the salvation that he earned when he "bore our sins in his body on the tree" (2:24). The resurrection is not simply resurrection from the tomb but resurrection from this abode of death. Thus it is of advantage to all generations from the beginning of time. The prophets of old had grasped this (1:10–12) but not all who heard them had believed. Now this message is given them anew by Christ himself. Baptism (3:21) enables Christians to make the journey with Christ through innocent suffering and into the glory of the resurrection. Thus their suffering may benefit not only the living but even the dead, since it is one with his.

As often occurs in reading the New Testament we may be disappointed in seeing the practical conclusions drawn from such considerations. In the end, servants are exhorted to submission as are wives, and citizens admonished to forbearance and obedience to the emperor. Nonetheless there is a freedom that comes with being servants of God (2:16) that colors all human and social relations. The intractability of social structure and cultural outlook puts limits on the action that flows from this, but the horizon offered for approaching human issues is eschatological and so beyond all limit. Readers of ensuing generations of believers are to think within that horizon rather than simply look for the practical solutions offered in the letter. In any case, the approach to suffering serves as a gloss on what it is to remember Jesus as the Suffering Servant, a remembrance embodied time and time again in the eucharistic memorial. It is a memory that can serve better than it does in the letter of Peter to express the solidarity of the Suffering Servant with the world's victims and with those who seem to have died in vain, and thus to bring to them the power to take a part in the shaping of the world's future.

Hebrews. In Hebrews some have found a reference to the Eucharist in 13:10: "We have an altar from which those who serve the tent have no right to eat." This seems unlikely since the author's whole argument leads to the exclusion of ritual sacrifices from the new covenant, all being consummated in the death of Christ. As in other New Testament books, holy lives and praise are the sacrifice of Christians.

On the other hand, the letter is more explicit than 1 Peter in giving a sacrificial interpretation to Christ's death. His solidarity with human suffering enters into his priesthood (4:15; 5:2, 7–8). Paralleling the liturgy of Yom Kippur, chapter 9 of the letter describes Christ's death as sacrificial shedding of his own blood and a priestly inauguration by way of entry into the heavenly sanctuary where he makes priestly and eternal intercession. The point of this for the readers is that through their own suffering and their "hard struggle" they may become one with Christ and come to share with him in the heavenly liturgy (10:19–22, 32–34). This is the ground of their perseverance and their good conduct (10:23–25). It ought to change their attitude toward suffering and allow them to unite it with their worship.

CONCLUSION: AN APPROPRIATED READING

The reading of New Testament texts in these two chapters has focused: (a) on the community context of eucharistic celebration; (b) on its relation to social setting; (c) on the significance of the bread and wine ritual in its biblical context; (d) on the identity of the community through its communion in Christ at the table; (e) on how the testamentary tradition complements the cultic; (f) on insight into memorial as prophetic remembrance; (g) on the use of historical images in making this remembrance, and (h) on how remembrance of Christ's suffering changes attitudes to human suffering.

This leads to certain observations that have a bearing on how we might celebrate Eucharist in our time. To use the headings indicated in the first chapter for a conversation with tradition, the *canon of remembrance* offered by New Testament texts is broader than the account of the supper in the Synoptic and Pauline narratives. It includes the Johannine testamentary tradition and the meal texts that point to how Jesus is to be remembered when his passover is commemorated. Furthermore, it is within the story of the covenant with Israel, as this is recalled by images such as those of pasch, servant, and sacrifice, that the death of Jesus is given meaning for his disciples. The canon of remembrance is enlarged to recall the stories in which these images are rooted, so that the meaning of Christ's death may appear in its relation to them. When Jesus himself, according to the tradition, celebrated the passover his words pointed to his own death as a turning-point in the history of God's deeds.

While obviously there can be no beginning similar to that of the Last Supper and cross, the church today lives at a crucial point of human history and of its own history when it is asked anew what God promised in Christ and how the present times are related to this promise. As at the time of the return of Israel to Jerusalem from exile, new contextual interpretation of Christ's death is called for that ought to be reflected in the reading of the scriptures and in blessing prayers. Drawing on the rich background of *todah* prayer, communities may find structural as well as metaphorical inspiration in composing eucharistic texts. More attention too needs to be given to the liberating power of the memorial of Christ's suffering for those who are life's victims, a liberating power that not only offers them ultimate freedom but draws them into the shaping of the future of the church and its canon of remembrance.

Taking up the second heading for conversation, we can say that the *ritual performance* indicated by the behavior of the early disciples of Christ includes these elements: blessing and gift, hearing the word, and a mutual upbuilding in charismatic service and table fellowship that constitute the context for the bread and wine ritual. Though blessing is clearly essential to commemoration, it is the common table, the common loaf, and the common cup that are put to the fore, not the action of one presiding. Some flexibility in the ritual observed strikes one today when diverse assemblies are seeking ways of gathering that draw in the lives of their members more fully. Now, as in New Testament times, the church needs to be careful of the measure in which its action is determined, not by the gospel, but by prevailing social models.

The Eucharist's *relation to Christian ethics* is indicated in several ways by a reading of New Testament texts. First, there is the importance of including the testamentary tradition along with the cultic. If the remembrance of Christ in liturgy is not founded in the living memorial of mutual love, Christ is not remembered as he pleaded to be. Second, the rite is necessarily complemented in some way by the elements of common life, in which communion is forged from service. Third, ritual performance or enactment has the power to question prevailing cultural and social suppositions and distinctions, but it can also incorporate these to the detriment of eucharistic practice. Fourth, attitudes to suffering are changed when it is seen in the light of the remembrance of the cross of Christ. While some of the attitudes reflected in the two letters examined are not adequate to the dilemma of suffering as it is posed in today's world, and may not have been adequate in their own time, the point is clear that the memorial of Christ speaks to all human suffering and to every situation in which people suffer. To face the realities of suffering at the heart of eucharistic memorial is an important challenge for churches around the world.

Retrieving the capacity for prophetic remembrance offers a new perception of organic development and challenges us to move beyond a too literal dependency on earlier ritual ordering, lectionary structures, and traditional blessings. This gives a rather different basis to what is understood by keeping memorial than derives from a more strictly cultic idea of ritual. It is perhaps also a better way to see how church tradition relates back to scriptural origins, with both continuity and change in rite and in perspective.

As far as the influence of *thought-forms* is concerned, most insights into the meaning of the Lord's Supper in contemporary studies come from a retrieval of the meaning of memorial in Semitic life and cult. While some Hellenic influence has to be accounted for, especially in Paul, the primary challenge is to retrieve the Semitic sense and forms of memorial and to draw not only theoretical but practical inspiration from this. It is of little use to include some pertinent ideas about memorial and representation in ecumenical documents if what we know about the Eucharist's Semitic background has no influence on how it is celebrated.

On the other hand, the discussion is a reminder that even within Jewish history keeping memorial was not uniformly understood and that it is presumptuous to think that biblical studies provide unequivocal insight into the meaning of eucharistic memorial. Biblical studies have always to be completed by understanding of the ways in which church traditions have led us to read the biblical texts. This is the matter for the following chapters.

Part III

_____

EUCHARIST IN THE
PRE-NICENE CHURCH

Chapter 4

THE PRE-NICENE CHURCH: EUCHARISTIC PRACTICE

Several factors obscure the reading of eucharistic tradition. First, it is often presented in broad sweeps covering several centuries, without giving sufficient attention to theological and cultural diversity within it. Second, there is a tendency to look for the orthodox and normative tradition in the post-Nicene church, much in the same way that christology is judged in reference to the councils beginning with Nicea. What comes later is then sought in some form in earlier literature.

In choosing to look at the pre-Nicene church, we are looking at a period when the tradition was in a formative state and still reflected considerable cultural, structural, and theological diversity. A sense of this diversity and richness derives from studies on particular authors, e.g., Irenaeus, Cyprian, and Origen, or on local churches, such as those of North Africa and East Syria, and from studies of early eucharistic prayer texts.

These studies shed light on eucharistic practices, on liturgical prayer, and on theological reflection. While they need to be examined separately, these three components have to be seen in relation to one another. An adequate liturgical theology cannot do otherwise. The available texts come from several regions, namely, Syria, Armenia, Rome, North Africa, and Gaul. They emerge in different religious and cultural contexts, showing some interaction with Judaism, Hellenism, and gnosticism. They show the impact of social circumstances on Eucharist, and the interplay of pastors and thinkers with the prevailing thought of their time.

As a minority group, the attitude of Christians to the world around them was by no means uniform and indeed differed from region to region.[1] In Syria, the relation to Judaism is a decisive factor in the for-

---

1. W. H. C. Frend surveys the period from 70 to 193 under the headings of relations with the synagogue, the position of communities within the empire, and the Hellenization that went on as a kind of response of the Christian faith within that culture to gnosti-

69

mation of Christianity. Jewish elements show up in morality and in worship, where synagogue prayer and table prayer continue to exercise an influence. In Rome, Christian meetings resembled other kinds of supportive groupings in Roman society. The situation was such that Christians needed to earn their living alongside others and so conformed in family and social matters to the prevailing mores. Their faith simply led them to disassociate themselves from public worship and immorality and to refuse certain kinds of occupation. Given their absence from public cult and the rather private nature of their gatherings, Christians were often seen as suspect, both by Jew and pagan. In face of suspicion and persecution, they had to remain steadfast in their faith. Martyrdom was preferable to any abjuration of the name of Christ.

Eucharist therefore was a commemoration of Christ and a nourishment which fostered a concern for unworldly matters, taught obedience to social practice and law in most things, and yet by communion with Christ's passion allowed the people to be firm in face of criticism and persecution. On the whole, one would not expect Christians to be prominent as social critics, and yet their readiness to renounce the world in fidelity to Christ's name and the hope of eternal life was a most profound criticism of all human power.

This chapter is devoted to a consideration of eucharistic practice. Under this heading there fall such things as the order of service, the place of assembly, the frequency of assembly, and communion outside the assembly. The evidence available is mostly from the churches of Syria and Rome, with some tidbits from other locations. The Syrian documents are the church orders known as the *Didache* and the *Didascalia*, and the apocryphal acts of the apostles. The Roman evidence is taken from the writings of Justin Martyr and the church order known as the *Apostolic Tradition of Hippolytus*. What comes in addition from North Africa is gleaned from the works of Tertullian and Cyprian.

Since this information is quite readily accessible there is no need here for a detailed study.[2] The material is rather summarized under four headings, in such a way as to underline its theological significance: (a) the order of service; (b) Eucharist and the observance of Sunday; (c) the remembrance of the dead; (d) the definition of eucharistic boundaries.

---

cism. This is quite a helpful overview of the varied world in which Christianity and its worship developed. See W. H. C. Frend, *The Rise of Christianity* (Philadelphia: Fortress Press, 1984), 119–228.

2. See, for example, Herman Wegman, *Christian Worship in East and West: A Study Guide to Liturgical History*, translated by Gordon W. Lathrop (New York: Pueblo Publishing Company, 1985); Robert Cabié, *The Eucharist*, vol. 2 of *The Church at Prayer*, edited by Aimé Martimort and translated by Matthew J. O'Connell (Collegeville, Minn.: Liturgical Press, 1986).

ORDER OF SERVICE

There is some doubt as to where information on the order of service begins. It would be pretentious to say that disputes about chapters 9 and 10 of the *Didache* are settled.[3] Whether they have to do with a community meal or the Lord's Supper within a meal, however, their pertinence to the eucharistic tradition is acknowledged since the work shows the forms of prayer adopted by an early Judeo-Christian community.[4] The order of service followed is the same as found in the supper narrative in Luke's Gospel: first there is the blessing of a cup, then a blessing of bread, and at the end of the meal a prayer resembling the Jewish blessing for concluding a meal. There is no mention of the inclusion of the supper narrative and memorial command, but there is an invitation after the blessing that calls on the holy to approach, to receive the holy things. Those who argue for a eucharistic celebration explain the absence of the supper narrative in different ways. Some think it could have been included within the meal, but not in the blessing. Others rightly point out that in the early church the supper narrative was not always incorporated into eucharistic prayers.

After the last of the three blessings there is an interesting rule that states: "Let the prophets give thanks as long as they wish." This means either that there could be other blessings than the three given, or that when a prophet prayed the final and longer blessing there was no limit on content and length. The option between set forms and improvisation within a canon may already have been an issue.

Chapters 14 and 15 of this same church order speak more clearly of the Eucharist, though critics think that they do not originally belong alongside chapters 9 and 10. They prescribe a gathering for Eucharist on the Lord's Day and the appointment of bishops and deacons to take the place of prophets and teachers. This indicates a church moving into the postapostolic age and needing to set up ministerial structures that give it continuity. It would appear that these officials can be chosen by the community, the usual practice known to us from early Christian centuries. The nonsacerdotal titles given to them is in keeping with the practice of the New Testament itself to give priestly dignity to the community of believers but not to ministers in virtue of their ministry.

With the later information on Christian services of worship obtained from the *Didascalia,* the writings of Justin Martyr, Cyprian and Tertullian, and the *Apostolic Tradition,* one sees emerging an order common to

---

3. For bibliography, see the introduction to the English translation of the pertinent texts in R. C. D. Jasper and G. J. Cuming, *Prayers of the Eucharist: Early and Reformed,* 3d ed. (New York: Pueblo Publishing Company, 1987), 20–24.

4. The dating is disputed, though it is placed as early as 80 C.E. by J.-P. Audet, *La Didache: Instructions des Apôtres* (Paris: Gabalda, 1958).

a number of churches, even while allowing for some diversity. The core elements are: reading from the scriptures (referred to as the Prophets, the Apostles, and the Gospels), prayers of supplication, the eucharistic prayer itself, and communion in the body and blood of Christ. Along with these, the documents mention psalmody, fraternal reconciliation through the kiss of peace, the instruction given by the presider, and the collection for the poor. This last was not taken up during the service but the people were expected to bring gifts for the poor with them and leave them with the deacons. In his commentary on the Lord's Prayer, Cyprian seems to indicate that in North Africa the prayer was already used in his time as an immediate preparation for approaching the communion table of the Lord's body and blood.[5]

Early communities assembled in places properly called house-churches, about which something is known from archeological discoveries as well as surmised from written texts.[6] The church order known as the *Didascalia* prescribes the positions to be taken by bishops, presbyters, deacons, widows, and the general body of the faithful.[7] The building was to face east and the bishop and presbyters were to be seated in chairs on its east side, joined by any visiting bishop who might be present. Men and women were separated, children apparently being placed where they would cause least disturbance. Since the dedication of widows to lives of prayer was considered important to the community, they had places to the fore of the faithful. Deacons were to welcome the people, assure proper order in the gathering throughout the service, and attend to the collection. Much of this is confirmed in the *Apostolic Tradition,* though it is mentioned there that deacons were to assist the bishop with the gifts in his service at the altar.[8] In such descriptions one can see how bishops and deacons were responsible for the ordering of the service, as well as the ideal of the one community, presided over by its bishop. Cultural influences are obvious in the separation of men and women and in the patriarchal role of the bishop.[9]

This testimony about the more common way of ordering the assem-

5. See Cabié, *The Eucharist,* 107f.

6. On early house-churches, see Robert Milburn, *Early Christian Art and Architecture* (Berkeley and Los Angeles: University of California Press, 1988), 9–18, 85–88.

7. See F. X. Funk, *Didascalia et Constitutiones Apostolorum* (Paderborn, 1905, reprint 1964). English translation in R. H. Connolly, *Didascalia Apostolorum* (Oxford: Clarendon Press, 1929, reprint 1971), 252.

8. *La Tradition Apostolique: d'après les anciennes versions,* edited and translated, with an introduction, by Bernard Botte, Sources Chrétiennes 11bis (Paris: Ed. du Cerf, 1968). This is the text, without the critical apparatus, as originally published in *La Tradition Apostolique de Saint Hippolyte: Essai de reconstitution par Dom Bernard Botte* (Münster: Aschendorffsche Verlagsbuchhandlung, 1963).

9. See the essay by Marcel Metzger, "The *Didascalia* and the *Constitutiones Apostolorum,*" in *The Eucharist of the Early Christians,* translated by Matthew J. O'Connell (New York: Pueblo Publishing Company, 1978), 194–219.

bly and its service needs to be completed by what is learned from some apocryphal writings of the period.[10] These have often been ignored in theological writings because of their association with gnosticism, but of late it has been more readily recognized that something can be known from them about early church practices. In the view of Georg Kretschmar, the *Acts of John* and the *Acts of Thomas* predate the *Didache* and along with it contain valuable evidence about Judeo-Christian churches.[11]

The pertinent passages indicate that there was a practice of celebrating the Eucharist in bread alone, or in bread and water, and they also give some blessing prayers that will be looked at later. These Eucharists are linked to the baptism of persons who accept the faith from wandering apostles and missionaries and are celebrated where there is no settled community or place of assembly. They offer no elaborate liturgy, but a simple blessing and breaking of the bread for persons newly baptized on receiving the word of the gospel from a preacher. In other words, they give a picture of what was done during periods of early evangelization and show a sense of adaptability in how the Eucharist is to be celebrated.

Thus the *Didache* and *Didascalia* reflect the practice of a settled community, while the apocryphal acts reflect practice in a time of evangelization. These latter are an integral part of the eucharistic tradition, the books themselves being such that they had a readership in the Christian church in both East and West for several centuries.[12] All three documents reflect Syrian Christianity and show the Jewish elements still present in Christian worship, particularly in the practice of table-blessing, whether in the formal setting of the house-gathering or the informal missionary situation of an open place.

From the *Apostolic Tradition* we learn that the blessing of fruits, olives, cheese, and oil could accompany the Eucharist, being placed at the end of the blessing over bread and wine.[13] The connection between the sacrament of Christ's body and blood and the blessing of the fruits of the earth was thus kept alive.[14] The description of community life in this church order describes a community meal, held in the evening sep-

---

10. English translations of the apocryphal texts are to be found in *New Testament Apocrypha*, edited and annotated by E. Hennecke, W. Schneemelcher, and R. Wilson, vol. 2 (Philadelphia: Westminster Press, 1965). Pertinent passages are *Acts of Thomas* 27, 29, 49, 120, 133 (pp. 457, 458, 470, 507, 512) and *Acts of Peter* 2, 5 (pp. 280, 285).

11. Georg Kretschmar, "Abendmahlsfeier I," in *Theologische Realenzyklopädie*, 1:234f.

12. See the introductions in *New Testament Apocrypha*, 268 and 427f.

13. *La Tradition Apostolique*, ed. Botte, nn. 5, 6, 54f.

14. The book, however, reserves the term *eucharistia* for the blessing over bread and wine and for what was thus blessed, namely, the body and blood of Christ. For other blessings and blessed things, it uses the word *eulogia*. This does not seem to reflect different prayer structures, but the desire to keep a distinct name for the sacrament of the Lord's body and blood. See David N. Power, "On Blessing Things," *Concilium* 178 (1985/2): 24–39.

arately from the Eucharist, with blessings of light and of food.[15] The
Christians who gathered for the sacrament were still accustomed to the
practice of community meal as an expression of union and service.

THE OBSERVANCE OF SUNDAY[16]

The Eucharist was the primary way of marking the Sunday, and as a
general rule it was celebrated only on that day, with a single gathering of the whole church. The people also gathered on weekdays, for
scriptural reading, instruction, and common prayer.[17] Some documents
also indicate the continued practice in some form of a community meal,
though not directly associated with the Eucharist. The Sunday observance, which entailed the gathering of the one assembly, for the one
Eucharist, professing the one faith, presided over by the one bishop,
thus belonged in a larger context of community gathering and community life.[18] This is important to its ecclesial significance and is part of its
living theology.

   Justin offers a brief explanation of why the eucharistic assembly took
place on Sunday, no doubt for the benefit of Jews and others who might
associate this gathering with less respectable purposes. He writes:

> And we all assemble together on Sunday, because it is the first day,
> on which God transformed darkness and matter, and made the
> world; and Jesus Christ our Savior rose from the dead on that day;
> for they crucified him the day before Saturday, and the day after
> Saturday, which is Sunday, he appeared to his apostles and disci-
> ples, and taught them these things which we have presented to
> you also for your consideration.[19]

   This explanation for holding Eucharist on the Sunday associates the
Eucharist itself with the creation of the world and with the resurrection
of Christ and his appearance to the apostles and disciples. It thus recalls

---

15. *La Tradition Apostolique*, ed. Botte, n. 26, 100f.

16. For a summary of discussions on the origins of Sunday, with bibliography, see
Thomas Talley, *The Origins of the Liturgical Year* (New York: Pueblo Publishing Company,
1986), 13–18.

17. *La Tradition Apostolique*, ed. Botte, nn. 35 and 41, 118f, 124f.

18. See Ignatius of Antioch, *Letter to the Philadelphians*, 4, in *Lettres: Ignace d'Antioche*, ed.
T. Camelot, 3d ed., Sources Chrétiennes 10 (Paris: Ed. du Cerf, 3rd ed., 1958), 142f. English
translation in *The Epistles of St. Clement of Rome and St. Ignatius of Antioch*, trans. J. Kleist,
Ancient Christian Writers 1 (Westminster, Md.: Newman Press, 1946), 86.

19. Justin, *Apologia* I, 65 and 67, 3–5. English translation in Jasper and Cuming, *Prayers
of the Eucharist*, 28–30. Original texts are given in Anton Hänggi and Irmgard Pahl, *Prex
eucharistica: Textus e variis liturgiis antiquioribus selecti*, Spicilegium Friburgense 12 (Fribourg:
Editions Universitaires, 1968), 70, 72.

the original creation and celebrates the beginning of the new creation. These ideas do not necessarily however constitute the original reason for choosing Sunday, and at that Sunday morning, as the time for eucharistic celebration. It may rather be evidence that there was some evolution in the theology of Sunday and of the sacrament.

The exact origins of the relation of Eucharist to Sunday are in fact obscure, particularly in the New Testament period. A key text in discussions is Acts 20:7–11. There it is described how Paul met with the Christians of Troas on the first day of the week, assembling in the evening and prolonging the gathering through the night, ending with "the breaking of the bread." There are differences of opinion about the hour intended in this description. Some think that the people assembled on the evening of Sunday, thus ending with the breaking of the bread early Monday morning. Others think that assembly was on the evening of the Jewish sabbath, so that the breaking of the bread took place in the early hours of Sunday morning.

The practical side of the question has to do with the relation of these early Christians to Judaism and with the reckoning of time that they adopted. If they met on the evening of the sabbath, this meant they took the Jewish stance that the first day of the week began on the eve of the sabbath. Against the background of Jewish belief and custom, this would have represented some deliberate harmonization between the sabbath and the celebration of the Lord's death and resurrection. If, however, the gathering began on the evening of Sunday, carrying over into Monday morning, the calculation of time could have been either the Roman reckoning of the day from midnight to midnight, or the Hellenic reckoning from dawn to dawn. In either case the first day of the week would have been more clearly distinguished from the Jewish sabbath, with a more wilful disassociation from its observance.

Though there is no solution to this historical puzzle, the question raised is important. The Christian Sunday and its Eucharist took some of its meaning from its practical relation to Jewish observance and to cultural time. The relation to time had a further effect when the Eucharist was placed, as noted by Justin, in the early morning of Sunday rather than in the evening. The reason for this may have been practical, but it had the effect of linking the Eucharist more directly with the image of the day as the first day of the new creation, the eighth day of time, and the day of eschatological expectation, all of this enhancing the commemoration of the resurrection of Christ. The Eucharist itself is as much proclamation of the Lord's death as it is commemoration of his rising from the dead, so that it is not by its nature associated with the day marked to commemorate the resurrection. Since however Sunday was the usual time for its celebration, the meaning given to the Sunday had its effect on the meaning given to the Eucharist.

Communion on weekdays was a possibility for all Christians. They took the body of Christ home with them and reserved it in their houses for weekday communion.[20] The practice of taking communion home is rooted in the nature of the sacrament as food. This is of course intrinsic to the nature of the sacrament, and the centrality of the communion table in the community celebration is obvious. Of itself, a more private form of communion on other days does not take away from the sense of the common food and the common table, to build the one communion in the body of Christ. Were it to substitute for the communion in common, that would be another matter.

The need for this food was even one of the reasons that led to weekday celebration of the Eucharist by presbyters. There is evidence for this in the letters of Cyprian. His conviction that the eucharistic food was essential to strengthen Christians suffering trial, and threatened even by martyrdom, made him allow its celebration in private homes and in prison cells, when circumstances warranted.[21] There is no indication of the rite observed on such occasions, but it must have been very simple. The need for more frequent Eucharist is connected with Cyprian's attribution of a priestly character to the presbyterium, whose members he dubbed *consacerdotes* with the bishop, able to celebrate the Eucharist if occasion arose without him, and celebrating with him on the Sunday in the community assembly.[22]

Apart from this extension of Eucharist to weekdays to supply the eucharistic food, there were other exceptions to the rule of the one eucharistic gathering on Sunday. Some of these were community gatherings, some perhaps of smaller groups. In North Africa there seems to have been a celebration of the Eucharist on what were called stational days, that is days of fast. These occurred on Wednesday and Friday and were marked by a gathering for prayer, which according to some evidence may have concluded with a Eucharist.[23] In Syria, besides the gathering in the house-church on Sunday, the *Didascalia* mentions a gathering in the cemeteries "on the departure of them that sleep,"[24] but this deserves special consideration.

---

20. *La Tradition Apostolique*, ed. Botte, n. 37, 119f.

21. Cyprian, *Epistula* 5, 2 (CSEL 3, 2:479) and *Epistula* 63, 16 (CSEL 3, 2:714). English translation: *Saint Cyprian: Letters*, Fathers of the Church 51 (Washington, D.C.: Catholic University of America Press, 1964), 5f, 213.

22. In one text Cyprian refers to the daily sacrifice, but in the Latin of his time *quotidie* does not necessarily mean every single day. See *Epistula* 57, 3 (CSEL 3, 2:652). English, *Saint Cyprian: Letters*, 159f.

23. Tertullian, *De Oratione* 19, 1–3 (CCSL 1, 267). English translation in *Tertullian: Disciplinary, Moral and Ascetical Works*, Fathers of the Church 40 (Washington, D.C.: Catholic University of America Press, 1959), 174.

24. *Didascalia*, ed. Connolly, 252.

REMEMBRANCE OF THE DEAD

Christian attitudes towards the future meant that with death there was no definitive separation between the living and the dead. All belonged to the one communion, the one body of Christ, and shared together in the expectation of final salvation in the reign of God and in the hope of the resurrection of the body. This was already bolstered in the understanding that the body and blood of Christ was nourishment for immortality, a strong note in early Christian writings, as will be seen.

The nature, occasion, and frequency of the gatherings in cemeteries in the Syrian church is not known. In the first Christian centuries there was no necessary connection between burial rites and the celebration of the sacrament. If it belonged in any way to those rites, it was not done on the day of death or burial but on the third day after burial and on the anniversary of death, the Christian *dies natalis*.[25]

The frescoes from the Roman catacombs that have often been taken as representations of the Eucharist are more likely to be paintings of the *refrigerium*, or funeral banquet held at graveside, a cultural custom that Christians saw no need to forsake. The Eucharist on the third and anniversary days took place in some proximity to the grave, in the space that cemeteries provided, but not at graveside. When the cult of the martyrs took on special vigor there were attempts to have spots close to their graves where Eucharist could be celebrated, just as many sought to be buried near them.

Remembrance of the dead within the Eucharist, even within the eucharistic prayer, which later was certainly common, may well have begun in this era. The observance of the anniversary, however, was something special. It is referred to by Tertullian as making "oblations for the dead."[26] The sense of this is not totally clear. The word *oblatio*, or offering, in the vocabulary of the time could substitute for the word *eucharistia*, since the prayer of thanksgiving was considered the great offering or sacrifice of the Christian people. However, it could also have the more distinctive meaning associated with offering, namely of doing something *for* somebody or for some special purpose. In the case of the commemoration of the dead, *oblatio* surely retained the meaning of thanksgiving for the redemption and grace of Christ, but in Tertullian it seems also to connote something done in favor of the dead, something from which they might benefit.

---

25. See Cyrille Vogel, "The Cultic Environment of the Deceased in the Early Christian Period," in *Temple of the Holy Spirit: Sickness and Death of the Christian in the Liturgy*, translated by Matthew J. O'Connell (New York: Pueblo Publishing Company, 1983), 259–76.

26. *De Corona* 3, 3 (CCSL 2, 1043). English translation in *Ante-Nicene Fathers* 3, 94.

Development in eschatological perspective and the understanding of the relation between the living and the dead in the Eucharist went hand in hand. Earliest attitudes to a great extent focused on the expectation of the final advent of God's reign and the final resurrection. Living and dead were considered one in this expectation. Later there was a greater interest in what happened to persons immediately after death. Besides designating the place to hold the funeral banquet, the term *locus refrigerii* was used to designate the place where the dead awaited the final resurrection in peace. In the case of martyrs, people expected them to be already with Christ, since they had given testimony to him in the shedding of their blood. Could others also expect such an immediate communion in the fullness of Christ's glory? In the early centuries of which we are writing, this question does not seem to have been resolved speculatively. Practically, there was increasing resort to the intercession of the martyrs on behalf of the common dead, as well as a tendency to look to the beneficial results of celebrating the Eucharist in their memory. Whether it was the remembrance by the holy people in the Eucharist, or the intervention of the holy person of the martyr that was thought to be the more beneficial is a mute question.

What the Eucharist meant in the community, in any case, was in flux. The memorial of Christ's death kept by the holy and redeemed people, where they gave God thanks and were nourished through their table communion with Christ, came to be perceived also as an action that could be done in behalf of others. While on the one hand this demonstrated the communion between the living and the dead in Christ, on the other it gave a somewhat different accent to the Eucharist as beneficial action rather than as communion. It is a matter of nuance, not contradiction, but in later ages the distinction was pushed much further.

DEFINING EUCHARISTIC AND CHURCH BOUNDARIES[27]

Beginning with the admonitions of Paul to the Corinthians, it was clear that giving or receiving the eucharistic elements was not to be done indiscriminately. Principles and rules were needed, principles that were not only about worthiness but about the church itself and its make-up. In the *Didache* we read of the offer of holy things to the holy, and by and large this could be said to be the all-encompassing principle. It was em-

---

27. See Kenneth Hein, *Eucharist and Excommunication: A Study in Early Christian Doctrine and Discipline* (Bern and Frankfurt: Peter Lang, 1973).

ployed in excommunication, that is, in deciding who was to be excluded from the table, to be readmitted only after due penance. Its application entailed views about grave sins, serious enough to warrant excommunication inasmuch as they were contrary to membership in the body of the holy. The classification of these sins expressed the church's sense of its own reality as the holy people, marking itself off from contemporary mores and outlook.[28]

Deciding on what constituted a proper celebration of the Eucharist when communities were set in opposition to each other was a different task. Assuring that the Eucharist was celebrated only by properly appointed ministers was one way around the dilemma. Ignatius of Antioch laid down the rule that there was to be no Eucharist without the bishop.[29] At a minimum, this meant that none should celebrate without the permission of the bishop and that no community outside his pastorate was to be recognized. By Cyprian's time there were rival bishops as well as rival churches, so that he stretched the norm for acceptable Eucharist to mean communion only with those churches that in discipline and creed were deemed to be in the orthodox tradition. How this norm is applied depends on who is defining orthodoxy, but in all cases it meant that eucharistic communion and ecclesial communion were seen to be intertwined.

In the New Testament period and for some time later, ministry, inclusive of presidency, was clearly related to eucharistic communion. Serving the *koinonia* of the church in any of its manifestations and functions centered around the one cup and the one loaf. It is sometimes said that in ancient times bishops presided over the Eucharist because they were appointed to preside over the community.[30] This is said in opposition to the idea that one ordained to Eucharist can take up ministry in any community in virtue of that power. On the other hand, it would betray the early sense of church not to see that Eucharist and community are reciprocal realities and that celebrating the Eucharist is essential to being pastor of the community. Perhaps then it would be better to say that any ministry, including episcopacy and eucharistic presidency, belonged within a eucharistic community shaped by many services, no ministry allowing for a difference in status or for some inner grouping that functioned in independence of other members. Such an attitude is in keeping with the idea that it is the table at

---

28. This is not the place to discuss the listings of sins that warranted excommunication and canonical penance, though their study is pertinent to ecclesiology as well as to moral theology.

29. Ignatius of Antioch, *Letter to the Smyrnaeans* 8, 1–2, in *Lettres,* 162; English translation in Ancient Christian Writers 1:93.

30. See Hervé Legrand, "The Presidency of the Eucharist according to the Ancient Tradition," in *Living Bread, Saving Cup,* edited by Kevin Seasoltz (Collegeville, Minn.: Liturgical Press, 1982), 196–221.

which all are equal that unites, regardless of the charisms to say the blessing or keep order or otherwise serve the faith and interest of the church.

Nonetheless, already in the pre-Nicene church, that is, by the time of the *Apostolic Tradition,* the distinction between clergy and laity is in firm place. The status and power of the former is defined by their tasks, especially those concerning the word and the table, giving them a certain power over the Eucharist rather than a place within it. It is startling to find that what started as a noncultic body should so soon have become one marked by cultic distinctions. The return to the central role of the common table of the blessed bread and wine may be the necessary way to move from a community defined in its inner boundaries by roles and powers to one that more clearly recognizes the priority of baptism and grace. Perhaps even after so many centuries this is still possible.[31]

CONCLUSION

Practice is a living theology, embodying belief and meaning. Within different the practices, we can note the ways in which through its manner of communion in the body and blood of Christ the church defines its understanding of the sacrament and defines itself.

The most noteworthy and most noted practice of these centuries is the gathering of the community on Sunday to keep this memorial. The normativity of the one assembly, however, allowed of exceptions that reflect an understanding of what the sacrament means to the church and the need for some flexibility. Such are the Eucharist to complete baptism in a missionary situation, the weekday gatherings in cemeteries to remember the dead, and celebration in the necessity to provide the faithful with the sacramental food. There was the risk that such practices would diminish the importance of the one eucharistic assembly that took place on Sunday. On the other hand, if kept in perspective they could play out more fully the meaning of what was done together on Sunday.

Some of these celebrations were connected with the desire to provide the faithful with the sacramental food of Christ's body. Taking communion home for weekdays was normal, even outside times of danger. It seems in good keeping with the stress, intrinsic to the celebration

---

31. See the article by A. Faivre, "Les premiers chrétiens interpellent le Synode des Évêques," *Revue des Sciences Religieuses* 63 (1989): 17–46. I have sought to explain the concerns behind the evolution of authority in early centuries in "Power and Authority in Early Christian Centuries," in *That They Might Live: Power, Empowerment, and Leadership in the Church,* edited by Michael Downey (New York: Crossroad, 1991), 25–38.

itself, that the body and blood are nourishment for the life of grace and for eternal life. Even when brought home, the sacrament is food of the common table, strengthening union with Christ and in him with others.

In its sacramental usage, the church also defined its own holiness, its eschatological horizons, and its inner order. Questions may be raised about some of the orientations noted under these categories, but they are three factors that are always at play when the church keeps memory of Christ and builds itself up as a body in him.

Chapter 5

THE PRE-NICENE CHURCH: EUCHARISTIC PRAYERS

Research on the origins and development of the eucharistic prayer over the last few decades has been enormous. It is next to impossible to account for everything written. Following current studies, the prayers are here presented by region. The purpose is not to review all the textual questions discussed by scholars, but to offer a theological reading on the basis of the state of the question. Special attention is given to three points: prayer structure, images of redemption, and cultural influence.

The idea of an *uranaphora,* either in the form of an original text or of an original structure, was at one stage important because of the attempt to discover the Semitic roots of the prayer. It has not been totally abandoned, but it does not now dominate studies. Rather than a genealogy that starts with Jewish blessings, a better line of investigation is to start with the Christian prayers in their diversity and then ask what relation these may have to Jewish texts. Comparison between one Christian prayer and another, or between Christian prayers and Jewish prayers, is more beneficial than genetic explanation. It is a richer way to uncover the flexibility of structure and meaning within a common tradition of memorial.

The prayers considered in this chapter are taken from East Syria, Rome, Armenia, and Egypt. None of them can be said to represent *the* liturgy of a church, since the period is still one that allows a measure of eucharistic improvisation,[1] but they do convey the tenor of what was deemed appropriate. As an addendum some consideration will be given to blessings that are not intended for the Lord's Supper but that give a sense of the general evolution in Christianity of a larger blessing tradition to which the Eucharist belongs.[2]

---

1. See Alan Bouley, *From Freedom to Formula: The Evolution of the Eucharistic Prayer from Oral Improvisation to Written Texts,* Studies in Christian Antiquity 21 (Washington, D.C.: Catholic University of America Press, 1981).

2. Even for later centuries, the Eastern churches point to the similarity between the

EAST SYRIA

The Prayer from the Didache[3]

As already mentioned, this church order has three table blessings in chapters 9 and 10, but it is the one at the end of the meal, "after you have had your fill," that has received most attention in studies on the genealogy of the Eucharist. It is compared with the Jewish *Birkat ha-Mazon*, sometimes thought to have provided the model for Christian Eucharist. The other two prayers, however, also deserve attention, for they too are Christian adaptations of Jewish blessing forms.

Relating the prayers of *Didache* 9, with what is later found in *Apostolic Constitutions* VII, 25, Enrico Mazza offers a theory that seems quite plausible, summarizing it as follows:

> We will recall that in *Didache* 9 there are three literary units: (1) a prayer (*eucharistia*) over the cup, (2) a prayer (*eucharistia*) over the bread, and (3) a prayer (of petition) for the church.
>
> Subsequently, the cup that here precedes the bread was moved to a position after the bread, giving the structure attested in the *Apostolic Constitutions* VII, 25, (i) *eucharistia* over the bread, (ii) prayer for the Church, and (iii) *eucharistia* over the cup.[4]

Whatever the validity of this historical reconstruction, the prayers are prototypically Jewish, both in language and in form. They are blessings addressed to God. In Greek translation the term used is *eucharistia*, whether this is a generic word for blessing or means more specifically thanksgiving being unclear. Each line of blessing ends with the typical summation, referred to as *chatimah*, and translated into English as "glory to you for evermore."

In the prayer of *Didache* 10, which corresponds to the Jewish *Birkat ha-Mazon*, there are three units. First there is the blessing for God's holy Name. This recalls Jewish reverence for the name of Yahweh and the theology of the glory of the Name linked with the work of creation and

blessing of water, the blessing of myron, and the blessing of the eucharistic bread and wine. Keeping such links in mind is salutary. See, for example, Emmanuel-Pataq Siman, *L'Expérience de l'Esprit par l'Église d'après la tradition syrienne d'Antioche*, Théologie Historique 15 (Paris: Éditions Beauchesne, 1971), 222–42.

3. An English translation of the prayer may be found in R. C. D. Jasper and G. J. Cuming, *Prayers of the Eucharist: Early and Reformed*, 3d ed. (New York: Pueblo Publishing Company, 1987), 20–24. It is usually studied in conjunction with the prayer in the *Apostolic Constitutions* VII, 25 (Funk, 412–14). Though in that context the prayer is presented as a thanksgiving *after* Eucharist, it is deemed to come originally from a eucharistic blessing and like the prayer of the *Didache* to show a Christian adaptation of a Jewish formula.

4. Enrico Mazza, *The Eucharistic Prayers of the Roman Rite*, translated by Matthew J. O'Connell (New York: Pueblo Publishing Company, 1986), 21.

with the work of salvation. Following Semitic idiom, in the *Didache* salvation consists in "knowledge," the knowledge of the Name being given in Jesus Christ and manifested in the church. Jesus himself is portrayed as *pais*, which could be translated as either child or servant. This echoes the conjunction in Mark's Gospel between the name of the Son and the Suffering Servant. There is, however, no specific mention of his death. In the prayer's soteriology, prominence is given to salvific knowledge.

Second, there is the blessing for food and drink, especially for the spiritual food and drink given to those who believe in Jesus. While this blessing puts the elements of the table to the fore, it actually changes the praise for created things and the land into a thanksgiving for the spiritual nourishment of eternal life given through Jesus.

The third unit is a petition for the church, but it is in the form of a blessing by reason of the doxology with which it closes. The church is here dubbed "the holy vine," which underlines the idea of divine election. It is a people gathered from the four winds into the kingdom, an eschatological gathering of God's chosen ones. This corresponds to the symbolism of the broken bread in the prayer of *Didache* 9 which with some artistry is made a metaphor for the gathering of the church. Instead of the grains of wheat being gathered for the one loaf, what is portrayed is the collection (in one basket?) of broken bread scattered over the mountains.

Addai and Mari[5]

This blessing, composed in Syriac, has its origins in the early East Syrian church, and like the prayers from the *Didache* betrays its Semitic roots. Since the earliest manuscripts come from as late as the tenth century and show additions to an earlier text, there is considerable controversy over the reconstruction of the original prayer. While it is not possible to resolve all the issues of form and content, enough is known to add to our information about pre-Nicene Eucharists.

In structure, the prayer is a sequence of three distinct units. These are the praise of God's name for creation, a thanksgiving for the work of redemption, and an invocation over the gifts of bread and wine. In its present state, this last invokes the gift of the Holy Spirit, but there

---

5. An English version of the text and a list of studies are noted in Jasper and Cuming, *Prayers of the Eucharist*, 39–44. The prayer is often compared with the Sharar, or Anaphora of Peter, which is of much later origin but apparently based on Addai and Mari. Jasper and Cuming offer a good bibliography, but the listing by Cesare Giraudo, *La struttura letteraria della preghiera eucaristica: Saggio sulla genesi letteraria di una forma* (Rome: Biblical Institute Press, 1981), 331, note 9, is more complete. For a more recent study, with some suggestions for a reconstruction of the text, see A. Gelston, *The Eucharistic Prayer of Addai and Mari* (Oxford: Clarendon Press, 1992).

is doubt as to whether such clear mention of the Spirit occurred in the original.

Ending with a doxology, each prayer would have constituted a blessing, but the present state of the text leaves this factor unclear. However, if the three prayers are taken separately, they may well represent three classical forms of blessing. The classical forms are those of praise (for creation), thanksgiving (for redemption), and invocation over the gifts (for divine blessings on humankind). Because of their early composition in Syriac, a Semitic language, not too much should be made of the difference between the verbs for praise and thanksgiving in the Greek text of the first two blessings.

More interesting is the address of the second blessing. There is a good argument that this blessing that invokes the *Lord* was addressed directly to Christ, while the first is directed to the triune God.[6] However, even if this form of address is granted, the invocations have to be seen in the context of a Syriac theology of the Name and its manifestation. The glory of the divine Name is revealed in what is recalled in each of the blessings, that is, in creation, in the redemption brought about through the Word incarnate, and in the life of the church. In the more developed form of the prayer this last is connected clearly with the work of the Spirit.

Redemption is celebrated as the restoration of human nature from its fallen condition. The divine nature is communicated through the putting on of human nature by the Lord. Remission of sins, enlightenment of the mind, and the gift of immortality are listed as the great benefits thus conferred.

The last of the three blessings is a prayer for the making holy of the gifts, here called the offering of the people, so that those who partake of them may be made holy and receive remission of sins, the hope of the resurrection, and life in the kingdom. That holiness comes to human beings through the medium of things made holy by invocation is in line with the tenor of Jewish blessings.[7] It is in this blessing that commemoration is made of the mystery of Christ's passion, death, and resurrection, rather than in the blessings of praise and thanksgiving. The power of commemoration is thus located in the request for the benefits of this work, conferred through the medium of the sanctified elements.

There is much argument as to whether the supper narrative, missing

---

6. See Albert Gerhards, "Zu wem beten? Die These Josef Andreas Jungmanns (†1975) über den Adressaten des Eucharistichen Hochgebets im Licht der neuren Forschung," *Liturgische Jahrbuch* 32 (1982): 219–30.

7. Sometimes it is suggested that rather than being made holy, things blessed are made profane through blessing, that is, withdrawn from the preserve of God, to whom all things belong, and placed at human disposal. Even in such perspective, things blessed carry the blessings of God to human beings. See Lawrence A. Hoffman, "Rabbinic *Berakah* and Jewish Spirituality," *Concilium* 1990/3: 18–30.

in extant manuscripts, belonged in the original text.[8] If, as seems likely, it was not part of the original blessing, one does find an oblique reference to it through mention of the tradition handed down, a tradition that gives the form or pattern of commemoration:

> And we also, Lord, your lowly, weak, and miserable servants, who have gathered and stand before you, *having received through tradition the form* [or example, or pattern] which is from you, rejoicing, glorifying, exalting, commemorating, and celebrating this great mystery of the passion, death, and resurrection of our Lord Jesus Christ, etc.[9]

This text may be more ample than the original version of the prayer, where such explicit reference to the passion, death and resurrection of Christ is hardly to be expected. However, the idea of a commemoration ordered according to apostolic tradition is probably original.

Acts of Thomas, John, and Peter[10]

The prayers found in these apocryphal sources may well predate either of the above. Though often neglected in studies on the early forms of the eucharistic prayer, to get a fuller idea of the tradition it is helpful to see them in relation to the more commonly cited texts.

Since they are not readily available prayers,[11] out of the six in the sources two are presented here, representing two different prayer structures. Both are pronounced over bread alone. The first is in the form of a thanksgiving, the second of an invocation.

---

8. See the studies listed in Jasper and Cuming, *Prayers of the Eucharist*, 41.

9. What later, theologically minded amplifications can do to a prayer appears in a comparison with the Anaphora of Peter, or Sharar, which turns the memorial of the mystery into a memorial of Christ's propitiatory sacrifice, an idea totally absent from Addai and Mari, which has a different imagery of redemption. See the text of the Sharar in Jasper and Cuming, *Prayers of the Eucharist*, 48.

10. The prayers are gathered together in French translation by Cyrille Vogel, "Anaphores eucharistiques préconstantiniennes: Formes non traditionelles," *Augustinianum* 20 (1980): 401–10. A Greek version is given in Anton Hänggi and Irmgard Pahl, *Prex eucharistica: Textus e variis liturgiis antiquioribus selecti*, Spicilegium Friburgense 12 (Fribourg: Editions Universitaires, 1968), 74–79. In *New Testament Apocrypha*, vol. 2, the texts are found on pp. 457, 458, 470, 507, 512 (Acts of Thomas), 253, 255 (Acts of John), 280, 285 (Acts of Peter). For a study of these texts, in conjunction with the other East Syrian formulas, see G. Rouwhorst, "Bénédiction, actions de grâces, supplication: Les oraisons de la table dans le Judaïsme et les célébrations eucharistiques des chrétiens syriaques," *Questions Liturgiques* 61 (1980): 211–40.

11. Jasper and Cuming do not mention them, but Hänggi and Pahl include them in *Prex eucharistica*, 74–79.

Acts of John 85[12]

[John] took bread, and brought it into the sepulchre to break it, and he said: We glorify thy name that converteth us from error and pitiless deceit; we glorify thee who has shown before our eyes what we have seen; we testify to thy goodness, in various ways appearing; we praise thy gracious name, O Lord; <we thank thee> who hast convicted those that are convicted by thee; we thank thee, Lord Jesus Christ, that we confide <in thy grace>, which is unchanging; we thank thee who hadst need of our nature that is being saved; we thank thee that thou hadst given us this unwavering <faith> that thou alone art <God> both now and forever; we thy servants, that are assembled and gathered with <good> cause, give thanks to thee, O holy one.

Acts of Thomas 133[13]

When they were baptized and clothed, [Judas Thomas] set bread upon the table and blessed it and said: Bread of life, those who eat of which remain incorruptible; bread which fills hungry souls with its blessing — thou art the one <thought worthy> to receive a gift, that thou mayest become for us forgiveness of sins, and they who eat thee become immortal. We name over thee the name of the mother of the ineffable mystery of the hidden dominions and powers, we name <over thee the name of Jesus>.

And he said: Let the power of blessing come and <settle upon the bread>, that all souls which partake of it may be washed of their sins.

It has already been noted that the Eucharist recounted in the acts belongs in a setting of itinerant apostolate, where converts are won to the faith by preaching. It is thus distinguished from the Eucharist of an already constituted domestic church. The sacrament is celebrated in bread alone, or in bread accompanied by water. It was at one time suggested that this was due to gnostic and encratistic influence, but two other reasons seem more persuasive.[14] First, the use of bread without wine fitted the informal setting wherein the converts were baptized. Second, in a Semitic context placing the accent on the bread blessing served to distinguish Christians from Jews.

---

12. *New Testament Apocrypha*, 253.
13. Ibid., 512.
14. See Georg Kretschmar, "Abendmahlsfeier I," in *Theologische Realenzyklopädie*, 1:240f., and in the same encyclopedia, "Abendmahl III/1," 69f.

The first of these prayers, a thanksgiving, is addressed to Jesus Christ, in praise of his name and in acknowledgment of his gifts.[15] The second, an invocation, is addressed to the bread, imploring the name of the mother and the name of Jesus. Among the six prayers mentioned, it is this last kind of blessing that dominates. Taking this in unison with the invocation found in the *Didache* and the third of the blessing prayers of Addai and Mari, this suggests that Palestinian Christianity gave great importance to blessing the bread as medium of the gifts of redemption. Thanksgiving and praise of God and of Christ clearly had their place, but as a sacrament the Eucharist stood out as blessed bread, food of soul and body in the kingdom of God.

As in the other East Syrian texts, remission of sins, knowledge, and immortality are the great blessings given to those who take the sacrament. The work of redemption is attributed more directly to the assumption by the Lord of human nature than to his death. The theology of the Name also stands out, but with a twist worth noting. Along with the name of Jesus, the name invoked is that of the mother or of the dove.[16] In East Syrian literature, for example in the Odes of Solomon, female imagery for the Father, for Christ, and for the Spirit is common. So also is some symbiosis between the names of Jesus and the Spirit. This highlights the double manifestation of the Name, namely, in the human nature of Christ and in the holiness of the church.[17]

Conclusion on East Syrian Prayers

Noting that in Jewish blessing, praise, thanksgiving, and invocation (or epiclesis) all fall under this category, we find that all three kinds occur in the sacramental celebrations of East Syrian Christianity. Because there is a problem in translating the Semitic words for blessing into Greek or into modern languages, there is no clear differentiation between praise and thanksgiving. If one form of blessing is given prominence over the others, it is the invocation of the name/names that sanctify the bread, making of it food for knowledge, the forgiveness of sins, and the gift of immortality.

In describing the work of redemption, it is the assumption and restoration of fallen human nature by Christ that is to the fore, rather than

---

15. This would confirm the possibility that the second blessing of Addai and Mari is indeed addressed to Christ.

16. Compare the invocation of the name of the mother in the second of the prayers quoted with this other text from the *Acts of Thomas:* " ... Holy dove that bearest twin young: Come, hidden mother ... Come and partake with us in this Eucharist which we celebrate in thy name ... " (*New Testament Apocrypha,* 470).

17. See Robert Murray, *Symbols of Church and Kingdom: A Study in Early Syrian Tradition* (Cambridge: Cambridge University Press, 1975), especially 314–16.

his death. The supper narrative is not part of the prayers, but it is apparent that what is celebrated is a commemoration done in keeping with apostolic tradition.

In present regard, these East Syrian blessings fare badly when placed alongside later texts, beginning with the prayer found in the *Apostolic Tradition*. Their recall may however enable us to note forgotten elements in tradition whose recovery can offer new possibilities for eucharistic prayer today. It is not a matter of reviving such prayers for use, but of drawing inspiration from them. They cut across the preference given to the later Antiochene type of Eucharist by showing other ways in which praise, thanksgiving, and invocation relate to each other in the sacrament. They show the possibility of the early reality of prayer addressed directly to Christ, contrary to the idea that this was introduced in response to later heresies. They show that the sacrament is not tied to the repetition of the words of Jesus at the supper but to the prayer over the food, and suggest the occasional possibility of Eucharist in only one element, when this is warranted by circumstances. We also see the diversity in the images used to commemorate the work of Christ and in naming the benefits of this work that accrue to humanity. A knowledge of all of these factors may serve current creative efforts by revealing that Christian eucharistic tradition is more pluriform than some currents in liturgical renewal have allowed.

EUCHARIST AT ROME

Prayer of the Apostolic Tradition[18]

The importance of this prayer comes from the influence that it exercised in the past and continues to exercise today, among other things in offering a common ecumenical point of reference. In ways this is odd, given the uncertainty of the origin of the document know as the *Treatise on the Apostolic Tradition* and the doubts whether the eucharistic prayer actually represents usage in the Roman church.

Read as a single literary unit, it is largely this prayer that has encouraged scholars to take the final blessing of the Jewish meal, or the *birkat ha-mazon*, as a model for the genesis of Christian Eucharist.[19] The

---

18. Since the text is not extant in its original Greek, there are historical problems concerning its exact form and wording. See *La Tradition Apostolique*, ed. Botte, n. 4, 47–53. An English translation and a list of studies is given in Jasper and Cuming, *Prayers of the Eucharist*, 31–38.

19. Among the problems that beset genetic studies of Christian Eucharist is the uncertainty over the form of the *birkat ha-mazon* in the early days of Christianity. It too is known only through reconstructions based on texts of a later age. For such reconstructions, see Jasper and Cuming, *Prayers of the Eucharist*, 10, and Lucien Deiss, *Springtime of the Liturgy:*

structure of Hippolytus, to use this convenient abbreviation, maintains the flow from thanksgiving to intercession in the Jewish prayer, but amplifies the form by injecting a supper narrative and an anamnesis that embodies an offering.[20]

As indicated above, the *birkat ha-mazon* included three blessings that flowed into one another. Blessing for creation and blessing for redemption led to an invocatory blessing or intercession for Israel. Each concluded with the *chatimah,* or praise of God's name for gifts bestowed. It is suggested that the third blessing may originally have been one of praise, but that it became a petition when Israel lost its sovereignty and the people begged for its restoration.

The prayer of the *Apostolic Tradition* moves easily from thanksgiving to intercession. In the thanksgiving there is a very brief mention of creation and an elaboration on the redemptive work of Christ. This is followed by an expanded prayer of petition, couched in the form of an epiclesis for the gift of the Spirit to the church.

There is nothing to correspond to the recurrent *chatimah,* except the final doxology. Thus the prayer reads more easily as a single unit than what is proposed as its Jewish model. This may prompt one to look for an alternative model in Giraudo's hypothesis that the Jewish background to Christian Eucharist is in the larger *todah* tradition.[21] In this tradition there is room for a single literary unit that moves from thanksgiving to intercession.

Whether the amplifications were made on the table blessing or on some other form of prayer, the role of neither supper narrative nor anamnesis is crystal clear. This is important to an understanding of the prayer and to eucharistic theology. Instead of acting on the prevailing assumption that a eucharistic prayer had to include the words of Jesus, some time ago Louis Ligier asked why a prayer, otherwise complete in itself, should incorporate the supper narrative.[22]

He resolved this problem by drawing a parallel with the additions,

---

Liturgical Texts of the First Four Centuries, translated by Matthew J. O'Connell (Collegeville, Minn.: Liturgical Press, 1979), 6–9. Deiss also gives the synagogue blessings, which helps the task of comparison.

20. *Anamnesis* or *commemoration* of course can be used to designate the entire Eucharist or the entire prayer. Here it is given the common technical sense of referring to that part of the prayer after the supper narrative, which begins "remembering." Similarly, though *epiclesis* means any kind of invocation, it is used technically to refer to the invocation of the Holy Spirit.

21. By way of ready reference, this is exemplified in the Bible in Nehemiah 9 and the psalms commemorating God's great deeds.

22. Among his studies on the matter, see Louis Ligier, "The Origins of the Eucharistic Prayer," translated from the French, *Studia Liturgica* 9 (1973): 161–85. The same question, now known as the question of the embolism, is brought up to date by Giraudo, *La struttura letteraria della preghiera eucaristica,* where the addition to basic prayer units is discussed at length.

or embolisms, introduced on Jewish high festivals, such as pasch or Purim, into either the second or third blessing of table prayer. This meant placing a specific motive, associated with the day's feast, either into thanksgiving for redemption or into the petition. By way of comparison the Christian Eucharist inserted the supper narrative, with its memorial command, as the motive for prayer made in commemoration of Jesus Christ. In Hippolytus it is directly related to the thanksgiving for redemption. In other prayers, of the Egyptian and later Roman traditions, it is entered into the intercessory part of the prayer.

Since Ligier's important contribution to the question, Cesare Giraudo has done a much more detailed study of the embolism in Jewish prayer, looking not only to table prayer but also to synagogue prayer, and to a number of biblical prayers, including psalms. Following a lead given by Henri Cazelles,[23] he suggested that *ydh* forms or *todah* prayer are more basic than *brk* forms or *berakoth,* for they are more readily connected with commemoration and with worship, including Temple worship. Thus he contends that any number of Jewish prayers, once they incorporate the elements of commemorative *ydh* or *brk* forms and oracle embolism, may serve to enrich Christian Eucharist. Presenting this hypothesis Giraudo points out that in its basic form *todah* consists of two related parts, namely, thanksgiving and intercession.

As with Ligier's hypothesis of an embolism to the *birkat ha-mazon,* Giraudo points to the recurrent embolisms to prayers of praise and intercession that commemorate God's salvific deeds. To cite one example, in a prayer from 2 Samuel 7:18–29 he places the embolism in the oracle of promise found in v. 27, which becomes the immediate foundation for petition.[24] This is important because Giraudo thinks that the embolism offers motivation beyond the deeds recalled. It is not simply a recall of a salvific event, for example the pasch or the foundation of the Davidic dynasty, that calls for praise or petition, but some form of command or oracle related to this event. It is this that engages both Yahweh's fidelity and the fidelity of the people.

In this light, Giraudo presents the supper narrative, inclusive of the memorial command, as the foundation for Eucharist, both as story and as command. It is also the assurance of God's fidelity and asks for the fidelity to praise and remembrance of Christ's followers. Within the total context of the act of thanksgiving, it is at the heart of the prayer, since it grounds the memorial. This avoids reducing these words of Jesus to a consecratory act, while still giving them their importance. Far from

---

23. Henri Cazelles, "Eucharistie, bénédiction et sacrifice dans l'Ancien Testament," *La Maison-Dieu* 123 (1975): 7–28.

24. *La struttura letteraria della preghiera eucaristica,* 143f. For the more complex introduction of this reminder of a divine oracle or institution into various kinds of discourse and prayer other than praise and thanksgiving, see 138–59.

reducing the Eucharist to a ritual act of constantly repetitious content, Giraudo sees the place given to the narrative as the basis for diversity in the rest of the prayer.[25]

In the church's eucharistic tradition, he points to the insertion of the narrative either into the thanksgiving for redemption or into the intercession. While the Antiochene is the best known of the former kind and the Roman of the latter, the difference appears already in the pre-Nicene repertory. The prayer of the *Apostolic Tradition* is an example of the narrative's inclusion in thanksgiving, whereas Addai and Mari gives reference to the memorial command in its intercession.

The anamnesis follows from the inclusion of the supper narrative. Once the memorial command has been recalled, the specific object of the commemoration is given, namely, Christ's death and resurrection. The anamnesis is thus one with the supper narrative, a kind of embellishment of the embolism within the prayer. The act of offering is inserted into the anamnesis, as well as thanksgiving for the ministry of the newly ordained bishop and of the people. This is in line with the understanding that commemorative thanksgiving is the Christian sacrifice, and that those who render it exercise a ministry at the altar, the people offering their prayer in the prayer of the bishop who presides and proclaims the blessing.

While this explanation of supper narrative and anamnesis is attractive and well grounded, another hypothesis merits mention. Leaving out the comparison with the embolism of Jewish blessing, one could read the recollection of the supper narrative as remembrance of one in the series of divine benefits of the new covenant. On this reading, the series of salvific acts closes not with the supper or gift of the Eucharist, but with the ministry that has here and now been accorded the bishop by the laying-on of hands and that dates back to apostolic origins and a divine ordinance. The list of benefits for which thanks is rendered thus includes creation through the Word, the incarnation, the death on the cross and descent into hell, the resurrection, the eucharistic sacrament, and the ministry that serves the church in its own service at the altar. The main difficulty with this conjecture is that the place of the anamnesis fits less readily into the reading of the prayer unless it is seen to flow naturally from the mention of the memorial command and to relate to the idea of memorial thanksgiving as sacrifice.

The prayer's intercession is essentially a request for the gift of the Spirit. Though some scholars dispute the mention of the Spirit in the original form of the prayer, Botte's reconstitution presents it as a petition

---

25. See *La struttura letteraria della preghiera eucaristica*, 357–60. Compare the same author's *Eucaristia per la Chiesa*, 359f.

over the offering of the church, asking graces for those who eat of the gifts in communion. Since the church's offering is the prayer over the bread and wine, it seems rather wrong-headed to argue whether the Spirit sanctifies the gifts or the people. It is better to see that it affects the inclusive act, whereby the people give thanks over bread and wine and eat and drink of them in the power of this blessing. No greater precision is given or needed.

The titles used to name Christ are of interest. He is Word, Savior, Redeemer, Angel, *Pais* (child or servant). They are a fitting entry to the imagery of redemption used in the prayer, which differs from that of the East Syrian tradition. Accent is on the voluntary death of Christ, on his descent into hell, and on his resurrection. Taking on flesh, the Word engaged in a struggle with the devil and with death, overcoming them both in behalf of humankind. This is a depiction of victorious suffering and death, whose conquest is manifested in the resurrection rather than of a passage through death into life. It has been surmised that the writing of Irenaeus had some direct impact on the composition of this prayer, but in any case it picks up on a theme that is common in early paschal homilies.[26] The name *pais* with its double reference to child and servant fits well with the recall of voluntary suffering, while angel or messenger ties in with the descent into hell, to bring the message of salvation to those bound by hell's captivity.

It is sometimes remarked that the prayer of the *Apostolic Tradition* gives little attention to creation, but develops the second and the third of the blessings of its Jewish model. Since, however, the age was still one of some improvisation the celebrant had room to amplify this if so inspired. In any case, if the influence of Irenaeus is correctly assumed, what counts is the identification of the redeemer Word with the creator Word. In his battle with the dualism and the hierarchies of the gnostic world, Irenaeus consistently affirmed the one mediation of the Word through whom the One God created and then redeemed the world. The mediation of the Word in redemption in itself exalts and restores creation. For Irenaeus, as will be seen further down, the restoration of the work of creation is so central to redemption that Christians give thanks to God by offering bread and wine, fruits of the earth, with thanksgiving and invoking the name of Christ. There is an echo of this incorporation of the things of the earth into the new covenant in the blessing of fruit, cheese, olives, and oil that the *Apostolic Tradition* inserts at the end of the eucharistic prayer.

---

26. See Enrico Mazza, "Omelie pasquali e birkat ha-mazon: Fonti dell'anafora di Ippolito," *Ephemerides Liturgicae* 97 (1983): 409–81.

Justin and the Eucharistic Prayer

Apart from all doubts about the use of the *Apostolic Tradition,* it is known from Justin Martyr that in the Roman church there was a place for thanksgiving for creation. Without giving a prayer formula, Justin lets the reader know something of the content of the great Eucharist. In the *Dialogue with Trypho* he says that thanks is given to God "both for creating the world with all things that are in it for the sake of man, and for freeing us from the evil in which we were born, and for accomplishing a complete destruction of the principalities and powers through him who suffered according to his will."[27]

The image of redemption as a destruction of deadly powers is not unlike that found in Hippolytus. Elsewhere in the *Dialogue,* where he finds in the Eucharist a fulfillment of the prophecy of Malachi 1:11, Justin mentions that in rendering thanks Christians make "remembrance of their solid and liquid food," as well as remembrance of "the suffering which the Son of God suffered for them."[28]

Thus the blessing for creation, which is so prominent in Jewish prayer, alongside the blessing for redemption, is maintained in the two sources quoted on eucharistic prayer in the church of Rome. It may not have been as much to the fore, but the imagery of redemption would be incomplete without the inclusion of creation. Creation and redemption are effected through the one Word of the one God, and the gifts of creation are necessarily included in the remembrance of salvation.

ARMENIA

The Prayer of Epiphanius of Salamis[29]

Only fragments of this Armenian prayer survive, and as they now stand they may not even represent the form and content of the original prayer. They are however thought to contain material that is pre-Nicene in origin.

Post-Arian concepts seem to have been pasted into the early text, but the affinity with the East Syrian tradition remains intact. Redemption is

---

27. For the Greek and Latin versions of this text, see Hänggi and Pahl, *Prex eucaristica,* 72–75. For an English translation, see Jasper and Cuming, *Prayers of the Eucharist,* 27f.

28. Robert Daly translates "kai ep anamnesei de tes trophes auton xeras kai hugras" as "in the remembrance *effected by* their solid and liquid food" (emphasis added). This is to emphasize the fact that the remembrance is made in the offering of the bread and the cup, which by reason of the commemorative thanksgiving are no common food and drink. See Robert Daly, *Christian Sacrifice: The Judaeo-Christian Background before Origen,* Studies in Christian Antiquity 18 (Washington, D.C.: Catholic University of America Press, 1978), 332.

29. Hänggi and Pahl, *Prex eucaristica,* 262–63, gives a Latin translation made not from the Armenian but from a Greek version. An English translation is given in Jasper and Cuming, *Prayers of the Eucharist,* 141f.

associated with the taking on and restoration of human flesh by God's child. As a result of christological controversies, the union of divinity and humanity in this child of God is much emphasized, with titles such as "co-eternal Son," or "perfect God the Word," who descended into the world from God's heavenly throne. Hence rather than accentuating the restoration of human nature, this prayer as it now stands elaborates on the perfection of both divine and human nature in the Word. Since much of this is obviously of later composition, may one suspect that the original thanksgiving for the incarnation was closer to the form that it has in Addai and Mari and that it is the perfecting of human nature that was celebrated rather than the perfection of the two natures in Christ?

The influence of the prayer of Hippolytus is apparent in the addition to the original Semitic theology of the imagery of Christ's "voluntary and glorious and life-giving death" and in the inclusion of the supper narrative. There is no sign of an anamnesis in the fragments that remain.

The prayer has thus a particular interest for the history of Christian Eucharist. It shows how in the course of time different patterns of remembrance are made to blend together and affected by ecclesial currents. Here we have the two pre-Nicene theologies of restoration of human nature and of victorious death brought together and completed in the wake of christological controversies by a high christology of the union of two natures in the one person of the Word.

EGYPT

The Strasbourg Papyrus[30]

This prayer from the church of Alexandria anticipates the Liturgy of Mark. It dates perhaps to around 200 C.E.

As in East Syria, its structure reflects that of Jewish blessings. It reads as a series of three blessings rather than as one structurally unified literary text. The prayers are prayers of thanksgiving for creation, of offering of reasonable and bloodless sacrifice through Jesus Christ, and of intercession over the offering for the church.

What is most interesting is how the blessing for redemption has become an offering of sacrifice. The text at this point reads:

Giving thanks through him to you with him and the Holy Spirit,[31]
we offer the reasonable (*logiken*) sacrifice and this bloodless service,

---

30. What is decipherable of the original Greek and a Latin reconstruction is given in Hänggi and Pahl, *Prex eucharistica*, 116–19. An English version is found in Jasper and Cuming, *Prayers of the Eucharist*, 52–54.

31. This naming of the Spirit may well not date back to the original text.

which all the nations offer you, from sunrise to sunset, from south to north, [for] your name is great among the nations, and in every place incense is offered to your holy name and a pure sacrifice.

This emphasis on reasonable sacrifice and bloodless service remains as a key feature of the later Alexandrian Liturgy of Mark and seems to have been the particular contribution to eucharistic prayer of the Egyptian church.[32] The idea is a development of Christian usage of Malachi 1:11 to explain the nature of Christian sacrifice and of eucharistic sacrifice in particular. The *Didache,* Justin, and Irenaeus all make use of this text to mark out thanksgiving for redemption in Christ as the unique type of sacrifice offered by Christians. It falls to this Egyptian prayer to make the offering of this reasonable and bloodless service of thanks over bread and wine the very form of commemorating Christ's suffering and death.

In the third unit, petition is made "over this sacrifice and offering" and God is asked to remember the church and all its members. There is no supper narrative, no anamnesis, no epiclesis, and no Sanctus in this early prayer. Some scholars think that as it stands it represents a complete prayer, and such an interpretation is bolstered by the comparison of its structure with Jewish blessing.[33] In that sense, though its theological imagery differs from the *Didache* and from Addai and Mari, along with them it represents an early tradition of a relatively short Eucharist, constituted by distinct units of blessing for creation, blessing for redemption, and blessing for the church, concluding probably with a doxology. Within this structure, each of these prayers offers its own form of remembrance, or in other words its own confessional interpretation of what is wrought in the work of Christ.

SUMMARY TABLES

A summary of this perusal of early eucharistic prayers can be given in two comparative lists. The first has to do with the structure of Eucharist, the second with its redemptive imagery.

---

32. It is also very prominent in the later liturgy of the Roman canon and in the texts of Ambrose that are connected with it. It is likewise integral to the Byzantine liturgy. However, in the commerce between churches the influence of early Alexandria may not be ignored.

33. See Ligier, "The Origins of the Eucharistic Prayer," 179; Enrico Mazza, "Una anafora incompleta?" *Ephemerides Liturgicae* 99 (1985): 425–36; Bryan Spinks, "A Complete Anaphora? A Note on Strasbourg Gr. 254," *Heythrop Journal* 25 (1984): 51–55. On this early form and the possible revival of a short anaphora based on it, see Geoffrey Cuming, "Four Very Early Anaphoras," *Worship* 58 (1984): 172. Cuming also attempts to read palimpsests of short anaphoras in later prayers, particularly the liturgy of John Chrysostom.

STRUCTURE OF EUCHARIST

[This table takes the longer text of Addai and Mari
to represent the East Syrian tradition].

	Addai and Mari	Apostolic Tradition	Strasbourg P.	Epiphanius
1.	Praise/creation	Thanksgiving/creation	Thanksgiving/creation	Thanksgiving/creation
2.	Thanksgiving/redemption	Thanksgiving/redemption Supper narrative Anamnesis/offering	Thanksgiving/offering	Thanksgiving/redemption Supper narrative
3.	Intercession/anamnesis Doxology	Intercession/epiclesis Doxology	Intercession [Doxology]	Intercession [Doxology]

This table, based certainly on reconstruction of original texts, shows that the more common format is that of three blessings, the third of which is an intercession. The anaphora from the *Apostolic Tradition* is the only one of these texts that reads as a clear and single literary unity, passing from thanksgiving to intercession and including the supper narrative with an anamnesis in the thanksgiving section of the prayer. Reference to the supper narrative and an anamnesis are found within the intercession in the prayer of Addai and Mari. This inclusion of the embolism in the intercession rather than in the blessing or thanksgiving is what is found in the later texts of the Alexandrian and Roman traditions.

Redemptive Imagery

This second list contrasts the images of redemption incorporated into the Eucharist:

1. Revelation of life and knowledge through Jesus Christ, God's child/servant: *Didache, Addai and Mari.*

2. Gathering of the church into the kingdom/into unity: *Didache* (kingdom), *Apostolic Tradition* (unity).

3. Restoration of humanity through the incarnation: *Addai and Mari* (includes forgiveness of sins and the gift of immortality), *Epiphanius* (later changed to confess the union of two natures in Christ).

4. Christ's voluntary and life-giving death through conquest of the powers of evil: *Apostolic Tradition, Epiphanius.*

5. Redemptive death aptly commemorated by the sacrifice of thanksgiving: *Strasbourg papyrus.*

In these early prayers there is no application of sacrificial imagery to the death of Christ. It is to be noted also that they do not express the idea that a representation or reenactment of Christ's mysteries is taking place. They look back to his death and its victory as the origin of the grace and the promise given in the gift of the body and blood. They look forward to the resurrection of the body and immortality as the consummation of what is received and to the heavenly worship in which earthly liturgy will be perfected. In that sense, they keep a clear distinction between past, present, and future realities, the present being the time in which by reason of what Christ has done in the past the church can look ahead to the fulfilment of his work in eternity.

The process of naming in these prayers is of interest to a theology of God and to the ways of addressing God in eucharistic prayer. The most elementary form of naming is found in the invocation of the Name in East Syrian liturgy. This indicates that because God is ineffable mystery all naming of God by human persons originates in the works of divine beneficence. Beyond this starting-point, there is a more explicit naming in the form of address directed either to the Father or to Christ. Such naming is also revelation. It is rooted in the experience of forgiveness, the eschatological reality of knowledge, victory over the powers of evil, and the promise of immortality. It is in the work of redemption, or of creation when considered in conjunction with salvation, that God is known and so named and thanked. Whatever praise is rendered, intercession made, or qualificative given to God, it is rooted in this experience of gracious gift and promise. The naming process holds in harmony the ineffable mystery of divine reality and the munificence of the revelation given in works.

OTHER BLESSINGS

While in the opinion of some all the Eucharists studied above are related to the final table prayer of a Jewish repast, for Giraudo this itself is tributary to a more fundamental form of commemorative blessing. It seems clear that some of the eucharistic prayers formulated in later centuries were influenced by Jewish blessings other than the *birkat ha-mazon*. To understand the emergence of Christian commemoration it is therefore helpful to take at least a brief look at some early Christian blessings that were not composed for use in the sacrament. Two examples are here offered. They come respectively from the document known as the *First Letter of Clement* and the canonical collection that goes by the title of the *Apostolic Constitutions*.

First Clement[34]

This letter is an exhortation from the church of Rome to the church of Corinth, occasioned by factional struggle in the latter community. It concludes with a lengthy prayer that may reflect the style of prayer in Rome when its church was still under heavy Judeo-Christian influence.

The structure of the first part of the prayer is as follows: (a) supplication for God's elect, to whom the gift of knowledge has been given in Jesus Christ (59:3a); (b) motivation for prayer in the kind of antithetical divine action attributed to the last days, e.g., casting down the mighty and exalting the lowly (59:3b); (c) appeal to God's providential care of the universe and of the chosen (59:3c); (d) petition for those who particularly need God's help, e.g., the sick and hungry, ending with a plea that all may come to acknowledge God and Jesus Christ (59:4). The remainder of the prayer praises God for the works of creation and providence and asks for the forgiveness of sins. It concludes with a doxology.

This prayer is seen by scholars as a Christian adaptation of Jewish blessings that extolled creation, providence, and the forgiveness of sins.[35] It is the mention of Jesus Christ that changes the content but not the form of the prayer. The prayer's ethical tone is strong, but it is mingled with eschatological expectation. The eschatological note suggests that it belonged within the community's liturgy, whereas the ethical bias is probably due to the use of the prayer that the author of the letter wants to make.

Apostolic Constitutions[36]

Though this canonical collection is usually dated as a collection in the fourth century of the common era, the prayers in Book VII are of earlier origin and are a Christian adaptation of Jewish prayers. The prayer in question is compared with the *Tefillah,* or eighteen blessings of the synagogue gathering. In particular, it is related to the seven blessings of this prayer for the sabbath and is a Christian way of marking that day, possibly prior to the observance of the first day of the week as the Lord's Day. Louis Bouyer sums up the form and content of these Christian blessings in this way:

---

34. *First Letter of Clement,* 59:1–61:3. See the English text in *The Apostolic Fathers: A New Translation and Commentary,* edited by Robert M. Grant and Holt A. Graham (London and New York: Thomas Nelson & Sons, 1965), 2:92–96.

35. See Otto Koch, *Eigenart und Bedeutung der Eschatologie im theologischen Aufriss des ersten Clemensbriefes* (Bonn: Peter Hanstein Verlag, 1964).

36. Book VII, 33–38. A Latin translation is given in F. X. Funk, *Didascalia et Constitutiones Apostolorum,* 1:424ff. The text is treated at length by Louis Bouyer, *Eucharist: Theology and Spirituality of the Eucharistic Prayer* (Notre Dame: Notre Dame University Press, 1968), 119–35, and by David A. Fiensey, *Prayers Alleged to be Jewish: An Examination of the Constitutiones Apostolorum,* Brown Judaic Studies 65 (Chico, Calif.: Scholars Press, 1985).

...the difference [between the Christian and Jewish text] bear especially on detailed enumerations, substituted for the global formulas of the Jewish prayers which prevailed. In each case... these exhaustive encomia (which are traditional in the Wisdom writings whose kinship with the Alexandrian Judaism of our formulas is obvious), that are also found in the Epistle to the Hebrews, furnish for the Christians who used them a final and ready-made place to insert the mention of Christ and his work.[37]

The first of the blessings, as found in the *Seder Amran Gaon*, is in remembrance of the covenant with the people through Abraham, Isaac, and Jacob. This is much amplified in the opening part of the corresponding prayer of the *Apostolic Constitutions*, but without any specific Christian note.

The second blessing of the seder is for God's work in creation, in healing the sick, and in quickening the dead. The second part of the Christian prayer develops this at greater length by drawing on Wisdom literature, and praising the divine Wisdom that is made manifest in creation, in the creation of human beings in particular, in the restoration of fallen humankind, and in the quickening of the dead. It is given Christian character by the simple device of inserting the phrase *through Christ* at the beginning and at the end of the acclamation: "You have abolished the decree of (our death), you who give life to the dead *through Jesus Christ our hope.*"

The third seder blessing is the one that incorporates the *Qedushah* and is the praise of God's glory, made manifest in Jerusalem and in the kingdom of God's rule. The corresponding Christian blessing again develops this theme at greater length by drawing on Wisdom literature and it also includes the Holy, holy, holy. Once again, the Jewish blessings are given Christian inspiration by the simple phrase *through Christ* and by this conclusion:

> ...You are the one who punishes the ungodly and who rewards the righteous, the God and the Father of Christ and the Lord of those who venerate him, whose promise is without deception, whose judgment is incorruptible, whose decision is impossible to decline, whose piety is unceasing, whose Eucharist is eternal, through whom there is owed a worship that is worthy of you, on the part of all holy and rational nature.[38]

What happens in this Christian adaptation of Jewish prayer is that the figure of Wisdom looms larger and the mediation of Christ is con-

---

37. Bouyer, *Eucharist*, 135.
38. Taken from Bouyer, *Eucharist*, 129.

nected with the work of divine Wisdom. One could thus speak of a Wisdom christology, in which creation is given a prominent place on the one hand and on the other the eschatological fulfilment of God's work in the reign ushered in through Christ. Within this context, the quickening of the dead has an important place. As far as Eucharist is concerned, one can see from this how Christian commemoration can draw on a prayer structure other than table prayer and on another set of images to express Christ's mediation.

CHRISTIAN PRAYER AND JEWISH BLESSING

It has been obvious throughout this chapter that comparisons have to be made with Jewish blessings. The comparison, however, has been done as each prayer warranted it, rather than through an attempt to trace a genesis of Christian prayer as such from Jewish. Several authors, and in particular Louis Bouyer, have persistently stressed that it is not the *birkat ha-mazon* alone that provides the model for Christian Eucharist. Even though the early prayers examined can be compared with it, it does not explain everything in them, nor does it explain some of the developments in post-Nicene prayers.

As already explained, Cesare Giraudo has tried to get beyond the dilemma of finding particular prototypes, either in the table prayer or in the synagogue prayer. He shows that there is a narrative and commemorative praise running through a variety of Jewish hymns and blessings, in whose variety and evolution these more formal prayers are but a point. He has shown too that an embolism, in the form of an appeal to a divine oracle of commemorative command and promise of fidelity, occurs in a number of such prayers.

One of the things that stands out in this hypothesis is the narrative basis of every commemorative blessing. Sometimes, as in certain psalms, the narrative is woven into the prayer in poetic recital. Sometimes, the narrative content of the blessing itself is only an allusion, but it has to be related back to the greater narrative. The order of the paschal seder is helpful in seeing one type of relation of blessing to narrative. The *haggadah* is a unit distinct from the blessing, but story and blessing complement and complete each other.

Some critics find that Giraudo has oversimplified the material and the issue of eucharistic origins.[39] However, even if one questions some

---

39. Giraudo's work is reviewed in Thomas Talley, "The Literary Structure of the Eucharistic Prayer," *Worship* 58 (1984): 404–20. For a criticism, see Paul F. Bradshaw, "*Zebah Todah* and the Origins of the Eucharist," *Ecclesia Orans* 8, no. 3 (1991): 245–60. While some of his criticisms seem to be justified, by sticking to the issue of the impossible genesis Bradshaw seems to miss some of the major points in Giraudo's study.

of the points that he makes, his work has made it clear that to Christian prayer there is a large background of commemoration, blessing, and praise in Jewish prayer, so that Christians did not have to draw solely on table blessing. The very attempt to arrive at a fundamentally simple structure has in fact served to show how much diversity of form and thought can occur within the commemoration of salvific deeds. It also shows that in revitalizing Christian Eucharist there is a rich inspiration on which to draw that can break the boundaries of set forms. A comparison between Christian prayers, and their comparison with Jewish forms of commemorative prayer, open up possibilities for Eucharist that are yet to be realized.

EUCHARIST AND CONTEXT

In examining tradition, it is inevitable that one isolates texts for examination. It can never be forgotten, however, that texts such as the eucharistic prayer emerge and develop in a much fuller context.

First is the meaning that they have within the order of service. The scriptural readings that preceded the thanksgiving and the communion were ordered in the sequence of Prophet (Old Testament), Apostle (or apostolic writings in the canon), and Gospel. This itself set the stage for a typological reading of the scriptures that relates everything to the person of Jesus Christ proclaimed in the gospel, whether it be Old Testament history or the life of the church. Everything too made it clear that this was a prayer over bread and wine, transforming them and preparing them as food and drink for the faithful, the one aspect never being isolated from the other.[40]

Second, the prayer would be better understood by relating it to the homiletic tradition, especially for the pasch or for the Great Thursday on which the supper was especially recalled. Some sense of the influence of the homiletic interpretation of Christ's mystery has been noted in the prayer of the *Apostolic Tradition*.

To pursue this point for the East Syrian church, one would have to go to the turning point between pre-Nicene and post-Nicene eras and look at the homilies and hymns of Ephraem the Syrian, in whom the orientation of the earlier Semitic Christianity is maintained and carried forward. In his homilies for the Great Thursday, for example, there is an accent on the teachings of Christ and on the food and drink of the

---

40. Account could also be taken of the differences in the prayer that may have been associated with the person of the minister. In the East Syrian church, we have seen mention of Eucharist rendered by a wandering missionary, a visiting prophet, and a resident bishop.

body and blood of Christ, as well as a heavily eschatological tone of expectation and impending judgment.[41] These orientations are similar to the imagery of the East Syrian prayers. In referring to the sacraments, some of his hymns recall the apocryphal blessings when they include an invocation of the mystery of the Spirit, as dove and mother, or the fire in the bread.[42]

Third, one needs to be attentive to the religious milieu of the prayers. The Semitism of the prayers of East Syria has always been noted. Looking at the (nonsacramental) blessing from the *Apostolic Constitutions*, it was seen how the Jewish sources reflect not only Palestinian Judaism but the wisdom tradition of Hellenized Judaism. In the prayer of Hippolytus we noted the influence of the response to gnosticism. Prayer formulations and even their doctrinal content are influenced by their contact with prevailing religious belief and practice. As a central and foundational confession of faith in the life of the church, Christ is proclaimed in the prayer in a way that expresses the response to the religious situation of the culture. It is thus appropriate to move at this point to a consideration of what may be generically called the theology of Eucharist in early times.

41. There is a text for the Great Thursday that could serve as an example in *The Eucharist*, edited by Daniel J. Sheerin, The Message of the Fathers of the Church 7 (Wilmington, Del.: Michael Glazier, 1986), 137–43.

42. See "Hymn of St. Ephrem to Christ on the Incarnation, the Holy Spirit, and the Sacraments," translation and notes by Robert Murray, S.J., *Eastern Churches Review* 2 (1970): 142–47. See also Peter Yousif, "St. Ephrem on Symbols in Nature: Faith, the Trinity and the Cross (Hymns on Faith, No. 18)," *Eastern Churches Review* 10 (1978): 52–60.

Chapter 6

THE PRE-NICENE CHURCH: EUCHARISTIC THEOLOGY

It has become quite popular to contrast the eucharistic theologies of the first and second millennia, dubbing the first liturgical and the second doctrinal and dogmatic. The distinction is meant to point to the liturgical context of theological elaboration in early Christian churches. It ought not obscure the cultural influences on eucharistic theology in those times, nor the relation of theology to eucharistic practice in later centuries.

Granted the clear reference to celebration in pre-Nicene theology, account must be taken of styles of interpreting the scriptural tradition, of the need for a public apologetic in defense of eucharistic worship, and of the influence of philosophical modes of thought.[1] The material is presented here under the following headings: (a) the understanding of the sacrament as memorial of Christ; (b) the application to the Eucharist of the notion of sacrifice; (c) the discourse on sacramental food and drink; (d) the grasp of the Eucharist as sacrament of the church; (e) the thought patterns followed by church writers in addressing these questions.

MEMORIAL OF JESUS CHRIST

It has been suggested that for the early church one of the principal contexts in which an understanding of Christ's redemptive action evolved was the celebration of the Eucharist.[2] Certainly the selection of scriptural

---

1. Though it is dated, there is a helpful survey of early eucharistic theology in Darwell Stone, *A History of the Doctrine of the Holy Eucharist*, vol. 1 (London: Longmans, Green & Co., 1909). A useful set of essays on individual writers in the early church is provided by *The Eucharist of the Early Christians*, translated by Matthew J. O'Connell (New York: Pueblo Publishing Company, 1978).

2. See, for example, Louis-Marie Chauvet, "Sacramentaire et christologie: La liturgie, lieu de christologie," in *Sacrements de Jésus Christ*, edited by J. Doré (Paris: Desclée, 1983), 228–36; Charles Perrot, *Jésus et l'histoire* (Paris: Desclée, 1979), 304–9.

readings for proclamation and the redemptive imagery used in thanksgiving and blessing served to shape Christian belief. As a memorial of Christ's pasch, the eucharistic confession of faith expressed the meaning of salvation.

One early expression of what it meant to call the Eucharist a memorial is found in Justin's figural reading of a scriptural image:

> The offering of fine flour that was prescribed for those cleansed of leprosy was a prefiguration of the bread of the Eucharist which the Lord Jesus commanded us to offer in memory of the passion he underwent for the sake of those whose souls are cleansed of all evil. He so commanded us in order that we might at the same time thank God for creating the world and all it contains for humanity's sake, for freeing us from the evil in which we were born, and for destroying utterly the principalities and powers through him who became subject to suffering in accordance with God's will.[3]

To explore the meaning given to memorial further, four trends can be noted during this period. First, the Eucharist is presented as a mediated share in the new creation of the paschal night. Second, it is directly related to Christ's will and action at the Last Supper. Third, antignostic polemic appeals to the Eucharist as the sign that the work of both creation and redemption are the work of God's Word. Fourth, spiritual theology shows how the Eucharist operates in the life of the true gnostic, who passes over from this world to the spiritual table of the Word.

Memorial as Paschal Fulfillment

This orientation is found initially in early paschal homilies. This homiletic tradition is developed principally through the use of two symbols or images of Christ, namely, the paschal lamb and the new creation. In proclaiming the mystery of the paschal night, one such homily begins by rejoicing in its effulgent light:

> For us, his faithful, [Christ] has initiated a bright new day, long, eternal and inextinguishable; it is the mystical pasch, celebrated in figures under the Law, but fulfilled in very truth by Christ, the marvelous pasch, the wonder of divine virtue, the work of power, truly a feast, an everlasting memorial, impassibility born of suffering, immortality born of death, life born in the tomb, healing born

---

3. *Dialogue with Trypho*, 41, 1. Original text in Anton Hänggi and Irmgard Pahl, *Prex eucharistica: Textus e variis liturgiis antiquioribus selecti*, Spicilegium Friburgense 12 (Fribourg: Editions Universitaires, 1968), 72–73. English translation in R. C. D. Jasper and G. J. Cuming, *Prayers of the Eucharist: Early and Reformed*, 3d ed. (New York: Pueblo Publishing Company, 1987), 27.

from wounds, resurrection born from the fall, ascent to heaven born from descent into hell.[4]

The homily was given during the night vigil of the paschal feast. The context is thus one of word and sacrament and the natural symbolism of light and darkness. The scriptures are heard to proclaim the prefiguration of Christ in the work of creation and in the blood of the paschal lamb. Possibly the readings included other figures of Christ, such as Abel and Isaac, in whose blood and sacrifice respectively Christ's own death is foreshadowed.[5] The mystery is manifested through the way in which word and sacrament belong together. Note how the two are linked in this passage:

> This is for us the celebration of our sacred feast, this is our spiritual banquet, this is our immortal and delightful nourishment. Since we have been nourished on the bread come down from heaven and have drunk of the chalice of joy, that chalice which is full of fervour and warmth, containing blood signed from on high with the glow of the Spirit, let us speak first on what is the Law, what is the economy of the Law, for in this way we will learn in parable the meaning of the Word and the economy of the Word.[6]

The homilist explains that the incarnation is the assumption by the Word of our "miserable and mortal flesh," in order to fill it with the Spirit. He then relates the passion to the Eucharist:

> This was the pasch which Jesus desired to suffer for us. His suffering freed us from sufferings, his death has vanquished death,

---

4. A. Hamman, *The Paschal Mystery: Ancient Liturgies and Patristic Texts,* translated by T. Halton (New York: Alba House, 1969), 50. Original text: *Homélies pascales* I, edited by P. Nautin, Sources Chrétiennes 27 (Paris: Ed. du Cerf, 1950), 117.

5. The central reading for the vigil in early times was Exodus 12. The Armenian lectionary, which reflects the order of service in Jerusalem between 417 and 439, includes Genesis 22, the story of Isaac. There was clearly room for the evocation of other figures that underline the suffering of Christ, as in this text from Melito of Sardis, *On Pascha and Fragments,* edited by S. Hall (Oxford: Clarendon Press, 1979), 37:

> He is the Pascha of our salvation.
> It is he who in many endured many things:
> it is he that was in Abel murdered,
> and in Isaac bound,
> and in Jacob exiled,
> and in Joseph sold,
> and in Moses exposed,
> and in the lamb slain,
> and in David persecuted,
> and in the prophets dishonoured.

6. Hamman, *The Paschal Mystery,* 54.

the visible nourishment has procured his eternal life for us. Such is the salutary desire of Jesus, such his love which is the Spirit; to show the figures as figures and no more; to offer in their place his holy body to his disciples. Take and eat; this is my body . . . drink of this for this is my blood of the new covenant which is being shed for many unto the remission of sins. Therefore he desires not so much to eat as to suffer so that he might deliver us from suffering in eating.[7]

The homilist goes on to proclaim the death of Christ as a cosmic struggle in which an end is put to death. The descent into the tomb is a breaking of the bonds of death through Christ's kingly power. The resting in the tomb for three days shows the universality of redemption, for those before the Law, under the Law, and after the Law. Christ's rising from the dead is the rising of the firstborn of the new creation.

Placed in this context, the bread and the drink of the sacrament give a share in the economy that is proclaimed through the scriptures and their interpretation. It is through the sacrament that Christians share the victory of Christ's suffering, which is the climactic moment of a cosmic struggle.[8]

Memorial and the Supper: Christ's Passion

Though biblical images are plentiful in the third-century work of Cyprian of Carthage, his theology depends on the relation that he traces between the Eucharist and the Last Supper.[9] By stressing that in the Eucharist the bishop prays the prayer that Christ prayed, he offers a distinctive interpretation of memorial. Like the homilist quoted above, Cyprian makes the voluntary suffering of Christ central to his understanding of the Eucharist, but he gives the theme a different twist. For him, the *passio* is located in the action of Christ at the supper, because it was there that he showed his suffering and death to be voluntarily undertaken. While the Eastern paschal homilies ponder the passion of Christ as obedience, struggle, suffering, and victory, Cyprian traces the passion back to its roots in the will of Christ. He also makes more use of the vocabulary of sacrifice, finding in the voluntariness of the passion the acme of true sacrifice. Of the Eucharist, he then says that it is the sacrifice of the church in which mention is made of the passion of Christ

---

7. Hamman, *The Paschal Mystery*, 64.

8. The similarity between this imagery and the imagery of the prayer in the *Apostolic Tradition* is clear.

9. *Epistula* 63 (CSEL 3, 2:712). An English text is found in *The Eucharist*, edited by Daniel Sheerin, Message of the Fathers of the Church 7 (Wilmington, Del.: Michael Glazier, 1986), 255–68.

which is commemorated. Of the bishop he states that in the prayer that expresses the offering he acts in the place of Christ:

> If Christ Jesus, our Lord and God, is himself the High Priest of God the Father, and first offered himself as a sacrifice to the Father, and commanded this to be done in commemoration of himself, certainly the priest [*sacerdos,* i.e., the bishop] who imitates what Christ did and then offers the true and full sacrifice in the church of God the Father, if he thus begins to offer according to what he sees Christ himself offered, performs truly in the place of Christ.[10]

The full reality of the sacramental communion of the faithful in the sacrifice of Christ emerges in martyrdom. They are prepared for this by drinking of Christ's blood, for thus they confess their communion in his passion and immolation. Cyprian finds a curious timidity in the fear to drink of the wine early in the morning, lest one's breath, redolent of wine, betray one to be a Christian:

> All of the discipline of religion and of truth is subverted unless that which is prescribed spiritually is kept faithfully, for in the morning sacrifice that which each one fears is that he should be redolent of the blood of Christ through the savour of the wine. Thus, therefore, the brotherhood begins also to be kept back from the passion of Christ in persecutions while it learns in the oblations to be ashamed about his blood and his bloodshed ... For how can we who blush to drink the blood of Christ shed our blood for Christ?[11]

There is a decidedly practical turn to Cyprian's eucharistic theology. He was deeply concerned to make communion available to the people in times of trouble as the sacramental food of Christ's passion, and this moved him to modify the rule of the one Sunday assembly. He saw the Eucharist as the source of the unity of the faithful with the church and with Christ, a unity that he found signified in the mixing of the water with the wine. Communion with the church is communion with the bishop, and Cyprian's sacerdotal characterization of his office related him directly to Christ, underlining the importance of the episcopacy in the church at the central moment of its worship.

---

10. *Epistula* 63, 14 (CSEL 3, 2:712). The Latin phrase to describe the bishop's relation to Christ is *vice Christi.*

11. *Epistula,* 63, 15 (CSEL 3, 2:713f.).

Memorial of Creation and Redemption through the Word

The thought of Irenaeus on the Eucharist was elaborated in his polemic against the gnostics. He found in it an argument against their doctrine and their ideas of mediation.[12] Of the resurrection of the flesh in particular his text says: "Our manner of thinking is conformed to the Eucharist, and the Eucharist conforms to our manner of thinking."[13] This principle underlies an appeal to the Eucharist on all matters concerning the economy of creation and redemption.

The gnostics included many groups and professed a variety of teachings. As we learn of them from Irenaeus, what was common was their belief in a hierarchy of beings and mediators between God and the world, and the distinction between the creative principle of spirit, source of good, and the creative principle of matter, source of evil. In enunciating the Christian faith, Irenaeus's basic purpose was to affirm the One Creator God and the One Word, through whom the Father created the entire universe and through whom the world is redeemed and recapitulated. This is the rule of faith,[14] the tradition of the elders, and the apostolic teaching, and outside it there is no truth. On the basis of this truth, Irenaeus affirmed the unity of the human person, spirit and matter, and the eternal redemption of soul and body.

A practical matter for worship is the offering of sacrifice. The pagan religions and the gnostic cults practiced sacrifice, and of course it was at the center of the Law. In the context of discussing sacrifice Irenaeus wrote of the Eucharist, the sacrifice of the new covenant commanded by Jesus Christ.[15] It is the only true sacrifice, of which Malachi prophesied, and it is made to the one true God. He appealed to this sacrifice to affirm the goodness and unity of all creation and the access to God through the invocation of the Name of Christ and through the food and drink of immortality. True sacrifice is not propitiation of mediators less than God, nor indeed propitiation of the anger of the God of the covenant, as some of the Jewish people mistakenly took the legal sacrifices

---

12. The texts on the Eucharist are translated in *Irenaeus of Lyons on Baptism and Eucharist: Selected Texts with Introduction, Translation and Annotation,* by David N. Power, Alcuin/GROW Liturgical Study 18 (Bramcote, Nottingham: Grove Books Limited, 1991). For the Latin text and a reconstruction of the original Greek, see *Irénée de Lyon: Contre les Hérésies,* critical edition by Adelin Rousseau and Louis Doutréleau, book 4, vol. 2, Sources Chrétiennes 100 (Paris: Éd. du Cerf, 1965), and book 5, vol. 2, Sources Chrétiennes 153 (Paris: Éd. du Cerf, 1969).

13. *Adversus Haereses* IV, 18.5; Power, ed., *Irenaeus of Lyons on Baptism and Eucharist,* 21.

14. The importance of this rule of faith stands out in a special way in his work, *Proof of the Apostolic Preaching,* translated and annotated by J. S. Smith (Westminster, Md.: Newman Press, 1952) in which he gives an exposition of Christian teaching based on the rule of faith invoked in baptism. The original Greek is lost. Smith translates from an early Armenian text.

15. See *Adversus Haereses* IV.17 and 18; Power, ed., *Irenaeus of Lyons on Baptism and Eucharist,* 14–22.

to be. It is rather an offering in gratitude. First it expresses gratitude for creation in the offering of bread and wine, first-fruits of the earth. Then it expresses gratitude for redemption, being the action of a free and redeemed people in which they invoke the Name of Christ. The Name of Christ is to be taken as the Name of the Father, because Christ is the Son and because he received the name of Lord from the Father.

Central to this theology is the idea that the blessing prayer is the invocation of Christ's name to the Father's glory. As such, it sanctifies the bread and wine, so that they are no ordinary food and drink but the table of the body and blood of Christ. In receiving this nourishment, Christians receive forgiveness of sins and the guarantee of the resurrection of the flesh.

Thus invocation of the name of Christ and participation in the flesh and blood whose reality is mediated by this blessing stand at the heart of the teaching of Irenaeus on the eucharistic memorial. To this he related the remembrance of Christ's voluntary suffering in the imagery that he shared with the paschal tradition. To invoke the name is to remember the suffering of the just one, and to remember the suffering of the just one is to find the world restored through it. To offer this sacrifice is likewise to be ready to suffer with him in Christian life.

So understood, the Eucharist confirms the doctrine of the one God, creating and redeeming the world through the one Word. It confirms the incarnation, for how could it be offered if the Word had not truly taken on flesh? It confirms the goodness of creation, for how else could God be offered the material things of this earth if they were not God's own? It confirms the resurrection of the flesh, since in it our very bodies are nourished with the flesh and blood of Christ.

Memorial as True Gnosis

In contrast with the esoteric knowledge of the gnostic sects that claimed special enlightenment and veered from the truth of the apostolic tradition, Christian writers found the true gnosis in those who sought wisdom in the Logos, the eternal Word of God who took on flesh as humanity's teacher and redeemer.

Inherent to this trend in Christian thinking and practice was the idea that it is by overcoming the concerns of this world that one may contemplate the revelation given in the Logos. A very ascetical form of this gnosis is associated with the Eucharist in the apocryphal *Gospel of Philip*.[16] The meaning of salvation is summed up in the saying that Jesus

---

16. On this work, see A. H. C. van Eijk, "The Gospel of Philip and Clement of Alexandria: Gnostic and Ecclesiastical Theology on the Resurrection and the Eucharist," *Vigiliae Christianae* 25 (1971): 94–120; Willem Cornelis van Unnik, "Three Notes on the Gospel of Philip," *New Testament Studies* 10 (1963/64): 465–69.

came "crucifying the world." One modern interpretation of this teaching is that for the letter's author the cross revealed the world's infamy.[17] Another finds there an evocation of the phrase in Galatians 6:14 that refers to Christ "by [or through] whom the world has been crucified," which means putting to death the wisdom of the world.[18] According to this Gospel, just as Christ took on the flesh and the sins of the world to save us from their enslavement, so in the Eucharist the Christian must put off the flesh and the world, crucifying them in Christ. Flesh and sacrament are in the same order; they have no ultimate eschatological significance, but only serve towards the attainment of the truth. The link between the cross and the Eucharist is nicely expressed through the use of the Syrian word *pharisatha*, which literally means a flat cake and comes from the verb *to extend* or *to stretch out*. It is used both for the eucharistic bread, and as an image of Jesus stretching out his hands on the cross.

This was still a rather crude way in which to respond to the desire of those who sought spiritual wisdom, beyond the things of the world. The Alexandrian writers Clement and Origen responded less directly to a popular desire for gnosis. They appealed instead to philosophical currents to express the unique character of the truths of revelation. For them, participation in the Eucharist belonged to the quest for the true gnosis of contemplative communion with the Logos.

The vision of redemption found in Origen's writings is as complete and cosmic as is that of Irenaeus, but his work concentrates much more on the life of the spirit, much less on the things of creation and on the flesh. His thought about the Eucharist is inseparable from his thought about scripture. The bread of the word and the bread of the Eucharist are both modes of communication of the soul with the divine Logos. In fact, there is a certain superiority to the word of scripture, which when spoken and proclaimed in the church embodies the divine Word or Logos. Origen even warns the faithful against obscuring the word through excessive reverence for the eucharistic elements. In keeping with such an outlook, he looks on the rites of the eucharistic celebration as a kind of ascesis, a way of liberating the spirit from the things of the flesh. Actions such as genuflection, prostration, and incensation free the mind from the exigencies of the body.

His spiritual ideals encroach upon his soteriology and sacramentology, so that he is less concrete than Irenaeus in what he says about the body and blood of Christ in the sacrament. What he says emphasizes a spiritual presence, but it would be wrong to see this as nonincarnational, for it is the result of the mystery of the Word's descent into the world. The following is a rather typical statement:

---

17. Georg Kretschmar, "Abendmahl III/1," in *Theologische Realenzyklopëdie*, 60.
18. Thus van Unnik, "Three Notes on the Gospel of Philip."

This bread which God the Word declares is his body is the word which feeds souls, word proceeding from God the Word, and bread from heavenly bread.... For God the Word was not saying that the visible bread which he was holding in his hands was his body, but rather the word in whose mystery the bread was to be broken. He was not saying that the visible drink was his blood, but the word, in whose mystery the drink was to be poured out. For what else could the body and blood of God the Word be, except the word which nourishes and the word which "makes glad the heart" (Ps. 103:15).[19]

What Origen argues against here is any simple identification of bread and body. The mystery of eucharistic presence is inherent to the mystery of the manifestation of the Word in the scripture, and what it means cannot be considered except in the light of the word spoken and proclaimed. What is given in the sacrament cannot be different from that which is given in the word.

We have seen how paschal homilies, the anaphora of the *Apostolic Tradition*, and Irenaeus emphasize Christ's struggle with evil. In contrast, the image of pasch that Origen adopts is that of passover.[20] The key scriptural reading for such an interpretation is Exodus 14, the story of the crossing of the Red Sea. Even in using the story of the eating of the paschal lamb as a prefigurement of Christ, pasch is understood as passover. Christ's death is a passover from this world to the Father. It is in keeping memory in the sacraments of baptism and Eucharist of Christ's passover from this world to the Father that Christians pass over from earthly to spiritual things. The word that they hear and that they receive sacramentally nourishes them for this journey.

Though in his homilies for the pasch or on the scriptures he speaks of the passion of Christ, his descent into hell, and indeed of the immolation of Christ as our pasch, Origen insists that these things are fulfilled in us spiritually. Thus of the phrase, "Christ our pasch has been sacrificed," he says:

For the one who understands that Christ our pasch has been sacrificed and that it is necessary to make feast in eating the flesh of the Word understands that there is not a moment in which one does

---

19. *In Mattheum* 85. See *The Eucharist*, ed. Sheerin, 187f., for the English translation. The original Greek may be found in *Origenes*, 11, Die griechischen christlichen Schriftsteller der ersten Jahrhunderte (Leipzig, 1903), 196–200.

20. See *Origène: Sur la Pâque*, edited by Octave Guéraud and Pierre Nautin (Paris: Beauchesne, 1979), 154–57. See also *Trois homélies dans la tradition d'Origène*, edited by P. Nautin, Sources Chrétiennes 36 (Paris: Ed. du Cerf, 1953). For an English translation, see *Origen: Treatise on the Passover*, translated and annotated by Robert J. Daly, Ancient Christian Writers 54 (Mahwah, N.J.: Paulist Press, 1992).

not make pasch, that is, passover. Such a one in every thought, word and action passes from the things of this life to God and hurries towards the city of God.[21]

In his spiritual theology Origen gives a special place to *eulogia*, or praise of God. The true gnostic reaches contemplative communion with the mystery of the Logos and joins with it in praise of the Father. This is the true sacrifice of the new covenant. Though he does not speak of the eucharistic prayer in this way, he does find that the celebration in which the word is received scripturally and sacramentally has its peak in the hymn sung to God, the offering of a spirit who sees the Father's glory in the Word. Preaching of the night of Christ's supper with his disciples, Origen concludes:

> Then [Jesus] taught the disciples who had celebrated the feast [of passover] with the Master and had received the bread of blessing and had eaten the body of the Word and had drunk the cup of thanksgiving. He taught them to sing a hymn to the Father in return for all these things, and to pass from height to height, for the faithful can never do anything in a valley.[22]

The eucharistic celebration as the memorial of Christ thus includes the word, the thanksgiving, the sacramental nourishment, and the *eulogia* of the liberated spirit. Sacramental memorial is mediation of the true gnosis that leads to the contemplation of the eternal Logos. The mystery of the three days of Christ's passion, burial, and resurrection is commemorated in what it signifies for the spiritual life of passage to the Father.

Conclusion

There are some common elements to these four ways of understanding the eucharistic memorial. The first is that all four see it as a way of participating in the mystery of Christ's death, descent into hell, and resurrection. It is not a mimesis of this mystery but a means of participation in what it has brought about. Second, each connects a particular way of understanding the passion with the understanding of the Eucharist. Third, in all four explanations certain practical concerns emerge, showing the need to see eucharistic development in the context of broader interests. For that time, these practical interests had to do with a specific

---

21. *Contra Celsum*, 8.22, edited by M. Borret, Sources Chrétiennes 150 (Paris: Ed. du Cerf, 1969), 222–24.

22. *In Mattheum* 85; text in *The Eucharist*, ed. Sheerin, 191. The valley in the simile is the valley of Hebron through which Jesus and the disciples passed on the way to the mount of Olives.

Christian spirituality, with protection in time of martyrdom, and with the defense of the faith against heterodox trends.

Indeed, the differences between the four theologies are connected with practical concerns. The homiletic tradition relates primarily to the transition from the pasch of the old covenant to the pasch of the new, and thus concentrates on the interpretation of the mystery of Christ through use of the scriptures. For Irenaeus, the great practical concern is the rule of faith and the place of the Eucharist within an antignostic apologetic. Christian rites must be clearly distinct from gnostic rites and yet appeal to people's religious sense. For Cyprian, the context is the concern for church unity and the risk of martyrdom. For Origen, as for the entire School of Alexandria, the Eucharist belongs to the way of true wisdom, to a spirituality that is enhanced by its contact with the way of the philosophers and yet finds its whole reason in the revelation of the Word of God. Since all of these theologies make some use of the image of sacrifice it is to this interpretation of memorial that it is now time to turn.

EUCHARISTIC SACRIFICE

Before considering how these theologies of memorial incorporate the notion of sacrifice, a word needs to be said about the New Testament background.[23]

New Testament Background

The starting-point for the use of cultic vocabulary is neither the designation of Christ's death as sacrifice, nor the similar designation of the Eucharist. It is rather the spiritualization of sacrifice, associated with the eschatological character of the community brought together in the Spirit of the risen Christ. While this position is particularly notable in the New Testament, it had its antecedents among the Jewish people. Even in the practice of the Temple cult, the rituals of sacrifice were not solely those of offering. They included forms of communion and sprinkling rites that indicated the action of God's redemptive and covenant mercy and were accompanied by songs of praise. In particular, however, there was a movement in Jewish companies to emphasize the spiritual sacrifice of the observance of the Law above all acts of cult.

---

23. See Robert J. Daly, *Christian Sacrifice: The Judeo-Christian Background before Origen* (Washington, D.C.: Catholic University of America Press, 1978), and the shorter work, *The Origins of the Christian Doctrine of Sacrifice* (Philadelphia: Fortress Press, 1978). See also Hans Moll, *Die Lehre von der Eucharistie als Opfer: Eine dogmengeschichtliche Untersuchung von Neuen Testament bis Irenaeus von Lyon* (Hanstein, 1975).

For New Testament writers, several ideas worked simultaneously to stretch the use of priestly vocabulary. Peoples' obedience to the gospel (Rom. 12:1; 15:16), their deeds of charity towards each other, their prayer and thanksgiving, were called offerings or sacrifices, because in them honor was rendered to God in the freedom and power of the Spirit. Not only that, but the people themselves as an eschatological community were dubbed a living sacrifice, a royal priesthood, a temple holy to God (1 Peter 2:4–10). Ministers were not given priestly names but rather bore secular designations, such as elder or bishop or deacon or presider, intended to underline their service to the community.

As far as Christ's death is concerned, as is well known it was primarily the Letter to the Hebrews that developed the analogy with the rites of Yom Kippur and with the daily levitical sacrifices. The image of Christ as the paschal sacrifice is first indicated by Paul in writing to the Corinthians, but it was not highly developed until the postapostolic period. Along with the prophecy of Malachi 1:10, both these images are important to the reading of early Christian writers on sacrifice.

Paschal Homilies

The paschal homilies already mentioned celebrated the passion of Christ as the new pasch, basing their typology on Exodus 12. In Christ's death, the sacrifice of the first pasch receives its antitypal fulfillment. The transition from the old economy to the new is not a break in God's operation, but it is its eschatological plenitude. Thus, for those familiar with the scriptures, the Eucharist allows them to remember Christ in a figurative remembrance of all that preceded him.[24] Sacrifice and suffering are fulfilled in the sacrifice and suffering that usher in the new creation. Through baptism and through the body and blood of Christ, Christians share in this paschal sacrifice and the new creation that it inaugurated.

Irenaeus on True Sacrifice

As in other parts of the world, in the Rhone valley where Irenaeus was bishop sacrifice was one of the religious means offered by the practice of various cults. He responded to this need by showing that in the Eucharist Christians have themselves a sacrifice, one that exceeds and replaces all others. It is both concrete and spiritual. It is concrete for it includes the offering of bread and wine, things of the earth. It is spiritual because it is a confession, an invocation, of the name of Christ and an

---

24. Unfortunately, as in the homily of Melito of Sardis, this may take on a virulent anti-Jewish tonality, when the Jewish people are accused of forsaking their own heritage in crucifying Christ.

expression of gratitude, not of appeasement. It is fruitful, because when the thanksgiving transforms the material gifts the faithful can partake of the very body and blood that feed both spirit and flesh in the guarantee of eternal life. It is an education of the spirit for in a sacramental and tangible way it embodies the one rule of faith, conforming to it and being confirmed by it.

In elaborating on the Eucharist as sacrifice of the new covenant, superior to all sacrifices of the Law, Irenaeus used the text of Malachi 1:11, as well as Matthew 5:12. The first text is fulfilled in the Eucharist, because it is the sacrifice of thanksgiving in which the name of Christ is invoked, because it is offered by persons redeemed and made free in Christ, and because the lives of these people by reason of their spiritual sacrifices are conformed to what the Eucharist expresses. The second text is fulfilled because in keeping the remembrance of the sufferings of Christ, the just for the unjust, Christians approach the table only if they are reconciled and do not sully it with enmity for each other, as Cain sullied his offering when he harbored hatred in his heart for Abel.

The text of Irenaeus does not seem to intend an offering of the body and blood of Christ, but one of bread and wine. These are offered with thanksgiving and out of pure hearts, and thus through invocation of Christ's name become his body and blood, from which the people eat and drink. By a sacrifice of gratitude, the earthly first-offerings become first-fruits of the new creation, for the nourishment of believers.

Origen and Clement

It is in the Alexandrian writers that the spiritual ideal of sacrifice is furthest pursued. They carry the allegorical interpretation of Old Testament sacrifices beyond any other writer in relating it both to Christ and to the Christian.

The death of Christ is interpreted through the figures of Isaac, the paschal lamb, and, via the letter to the Hebrews, the action of the high priest in the sacrifice of the day of atonement. Origen does describe the passage of Christ into heaven, or the spilling of his blood akin to the blood of the lamb, as a sacrifice of humanity's atonement and reconciliation with God and of propitiation for sin,[25] but he emphasizes that the primary motivation of Christ's action is the Father's love.

As far as the Christian is concerned, communion with the sacrifice of Christ is communion with the pasch of Christ. The Christian's whole life is a spiritual offering. Clement of Alexandria explains this in the vocabulary of true gnosticism. As he writes, the true gnostic is one who makes the perfect sacrifice:

---

25. See *Homilies on Leviticus*, 9, 10, quoted in *The Eucharist*, ed. Sheerin, 179.

This is the function of the true gnostic who has been made perfect to converse with God through the great high priest, and who is being made like the Lord, as far as possible, in the whole service of God which tends to human salvation through its provident care for us, as well as through service, teaching and the active ministry.... Mildness, I think, and philanthropy, and eminent piety, are the rules of the gnostic assimilation. I affirm that these virtues "are a sacrifice acceptable in the sight of God" (Phil 4. 18).[26]

Such teaching lures Christian disciples away from ritual sacrifices by inviting them to true wisdom and to the perfect worship of the Father, in communion with the Word. We have already seen how Origen interprets the pasch as passover and gives a spiritual meaning to the Christian's participation in the immolation of Christ. We should not think that this doctrine of spiritual sacrifice, which is nourished through the bread of word and the bread of sacrament, means mystical individualism. It is indeed the very basis of an ecclesiology of unity, as this is expressed by Clement:

Breathing together is properly said of the church. For the sacrifice of the church is the word breathing as incense from holy souls, the sacrifice and the whole mind being at the same time unveiled in God.... The mixture of incense mentioned in the Law is something that consists of many tongues and many voices in prayer, or rather of different nations and natures, prepared by the gift bestowed in the dispensation for the "unity of the faith" (Eph 4:13) and brought together in praises, with a pure mind, and just and right conduct, from holy words and righteous prayer.[27]

Summary

From what has preceded, we can see how in time the metaphor of sacrifice served to draw together the elements of mystery: the redemptive work of the Word made flesh, prefigured in the paschal lamb and located in the humility, obedience, and suffering of his voluntary death; the recapitulation of humanity into communion with this mystery through the spiritual sacrifice of holy lives, obedient to the gospel; the offering of bread and wine as signs of gratitude for creation and acknowledgment of the one God of all things; the offering of the prayer of thanksgiving, in which Christ is remembered and invoked and spiritual sacrifice reaches its fine point of praise of the Father; the communion in Christ's pasch

---

26. *Stromata* VII.3. English translation in *Ante-Nicene Fathers* 2:526f.
27. *Stromata* VII. 6, *Ante-Nicene Fathers* 2:531.

at the table of his body and blood, for the forgiveness of sins and the resurrection of the flesh.

The pre-Nicene period did not end however without some sacerdotalization of ministry and some development of a more cultic view of the Eucharist. This is found principally in the words of Cyprian and in the ritual of episcopal ordination in the *Apostolic Tradition*, which alongside his ministry of teacher and pastor, underlines the high-priestly role of the bishop in making the offerings at the altar. Indeed, this cultic turn became the main basis for the increasing distinction between clergy and laity, a fact most curious since the baptized people were called priestly long before their officially designated ministers.

SACRAMENTAL FOOD AND DRINK

In looking at eucharistic prayers, the strong emphasis on sacramental food and drink was noted, as well as its designation as the body and blood of Christ. In the theologies under consideration, the difference between Irenaeus and Origen, for example, may already be apparent. Irenaeus, like Ignatius of Antioch and Justin Martyr, is very specific and very realistic in referring to the body and blood.[28] Origen, on the other hand, makes this sacramental reality fit the priority that he gives to word or scripture in mediating communion with the Word of God.

The realistic attitudes of one such as Irenaeus need to be put in their proper context. In his antignostic polemic, Irenaeus wanted to defend two things above all. First, he asserted the freedom of God in creating the universe against any idea of emanationism. Second, he upheld the goodness of the material earth and of the human body against dualism of matter and spirit. The incarnation was a matter of great importance since it demonstrated God's association with the material world. In like vein, the reality of the food and drink of Christ's body and blood showed that the resurrection did not separate Christ from this world, as

---

28. There is a similar fleshly realism in a passage of Hilary of Poitier's treatise *On the Trinity* VIII, 13–16: "If the Word was truly flesh, and if we truly receive the Word made flesh in the Lord's food, why should we not hold that he remains within us naturally.... He joined the nature of his flesh to the nature of his eternity in the sacrament of his flesh which he allows us to share." From there he goes on to see the unity of Christians with Christ in the flesh as a mediation of their unity with him in the union of Father and Son. He concludes this passage in a way that puts his discourse in context, saying: "Every comparison is chosen to help our understanding, so that we may grasp what is being discussed by means of an example. These then are the facts about our life: since we are made of flesh we have Christ abiding in us, because of his flesh, so that we can live because of him on the same condition as he lives because of the Father." The original text is found in CCSL 62A: 325–28. The English translation is taken from *St. Hilary of Poitiers: The Trinity*, translated by S. McKenna, Fathers of the Church 25 (Washington, D.C.: Catholic University of America Press, 1954), 284–87.

it showed how the human body was nourished by this sustenance for immortality.

Irenaeus looked for some explanation of the way in which the bread and wine were transformed into Christ's flesh and blood. He found this in the union of earthly and heavenly elements in the sacrament. This union first underlines the power of the word of invocation, the heavenly, over the bread and wine, the earthly. He also seems to have had some idea of comparing the sacrament with the mystery of the incarnation. Thus there is a communion between the bread and the risen body of Christ that makes it comparable to the union of the divine and human natures in the Word made flesh.

This comparison was very clearly enunciated by Justin:

> For we do not receive these things as though they were ordinary food and drink. Just as Jesus Christ our Savior was made flesh through the word of God and took on flesh and blood for our salvation, so too through the word of prayer that comes from him the food over which the thanksgiving has been spoken becomes the flesh and blood of the incarnate Jesus, in order to nourish and transform our flesh and blood.[29]

There is thus no reason to confuse the opinions of Justin or Irenaeus with crude physicalism, as though they conceived of a material change or a localized presence. Due moment is given by them to Christ's resurrection and the new state of his being. On the other hand, it would be difficult to explain the realism of their language by appealing to the influence of a Neoplatonic perception of the relation between symbol and reality, which takes the former as a participation and manifestation of the latter. This is sometimes used to explain the oscillation in later writers between straightforward references to the gift of the body and blood, and references to the figure or symbol of the body and blood. It does not seem to fit Irenaeus's argument or the nonphilosophical mode of his thinking.

If Irenaeus is accused of being crudely physical, Origen is doubted for his excessively spiritual explanation. The influence of Philo and Middle Platonism on his thought needs to be considered. He clearly parted from the Neoplatonic idea of emanation from the One to explain creation, since this would implicate both God's freedom and the reality of the incarnation. On the other hand, he kept the strong distinction between the material and spiritual worlds and the superiority of the latter. He was influenced by the explanation that knowledge and truth are acquisitions of the spirit when it rises above the things of the earth. He

---

29. *Apologia* I, 66.2. The original text is given in Hänggi and Pahl, *Prex eucharistica*, 70f. An English translation is given in *The Eucharist*, ed. Sheerin, 34.

tended to see the material as a hindrance to the life of the spirit, so that
he thought of human nature's relation to material things as in need of
purification. His explanation of the nature of the sacramental food fitted
with these presuppositions. In his commentary on Matthew, he states:

> The bread which God the Word declares is his body is the word
> which feeds souls, word proceeding from God the Word, and
> bread from heavenly bread. It has been placed upon the table....
> And this drink which God the Word declares is his blood is the
> word which gives drink and wonderfully intoxicates the hearts of
> those who drink.[30]

He affirmed the basic faith in the gift of the body and blood. His
elevation of the spirit above matter, of word above sacrament, led him to
greatly spiritualize the sense of this identification between sacramental
reality and the body and blood of Christ.[31]

It is within a common orthodox faith that both Alexandrian writers
and Irenaeus develop their thought on eucharistic reality, looking for
ways to express this mystery of faith. For both, the eternal Word's gift
of divine life through the incarnation, the scripture, and the Eucharist
is the point at issue. With a heavier emphasis on the transformation of
bread and wine into Christ's body and blood, Irenaeus offers analogies
from the realm of faith. By reason of the accent that they put on humanity's spiritual nature, the Alexandrines describe the sacramental gift
in terms addressed to this concern. Together, they serve to define the
nature of the question as posed in later times.

CHURCH AND SACRAMENT

Sacrament of Unity

In appealing to the Eucharist as center of church unity, Ignatius of
Antioch wrote:

> Be careful then to participate in only the one Eucharist, for there
> is one flesh [sarx] of our Lord Jesus Christ and one cup to unite
> us in his blood [tou haimatos autou], one altar just as there is one

---

30. *In Mattheum* 26.26–28. The translation is taken from *The Eucharist*, ed. Sheerin, 1871.
31. Clement of Alexandria shows the same tendency to concentrate on the spiritual
meaning of the sacramental body and blood. See André Méhat, "Clement of Alexandria,"
in *The Eucharist of the Early Christians*, 99–131.

bishop with the presbytery and deacons, my fellow servants, so that whatever you do, you do according to God.[32]

Various tenets of faith are related to each other in this text, the principal point of reference being the incarnation. In speaking of the flesh of Jesus Christ in the sacrament, Ignatius uses the Johannine term *sarx*, thus underlining the relation of the Eucharist to the incarnation of the Logos. Since the Logos took on flesh for the salvation of the whole human race, uniting all humanity in one human flesh, it is this that grounds the unity of the church in the Eucharist. This Johannine imagery is completed by the Pauline image of unity in the one cup of Christ's blood, that is, in his passion. The church is one because of its foundation in the incarnation and passion of the Word made flesh. This unity is both symbolized and engendered in the one eucharistic gathering where all partake of the one bread and cup. The ministry or service of bishop, presbytery, and deacons is to foster this sacramental unity. It is in this context that obedience to the bishop becomes a test of orthodoxy and fidelity to Christ's body.

In the letter of Cyprian on the Eucharist, it is in his ruminations on the mixing of water with the wine that we see his imagery of sacramental ecclesial unity:

Since Christ carried us all and bore our sins, we can see that the water rightly symbolizes the people, and the wine the blood of Christ. When the water is mixed with the wine in the cup, the people are being mingled with Christ, and the throng of believers are brought into union with him in whom they believe. The mingling and union of wine with water in the cup is indissoluble, just as the church, that is, the people who are the church and who faithfully and courageously persevere in the faith can never be separated from Christ but will remain bound to him by a love that makes of the two one.[33]

An Ordered Assembly

It was because the one table forms the one living reality of the church that communities and their pastors insisted on the principle of the one eucharistic assembly. This became not only an effective bonding but one of the criteria of orthodoxy. Those who attempted separate assemblies were thought to place themselves outside the communion of the one apostolic church.

---

32. *Letter to the Philadelphians* 4. The original text is found in *Ignace d'Antioche: Lettres*, edited and translated by P. Camelot, Sources Chrétiennes 10 (Paris: Ed. du Cerf, 1969), 122f. English in Ancient Christian Writers 1:86.

33. *Epistula* 63, 13 (CSEL 3, 2:711f). See *The Eucharist*, ed. Sheerin, 264.

While the tasks of teaching and of judging helped to forge the idea and image of episcopal ministry, this was essentially related to the sacramental ministry of presiding at this one Eucharist. The diverse roles of presbytery and deacons within the church also took on a sacramental and symbolic character within the Eucharist.

Ignatius of Antioch adopted symbolic imagery to relate ministry simultaneously to the work of redemption and to the unity of the church. He describes the bishop as the icon of God the Father, the deacon as the icon of Christ's service, the deaconess as icon of the Spirit, and the presbyters as icons of the twelve apostles. To describe the unity and harmony of the church, he uses the image of the harp whose strings make but one sound, this depending on the harmony of all in obedience to the bishop. Nonetheless, it is quite clear that unity in faith and unity at the one eucharistic table are what make church unity, not subordination to the bishop. His role is totally related to preserving the genuine foundations of harmony. Thus an author who is fully aware of the role of Ignatius in developing the model of monarchical episcopacy can say of him:

> Christian identity in this period was determined by willing subordination to the interests of the group.... The threefold ministry promoted by Ignatius is still more remarkable for its sense of solidarity with the community than for its emergence as a distinct segment of the group.[34]

Within the pre-Nicene period there is however an increasing tendency to make a firm distinction between clergy and laity, accompanied by a sacerdotalization of the ministry of the bishop within the Eucharist.[35] For all his development of a sacrificial interpretation of the Eucharist, it is interesting that Irenaeus shows no signs of this sacerdotalization. In his description of the eucharistic order, Justin Martyr mentions the one who reads and the one who presides, but he has no distinguishing name for either. On the other hand, Origen contributes to the use of sacerdotal imagery for bishops and presbyters in conjunction with their role in teaching. His concept of sacrifice, as seen, is highly spiritual and has to do with a communion with the Logos through the word. Hence, the ministers who serve the teaching of the word exercise a priesthood that serves the spiritual priesthood and sacrifice of the baptized.

---

34. William R. Schoedel, "Theological Norms and Social Perspectives in Ignatius of Antioch," in *Jewish and Christian Self-Definition*, edited by E. P. Sanders (Philadelphia: Fortress Press, 1980), 1:55.

35. On this development, see Alexandre Faivre, *The Emergence of the Laity in the Early Church*, translated by David Smith (New York: Paulist Press, 1990).

Sacerdotalization is marked in the work of Cyprian, as well as in the church order of the *Apostolic Tradition*. This is consolidated by accentuating the bishop's role as teacher and judge, determining the criteria and boundaries of assembly.

It is the particular way in which he incorporates the image of sacrifice into the Eucharist that permits Cyprian to describe the bishop as a priest (*sacerdos*). As has been seen, he locates Christ's sacrifice and priesthood first of all in the supper, in the voluntary offering of himself in the blessing of bread and wine. In the Eucharist, the bishop acts in the place of Christ when he pronounces this blessing in which the offering of the church and the offering of Christ are one. Hence his assumption of the role of priest, but also his own call to give if needed the supreme testimony of martyrdom.

The clear distinction between clergy and laity appears in the description of installation into church ministries in the *Apostolic Tradition*. While reader and widow have to be installed, the laying-on of hands is reserved to bishop, presbyter, and deacon. Only the two former are described as an exercise in priesthood, but the deacon is associated with them in the acceptance of the offerings of the faithful at the Eucharist. It is primarily the bishop who appears as a priest, due to his role of accepting and offering the gifts at the altar. The use of biblical typology serves to describe his relationship to Christ in the exercise of pastorate and high-priesthood. The spirit of high-priesthood that the bishop receives extends not only to his eucharistic function in making offering, but includes his "authority to remit sins ... to assign lots [i.e., to choose and appoint ministers] ... to loose every bond according to the authority [given] to the apostles."[36]

Though these developments in the imagery of ministry contribute to a clergy/laity distinction, throughout this period the ecclesiological context and purpose of ministry and office are uppermost. Ministry is located in the community, even to the point that the bishop is chosen or accepted by all the faithful united in assembly. The unity of the church is guaranteed by the communion table at which all are equally participants, and ministry is but intended to serve this unity. When the imagery of sacrifice or priesthood is used, the primary sacrifice is that of the baptized in their obedience to the gospel and their communion with Christ in his own offering of self. The trend to use this terminology in a special way of bishop and presbyter is an innovation, the meaning of which has to be subordinated to the primary and more scriptural meaning. When order begins to assume a greater prominence in keeping church unity, with a greater importance given to the exercise of church

---

36. *La Tradition Apostolique: d'après les anciennes versions*, edited and translated, with an introduction, by Bernard Botte, Sources Chrétiennes 11bis (Paris: Ed. du Cerf, 1968), 44–47.

leadership, it is a sign that the core sacramental reality and communion of the church has begun to weaken.

METHODOLOGICAL APPROACHES

The basic methodology of early writers lay in treating of the Eucharist as celebration and in relating its meaning to the incarnation and passion of Christ within a unified vision of divine economy, as this is revealed in the scriptures and in the apostolic teaching. None of them assumed that what is affirmed in faith could be explained by reason, even though in different ways they endeavored to defend the faith against its detractors, or to show the meaning of its tenets either to the body of the faithful or to its more sophisticated members. In their efforts to accomplish any of these purposes, some development of ideas and some external influences on their thought process need to be noted in order to grasp the nature of their teaching. In the interests of eucharistic theology, two things are here noted. First there is the use of scripture in expounding the faith, and second there is the interaction with culturally prevailing thought-forms.

The Use of Scriptures

While much appeal is made today to the term *typology* to cover the application of scriptural figures to Christ, to the church, and to sacraments, it is prudent to be reserved in its use to describe the use of scriptures in the pre-Nicene period. There are commentaries on and allusions to both Hebrew scriptures and the writings of the apostolic era. What is primarily at issue in the appeal to scripture, however, is the use made of the Hebrew scriptures to explain the place of Christ and church in the divine economy.

Much of what is included under the notion of typology is actually nothing more than proof-texting, done in the persuasion that the reading of any text in the light of Christ was legitimate. Thus in reference to the Eucharist there appear the sundry figures of the paschal lamb, the manna, and Melchizedech, which continued to carry weight in later times. There are also more fanciful images, such as those of the inebriated Noah, the washing of Judah's garment in wine,[37] the offering of fine flour in the levitical cult,[38] and the wood placed in the bread given to Jeremiah by his captors.[39] There is an appeal too to prophecies, the

---

37. Both figures are found in Cyprian, *Epistula* 63, 3–6 (CSEL 3, 2:702–5).
38. Justin, *Dialogue with Trypho*, 41, 1.
39. Tertullian, *Adversus Marcionem*, IV, 40, 3 (CCSL 1, 655–57).

most commonly used being Malachi 1:11, but prophecy is understood to include sapiential texts.[40]

Rather than finding in this a strong notion of salvation history, one might better remark a lack of any profound sense of history in envisaging God's relation with the world. It is true that writers find providential sequence between Old Testament events and Christ, in the light of whom all else is comprehensible. It is also true that human history is said to find its meaning and climax in Christ. However, there is neither keen insight into the nature of historical narrative, nor a grasp of the passage from one event to another within the history of salvation, nor any attempt to show how the events of common or particular history are related to the advent of salvation in Christ.[41]

Both Justin and Irenaeus related the mystery of the incarnation to a concept of creation that saw all divine purpose manifested in that primordial act. In the words cited from Irenaeus, redemption is a recapitulation of all things into the creator Logos, a reunifying of what had been dispersed through sin. History in this perspective is a working out of a divine intention in a sequence of events, thwarted only temporarily by the refusal of humanity's free collaboration. Beyond the discernment of this original divine intention, nothing is revealed in history qua history, or in its narration. Sequence dominated the notion of history, rather than anything internal to the form and narration of events. The image at play was that of a Word unfolding its meaning and fullness in a series of utterances. It would continue to unfold until the eschatological realization of the resurrection of the dead.

All biblical texts, whatever their literary forms, could serve to illustrate the fullness of this Word, in which the bounty of the original divine creation came to light and realization. Present historical time is the time of the church and the sacraments. It adds no events of significance to the fullness of Christ. It is a time of waiting for the final fulfillment. Ethical and sacramental acts are assessed in terms of its preparation.

It is only with the School of Alexandria, under the influence of Philo and particularly with Clement and Origen, that one finds a more philosophical basis to typology in the reading of scripture and sacramental symbol. This did not amplify a sense of history qua history but grounded a spiritualized reading of texts and symbols. While Origen usually held to a literal reading of historical narrative, he saw the meaning of events not in themselves but in the way in which they served to elevate the soul to a contemplation of God. Hence he did not preclude the possibil-

---

40. See Cyprian, *Epistula* 63, 5 (CSEL 3, 2:704).
41. See L. G. Patterson, *God and History in Early Christian Thought* (New York: Seabury Press, 1967).

ity that God might introduce historical error into the narration of events in order to meet the spiritual ends of scripture.[42]

This is a philosophically based typology that gives primacy to the life of the spirit and sees the spirit limited and impeded by the body rather than served by it. Historical events as such do not count for much, and though the scriptures have a literal sense and tell true stories, it is their spiritual sense that counts and that brings the spirit into communion with the Logos. As with Irenaeus, here too historical event serves to unfold the utterance of the Word. There is however a difference. Whereas Irenaeus let the inclusion of the flesh temper the more spiritual meaning of redemption and heavenly expectation, Origen let the dominance of spirit temper the inclusion of the flesh in incarnation and sacrament.

Christianity's Interaction with Worldviews

The influence of Neoplatonism and Middle Platonism on early Christian thought is much discussed, whether this has to do with creation, incarnation, or sacrament. The conclusions drawn depend in part on what is known of the story and versions of Platonism, which is itself rather a disputed field.[43]

It helps to note what was the primary difference between Christian writers and the prevailing worldviews of the time, since the stress on this difference did much to shape Christian explanation of the scriptures and the economy of salvation. This lay in the Christian belief that the supreme God created the world out of nothing and by an exercise of free will.[44] This distinguished the Christian worldview from others. Middle Platonism explained creation as an emanation from higher principles, variously explained, and thought the origin of lesser beings to be rooted in a divine necessity of nature. Gnosticisms of many kinds gave a literal meaning to myths and peopled the spheres with a hierarchy of emanations with which human beings sought communion. The Christian faith that God made the world out of nothing was a denial of emanationism in any of its forms, and the belief in God's free act belied any idea of creation's necessity. The incarnation of the Word and the reality of the church and its sacraments had to be consistent with this foundational article of the Christian rule of faith.[45]

The question of matter was problematic because of the tension

42. See Maurice Wiles, "Origen as Biblical Scholar," in *The Cambridge History of the Bible* (Cambridge: Cambridge University Press, 1970), 1:454–89.

43. For a survey, see E. P. Meijering, "Zehn Jahre Forschung zum Thema Platonismus und Kirchenväter," *Theologische Rundschau* 36 (1971): 303–20.

44. See Patterson, *God and History in Early Christian Thought*, 31–57.

45. See Irenaeus, *Proof of the Apostolic Preaching*, on the three articles of the Christian rule of faith.

between the world of sense and the world of spirit in Platonism. Gnosticism took the extreme solution to this issue by seeing matter as in itself evil, the emanation from a principle of evil and the basis of an opposition between Old and New Testaments. The emphasis that we see that Irenaeus placed on the oneness of creation, the reality of the incarnation, the truth of Christ's flesh in the Eucharist, and the resurrection of the flesh is worked out in clear opposition to this gnostic worldview.

For all his attention to the superiority of the world of spirit, in Origen too we see that his thought is distant from any form of emanationism in explaining the creation of the world and the mystery of the Logos. In ways reminiscent of Neoplatonism, he explained the way to communion with the Logos through contemplation of the forms of word and sacrament in which the Logos is manifested. However, the communion reached is with the one divine Logos, internal to the Godhead, not therefore a union with a being lesser than or extraneous to God. There is no gulf between God and the world, but the distance is bridged through the presence of the Logos in the word of the scriptures and in the eucharistic sacrament.

The logocentrism of worldviews, Christian and other, is apparent. Within this logocentrism history cannot be viewed as anything but an unfolding of truth, a sequence of utterances that complement each other. There is little room for a perception of how it itself pertains to being and becoming, or of what it says to the nature of God to be caught up, in freedom if not in necessity, with historical being. In such a perspective, eucharistic blessing may encapsulate the sequential revelation of the Word in creation, Old Testament, incarnation, and passion. It need not envelop human history as such, but may simply invite believers away from its travail to a contemplation of the divine goodness and the hope of eternal happiness.

RECAPITULATION AND CONVERSATION

Of the eucharistic theology of the pre-Nicene church we have noted its explanations of memorial, its relating of this to a developing concept of sacrifice, its ways of referring to the sacramental food and drink, and its ecclesiological implications. We have also noted methodological approaches to discourse on the Eucharist that are inherent to this theology.

It is now time to survey all that has been said about eucharistic practice, blessing, and theology in this period in the interest of focusing conversation with it in a contemporary retrieval of tradition.

Memorial

The starting-point for an understanding of eucharistic development in the pre-Nicene period is the obedience to the memorial command of the Last Supper. The genesis of eucharistic practice is somewhat obscure, but in the various churches the desire to keep memorial as the Lord commanded is the clear impulse for eucharistic action and for eucharistic understanding. The proclamation of Christ's death, "according to the scriptures," and done therefore through a reading of the scriptures, is united with elements of blessing for creation and redemption. The act of keeping memorial is the way of participating in the pasch of Christ and in its fruits. In the rites, there is no mimesis of the passion, descent into hell, and resurrection, but creative and prayerful interpretation of the paschal event leading to the communion table is the medium of remembrance and of participation in this mystery.

Interpretation of redemption, of what was accomplished in the death of Christ, colors the reading of the scriptures and the imagery and content of eucharistic blessing. The imagery of redemption relates in different ways to biblical and Jewish background, as well as to worldviews to which Christian faith is countertestimony. It is in face of divergent worldviews that the relation between creation and redemption became a key factor in keeping memorial. From a simple conjunction of blessings for creation and for redemption addressed to God who is the author of both, the move was to a more unified blessing prayer and to a theology of Eucharist that captured both in a harmonious theology of the Word.

It is helpful to us to note the cultural diversity, both in prayer and in theology, and to recognize that this is integral to the place of the Eucharist in the life of the church. One way of understanding this cultural diversity is to see that keeping memorial is a confession of faith that draws on a memory and tradition, but must find meaningful expression in face of the given realities and beliefs that dominate one's surroundings. What is it to confess the mediation of Jesus Christ, and a bonding with God in Jesus Christ, among those who see the world's relation to the transcendent in other and contrasting ways? Within this confession, how does a church draw its boundaries of conversation and contact with persons of other persuasions?

It is the very conversation with this tradition, the very appreciation of how faith was forged in remembrance, that obliges us to consider how this confession of faith may be formulated and explained in face of contemporary worldviews and in relation to the God questions that arise from current instabilities.

Ecclesial Action

The Eucharist was in fact, and not only in theory, the sacrament of the church. It was where the church came together, where it confessed the living presence of Christ and the Spirit, and where it forged the expression of the faith that unites and saves. It was where all were united as one body, and where limits were drawn to communion, as well as the center from which communion with other churches was formed or denied. In an age when eucharistic communities form for different reasons and in diverse cultural and geographical patterns, a naive theology of assembly patterned on early church practice is inadequate. It is rather necessary to critique these assemblies and to ask how they may serve as a center, within diversity, of internal and external communion.

One clear thing that we learn from early Christian experience is that mere ritual assembly in and of itself is a travesty. It must necessarily relate to other forms of bonding and engagement. Even when the early connection with a common meal waned, the relation to community interaction remained in a variety of ways. There were other kinds of assembly for teaching and prayer alongside the Eucharist. People brought their gifts to the assembly to be shared, particularly in the interests of the poor. The offerings of bread and wine came from the people and these were blessed in the power of Christ's Name or of the Spirit for communion in the body and blood of Christ? Even with a greater ordering of assembly, and a greater stress on ministries, the core action was the eating and drinking together at the common table of the blessed bread and wine, the communion of all in the flesh of the incarnate Word and the blood of the passion.

Efforts at eucharistic interpretation fitted this concern with a sacrament that is at the heart of Christian life. The imagery of sacrifice in particular served to integrate the whole obedience of life to the gospel into the sacramental action. Ethical observance, contemplation of the truth, gladness in the things of creation, reconciliation between members, charity and mutual service, suffering injustice and opprobrium in the name of Christ, the hope of immortality, communion with the dead, all became one with the eucharistic praise and sacramental table under the imagery of sacrifice. The whole of human reality was drawn into the sacrament and renewed through its celebration, just as humanity and creation in the words of Irenaeus were recapitulated in the passion of Jesus Christ.

Sacramental Food and Drink

In these days when forms of eucharistic devotion are bothersome and even a cause of dissent, it is expedient to note that in the early church the

Eucharist was essentially nourishment of spirit and body. Explanations of what happens through the blessing prayer have to do with what is served at the table. If this is no common food and drink, how is it to be received as the body and blood of Christ. The more fleshly language of some writers expresses a concern with the communion effected with the risen Christ through the sacrament, the nourishment for immortality in Christ of those who eat and drink. No explanation offered in that early age can be thought adequate to contemporary perceptions of reality. The lines of interpretation were however already drawn in the tension between emphasis on the reality of the gift and emphasis on the purpose of the gift in a spiritual communion of faith and truth with the risen Christ, living in the church in the power of his word, of the invocation of his name and of the Spirit. Furthermore, integral to the issue of Christ's fleshly reality in incarnation, on the cross, and in the sacrament is the destiny of all human flesh. To affirm the fleshly presence of Christ is to affirm the oneness with him of all human flesh. To affirm the spiritual nature of the communion is to acknowledge that the end of sacramental communion is communion in God and that in communion with Christ all flesh is transformed, like unto his.

Historical Reality

The greatest difficulty in any conversation with early eucharistic tradition comes from its approach to the historical. History and historical narrative are not well integrated into scriptural interpretation and eucharistic blessing or into an essentially logocentric theological explanation of creation, redemption, and sacrament.

Neither their sense of themselves as eschatological people, belonging to the end-time, nor the cultural milieu of the Greco-Roman world prompted Christian writers to look at the dynamics of history rather than at a sequence of events or episodes, realized according to a divine word and intent in whose decree all reality is fashioned. Certainly Christians kept memory of historical events, of the birth, passion, death, descent into hell, and resurrection of Jesus Christ. These, however, were often conceived according to mythical patterns, so that for example the descent into hell could have the same realistic configuration as the death on the cross. The relation between event, its mythic representation, and its narrative interpretation was not much considered, because of the logocentricism of the prevailing notion of God. From this viewpoint, what counted was salvation history and the larger human history was but the field in which Christians worked out their salvation in the hope of eternity. The relation between Jesus Christ and this larger history, whether in soteriology or in sacramental remembrance, was not a point given much thought.

Biblical scholars in recent times have helped us to make sense of Jesus' memorial command by way of appealing to a Semitic sense of history and narrative. This connects God's lordship and God's presence to the contours and even to the discontinuities of history, rather than to theophanies, so that the unexpected is not woven into an existing pattern but causes the memorial narrative to be refurbished and past events differently interpreted. Little of this carries over into postapostolic Christian thought. What is lacking is the use of a narrative form that roots the memory in what is here and now coming to pass, while at the same time keeping alive the faith in God's advent in Jesus Christ. In other words, is it possible to see the larger human history as more than the field in which Christians live out their faith? Can light be cast in remembrance on the way in which it is involved in the recapitulation not only of created things but of human life on earth in all its forms and varieties and historical patterns?

For all the enthusiasm that we now have for including creation in blessing, to some extent it seems to have been this inclusion that in early Christianity stifled a more vibrant sense of history. The way of looking at creation in the Greco-Roman world served as a pattern for the way of conceiving redemption. Christians influenced by Hellenism tended to look to created works for a divine image and a spiritual truth, leaving aside the mediated nature of truth through lesser spiritual beings or ideas that prevailed in forms of Platonism or in the mythical world of gnosticism and popular cult. They opted for the radiance of the one Word of the one eternal God, but they found in it the revelation of divine thought and the image of human being made in the likeness of God.

Now this way of conceiving the manifestation of truth could pattern the contemplation of the image of Christ, the very icon of God. It was as manifestation of divine truth and as a pattern of human homage and obedience that Christ was acclaimed. The events of his death and resurrection did not so much disrupt history as pattern all of human history. The meaning and prefigurements of past deeds could be unfolded in the light of Christ and the expectations offered in him would come about by living according to the spiritual pattern of the passover. The more the image of passover as entry into God took over from the image of pasch as struggle and victory, the less likely became the integration of the death and resurrection into history and into a dynamic tension with other historical events. They became increasingly a parahistory, a history of transcendent being lived out above the level of common events and deeds. To put it in fairly common terms, the incarnation, death, and resurrection came to be remembered as the appearance in history of what had been designed by God before the creation of the world and prepared by the figures and prophecies of the Hebrew scriptures. Taken this way, they served as the pattern of behavior for Christians who awaited the final eschaton. Out of this reading of early Christian memorial, the question of how today our faith in Christ relates his memory to the realities and issues of human history looms large. Tradition gives us no model for this, but brings forward the question that challenges the possibility of a vibrant hope emerging from our obedience to Christ's memorial command.

CONCLUSION

What does all of this say to the fourfold pattern for conversation mentioned in the introductory chapter? The *canon of remembrance* is constituted chiefly by the proclamation of the scriptures, the blessing prayer, and the table rite. There is no clear evidence of the particular scriptures read in any church, but the subordination of other readings to the reading of the Gospels is obvious. From the homiletic tradition we can see the role that the Hebrew scriptures played in memorial, for the gospel event was proclaimed and interpreted "according to the scriptures," giving room thereby to the use of figures and typologies in proclaiming Christ's pasch. At the same time, in Irenaeus and the prayer of the *Apostolic Tradition* or in the gradual adaptation of the language of sacrifice, one sees how the use of biblical figures and images is worked into an interpretation of creation and redemption that is a response in faith to views of the world that distance God from it.

This makes it quite evident that liturgy uses and interprets the scriptures in a cultural milieu, using the approaches to text and to history fostered by that milieu. Consequently the pattern of a former age may not serve well in the present, when it is necessary to get beyond a typological reading of scripture and sacrament in commemorating Jesus Christ. On the other hand, given the diversity in prayers and in interpretations, the evidence points to the inextricable link between culture and remembrance. Unless imbedded in culture, there is no transformation of a world, no effective memorial.

In the second place, the *ritual performance* that prevails is that of a domestic church, much influenced however by cultural perceptions of family structures. While the central ritual of participation is the place that all have in partaking of the sacramental food and drink, a gradual distinction between clergy and laity occurs that coincides with a sacerdotalization of church office. The presider and other clergy are given a ritual role that highlights this distinction and their distinctive character. It is a distinction put into question by a reading of the New Testament, so that the way in which fundamental baptismal equality at the table harmonizes with the necessity of specialized ministries constantly recurs in the form given to ecclesiastical structures.

On ritual performance, it is also noted that over this period there is an increase in the reverence shown the body and blood. This risks drawing attention to the reality blessed rather than to the sacramental action. However, the matter may not be of great moment since the reverence expected went with the liberty of Christians to take the sacrament home for their daily nourishment. In this sense, marks of reverence were a way of expressing the bounty and dignity of the gift that Christ gave to the faithful through the action of the church in keeping his memory. On this score of giving readier access to the body of Christ to the faithful, both within and outside the assembly, one can only say that the conversation with this part of tradition has carried benefits for present post-Tridentine usage.

As for the *relation to ethics*, the gathering remained one brought together in the faith and the love of Christ, one that firmly belonged within the life of the church as a community of service. It presented a variety of demands, such as the need for reconciliation before acceding to the table or even the call to witness to Jesus Christ with the shedding of one's blood. More than anything else, it was the language of sacrifice that brought out the integral place of Eucharist in Christian life and the transformation of life and life's attitudes through the blessing and the table of the body and blood.

That this ethic postulated some distance from human and social involvement rather than active engagement is due mainly to the logocentric *thought-patterns* that diminished the sense of history and gave a mirror-like sense of God's presence in history through the Word incarnate and the figures that prepared Christ's coming. Whatever explanations are given of memorial or of the sacramental reality of Christ's body and blood are tinged with this logocentric perception of God's action. Thus they cannot be taken as they stand to serve present practice and theology.

If there is any image incorporated into early Christian memorial that challenges us today, it may well be the imagery of Jesus Christ's conflict with the powers of sin and death and of his immersion in human suffering in the course of this combat. The oneness with all human suffering is brought out, for example, in Melito of Sardis's recall of biblical types or in Irenaeus's illustration of Christ's surrender to the law of the suffering of the just in his use of the figure of Abel. Solidarity with others in suffering as a way of defeating sin and death may well be one of those elements in tradition that can come back at another time to give focus to a more deliberately transformative involvement in human history.

Chapter 7

DEVELOPMENTS IN PRACTICE, PRAYER, AND THEOLOGY AFTER NICEA

This chapter bridges the gap between the pre-Nicene period and the later medieval world. The impression that there was a relatively uniform development is to be avoided, but it is often created by attempts to summarize history over several centuries, with primary attention given to a few specific doctrinal concerns. This obscures cultural, euchological,[1] and theological diversities. Though the chapter is no more than a broad survey, it is attentive to these diversities.

First, some reflections are offered on eucharistic prayers, which constitute a major element in the confessional witness of tradition. Second, a look is taken at developing eucharistic theologies, with as much attention to their methodology as to their content.

EUCHARISTIC PRAYERS[2]

The eucharistic prayer is a fundamental confession of faith, giving it expression within ritual, prayer, and doxology. It is at the center of the life of each church, the act in which it expresses its relation to God and its way of keeping memorial of Jesus Christ and celebrating his active presence. Oddly, the prayer retained its central place even when said silently, for then its recitation became a rite of priestly mystery, to which

---

1. The term used to refer to the form and content of prayer texts.

2. Many texts, but by no means all, are found in Anton Hänggi and Irmgard Pahl, *Prex eucharistica: Textus e variis liturgiis antiquioribus selecti,* Spicilegium Friburgense 12 (Fribourg: Editions Universitaires, 1968), and in R. C. D. Jasper and G. J. Cuming, *Prayers of the Eucharist: Early and Reformed,* 3d ed. (New York: Pueblo Publishing Company, 1987). In both of these works there is a bibliography on each prayer. The most ample study to date is that of Louis Bouyer, *Eucharist: Theology and Spirituality of the Eucharistic Prayer* (Notre Dame: Notre Dame University Press, 1968).

the faithful looked as to an expression of holiness in their midst. In churches ritually linked to Rome, it is only today when the prayer is once again proclaimed aloud that it appears to have lost its power to gather and unite a congregation. A better grasp of its public role in the past may raise some of the needed questions about its present frequent inefficacy. The points for consideration are its structure, its imagery of redemption, and its use of sacrificial language.

Structure

The prayer builds the life of the person and the community in their relationship to God, to Christ, and to the world through a particular form of address and proclamation. Attention to the structure of the prayer has so much to do with the structure of faith that it cannot be counted a secondary issue in eucharistic studies.

As already indicated in looking at early prayers, the vast number of studies having to do with their genesis lead to no clear conclusions. Nonetheless various debates continue about the most appropriate prayer structure. One, which pursues the relation between Jewish and Christian blessing, is between those who favor a bipartite structure of thanksgiving, and intercession and those who favor a tripartite structure of praise, thanksgiving and intercession.[3] Others pertain to the form in which the mysteries of salvation are recalled, to the need to include the supper narrative, and to the role of the anamnesis and epiclesis in defining the meaning of the action.

When people stand in face of God and remember the event of the Exodus or the event of Jesus Christ, their prayer is prompted simultaneously by this remembrance and by the concerns of their own situation. Laud or praise seemed to dominate when communities were more directly influenced by wonder in face of the works of creation. When this was connected with trinitarian belief, the prayer attributed creation either to the trinity of persons, or to the Father's work through the Word.[4] The awe inspired by creation then dictated the tone of the entire prayer, even though thanksgiving for the work of salvation was included. When the prayer focused on the work of redemption, then thanksgiving prevailed. Intercession is a natural consequence for those who see that all things are from God, or for those who seeing that the

---

3. See Thomas J. Talley, "The Literary Structure of the Eucharistic Prayer," *Worship* 58 (1984): 404–20.

4. See the text of the Anaphora of Basil in Hänggi and Pahl, *Prex eucharistica*, 230–43, or its English translation in Jasper and Cuming, *Prayers of the Eucharist*, 116–23. Compare the Anaphora of James, *Prex eucharistica*, 244–61, and *Prayers of the Eucharist*, 90–99. These pages need to be read with the prayer texts at hand.

eschatological promise is as yet unfulfilled, are moved to confidence by the remembrance of God's action and promise in the past.

When this basic structure of praise, thanksgiving, and intercession is kept in mind, it becomes clearer that the supper narrative, the anamnesis, and the epiclesis are in the nature of theological amplifications. They are insertions that give a kind of primary theological explanation of what is being done when Christian people offer praise and thanksgiving over bread and wine in remembrance of Jesus Christ. This affects the disputes about the relative consecratory power of the words of Christ and of the invocation of the Spirit.[5] Neither of these in fact has any significance except in the context of the great prayer and in relation to the act of communion in which the prayer reaches its ritual climax. An analysis of the words of the supper narrative, the anamnesis, and the epiclesis is always helpful to an understanding of the eucharistic action, but the power of the action is not to be identified with any one of them, for they but spell out the meaning of the prayer and action as a whole.

The placement of the Sanctus in the prayer is still explained by a number of different hypotheses.[6] If it is correctly linked with the *Qaddish* in the synagogue prayer of eighteen blessings,[7] it can be said to incorporate the images of divine covenant and of the presence of the holy into the eucharistic memorial. In that sense, it also is a theological elaboration on the nature of the Eucharist.

Imagery of Redemption

Since the Eucharist is the memorial of redemption, the ways in which it is imaged in the prayer are clearly important. This applies both to the work of Christ and to what is accomplished through this work. Some examples are appropriate.

As already seen, in the prayer of the *Apostolic Tradition* the dominant image is that of Christ's victory by his suffering over the powers of sin and death. In the much more elaborate text from Book VIII of the *Apostolic Constitutions* all of the deeds of Christ's ministry are recalled, culminating in his voluntary deliverance of himself over to death.[8] The remembrance of Christ is prepared by recalling God's saving action from

---

5. On the formula of consecration, compare A. Verheul, "La valeur consécratoire de la prière eucharistique," *Questions Liturgiques* 62 (1981): 135–44, and P.-M. Gy, "L'Eucharistie dans la tradition de la prière et de la doctrine," *La Maison-Dieu* 137 (1979): 81–102.

6. See E. C. Ratcliff, "The Sanctus and the Pattern of the Early Anaphora," *Journal of Ecclesiastical History* 1 (1950): 29–36, and more recently, Bryan D. Spinks, "The Jewish Sources for the Sanctus," *Heythrop Journal* 21 (1980): 168–79: id., *The Sanctus in the Eucharistic Prayer* (Cambridge: Cambridge University Press, 1991).

7. See L. Bouyer, *Eucharist*, 64f. and 230f.

8. Text in Hänggi and Pahl, *Prex eucharistica*, 82–95, and Jasper and Cuming, *Prayers of the Eucharist*, 104–13.

the promise to Adam through the history of the Old Testament. All of this salvific work reaches its climax in the death of the sinless one for the sinful, in the restoration to humankind through Christ of the image of God.

The Anaphora of Basil of Caesarea gives a clearly confessional and trinitarian form to the Eucharist.[9] In addressing praise to God the Father, this anaphora portrays the incarnation as the Word's self-emptying, using for this the text of Philippians 2:7. Turning to the death of Christ, it describes it as both a descent into hell in order to conquer death itself and as a ransom for captives. The resurrection of Christ from the dead is then the resurrection of the first-born, anticipation not only of the resurrection of all flesh but even of a cosmic redemption. The salvation achieved for the world is variously portrayed as a restoration of the original creation, a pouring out of divine mercy, the gift of grace and immortality, and the constitution of the church as a holy nation and a royal priesthood, through fellowship in the Spirit. The gift of the Spirit is given to the church in the sacrament of baptism and is thus active in its eucharistic celebration, by which it keeps memorial of Christ as the icon of the Father.

In the Anaphora of John Chrysostom, all of this imagery is condensed into two images: God raises up what was fallen and delivers the beloved Son to death on account of the divine love for the world.[10] In this prayer the anamnesis appears to take on a greater role in expressing what is remembered. After the words of the Lord, it recalls "this saving commandment [to eat and to drink][11] and all the things that were done for us: the cross, the tomb, the resurrection of the third day, the ascension into heaven, the session at the right hand, the second and glorious coming." Though a similar anamnesis occurs in the prayer of Basil, it follows the profuse thanksgiving already mentioned and does not include mention of the commandment to eat and drink. In John, most of the thanksgiving imagery is omitted with the result that the sequential listing of the events in the anamnesis stands out more boldly and is directly related to the saving commandment.

The Jerusalem liturgy of Holy Week with its more historical rep-

---

9. Hänggi and Pahl, *Prex eucharistica*, 230–43; Jasper and Cuming, *Prayers of the Eucharist*, 116–23.

10. Text in Hänggi and Pahl, *Prex eucharistica*, 189–98, and in Jasper and Cuming, *Prayers of the Eucharist*, 131–34. For a discussion of the anaphoras of Basil and John Chrysostom, see Hans-Joachim Schulz, *The Byzantine Liturgy: Symbolic Structure and Faith Expression*, translated by Matthew J. O'Connell (New York: Pueblo Publishing Company, 1986), 142–59.

11. The prayer gives the supper account but does not include the memorial command. Thus "the saving commandment" refers back directly to the words: "Take and eat . . . Take and drink." See Jasper and Cuming, *Prayers of the Eucharist*, 133. The memorial command is included in the narrative in Basil.

resentation of the mysteries of Christ's flesh had an influence on the Byzantine liturgy. It is this influence that appears to be at work in John's mystagogy and in his anaphora. When the remembrance is so clearly related to Christ's offer of his body and blood and to the ritual of eating and drinking them, this remembrance of the mysteries or their representation is given a much more ritual focus than when the remembrance belongs in the act of thanksgiving as such, followed by the ritual of communion.

As is well known, a distinctive character of the Roman canon lies in the variability of its thanksgiving section. If the comparison with other Latin texts from Ambrose and the Mozarabic liturgy is correct,[12] a prayer with variable thanksgiving and otherwise fixed components may well have existed prior to the introduction of the Sanctus and to the known Roman liturgy. In any case, the Roman liturgy that developed after the transition from Greek to Latin is now the unique example of a prayer variable only in the pre-Sanctus. The Gallican, Mozarabic, and Armenian liturgies have prayers that show differences within a basic framework, but these occur at different places, even outside the thanksgiving.

The Verona Sacramentary has well over two hundred different prefaces, whose dating is uncertain but which at least belong to the centuries prior to Gregory the Great, that is, before the end of the sixth century.[13] Apart from the prefaces proper to the great feasts of the liturgical cycles, most of these belong to the feasts of saints. Some of them actually turn thanksgiving into petition,[14] some show preoccupation with immediate events, such as the barbarian invasions of the city.[15] While subordination of memorial to such concerns is a regrettable turn, it raises the question of how the prayer needs to resonate with human situations rather than remain abstract from them, as though salvation belonged on a different plane.

Examples from the Roman liturgy that express the mystery of Christ more fully are to be found in the old Gelasian Sacramentary. In two prefaces, one for Christmas Day[16] and one for Easter Day,[17] the central image used is that of the paschal lamb. Though composed for different feasts, they both show how the mystery of salvation may be celebrated in its fullness within the context of a particular cycle.

---

12. See the comparative texts offered in Jasper and Cuming, *Prayers of the Eucharist*, 155–58.

13. *Sacramentarium Veronense*, edited by L. Mohlberg (Rome: Herder, 1956).

14. Thus, for example, *Veronense*, no. 416.

15. Note the preoccupation with enemies in *Veronense*, nos. 428 and 440.

16. *Liber Sacramentorum Romanae Aeclesiae Ordinis Anni Circuli*, edited by L. Mohlberg (Rome: Herder, 1960), no. 20.

17. Ibid., no. 466.

Moreover, in the preface for Christmas there is a development of a theology of sacrifice that under the rubric of praise brings together the Eucharist, the death of Christ, and Old Testament prefigurements:

[It is fitting to give thanks and praise]: unceasingly immolating the sacrifice of your praise, whose figure the just Abel established, the lamb offered under the Law revealed, Abraham celebrated, and the priest Melchizedech presented, but the true lamb, the eternal pontiff, the Christ born this day fulfilled.[18]

The text is so succinct, composed with such a careful choice of verbs, that it says much by rich innuendo. It embraces the entire economy of prefigurement, fulfillment, and eucharistic commemoration. By reason of the distinctive verbs (*instituere, celebrare,* and *exhibere*), each of the Old Testament types is shown to foreshadow Christ and Eucharist in a particular way. It is the figures of the lamb as victim and of the priest who offers that are realized in Christ. Together with the clear ritual terms of *immolare* and *hostia,* this unequivocally offers a sacrificial understanding both of Christ's death and of the Eucharist. Yet this is immediately tempered, and in rather a radical way, when both are embraced, along with all the figures, under the rubric of sacrifice of praise, not propitiation. In other words, the imagery and vocabulary of sacrifice are retained but given a new meaning. In his very death Christ undid the old forms of sacrifice and did away with the need to make propitiation, so that those who believe in him have access to God in spiritual, not ritual, sacrifice.

In the intercessory part of the Roman canon, the figures of Abel, Abraham, and Melchizedech recur. Abel is dubbed "the just," and the priesthood of Melchizedech realized in the offering of bread and wine is underlined. It is the patriarchy of Abraham, and so the assurance of God's promises, that are brought to the fore. In this part of the prayer these types are invoked not so much to highlight thankful praise as to bolster the church's petition when it asks for a part in the heavenly liturgy. This is guaranteed by the descent and ascent of the angel who brings the church's gifts to the altar on high, from which the faithful are to receive graces and blessings. It is its "reasonable service" in offer-

---

18. "Vere Dignum: tui laudis hostiam iugiter immolantes, cuius figuram Abel iustus instituit, agnus quoque legalis ostendit, celebravit Abraham, Melchizedech sacerdos exhibuit, sed verus agnus, aeternus pontifex, hodie natus Christus implevit."

The pertinent words of the Easter preface read: " ... quod pascha nostrum immolatus est Christus. Per quem in aeternam vitam filii lucis oriuntur, fidelibus regni caelestis atria reserantur et beati lege conmercii divinis humana mutantur." This is translated: " ... because Christ our pasch has been immolated. Through whom the children of light rise to eternal life, the halls of the heavenly kingdom are opened to the faithful and the blessed by the law of exchange [established in the incarnation] are changed in their human nature into divine beings."

ing praise in commemoration of Jesus Christ that allows the church to
make such petition.

While the preface for Christmas Day and the fixed part of the canon
are not likely to be from the same hand, there is nonetheless an interesting link between them in the use of sacrificial language and in their
appeal to the biblical types. One underlines praise, the other petition,
but in both cases it is the reasonable service of the church's praise in
commemorating Christ that constitutes the sacrifice or offering.

This relatively quick survey of some of the major prayers demon-
strates the part played in sacramental commemoration by an imaginative interpretation that places the passion of Christ within the divine
economy and signifies in different ways the result of this for human salvation. In other words, prayers allow churches to appropriate the reality
of Christ's mystery in different if complementary ways. One presents his
death as an act of self-abasement and voluntary suffering in which sin
and death are defeated, while another appropriates it within the contours of a greater attention to the reality and purpose of sacrifice in the
relation of God to humankind. It is this interpretative and prayerful act,
together with the ritual of communion, that is the medium of the living
presence of the mystery in the church. It is only within the context of
a larger liturgical and catechetical development that the idea of a reenactment of the mysteries crops up in the anaphora of John Chrysostom.
Otherwise, the prayers look back to the events that restored the economy of grace and forward to what they prefigure for eternal life, asking
for a present share in this economy.

Eucharistic Sacrifice[19]

Some reference has already been made to the sacrificial imagery of
the Roman liturgy. More needs to be said on this usage in eucharistic prayers as a whole, since it took on increasing importance in the
post-Constantinian liturgies. In general, one can say that from what was
primarily the language of gift and offering (*prosphora, oblatio*) the prayers
turned to a language more attuned to cultic service (*latreia, cultus, obsequium*) and even more particularly towards the specific language of
sacrificial ritual (*thusia, sacrificium, hostia*).

In the prayers of Basil and Chrysostom the eucharistic action itself is
called reasonable and bloodless service. On the one hand, this stresses
that as service it is due and proper worship of God. On the other, it is a
worship in spirit, quite different from the offering of bloody victims. In
the anamnesis it is said that the gifts are offered in memorial of Christ's

---

19. This matter is studied in detail by Kenneth Stevenson, *Eucharist and Offering* (New
York: Pueblo Publishing Company, 1986).

mysteries. Gifts here seem to include both the bread and wine brought forward and the prayer of the church over them. In the Anaphora of James, the language has become more clearly sacrificial, for instead of offering and of bloodless service mention is made of bloodless sacrifice.[20]

There is a more pronounced turn to sacrifice in the East Syrian tradition. From the commemorative offering of Addai and Mari there is a shift in the Anaphora of Peter, or the Sharar, to the pleading of Christ's propitiatory sacrifice in which he bore and cleansed humanity's sins. It is this sacrifice that the church now wishes, through Christ's expiation, to be made worthy to offer to his Godhead.[21] In this there is a new stress on the propitiatory character of Christ's death and of its eucharistic commemoration. The traditional images of the lamb and voluntary suffering are still employed, but now they are related to the language of propitiation and cleansing from sin.

In the Liturgy of Mark, it is the language of offering and of gift that prevails, though in a few places the vocabulary of sacrifice is intermingled with this.[22] It is very clear that the offering includes thanksgiving and the gifts of bread and wine brought by the people, as well as the other gifts that they present for the use of the church community. Where the more explicit language of sacrifice is used, it is in relation to the types of Abel and Abraham. That no narrowly ritual understanding is intended in this is clear in the juxtaposition to these sacrifices of the offering of the widow's mite as a model for Christian offering.

In the Roman canon, besides the use of types already discussed one finds a whole array of sacrificial words, occurring in the intercessory part of the prayer, both preceding and following the supper narrative.[23] They are used however in a way that makes English translation difficult, a straight dictionary rendering being inadequate to the sense given to them. The terminology arises from the fusion of cultural Roman terms with biblical Latin, this being peculiar to the uses of Christian Latin. This includes such words as *sacrificium*, here called reasonable and bloodless, *obsequium, hostia, munus, dona,* and *oblatio.* Literally these would be translated as bloodless and reasonable sacrifice, service, victim, gifts, and offering. They all belong within the language of Roman cult and are

---

20. Greek and Latin texts in Hänggi and Pahl, *Prex eucharistica,* 244–75. English translation in Jasper and Cuming, *Prayers of the Eucharist,* 90–99.

21. For the text of this anaphora, see Hänggi and Pahl, *Prex eucharistica,* 410–15, and Jasper and Cuming, *Prayers of the Eucharist,* 45–51. After the anamnesis, the text reads: "We adore you, only begotten of the Father, firstborn of creation, spiritual Lamb, who descended from heaven to earth, to be a propitiatory sacrifice for all humankind and to bear their debts voluntarily, and to remit their sins by your blood, and sanctify the unclean through your sacrifice."

22. Text in Hänggi and Pahl, *Prex eucharistica,* 101–15 (Greek), 135–139 (Latin translation of Coptic), and Jasper and Cuming, *Prayers of the Eucharist,* 57–66.

23. Text in Hänggi and Pahl, *Prex eucharistica,* 424–26, and Jasper and Cuming, *Prayers of the Eucharist,* 159–67.

used in Bible translations to translate Hebrew words from the levitical code of sacrifice.

These words are apparently used to refer to the eucharistic action as a whole, including the commemorative prayer of thanksgiving and intercession, the devotion of the people, and the bread and wine that are proffered for blessing. It is the resultant obviously metaphorical use of the words that makes translation difficult. If, for example, *hostia* is simply translated as victim, it can seem to mean the offering of Christ's body and blood as victim, in this sacramental manner, and so indeed it has often been understood. In effect, however, it is a cultic way of referring to Christian gifts that in comparison with the usual ritual are noncultic.

One needs therefore to ask what is conveyed by calling prayer and bread and wine and devotion "victim." What is happening is that the power connected with sacrifices of homage is attributed through metaphor to the actions performed by the church in commemoration of the death, resurrection, and ascension of Christ. On the other hand, the translation also needs to bring out that the homage is offered through the mediation of Jesus Christ and in communion with his heavenly liturgy, this being the reason why it includes confident supplication. If the sense of the metaphoric transfer is kept in mind, perhaps the word *hostia* ought to be translated as "gifts offered through Jesus Christ in service and petition."

This brief survey is enough to convey the way in which sacrificial language was adopted in eucharistic prayers. From one point of view, it may be said to be a continuation of the New Testament's nonsacerdotal employment of this metaphor. It is curious that the language of gift and offering is in some instances stronger than the explicit language of sacrifice, but even this may have been taken from sacrificial ritual.[24] As noted in the Sharar, sacrifice may also be given the more narrow meaning of propitiation.

The evidence of New Testament, eucharistic prayers, and theological texts together suggests that the initial intention in referring to the Eucharist as sacrifice was to indicate that this is indeed true worship and that it is the new worship of those redeemed in Christ. Employed of Christ's death, it first occurs within a context of typological fulfilment, antitype fulfilling type. On this dual basis, the metaphor could then expand and assume different meanings in different contexts, by reason of

---

24. Some anthropologists find that even in sacrificial ritual gift is more fundamental than immolation and propitiation, but caution is desirable in reducing the plethora of sacrifices in cultures to one common meaning. Some theologians suggest that in a Christian understanding of Christ's death and of Eucharist, an economy of gift exchange between God and humanity takes the place of sacrifice, as a kind of antisacrifice. See Louis-Marie Chauvet, *Symbole et sacrement: Une relecture sacramentelle de l'existence chrétienne* (Paris: Ed. du Cerf, 1988), 104–15, 273–96.

its use rather than because of a basic lexical meaning. The fundamental thing about Christian worship is that it draws together commemoration of Christ, ethical action, blessing of earth's gifts, and prayers of praise, thanksgiving, and intercession, all of this reaching a climax at the communion table of Christ's body and blood. To predicate offering or sacrifice of this complex reality is to interpret it by use of an image taken from a different kind of context, one however that has already picked up considerable resonance in biblical stories and prophecies. This is to enrich the meaning of the action, not to tie it down, but it is inevitably open to the risk of being reduced to clearly defined meanings. In the present context of ecumenical dialogue it is helpful to note that the soteriology of eucharistic prayers, either before or after Nicea, is not dominantly that of propitiatory sacrifice. There is a greater variety of ways in which to express the mediatory role of Jesus Christ in reconciling the world to God.

Eucharist and Spirit

The Byzantine anaphoras and the Anaphora of James relate the prayer to a developed trinitarian theology. The prayer as a whole is addressed to the Father, in wonder at the divine ineffability in which the three persons are united as one. The pre-Sanctus attributes the work of both creation and redemption to the triune God, thus distinguishing itself from the early baptismal form commented upon by Irenaeus that attributes creation to the Father, redemption to the Son, and the work of the church to the Spirit. The post-Sanctus then recalls the redemptive deeds of the incarnate Word, while the invocation of the Spirit points to its work in the sacrament and in the church, where the kingdom of God is realized in anticipation of eternity. This formulation adapts the commemoration of Christ to the requirements of trinitarian orthodoxy, showing how doctrinal concerns can modify this remembrance.

In the Anaphora of Basil mention is made of the gift of the Spirit in baptism in the part of the prayer that precedes the supper narrative and the epiclesis over the gifts. This highlights the presence and action of the Spirit in the church, making it the ground for eucharistic memorial and its efficacious action, as besought in the prayer's epiclesis. It is only in the power of the Spirit that it is possible to confess Christ as the icon of the Father and to offer worthy worship. The meaning of Christ's supper words and actions is apparent only in virtue of the Spirit's illuminating and creative power. At the same time, the Spirit can do no other than point to these words as the origin and heart of the memorial of Christ's death.

By way of contrast the Roman church never included the confession of the Spirit in its eucharistic canon. This lack of confessional balance led in time to an exaggerated attention to the power of repeating Christ's own words.

Texts and Ritual

This last point is itself a reminder that texts in themselves never tell the whole story of what is signified and intended. It is within a ritual complex that their meaning takes on new determinations, and over time ritual changes can actually modify the meaning of an otherwise unmodified prayer text. For this reason, no examination of eucharistic prayers is complete without attention to the ritual context that develops.

For example, as already mentioned, it is possible to relate the anamnesis in the Byzantine prayer to the influence of the Jerusalem liturgy and the consequent tendency to highlight representational symbolism. The meaning of the entire action is expressed in the ceremonies of the Great Entrance.[25] At that point of the service, the congregation is summoned to greet the entry of the great high-priest with the cherubic choirs. Then in placing the gifts upon the altar, the priest recalls the placing of the body of Christ in the tomb.[26] In such a liturgy, it is no longer enough to remember the historical events of the passion, but they have to be given vivid representation. Likewise, it is not enough to verbally place the congregation in communion with the heavenly liturgy, but this too has to be visually represented. In this kind of context, the words of the eucharistic prayer that recall the Christ event themselves sound differently.

In the development of all liturgies, the priestly character of prayer and action was highlighted in the rites affecting the role and person of the one presiding. The place in the building from which he gathered the people in prayer or prayed in their presence affected the sense of what he said. Performed behind the iconostasis or under the baldachin above a martyr's tomb, the rite assumed an awesome quality that underlined the mediatory role of the one who prayed in the name of the people.

An accumulation of words and actions that seem but small modifications to the text succeed in changing its point of reference. Since the ritual place and action already distinguish them, we are not too surprised to see a few small words brought into the Roman canon that distinguish the priest's offering from the people's: "qui tibi offerunt, vel pro quibus offerimus." The differentiation in the communion rite between clergy and people also changes the way in which each partake in the sacrifice and its communion.

---

25. On the symbolism of the Byzantine liturgy, see Schulz, *The Byzantine Liturgy*, 16–172.

26. Setting the paten and chalice on the altar, the priest prays: "The noble Joseph, taking down your spotless body from the wood and wrapping it in a clean shroud with aromatic spices, carefully laid it in a new tomb."

In the prayer itself, the development of intercessions in the Byzantine or Markan liturgy combined the special attention given there to clergy and to imperial officials with the special places reserved for them in the assembly, with the way in which they shared in making the offerings, and with the rank attributed to them in the order of receiving communion. The ecclesiastical and civic orders are drawn together to represent a godly disposition. The same effect follows from the embellishment of the place of worship, as for example in the mosaics of the sanctuary in San Vitale in Ravenna. The eschatology of intercession and disposition of place and rite thus tends to identify revelation with order and Christ's power with an order of ecclesiastical and civic hierarchies.

EUCHARISTIC THEOLOGIES

The range of theologies over these centuries is great. Three types that seem to have a continuing influence will here be considered. These are the eucharistic theology of mystagogical catechesis, that of Augustine of Hippo, and that of the pseudo-Dionysius.

Mystagogy[27]

Though many bishops and teachers practiced mystagogy, its high-point is usually associated with the persons of Ambrose of Milan, Cyril of Jerusalem, John Chrysostom (while he was at Antioch), and Theodore of Mopsuestia. Questions about attributing some of the texts to these authors are still under consideration, but need not delay us here.

The four sets of writings have in common that they are addressed to the instruction of neophytes and include an explanation of the rites of the Eucharist as well as of baptism. Common also is the way in which the instruction is tied to the ceremony by basing teaching, both doctrinal and moral, on the explanation of specific rites and texts. Efforts have sometimes been made to determine what was *the* meaning in the ancient church of some specific rite, for example, the anointing, by looking at these authors, only to find that they differ in their explanations and even in what they reveal about the location of the rite in the ceremony as a whole. The authors' concern is to offer instruction on the Christian mystery and on Christian life, and they attune the explanation of rites

---

27. A good treatment of this material, with ample bibliographical references, is offered by Enrico Mazza, *Mystagogy: A Theology of Liturgy in the Patristic Age*, translated by Matthew J. O'Connell (New York: Pueblo Publishing Company, 1989). An English translation of the patristic texts is given by Edward Yarnold, *The Awe-Inspiring Rites of Initiation* (Slough, England: St. Paul Publications, 1971). All references in the present text will be to this translation.

to this purpose. It is difficult in liturgy to tie down any action to a specific meaning, for every word and rite takes its meaning from the whole.

In seeing the contribution that this mystagogy makes to the understanding of the Eucharist within the economy of grace, four points are considered here: (a) the issue of appropriate language; (b) the relation of commemorative rite to historical event and to future glory; (c) the inclusion of moral concerns; (d) the relation of faith discourse to Neoplatonism.

The Problem of Appropriate Language. These teachers wrestled with the problem of finding the right terms in which to explain what they held in faith. The concerns that they brought from their faith had to do with the reality of the church itself, the gift of the body and blood of Christ in the sacrament, the relation of the sacrament to the event commemorated, the expectation of future glory, and the grace with which the Christian was endowed through the sacraments of the pasch. The basic problem was how to connect different orders of reality, relating time to eternity, and connecting present rites with events from the past.

The language that they used to explain the relation of one order of reality to another was that of symbolism and participation. In their instructions, there is a strong dosage of words such as *figure, type, symbol, similitude, image,* and *icon,* and the distinction between the reality as imaged and the reality as truth (*aletheia* or *veritas*). The distinction was not that between what we might call mere image or picture and reality, but between two different forms in which the reality existed. Hence the authors oscillate between a direct identification of what is on the table or what is offered in communion as the body and blood of Christ and terms such as *figure* of the body and blood or *similitude* of the body and blood. There is thus a tension between the language of symbol, intended to connect the original and its sacramental participation, and the more realistic or material language of straightforward predication.

This tension is found, for example, in Ambrose, who in one place talks of the sacrament as the similitude of Christ's body, but in another designates it simply as the body of Christ.[28] In support of the transformation of the bread and identification of the blessed reality with Christ's body, he uses some very concrete biblical examples, such as the division of the sea when Moses touched it with his staff or the sweetening of the waters when Moses put a piece of wood into the spring.[29] The purpose of these examples is to show the power of God's word, which operates also in the sacrament.

Cyril is similarly graphic in identifying the bread and wine as the

---

28. Mazza discusses Ambrose's vocabulary, *Mystagogy,* 114–23.
29. *On the Sacraments,* Sermon IV, 18 (Yarnold, *The Awe-Inspiring Rites of Initiation,* 135).

body and blood of Christ and even declares that in communion "his body and blood spread through our limbs," so that in this way we become "partakers of the divine nature."[30] Since this participation in divine nature is obviously the point of the sacramental mediation, he calls it "spiritual bread," thus removing the possible note of capharnaitic understanding.[31]

Theodore of Mopsuestia, in asking that the bread and wine be "received as the body and blood of our Lord" rather than as common bread and wine, gets over the problem of connecting reality with symbol by noting the transforming power of the Spirit. It is by the Spirit that Christ's body is united in the resurrection with his divine nature and by the Spirit that he himself enjoys immortality, not only for himself but for others. Having undergone change himself in his body by the Spirit, it is by the Spirit that the gift of the body and blood may also transform those who receive them.[32]

A tension similar to that found in his words on the body and blood is found in what Cyril says of sacrifice. On the one hand, he speaks of the eucharistic prayer, with special note of the Sanctus, as the church's spiritual sacrifice, but on the other he can say that the sacrifice of propitiation is on the altar and "we offer Christ who has been slain for our sins, and so we appease the merciful God both on behalf [of the dead] and on ours."[33] It is interesting that where more emphasis is placed on propitiation, more realism seems to be employed in regard to the offering of Christ's own sacrifice in the Eucharist.

Commemorative Rite and Historical Event. Inherent to this question as to what is offered in the sacrament is that of how the rites relate to past events. Emphasis on Christ's sacrifice rather than on other images, such as the victory over death, colors the way in which the historical event is seen to be represented in the ritual action.

The most figurative of the interpreters is Theodore of Mopsuestia. It is to him that we owe the explanation that spreading the cloth on the table is the image of Christ being laid in the tomb.[34] It is he also who tells us that "at the sight of the bishop we form in our hearts a kind of image of Christ our Lord sacrificing himself to save us and give us life" and that the deacons represent the angels who ministered to Christ.[35] Theodore is here appealing to imagery and affective response, but his explanations are in no way a suggestion that these images render present the

---

30. Sermon IV. 5 (Yarnold, *The Awe-Inspiring Rites of Initiation*, 85).
31. Sermon IV. 9 (Yarnold, *The Awe-Inspiring Rites of Initiation*, 87).
32. Baptismal Homily IV. 10–11 (Yarnold, *The Awe-Inspiring Rites of Initiation*, 215–16).
33. Sermon V. 6–10 (Yarnold, *The Awe-Inspiring Rites of Initiation*, 90–92).
34. Baptismal Homily IV. 26 (Yarnold, *The Awe-Inspiring Rites of Initiation*, 228).
35. Baptismal Homily IV. 24 (Yarnold, *The Awe-Inspiring Rites of Initiation*, 226).

events in any kind of time/space reality. In fact, Theodore's major concern in the relation between past and present is with what is anticipated of the future. Salvation is completed only in glory, in the same way that Christ's sacrifice and priesthood are completed in heaven. What is thus remembered or represented in the Eucharist is the sacrifice offered in Christ's death and completed in heaven. Theodore follows the letter to the Hebrews rather carefully on Christ's sacrifice. He says that "he offered himself in sacrifice when he gave himself up to die for us all." Following this, Christ enters into the sanctuary to exercise the high priest's function of entering the sanctuary first and performing the liturgy in heaven on our behalf. It is thus the act of sacrifice by which Christ passed into heaven and which is perfected in this ongoing liturgy that is represented in the sacrament.[36] Thus while Theodore says that Christians continue to offer the one and only sacrifice which is that of Christ, as long as they commemorate it and proclaim the Lord's death until he comes, he also says of the bishop at the altar that "he represents for you a visible representation of these indescribable heavenly realities and of the spiritual immaterial powers."[37]

Chrysostom uses some of this language of representation in his catechesis on baptism, but not in what he says there of the Eucharist. On the other hand, from his commentary on the Letter to the Hebrews we know what he thought of the eucharistic representation of Christ's sacrifice.[38] While Christ offered himself in his death, for John the sacrament represents not only the death but also the entry into heaven and the heavenly intercession in which the sacrifice of the cross is completed and given an enduring reality. The absence of this eucharistic theology in the mystagogical catechesis has to do with its more specific moral purpose.

In reading these texts, Mazza notes that they show a tendency to talk more than earlier writers of the conformity of the sacramental reality to a higher reality. This began on the cross and now goes on as an eternal exercise of Christ's priesthood.[39] In other words, while an older theology thought of sacramental participation in historical events in terms of spiritual configuration and fruit, fifth-century mystagogy speaks of an event that taking on supraterrestrial form is here and now present in sacramental form.

Inclusion of Moral Concerns. The most imaginative inclusion of the moral life is found in the work of Cyril. For him, in the baptismal act the faithful die and rise in Christ, not in reality (*aletheia*) but in mystery

---

36. Baptismal Homily IV.16 (Yarnold, *The Awe-Inspiring Rites of Initiation,* 221). See Mazza, *Mystagogy,* 72–100.

37. Ibid., 19–21 (Yarnold, *The Awe-Inspiring Rites of Initiation,* 223–24).

38. John Chrysostom, *In Hebraeos* 17, 2–3; PG 63, 129–31.

39. Mazza, *Mystagogy,* 165–74.

(*mysterion*). This is then the basis for participation in the Eucharist and eucharistic nourishment is nourishment of this new life in Christ.

Of the four writers, John Chrysostom is the most moralizing and the most specific about the asceticism required and the moral duties exacted by sacramental participation.[40] It is his insistence on the covenant and moral implications of baptism that leads John in his baptismal catechesis to emphasize the nature of the Eucharist as food and nourishment rather than draw out its representation of the mysteries of Christ's passion, death, burial, and resurrection, or emphasize its sacrificial character. A flight from earthly things and care for the poor are expected of those who weekly share in the eucharistic liturgy and table. He finds it odd that people would provide precious vessels to hold the body and blood of Christ while neglecting the poor, who are the body and the altar of Christ in the community.[41]

Faith Discourse and Neoplatonism. Much is written on the influence of Neoplatonism on ecclesiastical discourse, showing how church teachers share in the perception that symbols participate in the reality symbolized. It seems at first sight a simple explanation, but the issue is complicated because of questions about the kind of Neoplatonism that was in vogue in those centuries. Not all church writers were necessarily linked up with the same school of thought.[42]

In commenting on mystagogical catechesis, Enrico Mazza helpfully points out that a distinction between spiritual and sensible realities is the thread that runs through Platonic thought, with primacy given to the spiritual. Indeed, the material is ontologically structured as a manifestation of, and manuduction into, the spiritual. When this kind of thinking is taken over in sacramental discourse, attention is given to the relation of the earthly to the heavenly and of the material actions to the spiritual life.

In the economy of grace, the passion of Christ itself as an earthly action is related to the heavenly. It belongs within the realm of word that manifests divine intention and a participation of the Word made flesh in the life of the eternal Word. In representing the mysteries of Christ the sacraments must point above all to the way in which they participate in the heavenly and spiritual reality. There is thus an ordered relation of sacrament to the Christ event and of the Christ event to the truth of the Word.

This language of subordinate participation includes the nonidentity between the represented and the representation that justifies the

---

40. See Mazza, *Mystagogy*, 109–14.
41. In 2 Cor. X.10, Homilia XX: PG 61, 9–61. English translation in *Post-Nicene Fathers* (New York: Christian Literature Company, 1889), 12:372–74.
42. See Mazza's discussion, *Mystagogy*, 165–74.

language of figure and image. Thus it is that the church writers found something in the worldview of their time that helped them to explain sacrament's relation to historical and eternal reality. On the other hand, we find them straining against such explanation, especially in talking of the gift of the body and blood of Christ, for it did not seem to satisfy their desire to identify the gift with the reality, albeit given in a sacramental mode. It recurs to some extent in writing of sacrifice, most especially in Cyril, because of the emphasis that he puts on propitiation. Then the presence of the victim and of the once-for-all earthly offering seems more necessary than when the accent is put, as in Theodore and John, on the movement into heavenly high-priesthood.

A summary of the eucharistic issues addressed in this catechesis will help to see what must be continually addressed in appropriating the tradition. The fundamental concern is that of the church's communion with and in Jesus Christ, the mediator. Assumed is his own identity as the Word of God made flesh. Salvation is possible through him because in the incarnation he became one through the flesh with humanity. Though he has ascended back to the Father through his suffering and resurrection and his flesh has now become immortal, made new in the Spirit, Christians must continue to have communion with him through the flesh. One of the problems of this catechesis was to find a way of expressing sacramental mediation in bringing about this communion. It needed to be emphatic enough to stress the union in one flesh, but spiritual enough to bring out that the union is with Christ in his risen and spiritual body and that ultimately this is intended to mediate communion with the eternal high-priest in his communion with the Father.

Communion with Christ in his human nature is also communion with his sacrifice, both in the effects of the shedding of his blood and in its worshipful reality. It is in bringing this out that we find a tendency to see the rites as a mimesis of the historical events of passion, death, entombment, and rising, coupled however with a representation of the heavenly intercession and the second coming. The inclusion of the last two images shows as well as anything else what is intended by the commemoration of the historical events. We are warned not to take figuratively representational language too literally.

For the mystagogues, while the Word made flesh entered human reality and history, his salvific action had a transhistorical quality. While his sacrifice entailed the reality of his suffering and the willing surrender of his body to death, it was completed only in his passage to the Father and in the exercise of his high-priesthood in the heavenly sanctuary. It is this event in its unity, and therefore in its very passage from the earthly to the heavenly, that Chrysostom especially finds represented in the liturgy. Hence at one and the same time he could speak of the church's union with Christ in his voluntary death and union with him in his heavenly liturgy. They are so completely one reality that they cannot be separated.

The interpretation of liturgical acts as imitative action stirs up vivid memory so that the faithful are incited to imaginative recollection of Christ's suffering or of his rising from the dead. This, however, does not designate what is properly represented, which is the earthly/heavenly sacrifice and all of this imaginative commemoration is kept within these parameters.

When the bishop is presented as one in whom we see Christ himself, this seems to be taken in two ways. In a more realistic way, this is because through his prayer Christ mediates his own priestly prayer to the church and transforms through his words and invocation of the Spirit the bread and wine into his body and blood. The representational role of the bishop lies in the nature of the liturgical action that he performs. In a more figurative way, there are moments when some of his movements or the rites that he performs are dubbed with a more figural explanation that recalls the moments of Christ's passion or his rising from the dead. The realistic and the figurative in a way complement each other, but they are distinct, and it is the relation to the liturgy completed in heaven that is the core of the explanation of the rites.[43]

Augustine of Hippo[44]

Augustine wrote no formal work on the Eucharist. His thought is found in various places, principally in his homilies, in his commentaries on John VI and in Book X of *The City of God*. Since the issues of sacrifice and presence have dominated Western thought for centuries, Augustine is invoked on these as an authority for at times opposing views. However, his teaching on the Eucharist is more comprehensive and needs to be seen in its totality.

Ecclesial Perspective. The first thing to be noted is the ecclesial perspective within which he preaches about or discusses the Eucharist. The

---

43. There is something comparable in the way of explaining the actions of the deacons. In allegory, their laying of the cloth has them represent the holy men and women placing the body of Jesus in the tomb. When attention is given to the mediation of the heavenly liturgy, they represent the angels in whose praises the earthly church now joins.

44. There are a number of studies on Augustine's eucharistic thought. In particular, see Wilhelm Gessel, *Eucharistische Gemeinschaft bei Augustinus* (Würzburg: Augustinus-Verlag, 1966); M. Berrouard, "L'être sacrementel de l'eucharistie selon saint Augustin," *Nouvelle Revue Théologique* 99 (1977): 702–21; T. Camelot, "Réalisme et symbolisme dans la doctrine eucharistique de S. Augustin," *Revue des Sciences Philosophiques et Théologiques* 31 (1947): 394–410.

sacrament is the sacrament of the Body of Christ and is intended for the communion of the one Christ, head and members, a holy communion in the love of God. Practically, Augustine elaborates often on the symbolism of the one bread and the one cup to enforce the need for charity and unity in the church. That which is signified, or in other words the sacramental reality, is threefold, each signification requiring the truth of the others. It is the flesh and blood of Christ, received within the communion of the one Spirit and known only by living faith. It is the faithful themselves who have been baptized and invited to the table, receiving there that which is a sign of themselves.[45] It is finally the Body of Christ, the communion of head and members united in the Spirit.

From this complex signification and reality there follows Augustine's insistence on the necessity of spiritual eating, something which he emphasizes particularly in his tractates on John VI.[46] He opposes both a capharnaitic and a thoughtless approach to the sacrament. In the former, there is a failure to understand the spiritual nature of the gift offered and this leads to scandal at the thought of eating the flesh of Christ. In the latter, people are content with the externals of communion, neglecting the inner faith through which alone communicants have access to the reality signified.

There is a deep appreciation in Augustine of the relation between sign and reality. Sign of its nature belongs to the world of the spirit, even though it appears in the world of matter where humans have access to the spiritual only through the material. It is because it belongs to the world of the spirit that it is possible to say that the sign participates in the reality signified. Hence those who, through loss of faith or lack of inner consciousness, live outside the world of the spirit do not have access to the reality signified and cannot participate in it. Augustine belongs to that way of looking at the world which sees the reality of the material totally in terms of its relation to the spiritual. People can live in the material world without ever knowing what it really is, because they do not see it in relation to the things of the spirit. They can be so immersed in the material that they never see beyond it, and unfortunately it is possible for some to take part in the Eucharist in this way. These, it must be said, receive the sacrament but not the reality, for they are outside the Spirit.

Against this background, one can understand Augustine's definition of the sacrament as the union of the heavenly and the earthly, the acces-

---

45. *Sermo* 272, PL 38, 1246–48. English translation from Daniel Sheerin, ed., *The Eucharist,* Message of the Fathers of the Church 7 (Wilmington, Del.: Michael Glazier, 1986), 95: "If you are the body and members of Christ, it is your mystery which is placed on the Lord's table; it is your mystery you receive."

46. *Tractatus in Ioannem,* 26: CSEL 36, 265–69. English translation in Sheerin, ed., *The Eucharist,* 218–24.

sion of word to element in the formation of sign. The manifestation of the truth that is given in material reality has to be illumined by a word that appeals to faith and understanding, penetrating the soul of the believer. While he narrows the essential word of sacrament to such things as the profession of faith and the invocation of the Trinity in baptism or the blessing prayer in the Eucharist, it is evident that for Augustine the hearing of this word takes place in the context of the proclamation of the fullness of the word, for only this arouses faith.

Augustine demands a practical reverence for the material sacramental elements, in how they are treated, touched, and consumed. He asks for this reverence, at times calling the elements the body and blood of Christ, at times the reality of the people themselves who are his members. This does not indicate a materialistic approach but goes well with his more spiritual understanding of sacrament, which is such as never to take away from the importance of the material. Neither does it indicate an excessively spiritual approach, for Augustine shows full well that membership in the Body comes only through union with the human nature of the Word who descended from the Father and has now ascended back to his embrace.

Sacrifice. It is in the context of his teaching on the Eucharist as the Sacrament of the Body that his teaching on sacrifice is comprehensible. This is found in a more popular way in his homilies,[47] and in more discursive form in Book X of *The City of God.*

In a sermon given on the day of pasch, for example, he explains the mystery of the body signified in the one bread and stresses the unity in charity that this imposes. He then goes on to speak of the sacrifice by way of commentary on the eucharistic prayer and its opening dialogue.[48] It appears that he sees the prayer itself as the sacrifice offered by the priest, when he prays it on behalf of the people. This is to maintain the original Christian meaning of eucharistic sacrifice. In this prayer, Augustine explains, the people are to join their hearts with their head in heaven, as invited by the exhortation to lift up their hearts. It is not just the words that they offer, but their very selves. As he says in another paschal homily, the sacrifice offered is sanctified by God, who willed "that we ourselves should be his sacrifice."[49]

In these paschal homilies, he speaks of the one bread placed upon the altar, not many loaves on many altars, but one bread on one al-

---

47. Sheerin gives an English translation of three important homilies, *The Eucharist,* 94–102. References to the original text are given there.

48. *Sermo* Wolfenbüttel 7, edited by G. Morin, *Miscellanea Agostiniana* (Rome, 1930), 462–64. See Sheerin, ed., *The Eucharist,* 101f.

49. *Sermo* 227, *Augustin d'Hippone: Sermons pour la Pâque,* edited by S. Poque, Sources Chrétiennes 116 (Paris: Ed. du Cerf, 1966), 241f. See Sheerin, ed., *The Eucharist,* 98.

tar. By such images, he shows that the sacrament and sacrifice of every congregation is the sacrament and sacrifice of the whole church. Not much is said in these homilies to relate the Eucharist to the passion or paschal event that is commemorated, for it is the union of all in Christ the head that Augustine puts to the fore as the reality of sacrifice.

In the fuller and more sophisticated teaching of the *City of God*, Augustine presents a Christian view of sacrifice that contrasts with that of popular Roman cult or even with the erudite opinions of Porphyry.[50] In X, 6, Augustine defines sacrifices as works of mercy done towards self or neighbor, through which access is had to God in holy communion (*sancta societas*). In the same context, he states that "the congregation or communion of saints is offered as a universal sacrifice through the High Priest [Christ]." This is again to accentuate the sacrifice of the whole body through the mediation of Christ, so that sacramental signification and sacrificial reality coincide. It is also to incorporate into the eucharistic offering the spiritual sacrifices of daily life, especially works of mercy. Later, in Book X, 20, we read that the daily sacrifice of the church is the sacrament of the sacrifice of the passion.[51]

The rest of the book allows the reader to connect the eucharistic sacrifice with more specific ideas on the priesthood and sacrifice of Christ himself. Jesus Christ in his passion became priest, victim, and mediator. In chapter 24 Augustine expands on the Platonist notion of Principle. What is effected in the Principle is already true of what flows from the Principle. Brought up into heaven, Christ brought with him the whole human race, of which in descending to this earth he had become the principle, or head and representative.

The sacrifice of the passion is, as it were, sacramentally represented in that which it has brought about, namely, the communion of the one body in the body and blood of Christ, the one Spirit, and the one communion of offering both self and praise. For the ecclesial sacrifice, Christ's own sacrifice serves as principle and exemplar, expressive of that attitude and devotion of which the faithful are to give evidence. Christ's passion was a complete surrender to the Father, and thus a perfect sacrifice. Through the passion, "he cast himself into God's spiritual fire, burning with a holy desire for God's ineffable and mystical embrace."[52] This then is to be the sacrifice with which the faithful are united in holy congregation in the celebration of the Eucharist.

While Augustine emphasizes the surrender and love that Christ showed in his passion, where he acted as head and mediator of human-

---

50. *De Civitate Dei*, X. 6ff.: CCSL 47, 276–79. An English translation of the more pertinent texts of Book X is given in Sheerin, ed., *The Eucharist*, 42–49.
51. *De Civitate Dei* X, 20 (CCSL 47, 294).
52. X, 18 (CCSL 47, 294)

kind, there is more than an echo here of what was seen in John Chrysostom and Theodore, namely, the idea that the sacrifice is perfected with the ascension to God's right hand, where Christ continues his priestly mediation. Furthermore, on both sacramental reality and sacrificial reality there is no way of separating Augustine's discourse on Christ from his discourse on the church, if the sacramental signs of body and sacrifice are to be allowed their full import, and if the mediation of Christ is to be fully appreciated.

Vocabulary. A word needs to be said on Augustine's vocabulary, which became important in the Berengarian controversy and made a lasting impression on medieval theology.[53] Using the term *sacramentum* to refer to the rite of the church, he distinguished in it between the sign (*signum*) and the reality (*res*). The reality includes both the body and blood offered in communion and the Body that is the communion of head and members in the unity of the one Spirit. In the sign, Augustine distinguishes the material factor (*elementum*) and the word of faith (*verbum fidei*). In expressing what was signified, he also distinguishes between the *res* or reality of the sacrament and its power (*virtus*). This caused much confusion in later centuries, since some could read in this a reduction of the reality to an efficacious power. Some would contend that the power and the reality are identical for Augustine, or in other words that there is a metonymy whereby sanctifying power is necessarily included in the reality signified. Others would press for a greater distinction, allowing for a difference between the reality present, namely, the body and blood of Christ, and its sanctifying power. The discussion is perhaps rather alien to Augustine's comprehensive attitudes. It is a preoccupation only when the presence of the body and blood of Christ becomes a concern in itself, apart from their reception. This happens when it must be defended in the case of those who receive unworthily and are not sanctified, or when extrasacramental devotions take on more importance, so that the species themselves are talked of as the Blessed Sacrament.

Theologically Significant Eucharistic Practice. Interesting points of eucharistic practice emerge from two texts of Augustine. The first is a passage of his commentary on 1 Timothy 2. The second is his narration of Monica'a burial rites in the *Confessions*.

In commenting on 1 Timothy 2:1 in one of his letters, he divides the prayers of the rite of the Mass into "obsecrationes, orationes, interpellationes and gratiarum actiones."[54] It is under "orationes" that he

---

53. A brief summary on vocabulary is given by William R. Crockett, *Eucharist: Symbol of Transformation* (New York: Pueblo Publishing Company, 1989), 88–94.

54. *Epistula 149 ad Paulinum* (CSEL 34, 2:359–64).

includes the eucharistic prayer and the Lord's Prayer. He views this
as essentially a prayer for the sanctification of the gifts offered and of
self-offering on the part of the church and its members. This sacramental offering signifies the desire of the faithful to remain one in
Christ as his members, united in the unity signified by the one bread.
He places thanksgiving at the end of the liturgy, when all have received communion and are ready to sing their praises to God. It is
clear enough from this that for Augustine the central prayer had become primarily one of sanctification of the bread and wine and of the
church's self-offering. This meaning chimes with his stress on the nature of the sacrament as sacrament of unity, in which head and members
are united in one offering and the communion of one body. We do not
know what prayer was used in North Africa at the time, but Augustine's interpretation fits well enough with the emphasis on offering and
reasonable service of the Latin liturgies in the Ambrosian and Roman
churches.

In his narration of the burial rites for his mother, Monica, Augustine
mentions that the Eucharist was celebrated at the graveside before she
was laid to rest.[55] This was not the common practice in all churches,
for in many the commemorative Eucharist took place some time after burial rather than as an integral part of the actual burial rites.[56] He
speaks of this as the offering of a sacrifice for the forgiveness of Monica's sins, according to her own request before she died. Her request
is stated in interesting terms, for what she asked was "that we should
remember her at your altar, where she had been your servant day after day."[57] In this way she thought that it would be remembered to
her that in the Eucharist we receive the divine victim who paid the
price for our redemption and in whom we are fortified against the enemy. In this way, the prayer that the church makes for her is based in
her own reception of the sacrament. It is a pleading that what Christ
guaranteed her in sacramental communion should be efficacious against
any onslaughts of Satan that may follow death. This gives an interesting slant to "offerings for the dead," since it shows the practice to be
rooted in the communion with Christ assured in sacramental reception, the communion of being a living member of the one who paid
the ransom for our sins and in whom we have triumphed over the
enemy.

---

55. *Libri Confessionum* IX, 13, 32: CSEL 33, 221f.
56. There is some suggestion that this was a communion service, not a full liturgy, but
the argument is not compelling.
57. IX. 13, 36: CSEL 33, 224f.

The Pseudo-Dionysius[58]

This pseudonymous Greek writer represents a trend in sacramental thought which retained importance in both East and West. Few seem to have followed his thinking exactly, but aspects of it occur constantly, and his authority as a witness from apostolic days was a matter of contention at the time of the Reformation. Elements of his thought are found in Thomas Aquinas, who wrote a commentary on his work, and they may have influenced church architecture in the Western Middle Ages. Today there is a resurgence of interest in his work among those who espouse a more apophatic approach to language about God.[59]

The commentary on the eucharistic liturgy is found in *The Ecclesiastical Hierarchy.*[60] The key perception of that work is that the ecclesiastical hierarchy of bishop, presbyters, and deacons has distinctive roles in mediating the divine illumination, which proceeds from the source of all light, the Most Holy Trinity. In the treatise *The Divine Names,* the author shows that the names used of God serve principally on the way of negation.[61] Using them allows us to strip our understanding of God of any created predicates, so that the soul is opened to the divine illumination. God is the One, in a oneness not to be confused with human union, source of all that is, but ineffable and beyond human thought.

In the liturgy, symbols have a similar negating and purifying function.[62] All the ceremonies, beginning with the opening incensation of gifts, place, and people, serve to purify the soul, detach it from its bodily perceptions, and bring it into the spiritual world. There is something like a stripping down of form in order to allow the true light to penetrate.

In his thought on the liturgy the writer is most of all concerned with the contemplation to which it leads. In his thought on Christ and on Christ in the liturgy, it is the image of the Logos and of the incarnation, rather than of the passion, that dominate. He sees the eucharistic action as a representation of the Supper, at which the Logos incarnate took on sacramental form, in which he remains present in the church, and through which access to the eternal Logos is still offered. In expressing the nature of the mystery of redemption, he dwells on the incarnation. It was because the deity took on our human nature, in all but its sin, that

---

58. An English translation of the works of the pseudo-Dionysius may be found in *Pseudo-Dionysius: The Complete Works,* translation by Colm Luibheid (New York: Paulist Press, 1987). References to the Greek text in PG 3 are given in the margin of the translation.

59. See the short but helpful work of Andrew Louth, *Denis the Areopagite,* Outstanding Christian Thinkers Series (London: Geoffrey Chapman; Wilton, Conn.: Morehouse-Barlow).

60. *The Ecclesiastical Hierarchy,* in *Pseudo-Dionysius: The Complete Works,* 193–259.

61. *The Divine Names,* in *Pseudo-Dionysius: The Complete Works,* 47–131.

62. On the liturgy, see *The Ecclesiastical Hierarchy,* in *Pseudo-Dionysius: The Complete Works,* 210–24.

our nature is transformed, filling "our shadowed and unshaped minds with a kindly, divine light."[63]

Of the great eucharistic prayer, he says that in it, standing before the altar, the bishop "praises the divine works,...those sacred works wrought gloriously by Jesus, exercising there his most divine providence for the salvation of the human race."[64] On communion, he explains that the union achieved comes from the fact that "the most divine Word has taken the route of incarnation for us and, without undergoing any change, has become a reality that is composite and visible. He has beneficently accomplished for us a unifying communion with himself."[65] In the rites with which he surrounds the sacred symbols of the body and blood, unveiling them and lifting them up and distributing them to be consumed, the bishop presents this mystery for the contemplation of the faithful. The contemplative union with the Word, rather than union with his passion and death, is the aim of liturgical rite.

Maximus the Confessor follows the pseudo-Dionysius in his commentary on the divine mysteries by giving primacy to the soul's ascent to God rather than to the memory of Christ's redemptive death.[66] After Maximus, there was a turning point in Byzantine liturgical commentary in Germanus of Constantinople, who gave more attention to the historical events commemorated.[67] The accent on contemplation and on divine unity and enlightenment found in *The Ecclesiastical Hierarchy*, however, continued to have an influence in eucharistic understanding and practice in both East and West. The root of this influence is found in the metaphysical foundation that the writer gave to the concepts of order and hierarchy. Though he strictly avoided the emanationism of Neoplatonism, he adopted the idea of order in the universe and of an ordered return of all things to the One who is their creator. This general concept was applied to the church in the distinction of two hierarchies, one of function, the other of perfection. The order of perfection is found in descending order in the lives of monks, of the baptized, and of catechumens. The order of function is found in the unifying, enlightening, and serving roles of bishop, presbyter, and deacon respectively. This grounded the distinction in the church between the ordained and the

---

63. Ibid., 221.

64. Ibid.

65. Ibid., 222.

66. For an English translation, see *The Church, the Liturgy and the Soul of Man: The Mystagogia of St. Maximus the Confessor* (Still River, Mass.: St. Bede's Publications, 1982), 57–120. For a summary on Maximus and his relation to the Areopagite, see Schulz, *The Byzantine Liturgy*, 43–49.

67. For a complete analysis, see R. Bornert, *Les commentaires byzantins de la divine liturgie du VIIe au XVe siècle* (Paris: Institut Français d'Études Byzantines, 1966). For the work of Germanus and a note on his place in the tradition, see *St. Germanus of Constantinople on the Divine Liturgy*, the Greek text with translation, introduction, and commentary by Paul Meyendorff (Crestwood, N.Y.: St. Vladimir's Seminary Press, 1984).

faithful, positing all mediating function on the side of the ordained. Eucharist is the action of the bishop, assisted by the presbyters and deacons, something that they perform for the sake of the faithful to bring them to contemplation of the Word and on the way of return to communion with the One.

CONCLUSION

This survey was meant to underline approaches to the mystery of the Eucharist in the centuries after Nicea and to bring crucial questions to the fore. This is preferable to a narrow quest for positions on presence and sacrifice.

Attention was first paid to the development of eucharistic prayers. In all liturgical families its basic structure remained quite simple. Amplifications on this structure put more stress on historical representation and on sacrifice. Even when the written text changed but little, the accompanying ritual gave a sense to the prayer that cannot be gleaned from an analysis of the text alone. In the comments of Augustine and the pseudo-Dionysius on the prayer we see how its understanding in practice could be somewhat detached from the actual text. Neither pays much attention to thanksgiving for the death and resurrection. One attends more to offering and the sanctification of the bread and wine, the other writes as though the prayer spoke only of the incarnation. This is a salutary reminder to those who may think that the composition of texts is in itself the response to a good use of the eucharistic prayer.

If we look at a number of important theologies, the unique nature of sacramental reality stands out. There is always a tension between realism and the nonidentification of the sign with the signified. The prevailing idea of reality, which in this period owed much to Neoplatonism, influenced an explanation of sacrament that derived from a particular way of seeing the relation between matter and spirit.

The church itself is the sacramental reality, not simply an agent that celebrates sacraments. The abiding relation to Christ the Savior, and communion with and in him, constitutes the church in its being, so that in offering the body and blood to neophytes Augustine could truly say: "receive that which you are." New ideas that developed about the role of the ordained minister were also given sacramental meaning, though it was not until later in the Middle Ages that the full force of this distinction between clergy and laity appeared.

To explain the communion between Christ and members in the one sacrament different approaches were taken. One was to accentuate the incarnation of the Word in such a way as to attribute almost divine qualities to his human nature from the moment of his enfleshment. This is what we saw done by the pseudo-Dionysius. Another, more common, approach was to consider the mystery of the transformation of the bread and wine in the light of Christ's own transformation in the Spirit in the resurrection. The more robust language of eating and drinking the flesh and blood of Christ has to be placed alongside this appeal to the power of the Spirit or of God's word.

In explaining the liturgical representation of past historical events, there was a tendency to place the events in their essence beyond the historical plane. The idea of pasch as passover, such as was taught by Origen, took on a more powerful tone when Christ's own priestly act was seen to be perfected in heaven. Christian life was then seen as a way of living beyond the concerns of the present time, and the transformation of history itself through the advent of Christ did not emerge very strongly. This lack of historical consciousness is the greatest problem that we face today in appropriating the eucharistic patterns of these centuries.

In short, the canon of remembrance was enlarged to embrace a diversity of prayers, but their meaning was affected by ritual performance. In theology, much was dependent on a way of seeing the relation of the material to the spiritual.

Part IV

EUCHARIST IN
THE LATER MIDDLE AGES

Chapter 8

HIGH MIDDLE AGES:
THE ROLE OF
THE EUCHARIST
IN CHURCH AND SOCIETY

Part II of this work was addressed to the place of the Eucharist in the New Testament, and Part III to the evidence of the pre-Nicene church. This was complemented by a general overview of the following centuries. In this next major section of the work, the chief theological interest is in the work of Thomas Aquinas, but this has to be read in the context of all that was taking place in eucharistic practice during the centuries to which he belonged. There is no claim that his theology is the sole work that deserves consideration or that it fully integrated what was happening. However, his eucharistic treatise is an excellent example of the endeavor to give a systematic and scientific explanation of the sacrament, in keeping with the ideals of learning and with the practices of the time.

In the first two chapters of this part of the book, consideration is given to eucharistic practice and prayer in their cultural setting. It is impossible either to survey all the pertinent material or to give a clear and uniform picture. Studies on the Middle Ages show how difficult a time it is to understand and what differing assessments can be made of it. By taking examples, however, it is hoped to gain an insight into the prayer and practice that constitute the context to which a reading of the theology of Thomas Aquinas belongs.

To this purpose it helps to distinguish two aspects of eucharistic practice, the two of course being related to each other. The first has to do with the role of the Eucharist as public symbol, showing how as a sign of Christ's presence and power the Eucharist was at the center of a cultural vision of church and society. The other aspect of practice has to do with the way in which persons or groups integrated the sacrament into their spiritual lives. The material on prayer and practice is thus divided into two chapters.

This present chapter looks at the Eucharist as a public symbol and is divided into four parts. These treat in turn of the Eucharist as a priestly act, its architectural setting, its relation to the issues raised by the resurgence of the evangelical life, and the part that it played in the ordering of church and society.

THE PRIESTLY ACT

It is common knowledge that the celebration of Mass without a congregation, or what is now called private Mass,[1] had become an accepted custom before the time of Aquinas. It would however be a mistake to take this as the barometer on which to read the understanding of the priest's role, for it was as much consequence as cause of changing ideas on the celebration of the Eucharist. Some other examples will therefore be taken to illustrate how within communal celebrations the Mass came to be seen in a special way as the action of the priest. Only then is it possible to understand the growing regularity of private Mass.

The Consecration of Saint-Denis

The first example is provided by the story of the consecration of the chevet of the abbey church at Saint-Denis on June 11, 1144, as narrated by Abbot Suger.[2] For the occasion, this lordly abbot had gathered a magnificent assembly in a magnificent building for a magnificent liturgy. Many years had been spent and much treasure had been invested in restoring the building to what was deemed fitting for its saintly patron, whom Suger liked to identify with the Areopagite of the Pauline narrative (Acts 17:34) and the reputed author of works such as *The Celestial Hierarchy* and *The Ecclesiastical Hierarchy.* He had collected gifts in abundance for its adornment and invited royalty and nobility to its consecration. There were nineteen lord bishops to consecrate the twenty altars of the upper and lower levels of the church. The culminating point of this splendid service was the harmonized celebration of Mass by the

---

1. Originally, the term *private Mass* could mean a Mass at which only the priest took communion, whether celebrating alone or with any number of faithful present. This was the meaning of the term as late as the sixteenth century.

2. See *Abbot Suger on the Abbey Church of Saint-Denis and Its Art Treasures,* edited, translated, and annotated by Erwin Panofsky, 2d ed. (Princeton: Princeton University Press, 1979), under the title "De Consecratione."

nineteen prelates, each at his respective altar on the two levels of the building. Suger describes the action in these words:

> After the consecration of the altars all these [dignitaries] performed a solemn celebration of Masses, both in the upper choir and in the crypt, so festively, so solemnly, so different and yet so concordantly, so close [to one another] and so joyfully that their song, delightful by its consonance and unified harmony, was deemed a symphony angelic rather than human.[3]

This is a description that bespeaks the ideals of the time at their most majestic. Though the metaphors of harmony are alike, the occasion differs considerably from the one assembly augured in the letters of Ignatius of Antioch. The accent is now placed, not on the congregation, but on the role and performance of the prelates. In restoring the church, Suger had provided the many altars in honor of the Virgin Mary and of the saints, but placed them so that all converged as it were towards the principal altar in the apse of the building. Here on the back panel he had caused to be inscribed the words that summed up the meaning of the sacramental offering:

> With a great cry, the crowd cries out to Christ: Hosanna. The true victim [*hostia*] offered at the Lord's Supper has carried all the people. He hastens to carry the cross who saves all on the cross. Christ's flesh seals the promise which Abraham obtains for his offspring. Melchizedech offers a libation because Abraham triumphs over the enemy. They who seek Christ with the cross bear the cluster of grapes upon a staff.[4]

The opening line of the inscription echoes the song of the Sanctus, which precedes the priestly action of offering that true victim first offered at the Lord's Supper. The action commemorates the supper and the cross that sealed the salvation of all people. In his offering of bread and wine, Melchizedech represents the priestly nature of the Eucharist as it related to the promises of the covenant with Abraham. The other biblical image is that of the staff on which the scouts sent ahead into the promised land bore back a cluster of grapes (Num. 13:23). In this image the Eucharist's relation to the cross is represented.

---

3. *Abbot Suger*, 118–21.
4. *Abbot Suger*, "De Administratione," 62f. The Latin reads:
   Voce sonans magna Christo plebs clamat: Osanna.
   Quae datur in coena tulit omnes hostia vera.
   Ferre crucem properat qui cunctos in cruce salvat.
   Hoc quod Abram pro prole litat, Christi caro signat.
   Melchisedech libat quod Abram super hoste triumphat.
   Botrum vecte ferunt qui Christum cum cruce quaerunt.

At the consecration ceremony, the singing of the Sanctus and the other splendid chants provided by the assembled monks united all with the priestly act. It was however to the harmony of the priestly action of all the bishops that Suger principally pointed, one whose meaning was inscribed in the words quoted above.

The Mass Order

That this concurred with the spirit of the times is reflected in the history of the liturgical books and their description of the ceremonies of the Mass. The emergence of the special book called the *Pontifical* shows how bishops performed certain services that reflected their exalted place in church and realm. The choir books for monasteries and their ritual books show how monks were caught up in the daily and seasonal round of divine praise. The parish clergy could not compete with either cathedral or monastery in matters liturgical, but in the celebration of the Mass they were no different from bishop or monk.

Much evidence could be considered on this point, but here it may suffice to look at three influential Mass orders from the eighth and ninth centuries that show how even that early the priestly act of offering Mass had begun to mark off not only the bishop but even the simple presbyter from the people.[5] These rubrical works belong to an era when there was still the ideal of only one celebration and only one priest, be he bishop or presbyter, presided at the liturgy, with other clergy participating according to rank and seniority. However, even though the custom of one Mass, one altar, one presider, was kept, the rubrics demonstrate an understanding of the priest's act that distinguishes it rather clearly from how the role of the presider was seen in the early church. Once cut off from the action of the assembly, it was but another step to believe that the priest's action had a purpose in itself, even if celebrated without a congregation.

The three liturgical orders in question are found in the collection edited by Michel Andrieu under the title *Ordines Romani* (nos. I, IX, and XVII).[6] The first is dated by Andrieu between 700 and 750 C.E. It was originally intended for the use of the bishop of Rome around 700 but was transported north of the Alps and thus modified around 750. The second, dated between 880 and 900 C.E., is the

5. On the fundamental identity of presbyteral and episcopal eucharistic celebration, see Niels K. Rasmussen, "Célébration épiscopale et célébration presbytérale: Un essai de typologie," in *Segni e riti nella chiesa altomedievale occidentale*, Settimane di Studio del Centro Italiano di Studi sull'Alto Medioevo XXXIII (Spoleto: Presso la Sede del Centro, 1987), 2:581–604.

6. Michel Andrieu, *Les Ordines Romani du Haut Moyen Age*, vol. 2, Spicilegium Sacrum Lovaniense, Études et Documents 23 (Louvain: Spicilegium Sacrum Lovaniense, 1960) 3–108; 325–36, and vol. 3, Études et Documents 24 (Louvain: SSL, 1961), 157–93.

first Romano-Frankish order for an episcopal Mass. The third is actually dated about a century earlier than this, but is considered here in third place because it is the rite used in a monastery where a presbyter-monk presided at the conventual Mass. The papal Mass has become the prototype for the other ordinals, and though there is a difference in the degree of pomp displayed, the ritual gives similar importance to the central act of prayer and consecration in each case.

It is within the canon of the Mass that solemnity and mystery are attached to the prayer and action of the priest. In the first redaction of OR I, done for the bishop of Rome, it would seem that the word *canon* meant the entire eucharistic prayer, inclusive of the part before the Sanctus.[7] When transported north of the Alps, the redaction marked the beginning of the canon at the Te igitur. Though the prayer is still to be prayed in an audible voice, the rubric prescribes that the bishop should rise *alone* and *enter into* the canon.[8] By the time of OR IX, written for use by a bishop, this part of the Mass is designated as the *actio* and the directives are similar.[9] In the monastic ordinal (OR IX), there are clearer indications of the new ritual ways of marking this part of the action of the celebrant, now regularly referred to as *sacerdos*. He is to pray the canon in a low voice, and for the doxology at the end of the prayer he is to raise the oblations from the altar.[10]

Ordination rites also speak to the importance that was gradually given to the priest's consecration of the elements in the Mass.[11] Traced back to Celtic ordinals, the anointing of hands had become a regular part of presbyteral ordination by the thirteenth century. So had the presentation to the candidate of the bread and wine in their appropriate vessels, these being looked upon as the instruments for the exercise of the presbyteral order. In the assimilation of anointing into the ordination rite, appeal to the Old Testament priesthood as prototype was encouraged and the sacrificial understanding of the ordained minister's action in the Mass was bolstered.

The Consecration of Churches

Along with these developments we can note how elaborate services were devised for the consecration of churches, altars, and altar vessels. Though some of this ceremonial was restrained by the time it was

---

7. Andrieu, *Les Ordines Romani*, 2:95, no. 88. See Andrieu's footnote 88.
8. "Surgit pontifex solus et intrat in canonem."
9. Andrieu, *Les Ordines Romani*, 2:334, no. 32.
10. Ibid., 3:182, nos. 49, 53.
11. This is documented by Bruno Kleinheyer, *Die Priesterweihe im Römischen Ritus: Eine liturgiehistorische Studie* (Trier: Paulinus Verlag, 1962), 114–22 and 154–62.

inserted into the Roman Pontifical, the earliest medieval rites are illustra-
tive of how the Mass had come to be seen as a priestly action, conceived
on the model of Old Testament sacrifices.

This ceremonial of consecration is in marked contrast with attitudes
toward the place of worship in earlier centuries. The earliest thought
on the blessing of places of worship was that this came about through
the simple fact of celebrating the Eucharist. *Ordo Romanus* XLII, dated
in the ninth century, shows how this was then prepared for by a deposition of the relics of martyrs, with the martyrion of the church of
Jerusalem as prototype.[12] Not only were the relics of martyrs placed in
the confessional, but along with them there went three portions of the
sacramental body of Christ and three grains of incense, all sealed into
the anointed stone of the altar.[13] Only after this was done could the
Eucharist be celebrated.

There are still further elaborations on the service of consecration in
Ordo Romanus XLI[14] of the same century, and in the Frankish sacramentary of Angoulême.[15] Apart from the chrismation of walls and altar, the
most remarkable of these rites is the preparation of the water to be used
in sprinkling the pavement, walls and altar of the church. This water is
mixed with ashes and wine. When it has been used for the sprinkling,
what remains is poured out on the ground at the foot of the altar. All this
is apparently done in imitation of the sacrificial blood ritual described
in Exodus 29:12–18 and illustrates the priestly and sacrificial character
attributed to the action of the Eucharist.

In brief, what is developed in the rites of the Mass and in the ceremonies of ordination and consecration of churches is the notion and
image of priestly mediation. The role of the ordained minister in presiding over the eucharistic assembly has given way to a role of mediation
between the people and God, especially in the act of offering sacrifice
and consecrating the elements.

The Private Mass

It is this development that provides the background to the origin of what
came to be called the private Mass, covering both the Mass at which only
the priest communicated and the Mass celebrated without a congregation. There is considerable discussion about the extent of its practice

---

12. See Andrieu, *Les Ordines Romani,* 4:311–49 and 353–402.
13. Ibid., 400, no. 11.
14. Andrieu, *Les Ordines Romani,* 4:341–44, nos. 9–17.
15. *Liber Sacramentorum Engolismensis: Le Sacramentaire gélasien d'Angoulême,* edited by
Patrick Saint-Roch, CCSL 159C (Turnhout: Brepols, 1987).

before the late Middle Ages and about its motivation, but there is no doubt as to its increasing significance.[16]

It is clear that an increasing number of monks were ordained to the presbyterate so that there were large numbers of priests in monasteries. On the evidence of eleventh-century writers, some of these at least on occasion celebrated solitary Masses, even at times without a minister.[17] Piety had something to do with this accession of monks to the priesthood, since the call to holiness had come to be associated with a call to ecclesiastical rank.[18] Thus the devout offering of the sacrifice of the Mass had personal as well as ecclesial implications.[19]

However, it should not be thought that ordination of itself meant daily celebration of Mass. Despite the number of priests in monasteries, there appears to have been a liturgical restriction on the number of Masses to be celebrated each day. Angelus Häussling has offered compelling evidence to show that monasteries kept the principle of "one altar, one sacrifice," so that not more than one Mass was allowed to be celebrated each day on any individual altar.[20] Though, as at Saint-Denis, altars were multiplied in abbeys, the number of daily celebrations would never have exceeded the number of altars, regardless of the number of priests in the community. The liturgical model guiding the regulation of Masses was that of the stational liturgy in the city of Rome. Each altar, with the relics of its saint or saints, stood for one of the stations of the Roman church's liturgy, so that with a Mass each day at each altar the abbey liturgy, though celebrated more modestly, mirrored that of the great city of Rome. This of course harmonized with the move of the Carolingian era to make the Roman liturgy the liturgy of the entire em-

---

16. The debate is summarized in the English edition of Cyrille Vogel, *Medieval Liturgy: An Introduction to the Sources,* translated and revised by William Storey and Niels Rasmussen (Washington, D.C.: Pastoral Press, 1986), 156–59. The principal authors and works in this discussion are Otto Nussbaum, *Kloster, Priestermönch, und Privatmesse* (Bonn: Hanstein Verlag, 1961); Angelus Häussling, *Mönchskonvent und Eucharistiefeier* (Münster: Aschendorff Verlag, 1972); Cyrille Vogel, "Une mutation cultuelle inexpliquée: Le passage de l'eucharistie communautaire à la messe privée," *Revue des Sciences Religieuses* 54 (1980): 231–50; Arnold Angenendt, "Missa Specialis: Zugleich ein Beitrag zur Entstehung der Privatmessen," *Frühmittelalterliche Studien* 17 (1983): 153–221.

17. See Odo of Cambrai, *Expositio in Canonem Missae,* PL 160, 1056, where he mentions the "Missa solitaria"; Berold of Constance, *Micrologus de Ecclesiasticis Observationibus,* PL 151, 983, where he mentions the "sacerdos sine ministro sacrificans."

18. See David N. Power, "Church Order," in *The New Dictionary of Sacramental Worship,* edited by Peter E. Fink (Collegeville, Minn.,: Liturgical Press, 1990), 212–33.

19. This motivation was eventually summed up in the words well known to many priests of an older generation, "Agite quod agitis, imitamini quod tractatis." For their introduction into the service, see the Pontifical of William of Durand, in Michel Andrieu, *Le Pontifical Romain du Haut Moyen Age,* vol. 3, Studi e Testi 88 (Vatican City: Biblioteca Apostolica Vaticana, 1941), 339.

20. See *Mönchskonvent und Eucharistiefeier.* For a summary of his position in English, see Angelus Häussling, "Motives for Frequency of Eucharist," *Concilium* 152 (1982/2): 25–30.

pire, and at the same time prevented the purely personal devotion of priests from becoming the norm of celebration.

In the thirteenth century, there is still evidence, even outside monasteries, of this reluctance to let devotion dictate the practice of private Mass. In writing to his brethren, Francis of Assisi expressed the desire that all the friars in any convent, brothers and priests, come together for the one eucharistic celebration.[21]

It seems to have been the new stipendiary system that was the decisive influence in the spread of the custom of celebrating Mass without a congregation. Celebrating without a congregation was in fact a corollary to offering the Mass for the special intention of a donor. Offering for the intention of a donor was in turn a consequence of having special Masses for specific intentions.

There are formularies for these special Masses in the medieval sacramentaries.[22] They were distinct from the observance of the liturgies of the liturgical season or festal cycle. In the beginning they were not intended for use without a congregation but served the interests of a particular group of people. Many of the formularies were composed for Masses for the dead, but there are also texts for Masses of the sick, for penitents, and for the medieval ordeal. The practice gradually gave importance to the celebration of the Mass in itself as an act of mediation rather than to its congregational character. It was a way of mediating grace in time of need, particularly in behalf of the dead.

What emerged as the stipendiary system was the offering of a donation to have Masses said for specific intentions, as an act of mediation. Even though it eventually encouraged the practice of private Mass, within the cultural ambience of the time it expressed a strong sense of community and has to be related to an understanding of mediation that is larger than the mediation of offering sacrifice. It seems in fact to have some background in the commutations of penance into prayer that was part of the development of the church's penitential system. In getting away from the harsh penances of the canonical and then of the Celtic penitential order, people were directed to other ways of obtaining conversion of heart. One of these was through a more intense and frequent confession of sin. Another was through the benefit that one could obtain from the penances and prayers of others. Monasteries or convents of both sexes were often given endowments in return for prayers and penances done for the living and the dead. The poor too were given pro-

21. See Francis of Assisi, "A Letter to the Entire Order," in *Francis and Clare: The Complete Works*, translation and introduction by Regis J. Armstrong and Ignatius C. Brady (New York: Paulist Press, 1982), 58. For a discussion of the subject, see Octave d'Angers, "La messe publique et la messe privée dans la piété de Saint François," *Études Franciscaines* 49 (1937): 475–86.

22. See Angenendt, "Missa Specialis."

vision of food and clothing in return for a part in their prayers, deemed to have a particular worth before God.

It was thus within a cultural milieu that gave importance to acts of prayerful mediation that a special strength was attached to the prayer of priests, especially in offering the Mass. It was conceptualized as an offering of Christ's satisfaction, or of Christ's body and blood, for and ` on behalf of the people. Such mediation was obviously deemed to have more efficacy than any other form of mediation or satisfaction. It was in this way that the mediatory role of offering the Mass for the living and the dead was accentuated and that Mass practices radically changed.[23] The entire development is in keeping with a new cultural way of giving a communal and public character to the Eucharist.

ARCHITECTURE, ART, EUCHARIST

It is not simply in liturgical texts that one can appreciate how the Eucharist stood in the piety of the Middle Ages. How it fitted into the whole scheme of salvation and the devotion that it aroused can be seen in part from the public works of art and architecture. Looking at the entire disposition of churches, one sees how the recall of the whole history of redemption is made to converge on the celebration of the Eucharist. Since moreover the architecture and church art of the time brought the humanity of Christ into focus in new ways, one finds a link between the development of eucharistic practice and developments in devotion to the humanity of Christ.

Saint-Denis

Since some intimation of the architectural model of the abbey church of Saint-Denis has already been given, it is useful to take its renovation as a starting-point. Though only parts of the church as restored by Suger now stand, his description is still available.

From the majestic but sombre porch inward, everything in the building directed attention and movement towards the sanctuary, which

---

23. Angenendt sums up the thought of the Carolingian era on priesthood that led to later developments, as follows: "Nun aber, in karolingischer Zeit, entstand daneben eine neue Deutung des Messopfers: Die Gläubigen bringen Brot und Wein dar; der Priester nimmt diese Gaben entgegen und wandelt sie zu Leib und Blut Christi, und als gewandelte Gabe bringt er die dam Gott zum Opfer dar. Es schein dabei undenkbar, dass Gott sich dem Opfer seines Sohnes entziehen könnte. Darum war dieses Opfer unfehlbar und von höchsten Wert, gerade auch dann, wenn es von Gott etwas zu erlangen galt. Der Messpriester vollzog diese Opferung von Christi Leib und Blut an Gott und trug dabei die Bitten des Volkes vor. Nicht mehr das Sich-Anschliessen an das vergegenwärtigte Selbstopfer Christi stand hier im Mittelpunkt, sondern das Opfern des Herrenleibes und Herrenblutes als eines impetratorischen Opfers" ("Missa Specialis," 219f.).

was dominated by a large crucifix and whose panel inscription has already been seen. Stained-glass windows and sculptures the length of the building represented scenes from the Old and New Testaments, as well as the lives of the saints. Other chapels and their altars were placed in a circle, whose center was the main sanctuary. Masses in these chapels were part of the worshipping unity of priests, monks, and people, in celebrating the holy mysteries. Through the rear and side windows there was a play of light that reached its climax in the sanctuary, no doubt at its most magnificent when reflected in the actual celebration of the Mass, with its use of rich ornaments and vessels.[24] Suger describes the effects of the construction, done with the help of all the new arts of geometry, stressing that he has had created

> a circular string of chapels, by virtue of which the whole [church] would shine with the wonderful and uninterrupted light of the most luminous windows, pervading the interior beauty.[25]

The medallions in the stained-glass windows immediately surrounding the sanctuary showed how Christ and his sacrifice are the center of the divine economy. All three are described by Suger, and two are still extant.[26] In one of them Christ is placed between two female figures, representing the Old and the New Laws respectively. Seven doves, representing the seven gifts of the Holy Spirit, form an aureole around his breast. With his right hand, he places a crown on the head of the church. With his left, he raises a veil from the face of the synagogue. The inscription reads: "What Moses veiled, Christ reveals by his teaching."[27]

In a second medallion, the crucifix stands atop the ark of the covenant, which is borne on four wheels and surrounded by the four figures of the prophecy of Ezekiel, representing the four evangelists. The inscription here reads: "On the ark of the covenant is established the altar with the cross of Christ; under a greater covenant, life willingly dies."[28]

Suger describes a third medallion, no longer extant. This depicted Old Testament prophets pouring wheat into a mill, while Paul turned the millstone and gathered the flour. The inscription, as recalled by Suger, lauded Paul for milling the flour from the bran of the Law of Moses and turning it into the true bread, food for angels and for hu-

---

24. Abbot Suger's chalice is kept in the National Gallery of Art in Washington, D.C. The cup is carved from sardonyx and rests in a gold and silver setting, embedded with gems. At its base is a haloed Christ, recalling the Alpha and Omega of the Book of Revelation.
25. *Abbot Suger*, "De Consecratione," 100f.
26. See *Abbot Suger*, 72–77.
27. "Quod Moyses velat Christi doctrina revelat."
28. "Foederis ex arca Christi cruce sistitur ara;
    foedere majori vult ibi vita mori."

mans.[29] Standing as it did next to the altar, the imagery of this window drew together the revelation of the Word as bread from heaven, the work of preaching the gospel, and the gift of the eucharistic bread.[30]

The words on the back panel of the sanctuary, completing these inscriptions and highlighting the mystery of the eucharistic sacrifice, have already been cited. The light streaming in from the rear window is essential to the truth of the mystery. It is an invitation to see all in the light of the Word coming from the East and to go beyond all that is perceived in the light to enjoy this light itself. Suger saw the mystery expressed and celebrated in the church as the object of contemplation. It was for those who could not readily grasp the mystery that he had the words inscribed, so as to instruct them. As for himself, his text describes how he was enraptured in contemplation by simply looking on the interplay of light, ornament, and precious stone. Since this kind of bodily vision leads along the way beyond the senses to intellectual or spiritual vision, he deemed it superior to attention to the word. Some phrases of Georges Duby sum up Suger's ambition and theological vision:

The basilica of Saint-Denis stands for a form of Christianity no longer expressed solely in terms of liturgy and music, but also in those of a theology, a theology whose leitmotif is the Incarnation. This is why Suger's work opened up a new dimension, that of [the human person] illuminated by the *verum lumen*.[31]

In short, in reflecting on the building that he has provided Suger expresses a devotion to Christ that focuses on the humanity of the Word, whose glory shines in the works of his flesh and in the celebration of his mysteries. At the center of this devotion lies the celebration of the sacrifice, just as the sanctuary where it is celebrated is the point towards which everything in the church converges.

---

29. "Tollis agendo molam de furfure, Paule, farinam
Mosaicae legis intima nota facis.
Fit de tot granis verus sine furfure panis.
perpetuusque cibus noster et angelicus."
30. Emile Mâle offers other examples of how representation of the birth and crucifixion of Christ refer to sacrifice and Eucharist. The crèche and the cross are shaped like altars, and the blood and water that flow from the side of Christ on the cross are received into a chalice by the New Eve, the church, while the synagogue turns away, blindfolded. See Emile Mâle, *The Gothic Image: Religious Art in France of the Thirteenth Century*, translated by Dora Nussey (New York: Harper & Row, 1913; reprint 1958), 190–99.
31. Georges Duby, *History of Medieval Art*, part 2: *The Europe of the Cathedrals 1140–1280* (New York: Rizzoli, 1986), 17–19. On this theme, see also Otto von Simson, *The Gothic Cathedral: Origins of Gothic Architecture and the Medieval Concept of Order*, 3d ed. (Princeton: Princeton University Press, 1979), 21–58, 61–141. In his work, Duby indicates that though Cistercian architecture lacks the kind of munificence displayed in churches such as Saint-Denis, it retains the key orientation of the play of light and contemplation (*History of Medieval Art*, 60).

Saint Martin in Zillis

This architectural convergence on the mystery of the sanctuary and on contemplation of truth in the light of the Word was not confined to Gothic design nor to abbeys and cathedrals. An example of how the same approach existed at parish level and in Romanesque architecture is found in the parish church of Saint Martin in Zillis, Switzerland, which dates back to about 1200 C.E.[32]

Some of the building has had to be refurbished, but the original wooden ceiling remains. It is painted with scenes from the Old Testament, from the earthly life of Christ, leading from the annunciation to the crowning with thorns, and includes the legend of the church's patron, Martin of Tours. There are two remarkable things about this portraiture. First, the series of depictions begins at the east end of the church, where the sanctuary is located, and ends next to the main door at the west end. Thus if one looks from the door inward, the first set of scenes that one sees are from the life of Martin, the second from the life of Christ, and the third, nearest the sanctuary, from the Old Testament. This seems to be the wrong sequence. The second strange thing is that the life of Christ concludes on the ceiling with the crowning with thorns, so that there is nothing of the crucifixion or of the resurrection included.

The explanation for these two curiosities emerges when one takes note that this is a place for eucharistic celebration, where the altar and the sanctuary form the center of attention. There is a large window at the east end of the church, from which light streams in. The ceiling is intended to be looked at from within the sanctuary, where one sees it illumined by the light coming from the East. Thus the first scenes are those of the Old Testament in which Christ is prefigured and which are made clear in the light of the Word. The second set has to do with the Word incarnate, and the third depicts the life of his exemplary disciple, Martin, which is patterned on the model of the Word.

The omission of crucifixion, resurrection, and ascension from the ceiling also becomes clear when the church and ceiling are viewed from the sanctuary. Though these no longer remain, it has been suggested that the sanctuary would have been dominated by a large crucifix hanging over it and that an image of Christ the pantocrator probably decorated the vault of the chancel.[33] If this conjecture is accepted, it can be seen how the building as a unit represented the mystery of the Word made flesh. The light streamed in from the East through the chan-

---

32. See Ernst Murbach, *The Painted Romanesque Ceiling of St. Martin in Zillis*, edited and with photographs by Peter Heman, translated from the German by Janet Seligman (New York and Washington: Frederick A. Praeger Publishers, 1967). There is a brief description of this church in Rosalind and Christopher Brooke, *Popular Religion in the Middle Ages: Western Europe 1000–1300* (London: Thames & Hudson, 1984), 137–39.

33. See Murbach, *The Painted Romanesque Ceiling of St. Martin in Zillis*, 19–21.

cel window, the morning light thus constituting the first and dominant expression of the mystery of the eternal Word, made manifest in the earthly mysteries. The sanctuary held the principal images of this mystery, namely, the creator Word, the crucifixion, and the celebration of the Eucharist. It is almost literally in the light of these images that the rest of the church is viewed. Prefigurement is given in the scenes from the Old Testament. In the deeds of the Word incarnate and in his suffering, as in the crowning with thorns, Christians are offered the *exempla* of the virtuous life. These are then made more immediate in the life of Martin, whose entire story in art and legend follows the pattern of Christ's.

At this point it is useful to pause over some other depictions found in Romanesque and Gothic cathedrals, mixed in with the Old Testament, the mystery of Christ, and the lives of the Virgin and the saints. Such are the representations of human work through the seasons of the year and of the life-span of each individual, and ideal representations of such works of virtue as almsgiving, the visitation of the sick, and the burial of the dead. Included too are images of secular kings and rulers placed at the feet of Christ or of the saints, and on occasion even the sibyl who represents the fates of secular history.

The entire conception of the mystery of Christ began to take on a new perspective with the depiction of the last judgment that adorned the tympanum of the major Gothic cathedrals. In judgment the reign of Christ reaches its fulfillment, and he offers retribution to all for their earthly deeds. It is the Christ of the passion who is judge, for in the carvings his body is adorned with its wounds and the instruments of crucifixion are often included in the scene. Here, even before one enters the church, the work of Christ as creator and redeemer is seen in its fulfillment at the end of time, the justice of God is known to rule all things, and the moral lesson of doing good and avoiding evil is already graphically presented to those who come to worship.

Depictions of Christ Crucified

Emile Mâle compares the art of churches with the twelfth-century works of Vincent of Beauvais on nature and on history, gleaning from the comparison an idea of how nature and human history were viewed in that epoch in the light of Christ.[34] *Speculum*, or mirror, is the word to describe how things are seen in relation to the mind of God. Everything is included in the divine design, whose principal image or mirror is Christ, creator and redeemer. It is according to the image of Christ that all else is interpreted. The labors of the seasons and the work of rulers relate

---

34. See Emile Mâle, *The Gothic Image*, 260. See the work of Vincent of Beauvais, *Speculum quadruplex* (Graz: Akademische Druk-U. Verlaganstalt, 1964/65).

to Christ, because it is in performing the tasks allotted them that people live the virtues of the Christian life and prepare for eternal life. It is in just such a setting that the mediation of Christ's eucharistic sacrifice takes on its full meaning in the society of the time.

After the thirteenth century, the representation of the crucifixion in churches took on more emotional intensity, as did the depiction of the nativity or of scenes from the life of the Savior. This is something that has implications for eucharistic remembrance and devotion. To have a crucifixion painted by Cimabue hanging over the place of celebration invites emotions quite different from those incited by the ornate cross of the resplendent and now triumphant Word, whose light shines even through the instruments of his suffering.

Attention to Christ's poverty and suffering is the kind of devotion that we are wont to associate with Francis of Assisi and with the painter Giotto, but there are historical antecedents, especially in miniature painting dating back to the eleventh century. It is surmised that this devotion to the suffering humanity of Christ found early root especially in England. Frequent reference is made to a miniature from a Book of Gospels, now kept in a New York library. This is known as the Weingarten Crucifixion, because of its origin in an abbey at Weingarten, England, in the second quarter of the eleventh century. Here is how it is described:

> It is a splendid work of great poignancy, but what is so extraordinary about it is a quality which makes one think of late medieval art with the tendency towards a violent expression of the suffering of the Passion . . . [35]

Of this crucifixion miniature, Richard Southern has to say that it is the "high-point of compassionate tenderness for the suffering Christ in pre-Conquest England."[36] He finds its counterpart in the prayers of Anselm of Bec and Canterbury. One ready example to justify this comparison is this excerpt that Anselm included in a collection of prayers that he sent to the Countess Mathilda of Tuscany before his death in 1109:

> Kindest, gentlest, most serene Lord,
> will you not make it up to me for not seeing

---

35. See *Francis Wormwald: Collected Writings*, edited by J. J. G. Alexander, T. J. Brown, and Joan Gibbs, vol. 1, *Studies in Medieval Art from the Sixth to the Twelfth Centuries* (London: Harvey Miller Publishers; New York: Oxford University Press, 1984), 156. See plate 184 of the volume. To show that such representation at that time was not confined to England, this needs to be compared with the crucifixion in the *Hortus deliciarum* of Herrad of Landsberg, on which see Mâle, *The Gothic Image*, 199.

36. R. W. Southern, *The Making of the Middle Ages* (New Haven: Yale University Press, 1953), 237f.

the blessed incorruption of your flesh,
for not having kissed the place of the wounds
where the nails pierced,
for not having sprinkled with tears of joy
the scars that prove the truth of your body?[37]

But to quote such a prayer is to pass already from art representation to practices of devotion, which will be the object of consideration in the next chapter.

EUCHARIST AND THE EVANGELICAL LIFE

The flowering of the evangelical life in the twelfth and thirteenth centuries was primarily a lay movement. It was fostered by an ideal of evangelical poverty and simplicity in the following of Jesus and by a newfound interest in obedience to the gospel, and thus in its preaching. The apostolic ideal prompted numerous men and women to look for a part in preaching the gospel and even in hearing confessions as a way of bringing people to repentance according to the evangelical model of fraternal correction.[38] Because of the power and prosperity of the clergy and monks (communally rich, if not always personally), the movement prompted considerable criticism of priests and bishops, even to the point of questioning their authority. The followers of Peter Valdes, for example, when put to scrutiny defended themselves on the principle that one must obey God in preference to human authority.[39]

The movement had its impact on the celebration and theology of the Eucharist, but in different ways. What needs to be considered is the place of the sacrament both among evangelicals eventually condemned as heretical or schismatic and among groups who maintained submission to Catholic authority and a reverence for the priesthood.

---

37. *The Prayers and Meditations of Saint Anselm with the Proslogion*, translated with an introduction by Sister Benedict Ward (Harmondsworth, Middlesex: Penguin Books, 1986), 97. On the influence of Anselm and Bernard of Clairvaux on devotion to the humanity and suffering of Christ, see Sandro Sticca, "The Literary Genesis of the Latin Passion Play and the *Planctus Mariae:* A New Christocentric and Marian Theology," in *The Medieval Drama*, edited by Sandro Sticca (Albany: State University of New York Press, 1972), 45–46.

38. This is the principal reason why the norms for confession to lay persons became a matter for pastoral and theological directives. See A. Teetaert, *La confession aux laïcs dans l'église latine depuis le VIIIe au XIVe siècle* (Paris: Gabalda, 1926).

39. See Giovanni Gonnet, *Le Confessioni di Fede Valdesi prima della Riforma* (Turin: Editrice Claudiana, 1967). Gonnet takes obedience to God alone as the key principle of Waldensianism, right from the beginning. Accounts of the Waldensian movement are to be found in M. D. Lambert, *Popular Movements from Bogomil to Hus* (London: Edward Arnold Ltd., 1977), 67–91, 151–64; Gordon Leff, *Heresy in the Later Middle Ages* (Manchester, 1967), 448–71.

Schismatic Groups

Unfortunately much of the information about schismatics comes from hostile documentation, not from within the groups themselves. There are professions of faith imposed on various communities, polemical writings, and the records of the Inquisition, these last coming in large part from later centuries. Asserting their own rights to preach and to confess, some of the evangelicals not only challenged hierarchical authority but raised questions about the qualities needed to celebrate the Eucharist properly. These had to do mostly with clerical morality. If a priest was deemed unfit to preach or to minister penance, was he not unfit to consecrate the Eucharist? As in the days of the Donatist heresy, moral adequacy and sacramental power were confused.

It is therefore interesting to see that the confession of the transubstantiation of the bread and wine into the body and blood of Christ was included in the profession of faith imposed on the Albigensians and Cathars by the Fourth Lateran Council, and to see the way that this fitted into its context.[40] It was directly related to the question of priestly power. Those accused of heresy were required to profess belief in the one and universal church, outside of which there is no salvation. Within that church, the sacrifice of Jesus Christ is duly celebrated and in it the bread and wine are transubstantiated into his body and blood. To this two points are added. One is directed against the dualism of spirit and matter among the heretics and states that in this sacrament the faithful share in the reality of Christ, who in the incarnation deigned to share that which is human, including human flesh. The second is the statement that only an ordained priest has the power to confect the sacrament. Hence the challenge to the right of priests to celebrate because of their unworthiness and the claim to spiritual authority even in this matter are joined with the more fundamental dualism. The doctrine of transubstantiation was by no means an isolated issue.

The Eucharist is mentioned also in early action taken against the Waldensians, that is, when the movement was still centered in Lyons and before it moved across the Alps.[41] The followers of the movement actually had opposition to the Cathars and their dualistic beliefs as one of their early primary aims. Nonetheless, the questions that they raised about the celebration of the Eucharist appear to have had to do with the priority of evangelical charism over commissioned authority. At least among their accusers, they were thought to have too closely associated a priest's moral quality, including his commitment to the evangelical

---

40. DS 802.
41. On the Waldensian Eucharist, see K. V. Selge, *Die ersten Waldenser*, vol. 1, *Untersuchung und Darstellung* (Berlin, 1967) 159–63.

life, with his power to celebrate. As a result, the orthodox constantly reaffirmed the power that comes with ordination.

Some concern was also shown with what the Waldensians believed to take place in the Eucharist. Did they really see it as the sacrifice of Christ and the confection of his body and blood, or did they take it as a spiritual eating and drinking, which would have no value were the recipients unworthy? It is more than likely that among the unlearned of this and similar movements the requisite distinctions were not made in the pursuit of their desire for an evangelical propriety in the celebration of the Eucharist. On the other hand, while it can hardly be said that church authorities were globally unconcerned about reform, it is true that they showed a great readiness to reaffirm the power of the priesthood at every turn, just as they reaffirmed the jurisdiction of bishops and pope.

Two practical matters were of interest to schismatic groups. The first was the tendency to deny the chalice to the laity, which they found contrary to the gospel. The second had to do with the Maundy Thursday celebration, though on this issue historical evidence is not very clear. It would appear that on that day the poor of Lyons reenacted the simple supper of the upper room as a sign of their fidelity to Christ and to his way of life. It is described in the fourteenth century in the manual of the Inquisitor Bernard Gui, who claims to use evidence going back to the early days of the movement.[42] He notes that a signing of the bread and cup with a simple sign of the cross was the central rite of this supper.[43]

Gui had two problems with this practice. The first was that gatherings performed this rite even when no ordained priest was present. The second was that in his mind it seemed to be the only day in the year on which they allowed for the celebration of the Eucharist. His description of the ritual may be more or less accurate, but his interpretation is open to question for it is not at all clear that the poor of Lyons saw their supper as a sacramental celebration. In their time, as a meal of and for the poor, held in utter simplicity, it may have had parallels with today's washing of the feet on Maundy Thursday, in which some see a reenactment of the action of Jesus at the supper and others the obedience to his commandment to the disciples to do ever to each other as he had done to them. All in all, evangelicals openly critical of church authority had troubles in keeping the Eucharist alive as a central public symbol, since they were constantly in conflict with hierarchical power and thus found it hard to find the needed institutional legitimization of sacrament and

---

42. Bernard Gui, *Manuel de l'Inquisiteur*, edited and translated into French by G. Mollat (Paris: H. Champion, 1926), 1:42–45.

43. Notable is the fact that there is no idea of a prayer of thanksgiving but only a manual signing with the cross and a breaking of bread. Even those groups looking for reform at that time had no sense of the tradition of *eucharistia*.

symbol. Without institutional legitimization (whatever its ground) it is impossible for a group to maintain symbols as an integral part of its life and tradition.

Orthodox Groups

How the followers of the evangelical movement, such as the followers of Clare or Francis or the Humiliati, who remained in communion with ecclesiastical authority dealt with the issue of the Eucharist provides an interesting contrast. As will be seen more fully in the next chapter, they continually affirmed the power of the priest and reverence for the priest-hood. They also seem to have accepted the practice of communion in only one kind, as well as the rulings that curbed the frequency of com-munion. On their own account, however, they were able to find in the Eucharist a symbol of Christ's poverty that met their aspirations and sanctioned their way of life. While challenge to the power of the clergy seems to have been outside their ken, by various devotions, and even ec-static apparitions, women and men following the simple life developed a place for the sacrament in their lives that left them not entirely depen-dent on priests. Once priestly consecration had given them access to the reserved sacrament, they found creative ways in which to integrate love for Christ thus present into their spiritual lives, as confirmation of their evangelical poverty.

PUBLIC AND POPULAR DEVOTION

A difference between official liturgy and beliefs and the people's prac-tice is often noted, as between the attitudes of the devout or learned and those of the common populace. The latter are then treated under the heading of *popular devotion,* even while sociologists and ethnologists admit the imprecision of this term. Keeping away from arguments about the definition of what constitutes popular devotion, it is possible to con-sider what were some of the more salient eucharistic practices that gave the sacrament its primary role in the life of people and of society.

One thing to be avoided is the idea that all practitioners of a devo-tion believe the same thing about its meaning and efficacy. Indeed, rites that become public symbols often gain this position because within their general compass they allow considerable diversity in belief. However much authorities try by teaching and catechism to assure uniformity of belief, people in their own minds keep their own counsel. It is probably obvious enough that not all who professed faith in the real presence of Christ in the Eucharist and found grace in eucharistic adoration would have explained this presence in the same way. When church authority sanctioned orthodox professions of faith, it endeavored to establish some uniformity of belief, but it would be naive to think that a word such as *transubstantiation* translates in the same way in the minds of all practitioners. Hence this look at common practices is not an attempt to determine what all believed in adopting them. The purpose is rather to see what practices constituted the central role that the Eucharist played in church and society, in forms often different from those of early centuries. The forms will certainly be seen to have theological import in themselves, but one always has to recognize the limitations of such insight over against knowledge of what people actually believed.

Reservation and Processions

Reservation of the Blessed Sacrament for devotional purposes became a common thing in the thirteenth century.[44] In popular practice, there seems to have been some connection between it and the more traditional devotion to relics. At one time, altars used to be placed over the tombs of martyrs. Later it was expected that every altar contain a relic within it. While this was primarily intended to keep the memory of martyrs alive and to benefit from their intercession, in practice people often sought protection and safeguard from relics.[45] The connection between keeping relics and reserving the sacrament of Christ's body is already suggested in the curious ceremony, noted above, of sealing three portions of the sacrament in the stone of the altar.[46] Though this practice provoked unhappy reactions from church authorities and liturgical commentators and was not kept for long, it does show the tendency to equate the sacramental body of Christ with more earthly remains. The same thing emerges in the Holy Week practice of entombing the body of Christ from Good Friday to Easter Sunday, while monks or faithful kept watch by the tomb.[47] In what then became more conventional modes of reservation, beginning with ornate boxes placed on the altar, the altar was the privileged place whereon the most important relic of the body of the Savior was kept.

Processions of the Blessed Sacrament appear to have begun in monasteries. At Canterbury in the time of Lanfranc's episcopacy there was a custom of carrying the sacrament in the Palm Sunday procession, which

---

44. On what follows, see Nathan Mitchell, *Cult and Controversy: The Worship of the Eucharist Outside Mass* (New York: Pueblo Publishing Company, 1982), 163–84.

45. The example of somebody like Paulinus of Nola illustrates that even in early times this reliance on relics was not an affair of the ignorant. Paulinus kept quite a stock of relics and sent them with his letters to his friends. See David N. Power, "On Blessing Things," *Concilium* 178 (1985): 24–39.

46. As noted, *Ordo Romanus* XLII.

47. See the processional of Padua for early indications of this rite: G. Vecchi, *Uffizi dramatici padovani*, Biblioteca dell'Archivum Romanicum, series I, vol. 41 (Florence, 1954).

celebrated Christ's entry into Jerusalem. Lanfranc may well have prescribed for the church and monks of his diocese what was already a practice in the abbey at Bec from which he came.[48] It is likely that the great adversary of Berengar of Tours found this an effective ritual means of combatting heterodox sacramental ideas.

On the other hand, from the eleventh century onwards veneration of the reserved sacrament was closely woven into the Holy Week services commemorating the passion and death of Christ. Kept in reserve after the Holy Thursday Eucharist, both for the emergency of viaticum and for Good Friday communion, it was put in a place where it could be revered by the faithful and was carried there with some solemnity. Then in some local churches after the Good Friday memorial of the passion it was placed in the so-called Easter Sepulchre where people could keep vigil during the hours of Christ's entombment. On the one hand, this use of the sacrament was closely linked to the memorial of Christ's passion, death, and resurrection. On the other, it shifted attention away from the liturgical act of thanksgiving and communion to what was done with the reserved sacrament and eventually even gave way to popular devotions surrounding the death of Christ that no longer attended to the Christ's sacramental presence but found greater outlet in lamentation and in the honor given to effigies of the dead Savior.[49]

The establishment of the feast of Corpus Christi for the universal church in 1264 C.E. was the high-point of devotion to the Blessed Sacrament.[50] The feast had its beginnings in the eucharistic devotion of the Beguines in the city of Liège, where they were thought by church leaders to provide a concrete response to the influence of the Cathars. When the archdeacon of the church, Jacques Pantaleon, was elected pope and took the name of Urban IV, he made it a feast for the universal church. Though its initial divulgation was tardy, in time it took on great importance across continental Europe and in England and became the center of much religious and civic activity.[51] The bull *Transiturus* by which it

---

48. Mitchell, *Cult and Controversy*, 130–31.

49. On the development of the liturgical deposition on Good Friday across Europe from the tenth century onwards and on its eventual replacement in some places by the passion play and popular veneration of the dead Christ, see Solange Corbin, *La déposition liturgique du Christ au Vendredi Saint: Sa place dans l'histoire des rites et du théatre religieux* (Paris: Société d'Editions "Les Belles Lettres," 1960).

50. The origins, development, and devotional and cultural context of this feast have been studied in detail by Miri Rubin, *Corpus Christi: The Eucharist in Late Medieval Culture* (Cambridge and New York: Cambridge University Press, 1991). The dates envisaged by the study are 1150–1500.

51. The part of Thomas Aquinas in composing the office for the feast is much discussed and has probably in the past been exaggerated. See Pierre-Marie Gy, "L'Office du Corpus Christi et S. Thomas d'Aquin: État d'une recherche," *Revue des Sciences Philosophiques et Théologiques* 64 (1980): 491–507; id., "Bulletin de Liturgie," *Revue des Sciences Philosophiques et Théologiques* 69 (1985): 310–19,

was promulgated spoke readily of the heartfelt devotion with which the faithful were expected to recall the passion of Christ in venerating the sacrament.[52] With its accommodation to the affective remembrance of Christ's suffering and its promotion of devotion to his sacramental presence, the celebration of the feast became in the circumstances of the time a central cultural and civic symbol.

Hearing Mass (provided for in diverse ways), giving Mass offerings, and attending public eucharistic devotions were the primary ways in which the Eucharist entered the lives of the general body of the faithful. How such practices were integrated into the devout life remains to be seen before the context of theological reflection is fully grasped.

---

52. For excerpts from the bull, see DS 846–47. The full text is in *Sacrorum conciliorum nova collectio,* edited by J. D. Mansi, 23:1077f.

Chapter 9

HIGH MIDDLE AGES: EUCHARISTIC DEVOTION

To appreciate the role of the Eucharist in the order of the time even further, it is necessary to see the part that it played in Christian spirituality. Four things are here considered, namely, infrequent communion, the devout look and the manner of hearing Mass, the eucharistic devotion of women mystics, and the eucharistic devotion of Francis of Assisi. At the end of the chapter, conclusions will be drawn from these two chapters to show the extent of the cultural realization of eucharistic practice.

INFREQUENT COMMUNION

Over a period of time, looking replaced eating and drinking as the primary means of communion with Christ present in the sacrament.[1] Infrequent reception and intense desire to look upon the host went together. Not only did the general populace receive less often, but the more fervent, whether because of their own reluctance or because of ecclesiastical direction, did not use communion as the normal mode of participating in the eucharistic celebration. Not only were common folk, among poor and prosperous alike, fascinated with looking upon the host and with eucharistic miracles, but holy men and women expressed their love for Christ more and more through ardent gaze upon the species.

It is the almost normative character of infrequent communion that is noteworthy at the turn of the millennium. Difficulty in getting people to

---

1. The standard works are Peter Browe, *Die Verehrung der Eucharistie im Mittelalter* (Rome: Herder, 1933; reprint 1967); Edouard Dumoutet, *Le désir de voir l'hostie et les origines de la dévotion au saint-sacrement* (Paris: Beauchesne, 1926). For more on the link with devotion to the humanity of Christ, see Edouard Dumoutet, *Le Christ selon la chair et la vie liturgique au moyen-âge* (Paris: Beauchesne, 1932), 113–80. There is useful information in Nathan Mitchell, *Cult and Controversy: The Worship of the Eucharist Outside Mass* (New York: Pueblo Publishing Company, 1982), 86–119, 163–86.

receive communion had already arisen to some degree in the fourth and fifth centuries. Pastors such as Ambrose, John Chrysostom, and Caesarius of Arles found it necessary to exhort the faithful to take communion more often, apparently without great response.[2] The extent to which the problem had grown by 1215 is evident in the well-known ruling of the Fourth Lateran Council on annual confession of sins and communion.[3] Since to abstain totally from the sacrament made a person suspect of the Albigensian or some similar heresy, deprivation of Christian burial was the ultimate penalty for failure to do one's paschal duty. On the other hand, however, even church leaders did not seem to insist much on frequent or regular communion.

There is no doubt some truth in the reason for infrequent reception repeated by Thomas Aquinas, namely, a lack of faith and devotion that contrasted with the fervor of early Christian centuries.[4] This does not explain the hesitation to receive on the part of pious people, including mystics. Nor does it explain prescriptions like the one found in the Rule of St. Clare, which lays down confession of sins twelve times a year and communion only seven times.[5] This prescription was not unique. Many lay orders or confraternities in the eleventh and twelfth centuries asked more by way of confession than by way of communion, which in some cases is foreseen only three times a year.[6] One example is found in the *Ancrene Riwle*, which was written in England about 1200 C.E. for a group of pious women living as solitaries close to a church.[7] It takes infrequent communion for granted but devotes entire chapters to each of the subjects of penance and confession.

---

2. See Ambrose, *De Sacramentis* V, 25; John Chrysostom, *Hom. in 1 Tim,* PG 62, 529–30; Caesarius, *Sermo* 73, 2, CCSL 103, 307. Unable to awaken such fervor in his congregation and impeded in his efforts by the rigors of penitential discipline, Caesarius resorted to the expediency of dismissing noncommunicants before communion time, lest their presence disturb the devotion of those approaching the table.

3. Concilium Lateranense IV, DS 812: "Omnis utriusque sexus fidelis, postquam ad annos discretionis pervenerit, omnia sua solus peccata saltem in anno fideliter confiteatur proprio sacerdoti, et iniunctam sibi paenitentiam pro viribus studeat adimplere, suscipiens reverenter ad minus in Pascha Eucharistiae sacramentum, nisi forte de consilio proprii sacerdotis ob aliquam rationabilem causam ad tempus ab eius perceptione duxerit abstinendum: alioquin et vivens ab ingressu ecclesiae arceatur et moriens christiana careat sepultura."

4. *Summa Theologiae* III, q. 80, art. 10, ad 5m.

5. "The Rule of Saint Clare," in *Francis and Clare: The Complete Works*, translation and introduction by Regis J. Armstrong and Ignatius C. Brady (New York: Paulist Press, 1982), 214. The rule even prescribes the appropriate days for communion, namely, Christmas, the Thursday of Holy Week Easter, Pentecost, the feast of the Assumption of Mary, the feast of Saint Francis, and the feast of All Saints. Effectively this entails some long periods of abstinence, as between Christmas and Holy Week, and between All Saints and Christmas.

6. See G. Meerssemann, *Ordo Fraternitatis: Confraternite e pietà dei laici nel medievo*, 3 vols. (Rome: Herder Editrice, 1977).

7. *The Ancrene Riwle*, translated into Modern English by M. B. Salu (Notre Dame: Notre Dame University Press, 1956).

Some have attributed these attitudes to the reverential fear incited by the emphasis on the divinity of Christ that grew out of combat with various christological and trinitarian heresies. This is not found, however, to be a completely adequate explanation, and it seems even less adequate when it is recognized how much fervent devotion to the humanity and suffering of Christ went with infrequent reception. Preoccupation with the need to do penance may have had its influence, though the severity of penitential discipline had already waned. More emphasis had been placed on the purgative character of the actual act of confessing sins and on the prayer that the penitent shared with the confessor. This increased the frequency of confession, however, more than that of communion, so that it may have been the strongly felt need to confess one's sins that kept people away from communion.

The influence of Cathars and other dualists on the general populace and even on the devout is not to be discounted. The Fourth Lateran Council prescribed that annual confession be made to one's own priest. This was not simply a matter of respecting proper jurisdiction but carried the practical guarantee that the penitent would be known to the priest. Confession thus became one of the ways in which pastors could ascertain and control the presence among the people of dualist heresy, with its contempt for the things of the flesh, for the material world, and for the sacraments and priestly orders of the church. Not only was it felt necessary to root out the actually heterodox, but the effect of such persuasions among the mass of the faithful was thought an ever-present danger. There was an odd result from this in that two opposites together served to discourage frequent communion. One was the suspicion of the flesh, and hence of one's sinfulness, which many imbibed from the atmosphere promoted by a dualistic outlook. The other was the combined stress on the confessional practice and the preaching of penance used to combat this heterodoxy of belief or of disposition.[8]

The divisions that the order of the liturgy introduced between priest, clergy, and people or between monks and people also played its part in this development. It was not so much the barrier of the Latin language that set priest and people apart, as it was the mystery of the priest's role that allowed the language barrier to be erected. The mystery and the separation were at their most intense in the stillness that accompanied the celebrant's entry into the canon of the Mass and its silent recitation. The language barrier and the physical barrier between altar and people together kept the faithful away from direct participation in

---

8. See G. Devailly, "L'encadrement paroissial: Rigueur et insuffisance," in *La religion populaire en Languedoc du XIIIe siècle à la moitié du XIVe siècle,* Cahiers de Fanjeaux 11 (Toulouse: Privat, 1976), 392f.

the eucharistic action, leading thus to other forms of benefiting from the sacrament.

HEARING MASS AND THE DEVOUT LOOK

The ways of hearing Mass are best treated by taking three examples. One is from a rule provided for pious women, another from a book composed for use by the laity. In both of these cases special note is taken of the prayers that accompany the elevation of the host. The third example has to do with helping the unlettered to follow the Mass.

The Ancrene Riwle

As mentioned, the *Ancrene Riwle* was written for English solitaries who lived a rule of life in close proximity to a church where they could worship daily. From what is written about their prayer and daily discipline it seems to have been taken for granted that attending Mass would not necessarily mean receiving communion. It is significant that the rule's primary eucharistic concern is with the women's devotion to Christ present in the sacrament rather than with communion. Since Christ was always present in the sacrament, it was possible for them to reverence him there at all times, even when they were not physically present in church.

The rule directed their devotion to Christ on the altar from the moment of rising in the morning:

> When you are quite ready, sprinkle yourself with holy water...
> and turn your thoughts to the Body and precious Blood of God
> on the high altar and fall on your knees towards Him with these
> greetings: Hail, author of our creation! Hail, price of our redemp-
> tion! Hail, viaticum of our journey! Hail, reward of our hope! Hail,
> consolation of our time of waiting! Be thou our joy, who art to be
> our reward; let our glory be in thee throughout all ages for ever.
> O Lord, be always with us, take away the dark night, wash away
> all our sin, give us Thy holy relief. Glory be to thee, O Lord, who
> wast born of a virgin.[9]

The mention of the blood of Christ as well as of the body suggests that the women were asked to attend to a celebration going on in the church rather than to the reserved sacrament. Even if this is so, it is a devotion connected with attention to the mystery of Christ's coming on the altar rather than with communion. The same prayer was prescribed

---

9. *The Ancrene Riwle*, 7.

for use at the elevation during the actual hearing of Mass. It could also be used on the occasions when the women received communion by reciting it before the Confiteor that was said immediately before receiving. In other words, the same faith and devotion could be expressed, whether in turning one's mind to a celebration in progress, or at the elevation of the consecrated host, or in receiving communion, and this last act was less frequent than the previous two.

As a formula that embodies the traditional meaning of the sacrament, the prayer in question is very fitting. It combines acknowledgment of Christ's godhead with acknowledgment of his humanity. In the manner of early prayers and of the theology traced to Irenaeus, it connects redemption with creation. It looks to the sacrament for the forgiveness of sins, and it is intensely eschatological in its hope. The only peculiar thing about it is its frequent use in situations other than that of communion.

In giving the women directives on how to attend Mass, the rule adds other prayers to be said at the elevation, at the kiss of peace, and during the priest's communion. These are of an intensely personal nature and do not shun from using the language of sacramental feeding for the act of looking and reverencing. When the priest raises the host, the women are to pray:

> But what place is there in me into which my God may come, and remain in me, God, who made heaven and earth? Is there, O Lord my God, that in me which may receive thee? Wilt thou come into my heart and inebriate it, and shall I embrace thee, my only good?[10]

The elevation prayers close with a petition that uses the image of feeding:

> Grant we beseech thee, Almighty God, that him whom we see darkly and under a different form, on whom we feed sacramentally on earth, we may see face to face as he is, and that we may be worthy to enjoy him truly and really in heaven through the same Jesus Christ, etc.[11]

Finally, at the kiss of peace and when the priest receives communion, the women are instructed to pray in this manner:

> Forget the world [the rule admonishes], be completely out of the body, and with burning love embrace your Beloved who has come

---

10. Ibid., 13f.
11. Ibid.

down from heaven to your heart's bower, and hold him fast until he has granted you all that you ask.[12]

These prayers and prayer instructions, which are intended to accompany the devout look, in fact use the language of consuming the elements. They express a desire for an eternal union with Christ, or with the Word made flesh. There is certainly the emphasis on the godhead of Christ which Jungmann noted, but it is the fact of the incarnation that makes it possible to combine warm intimacy with holy reverence.

Lay Folks Mass Book

The sacramental value attributed to devout regard is likewise apparent in another work of the time, called the *Lay Folks Mass Book*.[13] This was originally composed in French in the twelfth century and shortly afterwards translated into English. It is really a catechesis on hearing Mass and about the attitudes and prayers appropriate to doing this. It offers a number of prayers for the elevation of the host. Hemmed in by Paters and Aves, the person hearing Mass is to greet the elevated host in this way:

Praised be thou, king, and blessed be thou, king,
of all thy gifts good and thanked be thou, king.
Iesu, all my joying, that for me spilt thy blood and died upon the rood,
Thou givest me grace to sing the song of thy praising.[14]

This prayer embraces the nature of the Eucharist quite fittingly. It offers thanks and praise and remembers the passion in the image of the spilling of Christ's blood upon the cross. It could well be part of a eucharistic prayer and is certainly suited to sacramental communion, even though placed at the elevation.

A shift in piety is more clearly marked in the prayers suggested for recital during the canon and during the period from the Pax to the rinsing of the chalice by the priest. During the canon the people are to unite themselves with the priest in praying for the living and the dead, asking that the offering be a medicine and a means for the forgiveness of sins. Beginning with the Pax, they are to offer prayers for peace and to ask the threefold love of God, self, and neighbor. These prayers conclude with the petition

---

12. Ibid.

13. *The Lay Folks Mass Book, or The Manner of Hearing Mass with Rubrics and Devotions for the People,* with appendix, notes, and glossary by Thomas Frederick Simmons, Early English Text Society, Original Series 71 (London: N. Trübner & Co., 1879).

14. Ibid., 40. The text is rendered here in more contemporary English.

that by this holy sacrament, that now is here present, and by virtue of this Mass, we might have forgiveness of all our guilt and all our misdeeds, and by thy help come to this bliss.[15]

Origin of the Prayers

Edouard Dumoutet was right in observing that there has been a dislodgment of the climax of the Mass from the communion to the elevation, so that desire and looking are more the means of communion than eating and drinking.[16] The examples given above show the association with the elevation of prayers that are more suited to communion. In fact among scholars there is some kind of consensus that the prayers in question were originally intended for use before sacramental communion, and this would explain their content. When communion became less frequent they were transferred to the moment of visual communion at the elevation.

The clue leading to this solution is found in the private prayers to be said by the priest immediately before communion. Of these three survived in the Missal of Pius V. Two were left in the Missal of Paul VI, allowing the priest to choose between them for a single precommunion recitation.[17] They are the kind of prayers that the people were invited to say at the elevation, so it may be surmised that they moved there from their original place before communion. This however does not mean that the people were invited to say prayers that had been originally intended for priests. The prayers in fact originated as a genre in collections of the Carolingian era that served the faithful as much as the clergy.[18] The significant thing therefore is not that the baptized began to recite prayers intended for priests, but that at the elevation they began to recite prayers originally intended to prepare for the act of sacramental communion.

Further understanding of the content of the salutations used, first for communion and then addressed to Christ in the sacrament at the elevation, derives from an early similarity between such prayers and prayers used for the adoration of the cross. For example, one sees a close con-

---

15. Ibid., 54.

16. Dumoutet, *Le Christ selon la chair*, 149f. On the importance of the elevation see also Peter Browe, "Die Elevation in der Messe," *Jahrbuch für Liturgiewissenschaft* 9 (1929): 20–66.

17. For such prayers, see V. Leroquais, "L'Ordo Missae du Sacramentaire d'Amiens," *Ephemerides Liturgicae* 41 (1927): 435–55; Adalbert Ebner, *Quellen und Forschungen zur Geschichte und Kunstgeschichte des Missale Romanum im Mittelalter: Iter Italicum* (Freiburg im Breisgau: Herder, 1896).

18. See Pierre Salmon, *Analecta liturgica: Extraits des manuscrits liturgiques de la Bibliothèque Vaticane: Contribution à l'histoire de la prière chrétienne* (Vatican City: Biblioteca Apostolica Vaticana, 1974). The pertinent material is in "Partie IV, Libelli Precum du VIIIe au XII siècle," 123–94.

nection between these two kinds of prayer in the *Ancrene Riwle*. When on rising in the morning the women are instructed to greet Christ on the altar, they are also exhorted to address this prayer to a crucifix:

We adore thee, O Christ, and we bless thee, because by thy holy cross thou hast redeemed the world. We adore thy cross, O Lord. We commemorate thy glorious passion. Have mercy on us, thou who didst suffer for us. Hail, O holy Cross, worthy tree, whose precious wood bore the ransom of the world . . . O Cross, O victorious Wood . . . Medicine of Christians, save the sound and heal the sick.[19]

Similar salutations of the cross are found in the pre-Carolingian and Carolingian collections that contain salutations to be addressed to Christ before sacramental communion. The salutations of the cross are in fact more numerous.[20] It looks therefore as though salutations of the cross such as that cited above served as models for later development of communion or elevation prayers.[21]

From the thirteenth century onward, the prayers for the elevation took a turn that concentrated less on the mystery of redemption and more on the glory of the Word made flesh. Thus in a thirteenth-century text words almost identical with those in the *Riwle* are followed by these:

Hail Jesus Christ, son of the Virgin Mary,[22] word of the Father, lamb of God, salvation of the world, holy victim, word made flesh, fount of piety.

Hail Jesus Christ, praise of the angels, glory of the saints, vision of peace, wholly God and wholly human, flower and fruit of the Virgin Mother.

Hail Jesus Christ, splendor of the Father, prince of peace, gate of heaven, living bread, parturition of the Virgin, vessel of purity.

Hail Jesus Christ, light of heaven, creator of the world, our joy, bread of angels, delight of our heart, king and spouse of the Virgin Mother.

---

19. *The Ancrene Riwle*, 7f.

20. See André Wilmart, "Prières médiévales pour l'adoration de la croix," and "L'office du crucifix contre l'angoisse," *Ephemerides Liturgicae* 46 (1932): 22–65 and 421–34.

21. See the texts for the elevation from the thirteenth and fourteenth centuries compiled by André Wilmart, "Pour les prières de dévotion," in *Auteurs spirituels et textes dévots du Moyen Âge Latin: Études d'histoire littéraire* (Paris: Bloud et Gay, 1932), 13–25.

22. As is evident in the texts collected by Wilmart, a stronger devotion to Mary develops as something integral to devotion to the sacrament.

Hail Jesus Christ, way most sweet, supreme truth, our reward, fount of charity, sweetness of love, our rest and eternal life. Amen.[23]

In conjunction with devotion to the Word made flesh, prayers to the Virgin Mother came to be associated with eucharistic veneration. Praised for her role in the incarnation, she was also asked to mediate with her Son or to unite the suppliant with him. One manuscript prayer follows up address to Christ with this address to Mary:

Rejoice, O gracious Virgin, for by your word you conceived the Word.

Rejoice, for as a fruitful branch you brought forth the fruit of life.

Rejoice, beautiful rose blossoming forth in the resurrection of Christ.

Rejoice, O mother made glorious in the ascension of Jesus into the heavens.

Rejoice as you flow with delights, for you are now a rose joined to the lily.

Wash us from our vices and join us to your son. Amen.[24]

Guiding the Unlettered

The ways of hearing Mass so far discussed suppose some literacy. The general populace had to be guided in other ways. It was to aid

---

23. This is taken from the Psalter of Lyre, end of the thirteenth century. Wilmart, "Pour les prières de dévotion," 23f. The Latin text reads:

Ave Ihesu Christe, fili virginis Mariae, verbum patris, agnus dei, salus mundi, hostia sacra, verbum caro, fons pietatis.
Ave Ihesu Christe, laus angelorum, gloria sanctorum, visio pacis, deitas integra, verus homo, flos et fructus virginis matris.
Ave Ihesu Christe, splendor patris, princeps pacis, ianua celi, panis vivus, virginis partus, vas puritatis.
Ave Ihesu Christe, lumen celi, principium mundi, gaudium nostrum, panis angelorum, iubilus cordis, rex et sponsus virginis matris.
Ave Ihesu Christe, via dulcis, summa veritas, premium nostrum, fons caritatis, dulcor amoris, requies nostra, vita perennis. Amen.

24. From a Troye manuscript, Wilmart, "Pour les prières de dévotion," 23. The Latin text reads:
Gaude virgo gratiosa Verbum verbo concepisti.
Gaude tellus fructuosa fructum vite protulisti.
Gaude rosa speciosa Xto vernans resurgente.
Gaude mater gloriosa Jhesu celos ascendente.
Gaude fluens deliciis nunc rosa iuncta lilio.
Emunda nos a viciis et tuo iunge filio. Amen.

them in prayer at Mass and in following Mass that in the ninth century Amalar of Metz had composed his allegorical treatise on the rites, much to the chagrin of Florus of Lyons. This became a model thereafter for the typical *Expositio Missae*, some of whose explanations Thomas Aquinas integrated into his treatise on the rite of the Mass, avoiding the excesses of dramatization to which Amalar and others had been prone.[25] What these expositions did, in a time when people had lost touch with the word proclaimed and the prayers offered and when communion was becoming less frequent, was to give them a means of focussing attention and prayer on the passion of Christ while Mass was being celebrated. Persons who could read were assisted by written prayer books, but many relied on what they could see.

Preaching on the Mass given to the people in the thirteenth century assumed that they were there "to hear Mass." Even on those occasions when the people received communion, this act fitted into the pattern of hearing Mass. Adolph Franz documented this preaching in his book on the Mass in northern Europe in the Middle Ages, which he wrote at the beginning of this century. In particular, he explains the graces of hearing Mass that preachers enumerated.[26] One listing may serve as an example.[27] The preacher first says that those who hear Mass go away in some way divinized (*quasi deificus*). This grace is obtained either through receiving communion or through the reverent salutation of Christ present in the species. The second fruit is that they leave more fully united with the mystical body, which is the unity of believers. The third grace obtained is the lessening of one's sins, and the fourth is strength against the devil and temptation to sin. In the fifth place, a person is made happier by hearing Mass, as are also the person's friends. The sixth and final benefit is protection against the misfortunes of life and against sudden death. These six graces are, according to the preacher, symbolized in the six times that the priest turns to the people and greets them with the words "Dominus vobiscum."

Alongside both the vision-aided devotion to the host and the figurative interpretations given to the actions of the priest, Mass-offerings became the principal way in which the laity took part in worship. The strong idea behind much Mass-offering however was not that the faith-

---

25. For an overview, see Angelus Häussling, "Messe: Expositiones Missae," *Dictionnaire de Spiritualité* X [published in 1980], 1083–90. Many such treatises from the eighth to the sixteenth century are included in the listing of liturgical references in Vogel, *Medieval Liturgy*, 12–17.

26. Adolph Franz, *Die Messe im Deutschen Mittelalter* (Freiburg im Breisgau: Herder, 1902), 3–72.

27. Ibid., 37f.

ful offered themselves along with the priest's offering, or along with Christ, but that by the stipendiary system they could obtain the benefits of the sacrifice, for themselves and for the living and the dead. Isidore of Seville in the seventh century had already in his etymologies defined Eucharist as *bona gratia*, to emphasize the grace that the people receive from the Eucharist rather than the liturgical action.[28] Isidore did not particularly associate this grace with the fruits of sacrifice, but that was what happened later.

That even the elevation of the host during the Mass could be interpreted to this purpose is seen in the *Rationale Divinorum Officiorum* composed by William Durand, bishop of Mende, and dated in 1296.[29] Durand gives five reasons for the elevation, which he associates with the consecration as the key moment of the sacrifice. These are: that all who look upon it may pray for what is profitable to salvation; that the superiority of this sacrifice to all other sacrifices may be observed; that it may serve as a sign of the lifting-up of Christ, the true bread; that it may be a sign of the resurrection; that all may reverence Christ who has just descended upon the altar. Associated though it is with other motivations for the elevation, sacrifice here takes pride of place.

Other evidence of the link made between elevation and sacrifice is found in illustrations in missals. In one such illustration, the priest is shown lifting himself up in the form of a small child, which he offers to God who appears above the altar.[30] It is not clear from the picture whether this is God the Father or Christ in glory. It could well be the latter since some liturgical commentaries on the prayers and rite of the canon held that after the consecration where his sacrifice was perfected, Christ took the offerings of priest and people along with his own to the heavenly altar. Some theologians gave a similar meaning to the elevation. Albert the Great took it as a sign of Christ's being lifted up on the cross.[31]

Within the thirteenth century, there was some resistance to the importance given to the elevation. Quite interestingly, there is no mention of it in Thomas's explanation of the visible actions of the priest in celebrating the Eucharist, though he did read signs of the passion in these various gestures.[32] In his revision of the Dominican ordinal during the thirteenth century the master general, Humbert, had directed that the elevation be of short duration and not be prolonged

---

28. Isidore, *Etymologiae* VI, 38: PL 82, 255B.

29. The text is quoted in Stone, *History of the Doctrine of the Eucharist*, 359f.

30. See the plate from a thirteenth-century missal in Dumoutet, *Le Christ selon la chair*, opposite p. 104.

31. *De Sacramento Eucharistiae*, dist. VI, tract. 1, cap. 1, no. 3.

32. *Summa Theologiae* III, q. 83, art. 5.

as some priests were wont to do.[33] It may well be therefore that in his own celebration of the mysteries, Thomas gave little prominence to this action.

The evidence from these texts on hearing Mass thus shows a number of converging and diverging interests. First, the move from eating and drinking the body and blood of Christ to viewing the host is obvious. Second, as is seen in the placement of communion prayers at the elevation, much the same kind of eucharistic purpose was at first attached to this visual symbiosis as was attached to sacramental communion. Third, devotion to the host incorporated a keen devotion to the passion and the cross, which was thus the way in which remembrance of the passion was expressed within eucharistic practice. Fourth, by the thirteenth and fourteenth centuries two factors seemed to change somewhat the nature of communion with Christ in the sacrament. The first factor was the increased attention to the offering of the sacrifice, by the priest and by the people in conjunction with him. The second factor was the heavier accent on adoration of the Word of God made flesh, now glorious in heaven. With this there went an increased devotion to Mary, honored so grandly by her Son and deemed fitting petitioner at his throne for the needs of the faithful.

Since the presence of Christ in the Eucharist was central to all devotion, including that of offering sacrifice, there was certainly much use of miracle stories in instructing the people on the sacrament. This goes back as far as Gregory the Great and Paschasius Radbertus. Sometimes it is taken to mean that people had a very materialistic belief in the real presence, one that could be associated with visions, miraculous cures, and even with the replacement of ordinary food by the body of Christ.[34] However, even in the use of these stories to encourage faith in Christ's presence among the faithful, the aim was faith rather than graphic explanation of the host and its properties. Stressing faith in the reality of Christ's presence in strong imagery was one of the ways of combatting intellectual tendencies that bordered on reducing the Eucharist to the order of mere sign. This could however be used to encourage a very spiritual reverence for Christ's passion and for his eucharistic presence. The picture of a populace chasing after the miraculous would be wrong, whatever exaggerations of piety there certainly were.

---

33. See William R. Bonniwell, *A History of the Dominican Liturgy* (New York: Joseph P. Wagner, Inc., 1944), 126.

34. For the period that she covers, Miri Rubin offers a number of these stories, *Corpus Christi: The Eucharist in Late Medieval Culture* (Cambridge and New York: Cambridge University Press, 1991), 108–29.

WOMEN MYSTICS

How strong physical imagery, and even bodily reaction, could be combined with a very ardent devotion to Christ in his passion stands out most clearly in the lives of women mystics. As is already clear, even devout women following a rule of life were generally not wont, or were not allowed, to practice frequent communion. The intensity of desire and the communion with Christ in his passion and cross expressed in the prayers cited above is at its strongest in the lives of the mystics, even when it is counterbalanced by lively protestations of unworthiness. Edouard Dumoutet has appositely observed that in the high and later Middle Ages holy women did more to advance reverence for the Blessed Sacrament and to counterbalance the trend to infrequent communion than did doctors of theology and church pastors.[35]

Eucharistic apparitions and miracles often figure in the accounts of their lives. Some women were able to live for long periods on no other food than the Eucharist. In some cases, as in that of Catherine of Siena, they received the chalice directly from Christ in ecstasy, even though they could not get it from a priest.[36] In other cases, as with Marie d'Oignies, spiritual guides felt compelled to grant communion more often because of the intense desire of the women and the fear that they could not live without this nourishment. In lauding the desire for communion that consumed Marie d'Oignies and her companions in the beguinage of Liège, Jacques de Vitry describes it in this way:

> Some of these [women] so sought after the odor of this great sacrament that they could not bear to be without it, taking no consolation or rest but languishing even in their bodies, unless their souls could be frequently nourished with the sweetness of that food. Let those faithless heretics blush, who receive the sweetness of this food neither in faith nor in their hearts.[37]

---

35. Dumoutet, *Le Christ selon la chair,* 118–26. He lists the following examples from the thirteenth and fourteenth centuries: Gertrude, Mechtilde, Luitgarde, Angela of Foligno, Margaret of Cortona, Catherine of Siena, Dorothy of Danzig, Emily Brichienni, and Lydwine of Schiedam.

36. On desire for the Eucharist and the ways in which Christ met these desires, see *Catherine of Siena: The Dialogue,* translation and introduction by Suzanne Noffke (New York: Paulist Press, 1980), 293–96.

37. *Acta Sanctorum Junii,* (Paris and Rome, 1867), 5:548. De Vitry's description of life at the beguinage and of Marie's piety is on pp. 547–72. He is adroit enough to use this example against the Cathars, who showed little esteem for the sacrament, just as Jacques Pantaleon, archdeacon of Liège, when he became Urban IV responded to heresies by promulgating the local feast of Corpus Christi, inspired by the Beguines, as a universal feast.

Some writing has used gender studies to gain insight into these phenomena.[38] Such explanation speaks of the place of food in the life of women of that age, and of their feminine capacity for compassion, that shows in their attention to Christ's suffering. Without entering into such theories, one might simply note how lay persons were able in prayer, without benefit of clergy, to fill in the want in eucharistic practice that the times imposed.

Gertrude of Helfta

A more detailed look at the place of eucharistic communion in the life of one saintly woman will serve better than an attempt to speak broadly of this devotion. There is in fact clear testimony of a connection between ecstasy, devotion to Christ's passion, and eucharistic desire in the writing of Gertrude of Helfta. This is to be found in the account of her mystical experience over the space of a year in the second book of a work entitled the *Legatus*, written either in 1289 or 1290.[39]

Gertrude's reluctance to take sacramental communion because of feelings of unworthiness is apparent.[40] This however only seems to have intensified her ardor and desire, and she is eventually led by her revelations to doubt whether she has not wounded the Lord's love in abstaining from reception.

Gertrude's account of this year of favors shows her intimate love for Christ, the Son of God. It is a love inspired by the suffering of his passion and by his invitation to her to unite with him in devotion to it. Her revelations were given to her at different hours of the day, sometimes in choir during the liturgy, sometimes when she was at prayer in the convent chapel, and sometimes even as she moved around the house. Some of them were directly connected with the celebration of Mass or with communion, while some were given her while she was in prayer before the crucifix.

Early in the book, in the form of an address to Christ, Gertrude describes the experience that she had of his intimate presence on those days on which she took communion:

> On those days on which I approached the living nourishment of
> your body and blood, you favored me with your visible presence;

---

38. See Carol W. Bynum, *Holy Feast and Holy Fast: the Religious Significance of Food to Medieval Women* (Berkeley: University of California Press, 1987).

39. Gertrude d'Helfta, *Oeuvres Spirituelles*, vol. 2, *Le Héraut*, introduction, critical text, translation, and notes by Pierre Doyère, Sources Chrétiennes 139 (Paris: Ed. du Cerf, 1968), book 2, 230–306.

40. It seems that at the Benedictine monastery of Helfta there may have been greater opportunity for frequent communion than in many other places. It is thus all the more interesting that Gertrude found this a problem.

even though I did not see you more clearly than when something is seen in the first light of dawn, this benign condescension did not cease to attract my soul to a more familiar union, by which I could see you more clearly and enjoy you more freely.[41]

As she recounts it, one time she asked a friend to pray for her to the crucified Savior, asking that her heart might be transfixed with the arrows of his own love. Subsequent to this request, when she was about to receive communion she felt her body pierced by an arrow of love. Returning to her place in choir after reception, she gazed upon the image of Christ crucified that she had in a book. It seemed to her then that a ray of sun came forth from the wound in his side and filled her with tender love. She recalls that this experience led her to meditate more often on the love that a heart ought to feel for the crucified. In her vocabulary, to exercise such love for Christ is to wash, anoint, and dress his wounds.[42]

On one occasion when Gertrude was due to receive communion, according to established practice, she heard Christ ask her in his thirst for a drink. Having made this request from her, he reversed their positions by offering her a golden chalice whose draught filled her with tears.[43] On the feast of the Nativity of that gracious year she received another favor when the Virgin handed her Christ in the form of a feeble child. To this favor she ascribes an increase in her devotion to the passion.[44]

Towards the end of the account of her revelations during that year, Gertrude narrates two episodes that prompted her to practice more frequent communion. One day, though hearing Mass, she did not go to communion, whether because she felt unwell or she felt unworthy is not clear, even it would seem to herself. In any case, Christ intervened to make her see that the gift of his body and blood expresses God's paternal love, and that she ought not to approach it as though risking divine judgment. She responded to this revelation by uniting herself more closely to the passion, offering her tears, and suffering to make up for her negligence.[45]

The second of the two episodes having to do with the frequency of communion is the last revelation narrated in this book of the *Legatus*.[46] It has to do directly with how often one ought to receive. In her ruminations, Gertrude reflects the common tendency of the time to fear unworthiness in receiving. Reverence and fear of damnation, she

41. Book 2, chap. 2, 233. Translations given here are done directly from the Latin text in the Sources Chrétiennes edition.
42. Book 2, chap. 5, 248–51.
43. Book 2, chap. 9, 276–78.
44. Book 2, chap. 16, 290–92.
45. Book 2, chap. 18, 300–302.
46. Book 2, chap. 19, 304–6.

notes, would seem to prompt eucharistic abstinence.[47] Christ however answered these fears and doubts for her by showing her that her very fear of being unworthy provided her with a motive to receive more often. If she knew her unworthiness this only made God's condescension in giving this gift to sinners clearer. Indeed, Christ's own majesty and glory shine forth in the piety and condescension of his heart in offering himself in sacramental nourishment to sinners.

These meditations of Saint Gertrude reflect all the trends and aspirations of her time. On the one hand, she is prone to think herself unworthy before the Lord. On the other hand, she is consumed by the longing created by a desire for intimate communion. On the one hand, she is deeply reverential of the majesty and glory of Christ, the Son of God ascended into heaven. On the other hand, she is filled with tender compassion for his sufferings. How is it possible to combine vivid remembrance of the passion with the knowledge of Christ's person and of his present glory? How can one satisfy the need for penance and the desire for frequent communion simultaneously? How is it possible to foster reverence for the body and blood of Jesus Christ and still allow ready access to it?

The eucharistic practice and devotion of women such as those of the *Ancrene Riwle*, and especially of the women mystics of these centuries, is a very important part of eucharistic tradition. Power, both ecclesiastical and scholarly, was held by men and the liturgy was controlled by men. While not resisting this power, as the dissident evangelicals did, these women demonstrated an alternative to male power in the influence that they had because of their gifts, their learning, and their communion with Christ. They contributed enormously to the meshing of devotion to Christ's humanity, eucharistic symbolism, and spirituality. Thus they led the way in an integration of eucharistic practice and culture that reached its highest levels of communion with Christ. The deficiency of the age, not theirs, was that the social and ecclesiastical forms of power and the official performance of liturgy were unable to absorb their influence.[48] It is the kind of alternative practice to which attention can be profitably given in our time, in the hopes of better integration.

---

47. Caroline Bynum points out that Gertrude had a strong sense of God as judge, who would justly condemn sinners. In that light, these reflections on frequent communion are all the more interesting. See Carol Walker Bynum, *Jesus as Mother: Studies in the Spirituality of the High Middle Ages* (Berkeley: University of California Press, 1982), 189.

48. See Caroline Walker Bynum, "Women Mystics in the Thirteenth Century: The Case of the Nuns of Helfta," in *Jesus as Mother*, 170–262.

EUCHARIST AND THE SPIRIT
OF FRANCIS OF ASSISI

While the evidence from women's lives is the most abundant, some men were also able to find resources that allowed a relative independence from clergy. Though the Eucharist required priests to consecrate, the reservation of the sacrament in effect gave lay persons a certain freedom in their eucharistic devotion.

Gertrude demonstrated how new forms of eucharistic devotion could become part of the monastic life. The place of the Eucharist in the spirituality of the new forms of evangelical life is found in the life of Saint Francis of Assisi. In effect, he found a way of putting the sacrament at the heart of evangelical aspirations without indulging criticism of the clergy and dissent from their authority. Remaining in communion with the church and its pastors, he was able to bring devotion to the sacrament into a new kind of life, in his own way bypassing its clericalization.

Like the women mentioned, Francis was deeply affected by what he experienced as Christ's condescension and by his devout attention to his sufferings. He gave this piety a distinctive note however by linking it with his aspirations to evangelical poverty. Obedience to Christ's call and the imitation of his poverty fitted into the sacramental devotion that he sponsored among his followers.

Francis placed the humility of Christ at the heart of this piety, so that we see an affinity between his devotion to the cross, his devotion to Christ's infancy, and his devotion to the Eucharist. Combining these three devotions made Christ accessible in popular ways that became the less learned. Developed through the use of vernacular languages, these devotions remained tangential to the official liturgical practice of the time, even though they followed the rhythm of its calendar.

Though the crucifix that he embraced at San Damiano represented Christ's victory over the sleep of death, Francis showed it the tender love of compassion. The example of this compassion with Christ's suffering inspired later more imaginative depictions, such as that of Cimabue. In relating the nativity and the crucifixion, Francis took the incarnation less as a manifestation of the divinity than as a self-emptying and humility on the part of the divine person of the Son. His kind of eucharistic devotion went very well with devotion to the mysteries of Christ's life, especially to his birth in poverty, which Francis displayed to the people on Christmas night in the nativity scene at Greccio. It is to this that he compares the mystery of the Eucharist, wherein:

> ... daily [the Son of God] humbles himself as when he came from
> the royal throne into the womb of the Virgin; daily he comes to us
> in a humble form; daily he comes down from the bosom of the Fa-

ther upon the altar in the hands of the priest. And as he appeared to all the apostles in true flesh, so now he reveals himself to us in the sacred bread.... And in this way the Lord is always with his faithful, as he himself says: Behold I am with you even to the end of the world.[49]

The accent in this text is on Christ's humility, evident not only in the birth from the Virgin but in the sacrament. It singles out the presence in the host, or bread. Christ is more accessible under this species as it were, being visible thus to sight and being always present wherever the host is reserved. Francis wanted his followers to constantly reverence Christ in the sacrament, even as they travelled along the roads and turned at opportune moments to the churches where the sacrament was kept. He found a reason for the institution of the sacrament in the promise given by Christ in Matthew 28:20 to remain always with his followers.

Though he expected the priests among his brethren to live the same poverty as the other friars and was even reluctant at first to allow them books for the divine office, Francis was too much a man of his time not to show great respect for the priesthood. For him, the sacrality of priestly action and the humility of Christ shown in the sacrament went together:

Let all [hu]mankind tremble, the whole world shake, and the heavens exult, when the Christ, the Son of the living God is on the altar in the hands of the priest. O admirable heights and sublime lowliness! O sublime humility! That the Lord of the universe, God and the Son of God, so humbles himself that for our salvation he hides himself under the little form of bread! Look, brothers, at the humility of God and pour out your hearts before him. Humble yourselves, as well, that you may be exalted by him.[50]

As far as liturgy is concerned, the preaching of Francis and his popularization of devotion to the newborn infant and to the crucified Christ show how difficult it was to integrate liturgy and devotion, due largely to the ecclesiastical divisions between clergy, monks, and faithful. In these circumstances, the visual role that the Eucharist had begun to assume as a public symbol in the life of the church fitted the devotion of the followers of Francis and allowed them to keep the sacrament at the center of their practices, despite the disparity between what was prescribed by the liturgy of the official books and the more popular practices that Francis fostered.

These diverse examples of eucharistic piety are good illustrations of how the Eucharist could in the manner of the time become part of

---

49. "The Admonitions," in *Francis and Clare: Complete Works*, 26f.
50. "A Letter to the Entire Order," in *Francis and Clare: Complete Works*, 58.

emerging forms of spirituality, even as frequent communion was on the wane. Indeed it may well be its accommodation to diversity that shows best how the Eucharist was such a powerful and vibrant common symbol. In the new forms of practice, it was a focal point of reverence for all, a symbol of ecclesiastical and even civic unity, and at the same time a support for new forms of the spiritual life.

EUCHARIST, COMMUNITY, SOCIETY

On the basis of what has been presented in these two chapters, it is time to reflect for our own benefit on the place of the Eucharist as public symbol and on the implications of this for an understanding of the sacrament. The capacity to join people together in their individual lives of grace and in their ways of conceiving the public domain belongs to the very nature of the sacramental memorial of Christ's passion, but the variations on this will inevitably be related to the prevailing social and cultural milieu.

By the thirteenth century the *canon of remembrance* was no longer determined by the text of the liturgy. It was no longer constituted in practice by the word of the scriptures, eucharistic prayer, and communion, though these remained on the books. Remembrance was focused on priestly consecration and offering and on the elevation of the host. It was given expression in the personal prayers addressed by either people or priest to Christ, in veneration of his incarnation and remembrance of his passion. In that regard, this was an age when *ritual performance* had virtually changed the canon of remembrance or had substituted new elements for the old in evoking remembrance of Christ and his passion. For some, the *relation to ethics* was that of the symbol's power to uphold or restore order within a remembrance of the justice of Christ. For others, it was the power of the call to the evangelical life found in the symbols of the suffering and poverty of the Word Incarnate. As for the appropriation of *modes of thought,* discussion will have to await the chapter on theology, though it is already clear that concepts of order had a keen part to play in underpinning eucharistic practice.

Given the position of the church in the world of its time, the high Middle Ages was a time in which the social role of eucharistic rites was intensified. This was not done through the kind of participation in prayer and communion that marked the early centuries but through the new rites that centered on looking and on Mass-offering. In recent years there have been several studies done from a sociological and cultural perspective that consider the place of the Eucharist in society from about the beginning of the second millennium to the Reformation. This is quite helpful in allowing us to appreciate its role as a public symbol, as well as letting us see on what score the prevailing order was challenged by dissenters, but it does not get to the heart of faith, belief, and devotion.

The move from sociology to theology attempted or at least suggested by some of these studies is not so easily made. Perhaps this is cultural anthropology's or sociology's inner problem in addressing the values and beliefs that are the foundation of shared life in any community or society. These human sciences are of their nature more successful in observing structures and processes than in discoursing on the deeper human realities that lie beneath them. Knowledge of how Christ, church, society, and history are represented in art and architecture, of the devotions practiced, of the prayers said, or of the preaching offered gives us more insight into how faith or belief in Christ brought people together in all the affairs of life.

The contribution of sociological study and theory is to help us see how the order of the Middle Ages held together and how the Eucharist served that cohesion.[51] To begin with, one can simply note how the great occasions of Easter and Corpus Christi brought people together in worship and festivity. Annual confession and annual communion were related to Easter, tithes or dues were then paid, and it was a time for reconciliations to be effected. Corpus Christi was marked by the procession of the Blessed Sacrament in which all took part according to their respective positions in society, so that it upheld social as well as ecclesiastical order. Parish and town confraternities that served the religious and at times material needs of their members were set up around devotion to Corpus Christi.[52] The mystery plays were later added to the Corpus Christi festivity, calling for greater participation. They were a means of religious instruction, doctrinal and moral, though with time some of the plays took on a secular rather than a religious tone. In the thirteenth century this festive organization was only at its beginning, but as it continued to develop it was in continuity with the kind of eucharistic piety that had already woven its way into society.

Of the Mass liturgy, John Bossy notes that though not all communed regularly at the table, there were other signs of both order and communion. With the papal and then episcopal liturgies serving as the model for parish and monastic liturgies, the clergy and people took their places in church assigned to them by their diversification in order. Within the distinction between clergy, monks, and faithful, officials of the social

---

51. For the period from 1150 to 1500 there is a vast bibliography in Rubin, *Corpus Christi*, not confined to the feast of Corpus Christi though mostly connected with it. For a sociological perspective on the Mass, see John Bossy, "The Mass as a Social Institution 1200–1700," *Past and Present* 100 (1985): 29–61.

52. See for example, Y. Dossat, "Les confrèries du Corpus Christi dans le monde rural pendant la première moitié du XIVe siècle," in *La Religion populaire en Languedoc*, 357–85.

order were allowed their due ritual distinction, much as in earlier times magistrates of the imperial rule were recognized by the pontiff at moments such as the presentation of gifts and the kiss of peace. With the infrequency of communion, the penitential rite, adoring the elevated host, and the kiss of peace were the primary moments of ritual communion that united all in the oneness of Christ's body. Bossy also contends that the emphasis on sacrifice served ecclesial and social unity, since the offering of sacrificial satisfaction helps to overcome divisions. Sacrifice recognizes the need for reparation, whereas rites of the common table may continue while overlooking the need for reconciliation.[53]

In using cultural anthropology to bolster a theological point of view, some turn to the work of Victor Turner, especially to his basic ideas on society and *communitas*.[54] His work seems to allow some way of seeing how different rituals interrelate and how together they serve the ultimate purpose of a transcendental community. In Turner's perspective it is what he terms *communitas* that truly gathers people together in a shared life, with its beliefs, values, and hopes, and the trust in a oneness that goes beyond any ritual power to express, though some rites do come closer than others to doing so. In a society that fosters *communitas* there has to be order and there has to be some freedom from order, or, what he terms in the title of his book, structure and antistructure. An ideal ritual sequence will allow for both, as indeed a well-ordered society both needs members who express antistructure and allows them to have their place. They serve as a symbol to others of a greater reality and of alternative values. For the Middle Ages, Turner thought that the mendicant movement, of which Francis became the primary symbol, represented antistructure and in a privileged way pointed to the *communitas* beyond all structure to which the age aspired in its veneration of Christ.

Unfortunately this theory is sometimes used to foster resistance to contemporary liturgical renewal. Turner himself, rather quaintly, thought that it is impossible to improve on the ritual flow whereby the medieval and then Tridentine Mass order symbolized *communitas* in its Gregorian chant, its use of the Latin language, and in the moment of the elevation.[55] He thought that it was at the elevation that the Mass passed

---

53. In the early church of course this was obviated by excommunication and by a closer scrutiny of members' lives in the call to penance that opened the liturgy. Later on, Calvin and Zwingli were adamant on keeping away the unworthy, but it is asked whether without sacrifice they could find a good way of effecting the reconciliation that could bring sinners back to the eucharistic table.

54. While his ideas are developed in a number of works, what seems to have caught most attention is Victor W. Turner, *The Ritual Process: Structure and Anti-Structure* (London: Routledge & Kegan Paul, 1969).

55. See Victor Turner, "Ritual, Tribal and Catholic," *Worship* 50 (1976): 504–26.

beyond structure to unite all in *communitas,* that is, in a profound unity with Christ in his sacrifice and in his honor of the Father.

It is remarkable how the faith of early eucharistic tradition survived in changed form. The new rites continued to serve communion with Christ and among Christians. They allowed freedom to some believers to pursue more personally characteristic spiritualities within the diversities of one generally common practice, though cruel oppression was used towards those who dissented from public authority. Stress on the real presence did not take away from the memorial character of the Eucharist because devotion so closely wed adoration and remembrance of the sufferings and passion of Christ. The sense of communion among the living and among the living and the dead found in the offering of Mass was strong and its model of satisfaction served sinners and social interests in suggesting a model of justice and reconciliation. It may well have been an age of stronger piety than ours.

The use of cultural and sociological studies however leaves some problems unresolved. More needs to be said about what it means to satisfy a diversity of attitudes within a common and ecclesiastically ordered eucharistic practice. On the one hand, this is good because it allows people to relate simultaneously to the public symbol and to their own personal reality. On the other hand, it carries within itself the seeds of division over against that moment when differences may surface and come into conflict with an ideal of order that looks for both internal and external uniformity. In other words, though the social model may for a time serve all, it has to legitimate diversity in unity if it is not to cause eventual conflict in face of claims to freedom. Hence, one has to go beyond sociological theory to a critique of the ideology that served the dominant order and so the interests of some over others. It is also necessary to critique the ritual moves that vastly changed eucharistic communion, in both expression and reality, by shifting attention from the table and the word to the visual.

The sociological notion of *communitas* is too vague to serve much insight if it is not filled out with whatever are a society's or community's prevailing perceptions of reality. Aspiration to a communion in being never exists except as expressed in rites and symbols, in values and beliefs. When it is possible to clarify what these are, it may actually appear that outward unity camouflages internal disunity. It is not enough to allow some social play to antistructure. What is expressed in symbols and rites and witnesses of antistructure needs to be integrated more fully into the life of the church, as a community that models a transformation of human reality. When its witness serves the prevailing social order too readily, it may find that it has compromised its own most fundamental beliefs and values.

The challenge to what was expressed in the ordering of the Eucharist came with the evangelical movement of the twelfth century and emerged most forcefully in the disparagement of priestly power by the Cathars and Waldensians. The story of these groups is of course compounded by the dualist heresies that did indeed find place within them, but the roots of their ecclesial critique needs better appreciation.

For these dissidents the issue of eucharistic celebration could not be reduced to a question of validly transmitted powers. If its celebration did not appear to be in harmony with the witness of a way of life true to the scandal of the gospel, it was a suspect representation of communion with Christ in his passion. As the Middle Ages progressed, it became more and more clear that the issue of eucharistic celebration surfaced wherever there was a challenge to ecclesiastical authority and its foundation. The challenge was founded in ideas about the nature of Christian community and of its fidelity to the evangelical way of life. While one can rue the nature of some of the opposing ecclesiologies,[56] as well as the attitudes towards the created world that heterodox groups entertained, one must needs admit that the exaltation of priestly mediation was too great in the medieval church. By relying so heavily on the notion of ordered distinction, celebration of the Eucharist failed the very communion in the grace of Christ and at the table of Christ that it was meant to serve. The challenge of the evangelical movement, whether expressed with the simplicity of Francis or with the persistence of Peter Valdes, is ultimately a critique, through praxis, of the church's sustaining concept of order as it influenced participation of the faithful and the manner of eucharistic remembrance.

Cultural integration was in fact brought about less through liturgy than through what liturgically speaking are subsidiary rites and practices. It was achieved at the great expense of the loss of the communion table's centrality to the communion of the faithful in and with Christ. The elevation does not do what the common table does. Holy gaze and common table may both refer to Christ's passion and glory, but they do not signify the same kind of participation in it. While it served the needs of the cultural moment and must always be given attention, the visual is a less appropriate way than access to the table to express eucharistic communion. To give it precedence over eating and drinking is in effect to change the Christian reality, whatever dogma or theology may protest about real presence and about losing nothing of the grace essential to salvation. Reconciliation through priestly mediation and reconciliation through a just sharing at the common table do not effect the same communion in faith, if it is true that reality comes to expression and comes to be through its symbols.

In the light of the foregoing, one final comment is pertinent. Inas-

---

56. More will be said of this in the chapter on the development and place of doctrines.

much as a tradition is a living tradition it has its alternate voices. There are many such to be heard in the times we have considered. There is the voice of the common faithful who could find a vivid expression of the communion of the living and the dead in their Mass-offerings, at a time when it was hard for them to find this in an active participation in the liturgy. There is the voice of the evangelical movement, in all its diversity, with its concern for the part of the baptized in the church, with its adherence to the word of the gospel, and with its witness to the following of Christ.

There is the voice of the women of the *Ancrene Riwle* and of women such as Gertrude and Marie, with their ardent love for the suffering Christ and their personal intimacy with him beyond the existing sacramental boundaries of the time. In their prayer to Christ in the sacrament and on the cross, these women found ways to combine awesome reverence and compassion. Christ allied himself with human suffering, with human desire, and with the feminine through ways that were not possible in formal liturgy.

The history of the medieval Eucharist is not simply the history of its formal liturgies. It includes these alternate voices. Failing to attend to them would cause us to miss much that is pertinent, vital, and challenging in the eucharistic practice of the Middle Ages.

Chapter 10

THOMAS AQUINAS ON THE EUCHARIST: FOCAL POINT OF MEDIEVAL THOUGHT

There was considerable diversity in the eucharistic theology of early scholasticism, but special attention is given here to that of Thomas Aquinas. This is because of the way in which he incorporated the new learning of his time and because of the role that his work has had in recent theological renewal. After careful study of the text, it can be asked how it appears against the background of the practical and cultural developments already described.[1]

THEOLOGICAL BACKGROUND

The devotional and evangelical context of eucharistic development has already been noted. The literature on the Eucharist produced in the centuries immediately preceding Saint Thomas is quite extensive. In its variety it reflects a developing theological methodology,[2] as writers brought

1. Though the focus here is on the *Summa Theologiae* III, qq. 73–83, it should be remembered that this treatment was preceded by other works. There were the systematic reflections of the commentary on the Sentences of Peter Lombard, the disquisition on the Eucharist in his lectures on John (*Super Evangelium S. Ioannis lectura*, rev. ed. [Turin: Marietti, 1953] and his compilation of authorities in the *Catena Aurea* for the four Gospels (*Expositio Continua [Catena Aurea] in quatuor Evangelia*, rev. ed. [Turin: Marietti, 1953]). There is further material in the notes from his lecture commentary on 1 Corinthians published posthumously by friar Reginald (*Expositio in S. Pauli Epistolas*, 8th rev. ed., vol. 2 [Turin: Marietti, 1953]).

2. For studies of this literature, see Joseph R. Geiselmann, *Die Eucharistielehre der Vorscholastik* (Paderborn, 1926); Joseph de Ghellinck, "Eucharistie au XIIe siècle en Occident," *Dictionnaire de Théologie Catholique* V/2, 1233–1302; Ferdinand Holböck, *Der eucharistische*

reason to focus on the mystery professed in faith. It includes: polemical works against novel ideas or heretics; the documents of church councils; sermons; exegetical works on the scriptures; liturgical treatises, commenting on the rites of the Mass; systematic works, inclusive of collections of patristic texts, canonical works, and *summae*.[3] The work of erudition was crowned by the *summa*, whose purpose was to order everything in a comprehensive synthesis.

Presence in Truth and in Mystery

Theological questions on the Eucharist at the time when Thomas was writing centered on the truth of Christ's presence, the manner of his presence, the efficacy of the sacrament, and the representation of the passion. Though Paschasius Radbertus is often remembered for the crudity of the stories used to support belief in the real presence, he had in fact made a useful distinction between mere figural representation, presence in truth (*in veritate*), and presence in mystery (*in mysterio*).[4] The action of breaking the bread or pouring the wine was mere figural representation, pointing to the sufferings and death of Christ in his passion. True presence had to be predicated of the body and blood of Christ and presence in mystery of his passion.

The idea of presence in mystery was common in monastic theology.[5] It refers to the communion of the faithful with Christ in the mystery of his passion, both in the love of God for creatures that this signifies and in the self-offering or movement of the heart of Christ towards God. Paschasius used the metaphor of *passover* to express this communion and the conversion which it entailed on the part of the faithful, leading

---

und der mystische Leib Christi in ihren Beziehungen zueinander nach der Lehre der Frühscholastik (Rome: Officium Libri Catholici, 1941); Henri de Lubac, *Corpus Mysticum: L'eucharistie et l'église au moyen âge: Etude historique*, 2d ed. (Paris: Aubier, 1949); Gary Macy, *The Theologies of the Eucharist in the Early Scholastic Period: A Study of the Salvific Function of the Sacrament according to the Theologians c. 1080–c. 1220* (Oxford: Clarendon Press, 1984). For a general survey of theological literature, indicating the different types of work, see Joseph de Ghellinck, *Le mouvement théologique du XIIe siècle: Sa préparation lointaine, avant et autour de Pierre Lombard, ses rapports avec les initiatives des canonistes, etudes, recherches et documents*, 2d ed. (Brussels: Culture et Civilisation, 1969).

3. This is the listing used by de Ghellinck in the article "Eucharistie," *Dictionnaire de Théologie Catholique* V/2. The different kinds of work that belong to the corpus of Aquinas's writings are put in the context of developing methodologies by Marie-Dominique Chenu, *Toward Understanding Saint Thomas*, translated with authorized corrections and bibliographical additions by A.-M. Landry and D. Hughes (Chicago: Henry Regnery Company, 1964), 79–96.

4. See Paschasius Radbertus, *De corpore et sanguine Domini, cum appendice Epistola ad Fredugardum*, edited by Beda Paulus, Corpus Christianorum, Continuatio Mediaevalis 16 (Turnhout: Brepols, 1969).

5. For a study of mystery in monastic theology in the twelfth century in that this focus still prevails, see Alf Härdelin, "Pâques et rédemption: Etude de théologie monastique du XIIe siècle," *Collectanea Cisterciana* 43 (1981): 3–19.

finally to communion with the Word of God in eternity in the love of the Father.

Though the truth and manner of Christ's presence dominated theological debate and drew most attention in later centuries, we would misapprehend these debates were we not to see them within the framework of the participation in the mystery of the passion that writers took to be the end and purpose of the eucharistic sacrament. Though they devoted much explanation and even acrimony to the question of Christ's presence, the key writers such as Paschasius, Ratramnus, and Lanfranc worked within this horizon. It is an important part of the legacy of monastic theology that this horizon prevailed through the high Middle Ages. It was more obvious in monastic writers such as Baldwin of Forde,[6] but in Thomas Aquinas himself we will see how it was maintained even in scholastic theology.

As the debate over presence in truth was argued in the ninth century, it had to do with the identity of the eucharistic body with the historical body of Jesus Christ, taken from the womb of Mary, done to death in the passion, and raised up by the Father to his right hand. While Paschasius Radbertus had affirmed this identity, the monk Ratramnus, of the same monastery of Corbie, had denied it and affirmed a presence of the body and blood in figure.[7] The question ultimately had to do with the manner of Christ's presence. Paschasius's chief concern was to affirm the fact or truth of the presence. Ratramnus on the other hand was conscious both of the glorified state of Christ's body, which made it different from the way in which he had lived and suffered on earth, and of the figural or sacramental manner of his presence in the sacrament.

In ensuing centuries it was the question of the body's presence in truth rather than of the passion's presence in mystery that generated most debate and discussion. The debate came to its highest point in the Berengarian controversy of the eleventh century.[8] At that time, in countering the dialectic of Berengar between figure and truth Lanfranc of Canterbury used several distinctions of his own.[9] First, he distinguished

---

6. See the edition of his treatise on the sacrament of the altar, *Beaudoin de Forde: Le sacrement de l'autel*, edited by J. Morson, original text and French translation, with an introduction by Jean Leclerq, 2 vols., Sources Chrétiennes 93 and 94 (Paris: Ed. du Cerf, 1963). Writing of the Eucharist as a *sacrifice* in which the mystery of Christ is represented, Baldwin states that to participate in it, it has to be offered, eaten, and imitated (nos. 138 and 224).

7. Ratramnus, *De corpore et sanguine Domini: Texte original et notice bibliographique*, edited by J. N. Bakhuisen van den Brink (Amsterdam: Verhandeligen der koninklijke Nederlandse Akadamie Wetenshappen, 1974). For a discussion of his work, its purpose, and significance, see Jean-Paul Bouhot, *Ratramne de Corbie: Histoire littéraire et controverses doctrinales* (Paris: Etudes Augustiniennes, 1976).

8. See Jean de Montclos, *Lanfranc et Bérengar: La controverse eucharistique du XIe siècle* (Louvain: Spicilegium Sacrum Lovaniense, 1971).

9. See his work *Liber de corpore et sanguine Domini*, PL 150, 407–42.

between what is seen and what is known. In the case of mysteries of faith, it is not the rite in itself or the thing seen that leads to knowledge but rather the authority of the faith as taught by tradition. In explaining Christ's eucharistic presence, he distinguished between primary essence and secondary essence to show first what remained of the bread and second how Christ is present. After the consecration, the primary essence of what is present is the body and blood of Christ. Of the bread and wine only the secondary essence remains, this corresponding to what we would call the appearances.

A parallel distinction is the one between substance and appearances. Where there had been bread and wine, after the consecration there is the substance of Christ's body and blood and only the appearance of bread and wine. There is no suggestion of the use of Aristotelian metaphysics in this distinction. It results rather from a use of dialectic to find an apt vocabulary whereby to uphold the identity between the eucharistic body of Christ and his historical body, without supporting the crude realism of a change in taste, color, form, and appearance. Berengar's adversaries allowed for a consumption in figure or in sacrament of what was present and given in truth or substance, responding thus to what they read as his contention that truth or reality must always follow appearances, even in the Eucharist. It was in the nontechnical sense of Lanfranc's use of the word *substance* that *transubstantiation*, or substantial change, was introduced into eucharistic vocabulary, then to be employed by Lateran IV in its dogmatic proscription of the Albigensians.

In expressing the identity between what is present in the sacrament and the historical body of Christ, not all theologians or spiritual writers wrote the same way. Some continued to stress the identity between the body present in the Eucharist with the historical flesh taken from the Virgin Mary, and of the blood in the Eucharist with the blood that flowed from the cross. Others took more note of the transformation undergone by Christ's body in the resurrection, as well as of the difference between the manner of his presence in heaven and the manner of his presence in the sacrament. The accent on his glorified state made it easier to explain the spiritual quality of the sacramental reality.

In this latter way of speaking, more is asked by way of rising above the evidence of the senses and the workings of the imagination. Where a straightforward identification is affirmed, though the need for faith is accentuated the imagination is more ready to indulge stories of miraculous appearances and bleeding hosts, which either prompt or reward the obedience of faith. A test question of the time had to do with what a mouse would eat were it to get at the species of bread.[10] For those who

---

10. See Artur M. Landgraf, "Die in der Frühscholastik klassische Frage *Quid sumit mus*," *Divus Thomas* 30 (1952): 33–50. Reprinted in Landgraf, *Dogmengeschichte der Frühscholastik*

stressed that a sacramental mode of presence is totally distinct from a material mode, the answer was that it would eat the species of bread without touching the physical reality of the body of Christ, since in the sacrament Christ makes himself present for human beings and not for beasts and animals. Those who clung more to the image of flesh hidden under the appearance of bread, either bewailed the offense done to Christ or postulated a kind of reverse substantial change whereby God's power could avert the desecration.

A question also arose about what was present under each species. To answer the question, writers introduced the idea of concomitance. Though the sign of the bread refers primarily to the body and the sign of the wine to the blood, because of Christ's own essential unity the reality of body, blood, soul, and divinity is present by concomitance under either kind. In effect, this theory minimized the importance of ritual action and signification in favor of the reference to what is contained in the sacrament.

Sign and Sacrament

In the decades preceding Aquinas, the schoolmen refined the definitions of sacrament, principally by working from the cases of baptism and Eucharist to general sacramental theory.

Much of the agenda to be taken up by the summists is already found in the sentences of Anselm of Laon.[11] He treated the Eucharist under seven headings: its institution, the reason for this institution, the nature of the sacramental elements and their symbolism, the reality of the sacrament, the manner of consecrating, the manner of consuming the sacrament, and the nature of spiritual consumption.

It was however the work of Hugo of St. Victor that set the precedent for later authors. In his treatise *De Sacramentis*, he dealt first with the Eucharist's importance and then with its institution.[12] Next he took up some issues pertaining to what happened at the Last Supper, asking whether Christ gave the disciples his mortal or his immortal body and whether communion was given to Judas. He then explained how the paschal lamb was a figure of the presence of Christ in the Eucharist. In

---

III/2 (Regensburg: Pustet, 1955), 207–22. For a somewhat different view on the reasons for this discussion, see Gary Macy, "Of Mice and Manna: Quid Mus Sumit as a Pastoral Question," *Recherches de Théologie Ancienne et Médiévale* 58 (1991): 157–66.

11. For an edition of Anselm's sentences, see F. Pl. Bliemetzrieder, *Anselm von Laon systematische Sentenzen* I. *Beiträge zum Geschichte der Philosophie des Mittelalters*, vol. 18 (Münster, 1919). For his place in the literature, see Geiselmann, *Die Eucharistielehre der Vorscholastik*, 431–41.

12. Hugo of St. Victor, *De Sacramentis*, II, VIII: PL 176, 462–72. English translation by R. J. Deferrari, *On the Sacraments of the Christian Faith* (Cambridge, Mass.: Medieval Academy of America, 1951).

the four following questions he settled issues about the nature of sign, about what is signified, and about the nature of the change of bread and wine into Christ's body and blood. After that, he explained why it is appropriate to use bread and wine and the meaning of the fraction of the host into three parts before communion. From there he went on to say that what happens to the species after consecration, including their corruption in the stomach, does not affect the body of Christ in itself. Finally, he introduced a brief title dealing with the name *Mass* and with the rite of celebration, especially offering.

What he said in the sixth and seventh chapters about sign and signified had an important influence on the work of other scholars. Hugo explained that in the sacrament of the altar there is figure inasmuch as there are the appearances (*species*) of bread and wine, but that the reality (*res*) is that of the body and blood of Christ. He then distinguished three things in the sacrament: the species or appearances of bread and wine, the truth of the body and blood of Christ, and the spiritual grace, which is the invisible and spiritual participation in Jesus Christ, perfected by faith and love in the heart of the communicant.

These distinctions continued to be elaborated by other writers. Thus Peter Comestor defined a sacrament as a sign of a sacred thing by which something unknown is made known.[13] For him, there is a difference between signifying and containing. That which is signified and contained in the Eucharist is the body and blood of Christ, whereas the unity of the church is signified but not contained. He also distinguished between that which is sacrament alone, namely, the species; that which is sacrament and reality, namely, the body and blood; and that which is reality but not sacrament, namely, the mystical flesh of Christ, the church.

Peter Lombard used these same distinctions in his influential treatise, the *Sententiae*.[14] He also tackled the question of how the sacramental change comes about, offering a useful summary of positions taken on this. First there are those who find a change similar to the change of food and drink into the reality of the one who consumes them. Then there are those who say that what was the substance of bread and wine becomes the substance of Christ's body and blood. Third, Peter records the view that the former substance is destroyed in order to give way to the substance of the body and blood. Finally, he mentions the theory of impanation, upholding the coexistence of two substances under the same appearances. Peter finds that the acceptable theory is that of the

---

13. See Raymond Martin, "Pierre le Mangeur *De Sacramentis*," appendix to *Maître Simon et son groupe de Sacramentis: Textes inédits*, edited by Henri Weisweiler (Louvain: Spicilegium Sacrum Lovaniense, 1937), no. 12, 41.

14. *Magistri Petri Lombardi Parisiensis Episcopi Sententiae in IV Libros distinctae*, edited by the Collegium S. Bonaventurae, Book 4 (Rome, 1916), dist. 8–13. Also found in PL 192, 856–68.

change of one substance into another, without change in appearances. This is essentially the position adopted by Thomas Aquinas, for which however he was to offer a more elaborate explanation.

The format of Thomas's treatise on the Eucharist reflects the common division of questions. He treats first of its institution, dedicates the bulk of argument to the questions of sacramental presence and sacramental effects, and adds briefer considerations on the rite or celebration, where the representation of the passion is taken up. It is in his use of Aristotelian philosophy that Aquinas shows his greatest originality. It was this that gave him a philosophical basis whereon he could explain both Christ's presence and the efficacious representation of his passion.

Influences

It is helpful to place the theology of Saint Thomas within a certain worldview. Indications of this are found in his deference to Augustine and in his commentaries on Aristotle and on the pseudo-Dionysius. Much of what he wrote on sacrament can be understood within the dialectic between these perceptions of reality.

Augustine's definitions of sacrament, as well as his definition of sacrifice, clearly have a place.[15] The idea that the word acceding to the element makes a sacrament received further elaboration in the explanation of the composite between matter and form. Augustine's interiority allowed him to see the image of God in Christ reflected in the human soul, so that sacraments actually helped the journey inward to the God who is more intimate to one than one is to oneself. Augustine was fond of figurative explanations of the scriptures on the basis of his idea that all things ultimately participate in the divine and find their inmost reality when this is revealed in the reality of the Word made flesh. In Thomas's schema of the coming forth from and return of all things to God there is an Augustinian influence that allows him to find the journey of the human soul in following that process.

The Neoplatonism of Augustine however was not the same as the Neoplatonism of the pseudo-Dionysius, whose influence is also found in Aquinas.[16] In the latter, there is a strong strain of notions associated with Plotinus and Proclus, with their idea of the One from which all things emanate and to which all return, while it itself remains veiled in obscurity and inaccessible to human thought. Though the pseudo-

---

15. It is the definition from *The City of God*, Book X, VI, that Aquinas quotes in explaining how the death of Christ is a sacrifice. This gives clear priority to the purpose of bonding in communion (*sancta societas*) over making retribution.

16. See the comparison in M. Chenu, *Nature, Man and Society in the Twelfth Century: Essays on New Theological Perspectives in the Latin West*, selected, edited, and translated by J. Taylor and L. K. Little (Chicago: University of Chicago Press, 1979), 49–98.

Dionysius incorporates this into faith in Christ as the Incarnate Word, in the language used of God he prefers the apophatic and in the mediation of the senses through the rites that appeal to them he finds purgation rather than manifestation. The imagery of light plays an important part in the work of the pseudo-Dionysius. The light from the Godhead illumines and attracts, but though source of all light it cannot be known in itself. The world of the sensible is the only way of return to the light, but this is more by way of a manuduction beyond the sensible than of a manifestation that allows for analogous explanation. Sacramental ritual is a purification of sense, allowing for the freedom of the attraction of light to contemplation.

With the assimilation of an Aristotelian outlook into theology, there was more room for attention to the things of sense in themselves rather than only to a superimposed spiritual meaning. Ever since Paschasius, writers had grappled with the relation between what is empirically observed and what is affirmed as truth or reality.[17] Thomas's use of Aristotle made it possible for him to relate sense perception to intellectual insight, while still distinguishing clearly between the twofold operation. In the case of the Eucharist, it also allowed him to distinguish between what is perceived and what is known to be true on the basis of authority rather than reason. On the other hand, he took more account of the intrinsic nature of things in themselves in explaining their role as signs than did Augustinian typology or allegory. The images that things convey allow insight into the things to which they refer. Any figurative sense attributed to sign has to have an adequate basis in the nature of that which serves as sign. Rather than indulge fanciful allegories, Thomas was inclined to stand by those significations that could be clearly related to what belonged to the nature of the reality that served as sign.

In his introduction to the work and thought of Thomas Aquinas, Marie-Dominique Chenu suggests that within the Aristotelian framework Thomas reversed Dionysius.[18] The latter had said that we rise to God by removing every created thing from the notion of the Godhead, and this done we can affirm God as cause. Thomas put the knowledge of God as cause first, then negation, then affirmation by way of eminent attribution. However, the enduring influence of the pseudo-Dionysius constituted a dialectic in Thomas between the analogies drawn from knowledge derived from the relation of effect to cause on the one hand, and the movement of return to the One beyond such knowledge on the other. As far as sacramental theology is concerned, this meant that

---

17. See the interesting essay "The Eucharist and Nature," in Brian Stock, *The Implications of Literacy: Written Language and Models of Interpretation in the Eleventh and Twelfth Centuries* (Princeton: Princeton University Press, 1983), 241–325.

18. Chenu, *Toward Understanding Saint Thomas*, 229.

the need to purge sense and sense-image is as great as the possibility of knowing the things manifested through the perceptible signs and words. As will be seen, it is above all in his explanation of Christ's sacramental presence that one finds the appeal to rise above all sense perception and analogy in order to have access to the Christ present.

All in all, Thomas had three perspectives to coordinate. These were the grasp of the incarnation in its relation to the life of the spirit taken from Augustine, the contemplative pursuit of the One drawn from the pseudo-Dionysius, and the recognition of the form of things in the world that offered a way of dealing with signification and the relation of effects to cause, brought in from Aristotle. It was his way of bringing these together that give a distinctive and fresh approach to sacramental and eucharistic theology.

With these preliminaries, it is possible to present his thought on the place of the Eucharist in the economy of grace, on the presence of Christ in the Eucharist, and on the representation of the passion that he relates to his theories of causality.

THE EUCHARIST IN THE ECONOMY[19]

For all the subtlety of the treatment of the sacrament of the Eucharist in the *Summa Theologiae*, it is impossible to overlook the references to practices and assumptions of the age in which it was written. Thomas took some ritual developments for granted, for example, the silent recitation of the canon and the separation of the prefatory thanksgiving from the rest of the great prayer.[20] He was familiar with the offering of Mass for the living and the dead.[21] He explained the relative infrequency of communion by appealing to the difference in zeal and faith between his own time and that of the early church.[22] He knew of the practice of giving communion in one kind only[23] and of the use of spiritual communion as distinct from sacramental.[24] One of his questions has to do with miraculous apparitions of Christ in the host,[25] and he looked for reasons why other materials may not be substituted for wheaten bread and grape wine.[26] Finally, in explaining the prayers and actions of the priest cele-

---

19. *Summa Theologiae* III, q. 73.

20. Q. 83, art. 4.

21. Q. 79, art. 7.

22. Q. 76, art. 8.

23. Q. 74, art. 5.

24. Q. 74, art. 4.

25. Q. 76, art. 10.

26. Q. 74, art. 3. He thinks that only wheaten bread has truly nutritive qualities and that bread made from other substances is at best a substitute for it. He is optimistic about the possibility of importing grape wine into regions where vines do not grow.

brating, he drew to a moderate extent on expositions on the Mass and on the canon that guided the catechesis on the Mass for the people.[27] Liturgical reform was not his agenda. His interest was rather in a good explanation of the sacrament as known to his times, settling disputed theological questions, and explaining how all aspects of the sacrament and its celebration held together in an organic intelligibility.

Though his discussion of Christ's presence is lengthy, it is important to note that all the questions on the sacrament are placed within the context of the eucharistic action. This appears from the way in which the opening and closing questions frame the treatise. The opening question, q. 73, places the sacrament within Thomas's vision of the economy of grace. The treatment concludes with q. 83, in which he explains the rite of celebration, in which "the entire mystery of our redemption is contained."[28] All other matters are held together through this dual reference to the economy and to the rite. As with other matters, in writing of the Eucharist Thomas follows the *ordo disciplinae*, that is, he takes an ordered approach in explaining the truths of the faith, setting each element within a picture of the whole.

The Reasons for This Sacrament

In q. 73, Aquinas shows how the mystery of the Eucharist as the sacrament of Christ and of the church has its figures or types in the Old Testament[29] and how it points forward to future glory.[30] Thus as a sacrament of the church it is placed within the economy of salvation. For the individual person, it is nourishment of the spiritual life,[31] communion in Christ's passion,[32] and communion in the sacrament and grace of the unity of the church, Christ's mystical body.[33]

Art. 5 offers three reasons for which Christ instituted the Eucharist. The first is that in departing from his disciples *in propria specie*, he wanted to remain with the church *in sacramentali specie*. In his *Commentary on the Sentences* Thomas had followed those who found in the Eucharist the fulfilment of the promise that Christ made to remain always in his church, as recorded in Matthew 28:20.[34] In the *Summa* that text is not

---

27. Q. 83, art. 4 and 5.

28. See q. 83, art. 4, c.: "in hoc sacramento totum mysterium nostrae salutis comprehenditur."

29. Q. 73, art. 6.

30. Q. 73, art. 4.

31. Q. 73, art. 1.

32. Q. 73, art. 4.

33. Q. 73, art. 3.

34. *Scriptum Super Sententiis* IV, Dist. VIII, q. 1, art. 3, ad 3m. This text was also used in the bull *Transiturus*, in reference to a corporeal presence: "Adscensurus enim in caelum dixit Apostolis *et eorum sequacibus*: Ecce ego vobiscum sum omnbius diebus usque ad con-

mentioned and there seems to be more emphasis on the difference between the ordinary mode of presence and the sacramental. The issue is not simply that Christ remains even though he has taken his place in heaven, but that it is better for the church that he remains in this distinctive sacramental way. Contact with Christ in this sacrament through faith includes no resemblance to usual corporeal presence, nothing that would make Christ perceptible to the senses in his own bodily form. Both the glorified nature of his body in heaven and the sacramental mode of presence exclude this comparison. Those who used Matthew 28:20 did not emphasize the difference between the earthly presence and the sacramental presence as much as Thomas, which is probably the reason why the text is omitted from the *Summa*.[35] This sets the stage for his subsequent elaborations on the presence of Christ in the Eucharist and shows how central this question is to his eucharistic thought.

The second reason given for the institution in q. 73, art. 5 is that since salvation is through faith in the passion of Christ, a sacramental commemoration of this is necessary. Saving faith is in the passion, and faith and grace come from the passion. Hence the need for an effective commemoration. He fills this out later in the treatise by incorporating his general sacramental principle that the passion is efficacious for redemption through the instrumentality of the sacraments.

The third reason that he gives has a more subjective note to it. He explains that on the eve of his passion Christ desired to leave a kind of testament to his disciples, commending to them a way of remembering him that would inspire friendship and even affection. In giving this reason, Thomas is in line with the thought found in the writings on the Eucharist of such as William of Thierry[36] and Peter the Venerable,[37] for whom there is a strong affective note to memory. This third reason is complementary to the need for a sacrament of commemoration, rather than distinct from it. In postulating the need for a sacrament in which faith may be exercised Thomas is more concerned with an objective order of reality, whereas in writing of memory he refers more to the subjective disposition of participants in the sacrament. This emphasis on the subjective was stronger in the *Commentary on the Sentences*, where he had more to say about the rite of celebration and the memories

---

summationem saeculi [Mat 28:20], benigna ipsos promissione confortans, quod remaneret et esset cum eis etiam *praesentia corporali*" (DS 846; italics added).

35. On this point see the article by Pierre-Marie Gy, "La relation au Christ dans l'Eucharistie selon S. Bonaventure et S. Thomas d'Aquin," in *Sacrements de Jésus Christ*, edited by J. Doré (Paris: Desclée, 1983), 82–86.

36. *De corpore et sanguine Domini*, PL 180, 346–66.

37. Peter the Venerable, *Contra Petrobrusianos hereticos*, edited by James Fearns, Corpus Christianorum, Continuatio Mediaevalis 10 (Turnhout: Brepols, 1967).

that it elicits.[38] In the *Summa* this remains only in the discussion of the signs of the cross made by the priest in the course of celebration. These serve to evoke memories of the cross of Christ's suffering,[39] whereas the essence of the sacramental representation is to be found in the matter and form of Christ's words over the bread and wine. It is in this that he finds the sacramental efficacy of the passion's representation, an efficacy related to the way in which the death is signified in the twofold and separate consecrations.[40]

To this way of setting the Eucharist within the economy of redemption, and to the subsequent explanations of distinct points of doctrine, some things already established in part III of the *Summa* are pertinent. In q. 8, Thomas had written of the grace of Christ's headship, which makes of Christ and his members as though one person, "quasi una persona."[41] In q. 22 he established the mediation of Christ's priesthood, now operative through the church. Within this perspective, he located the sacraments within the cult of the church, which is a sharing in the cult rendered by Christ himself.[42] In q. 48 he explained the efficacy of Christ's passion by way of merit, satisfaction, sacrifice, redemption, and efficient causality. In explaining these categories he heavily emphasized how through love the requirements of mercy and justice are both satisfied and how this reflects the entire order of redemption. These points of doctrine are important to what he writes of the Eucharist and serve as background to its understanding.

The centrality of sign to the definition of sacrament which Aquinas established in his opening question on sacraments continues to play its part, both in explaining Christ's presence and in explaining the causal efficacy of representing his passion.[43]

THE PRESENCE OF CHRIST
IN THE EUCHARIST

As q. 83 makes clear, the sacrament is the commemorative and ritual celebration of the mystery of redemption, and hence an act of Christ in the church, whereby the faithful share in this mystery. Aquinas certainly responded to the interests of his time in giving so much thought to the manner of Christ's presence, but beyond that it is clear that in his vision

---

38. *Scriptum Super Sententiis:* "Quarta ratio sumitur ex ritu quo frequentandum est hoc sacramentum, ut ultimo traditum magis memoriae teneretur."

39. Q. 83, art. 5.

40. Q.83, art. 1, c.

41. Q. 8, art. 2, c.

42. Q. 63, on the sacramental character of order and baptism.

43. See Q. 60, art. 1, c.

the presence of Christ himself, rather than only of his saving power, was important to the efficacy of the sacrament both as communion and as representation.

Aquinas stresses that the Christ present in the sacramental commemoration of the passion is the whole Christ, body and blood, soul and divinity.[44] Following up on the need to keep sign and signified in relation to each other, he explains what is present under either kind by way of signification and what by way of concomitance.[45] This notion of concomitance, however, is not meant to draw away from the importance of signification.

Two things need to be noted about the relation between reality and signified. First, in affirming the truth of Christ's presence and in probing its manner, one does so by way of reference back to Jesus' words at the supper and what they signify. The logic of the words has to be respected by anyone who would better understand the doctrine that they convey.[46] The starting-point for explanation is the words of Christ and what they affirm. Though the appearances are still those of bread and wine, the words themselves show that the body and blood are present in truth and are given in communion, that they are not just figuratively represented by the gift of bread and wine. The words show furthermore that this gift of the body and blood draws the communicant into the salvific reality of the passion to which Christ delivered himself and which is sacramentally commemorated.

Second, what the communion rites signify shows that the Eucharist is the sacrament of unity, uniting the faithful with Christ and uniting the church as one in charity. In other terms, the Word Incarnate is present and united with the church, as though one person, through the mediation of the signs of his passion and of the signs of communion in one reality.

It is of the highest importance that Thomas gives primacy in his considerations of the Eucharist to the presence of the person of the Word, who became incarnate and suffered for humankind. He is present in the sacrament in the humanity in which he suffered and died for the redemption of the world and in which he is now glorified, having opened the way to eternal life for one and all. The end of the sacrament is communion with this Christ, in faith in the saving power of his passion and in a communion of love, which prepares the way for a communion in glory.

---

44. Q.76, art. 1.

45. Q. 76, arts. 1 and 2.

46. See Karl Rahner, "Word and Eucharist," *Theological Investigations* (New York: Crossroad, 1982), 4:253–86.

The Mode of Christ's Presence

Once the presence has been posited, in due regard for its link with the sacramental signs, the issue arises of the mode or manner of this presence. From authorities to which he owed his doctrine, Thomas took the notion that presence in truth meant presence *per modum substantiae,* or substantial presence. At the same time it is noteworthy that from the outset of his explanation Aquinas saw this as an essentially spiritual presence.[47]

In the *Commentary on the Sentences,* he followed the order of Peter Lombard's *Sentences* and started by explaining this presence. Only then did he move on to explaining substantial change. In the *Summa,* he reverses the order of treatment. This is apparently because he thought that to understand the presence it was necessary to understand how Christ becomes present. If not simply faith but intelligibility is to be sought, what is affirmed and explained about the change is essential to the grasp of the manner of the presence. To this purpose, he set out to use the Aristotelian thought that served to give sacred doctrine or theology a credible place in the universe of science and to show that faith can be enlightened by reason.

The starting point of the analogy that he employed is the distinction between substance and accident in composite beings. The distinction starts with the logic of predication that allows us on the one hand to point to appearances to define qualities and on the other hand through a reasoning process to define a thing by its core reality. What a thing is, is not identified with what moves the senses. Though it is generally known through sense perception, a reasoning process is necessary to come to this knowledge. Substance describes the core reality known to intellect, accidents whatever touches the senses. Aquinas uses this analogy to explain how the body and blood of Christ are known to faith and are indeed the reality present, though sense perception points to bread and wine

His treatment of this question is a good example of the diachronic nature of analogical predication. What is offered is not so much a synthesis or a single core concept as a play between negation and affirmation. In the invitation that Thomas extends to the reader to understand something of Christ's presence, he insists on the appeal to the intellect, not the imagination.[48] In using analogies to explain sacrament, one is not dealing with physical reality or with physical change. The concern is to see how things that happen in the physical order and that have them-

---

47. See q. 75, art. 1. ad 1m and ad 4m: "idest invisibiliter, modo et virtute spiritus."

48. He makes this clear in introducing the notion of substance, affirming that this is the "proprium obiectum" of the intellect. See q. 75, art. 5, ad 2m.

selves a proportionate intelligibility for the human mind may serve as comparisons whereby to proceed to insight into something that is true in a totally different order of things.

Though his focus is on what is represented in sacrament, in an earlier question Aquinas had made it clear that the sacramental has a reality beyond what is explained through sign-activity as such.[49] What happens, though known through signs, cannot be wholly accounted for through their operation as signs. What takes place in sacramental action is in the realm of being, not only in the realm of mind and understanding, where signs by their nature work. One can learn through signs of what takes place, but without reducing the reality to the intelligibility expressed through signs.

Negation and Affirmation

In the articles of the *Summa* on Christ's presence, the way of negation is foundational to the reasoning process that leads to understanding. Thomas eliminates various possibilities that would contradict the truth of Christ's presence. On condition that this dialectic is engaged, the idea of substantial change can be adopted, for it is comprehended only on the grounds of the negative affirmation that Christ does not become present in any of the ways mentioned. These include movement from place to place, taking presence in a place alongside bread and wine, coming to be present through a process of corruption and generation. Of all of these processes, the one that presents the closest similarity to sacramental change is that of corruption and generation, because in this case one substance replaces another within the same quantitative dimensions. Here too however the process of change must be excluded with the affirmation that sacramental change is total conversion, touching the whole being of bread and wine, without any intervening process and without any natural comparison that would allow it to be imagined.[50]

Through the negation of any natural process of becoming and the affirmation of total substantial change, one comes to the idea of presence *per modum substantiae* as an intellectual, not imaginative, representation. The first positive insight from this analogy comes from an appreciation of grammatical use. One predicates the body of Christ of what is seen, touched, tasted, weighed, in the way in which one predicates substance of any sense mass,[51] except that here in virtue of words,

---

49. Q. 62, for his basic treatment of sacramental causality.

50. See q. 75, art. 4, c.: "...tota substantia panis convertitur in totam substantiam corporis Christi, et tota substantia vini in totam substantiam sanguinis Christi."

51. See q. 76, arts. 1–3.

not appearances, the sense mass represents a reality distinct from the appearances.

Given this important notation, substantial change means that the rules of grammar must be applied to the sacrament in accordance with the usual modes of predication. Change in the secondary aspects of appearances does not nullify the predication. Of a large or a small loaf, of a whole loaf or part of a loaf, of a slice or of a crumb, one says that it is bread. In the sacrament, the substance is that of Christ's body, not that of bread. Given the difference, the rules of predication are the same. Of anything that retains the external qualities of bread one says that it is the body of Christ.

The next step comes in distinguishing substance from appearances and qualities, or what Aquinas refers to as accidents. The substantial form and the accidental form of a thing are not identical. One already notes this in being able to predicate breadliness of any portion of bread or of breads of different textures. Though connected, the intelligible reality and the appearances are not identifiable one with the other. Having learned to differentiate between substance and accident, of the sacrament one can then predicate a substance that is not at all displayed through its own accidents but that is known to be present through those of another substance. Accidental predications still have to do with the weight, taste, color, etc., of bread and wine. Once the sacramental action has been performed, one predicates of what appears that which is is substantially, namely, the body and blood of Christ, not bread and wine. The predication follows the truth of the words spoken, not that of the appearances of things to the senses.

Though the language of substance and accident is that of Aristotle, in all of this there seems to be not a little of Dionysian negation in regard to the role of the senses. To come to the truth and to communion with Christ in the sacrament, one has to rise above what the senses communicate and what imagination can represent. The truth of the predication and the response of faith lie totally in holding the negations in balance. Christ's presence is in no way a localized presence, a hidden presence, a presence beneath or in the accidents of any physical being. As Aquinas says, it is a spiritual presence, one that defies imagination, one inconceivable to reason alone, one not to be found at all in the order of nature. It appeals wholly to the intellect, whether this be to the affirmation of faith or some degree of intelligibility. Yet it is the true presence of Christ, not just a communion in mind or in spirit, for it is the person of the Word Incarnate, the whole Christ, who is present and gives himself in communion.

This stress on the personal presence of Christ explains why Christian life is totally ordained to the Eucharist. Baptism into Christ leads to communion with him in the Eucharist, so that even a baptized infant is oriented in this direction.[52] Every act of charity is linked with a desire for the Eucharist.[53] When Thomas writes of the desire, or *votum*, for the sacrament, this is not a purely mechanical notion. It expresses the orientation to communion with Christ that is a necessary part of charity, that toward which charity carries one, even if unknown to the one who elicits such an act. Furthermore, communion with Christ in the Eucharist is for those on the way. Of its very nature it is eschatological, that is, it ordains one to the fuller communion with him in glory.[54]

To see its pertinence to sacramental devotion, one might fruitfully compare this explanation of sacramental presence with what Thomas wrote in the IIa IIae of contemplation and of voluntary poverty, where the same need to rise above the senses and the direct perceptions of reason in order to commune with God as revealed in Christ is affirmed. In the IIa IIae, q. 180, art. 4, ad 3m, he wrote of the six degrees or steps through which one ascends through creatures to the contemplation of God. These represent a very similar process of negation until one reaches perception without imagination or ratiocination.[55] In q. 186, art. 3, writing on voluntary poverty, he finds in it the foundation of perfection inasmuch as it draws humans completely away from the attraction of the mundane or earthly, even of what is in itself good. Though God approaches human beings through the things of the senses, the final communion with God is an act that goes beyond them. Though it is a gift, it has to be prepared for by the way of negation. In a similar way, for Christ to present himself to the faithful through the sacrament of bread and wine is to invite them to a way of negation. On this road, through what faith comes to affirm in denying, the person is prepared for the gift of contemplation that is no longer contained within the sacramental act.

The way of negation and affirmation also requires that we refrain from imagining what happens to Christ in becoming present. Becoming present in the sacrament in no way affects change in his being. What is done to the bread or to the wine is not done to Christ. If it is subject to physical action, he is not. Though he is present whole and entire and therefore *with* his own "quantitas dimensiva," he is not present *through* his quantity or in a quantitative way.[56] Taking up the litmus test of scholastic theology, "quid sumit mus," or what is eaten by a mouse that gets at the sacramental bread, he says that the mouse does indeed eat the body of Christ, but only *per accidens*. That is, it eats the accidents

---

52. See q. 73, art. 3.

53. Q. 75, art. 1.

54. Q. 73, art. 5.

55. On contemplation and the relation to it of reasoning, see IIa IIae, q. 180, art. 1.

56. See q. 76, art. 5, c.: Christ is not present "secundum proprium modum quantitatis dimensivae, sed magis secundum modum substantiae."

through which the body is present but does not get at the substance that is sacramentally present.[57] It is only humans that attain in the sacrament to the substance, whether they receive well or badly, once they act with the knowledge of faith. Indeed, were a person to eat a host that is consecrated without knowing this, the person would consume the accidents under which Christ offers himself but would not receive what is offered, or in other words would have no contact with the reality itself.

The Christ Who Is Present

Asking what reality eucharistic presence implies in Christ himself in his glory, Thomas answers that it is a *habitudo*, or relation, to the sacramental species.[58] He does not elaborate on this, but it is a profound insight that can perhaps be better grasped by seeing that the sacramental relation to the church is like the transcendentals are to being. One cannot think being without thinking one, true, and good. Similarly, one cannot think of Christ in glory without taking account of his relation to his sacramental being in the church. This habitual relation to the eucharistic sacrament belongs to his being in glory until the consummation of the economy of redemption. It is now true of him as he is seated at God's right hand that he communicates himself in sacrament to his church, associating it thus with himself in his communion with the Father. In the eternity of glory, this becomes a relationship in a more perfect communion to all the blessed. It is then without the need of sacrament, but it is still a communion with the Father through the Word in the glory of his perfected humanity. Common to Eucharist and to glory is the mediation of communion with the Word through the humanity in which redemption was won. Different is the form of mediation, one being through a sacramental mediation, the other through a vision of the Word Incarnate in glory. The mode of Christ's being in the sacrament is such that it invites the faithful to strain in faith after the form of communion in glory, of which it is the foretaste and hope.

In writing of the grace of the sacrament, Thomas draws on the images of eating and drinking to go beyond them to the manner of communion with Christ.[59] They nourish life, repair failed strength, and in the case of the wine offer sweetness and inebriation. However, to be nourished and strengthened by Christ, to enjoy the sweetness of his presence, one cannot allow oneself to be tied to anything localized or carnal. At the same time, the words spoken over the elements are words said in remembrance of Christ's passion. They recall the immensity of

---

57. Q. 80, art. 3, ad 3m.
58. Q. 76, art. 6, c. and ad 3m.
59. See q. 79.

his pain and the immensity of his love, which in sacrifice opened access
to God and to communion with God, through the communion in the
body of Christ.[60] Though Aquinas explains the effects especially in relation to the individual person, from the signification of the one bread
made from many grains of wheat and of the wine made from many
grapes he relates communion with Christ to the unity and charity of
the church.[61] To be one with the mystical body that includes the blessed
and the church on earth is the final end towards which we journey. Life
in this body is nourished by the sacrament and reaches its climax in
contemplation.

REPRESENTATION OF CHRIST'S PASSION

Representation and Immolation

Though Lanfranc and Baldwin explained the presence of Christ in the
language of substance, they continued in the monastic tradition to write
of the presence of the passion as its presence in mystery. Thus they juxtaposed a more patristic style of expression with one that anticipated the
scholastic usage. In Thomas Aquinas there is more uniformity in the language used for both aspects of the Eucharist. In the case of both presence
and reference to the passion, he used many expressions that are taken
from patristic writers, just as he accounted for the traditional types of
the Eucharist, such as the paschal lamb and the manna. Going beyond
that language, however, he found the means to explain both presence
and efficacious commemoration in the philosophy of Aristotle. Having
explained the mode of Christ's presence by appealing to the distinction
between substance and accident, he employed the Aristotelian notion
of efficient causality to explain the presence of the passion.[62]

In q. 48, when he explained the ways in which Christ redeemed
humanity through his passion, Thomas had ended the question by sub-
suming the explanations of redemption through merit, satisfaction, and
sacrifice under the category of efficacious causality. The signification and
exemplarity of Christ's passion as spelled out in these ways belong to its
efficacy, and they in turn are best understood for Aquinas when subsumed under the category of efficacious causality. What is signified and
exemplified on the one hand and what is caused on the other concur,
and in order to be part of our human reality, what is caused must be
signified and must have its human agent who works as one with the
divine intention.

---

60. Compare Q. 48, art. 2 and 3.
61. See q. 79, art. 1, c.
62. Q. 62, art. 5.

Aquinas follows a similar line of thought in writing of the Eucharist, though the procedure is less formal and less consistent. In q. 83, the category of sacrifice is effectively subsumed into the causal explanation of the relation between the passion and the sacrament, with proper attention to how this sacrifice is signified or represented.

Q. 83 treats of the rite of celebration. In the first article, Thomas asks whether Christ is immolated in the celebration.[63] He responds that in the Eucharist the passion, or immolation, is represented. Thomas's idea of representation as such seems to be that of an image. He compares the presence of Christ's passion to the presence of the one portrayed in a portrait.[64] While he uses the same comparison elsewhere to refer to Christ's own personal presence, the context there shows clearly that it is a loose image to refer to the sign aspect of substantial presence.[65] In q. 83, art. 1, it is the notion of figural representation that comes to the fore. Thomas says that the representations of the Old Law and the eucharistic representation are alike in that they are both figures of Christ's immolation. The Eucharist, however, differs from the Old Testament types not in its capacity to represent but in that it is efficacious of grace, or in that through it the faithful receive the fruits of the passion.[66]

In q. 73, art. 4, he had also given the presence of the Christ who suffered, or Christ the victim, as a reason for calling the Eucharist a sacrifice,[67] but he does not repeat this in q. 83, art. 1, when he asks whether Christ is immolated in the celebration of the rite. To show that there is more than figurative representation of the passion involved, he appeals to the role of the priest. He mentions that the priest in consecrating bears the image of Christ, so that priest and victim are as it were one.[68] That is to say, since Christ consecrates through the words of Christ himself spoken by the priest, and since it is the Christ who was victim on the cross who is present, priest and victim in the eucharistic sacrifice are one. This however is not to predicate any presence of the immolation other than in its figural representation and in its efficacy.

How does this efficacy work? The sacramental sign that represents Christ's immolation consecrates the bread and wine so that Christ himself is present in the sacrament. The consecration of the offerings is what makes the Eucharist a sacrifice, one that is commemorative and representative of the cross. The figural representation does not give

---

63. *Immolation* belongs to the language of sacrifice. By using it here, Aquinas takes account of the tradition that calls both Christ's death and the Eucharist sacrifices.

64. Q. 83, art. 1.

65. Q. 73, art. 5. c.: Christ is present in the sacrament "... sicut in absentia imperatoris exhibetur veneranda eius imago."

66. See also Q. 83, art. 2, ad 1m.

67. Q. 73, art. 4, ad 3m.

68. Q. 83, art. 1, ad 3m. The image is predicated not of the person of the priest as such, but of his action of saying the words of Christ over the bread and wine.

the passion itself substantial presence, but makes present the Christ who suffered. The gift that Christ then makes of himself to the faithful through communion is the sacramental act in which the passion is represented as cause of grace. The same love and intention of Christ that were operative in his sacrifice on the cross are operative in this sacrament that represents and commemorates the cross. In other words one could say that while Christ himself is substantially present, his passion is present as efficacious cause because of the intention and love that he had in the passion. It is in the power of the passion or immolation that the offerings, the bread and wine, are consecrated and become Christ's body and blood. It is through the eucharistic sacrament in which Christ himself is received that the faithful are made sharers in the fruit of the immolation.[69] The coherence between sacrifice and sacrament is obvious. On the one hand, what is effected must be sacramentally signified. On the other, it is in receiving Christ, who died for humanity in the sacramental sign, that the grace of the passion that is represented is received.

Both the second and third reasons for which Christ instituted the Eucharist refer to this representation of his immolation. The second reason is verified because of the effectiveness of the sacrament as cause of grace, uniting communicants with Christ's death in faith. The third reason is verified in the passion's figurative representation. This is found first and foremost in the dual consecration, but it is spread in some way over the rite of the Mass through the use of allegorical explanation. In Thomas this is mainly restricted to the signs of the cross executed by the priest, so that he is quite sober in the way in which he predicates imagery of the eucharistic rite.[70]

Eucharistic Sacrifice

For Thomas, despite the practical tendencies of his time that we have noted, the efficacy of Christ's sacrifice is primordially communicated through sacramental communion. Nonetheless, given the practice of priestly offering it was necessary to explain in reference to this how the Eucharist is not only sacrament but also sacrifice.[71] This introduced a measure of ambiguity into his treatise since he had to account for an efficacy in offering that is made through a ritual performance in which

---

69. Q. 83, art. 1, c., where he quotes the prayer from the Missal: "Quoties huius hostiae commemoratio celebratur, opus nostrae redemptionis exercetur." It is with the reception of the fruits that he identifies the exercise or enactment of the work of redemption.

70. See q. 83, art. 5.

71. Q. 79, art. 7, asks whether the Eucharist may benefit persons who do not receive communion. The answer is that it may do so, not as sacrament but as sacrifice.

beneficiaries of the sacrament do not receive communion, whether it be offered for the living or for the dead.[72]

It is because of the representation of Christ's death that Thomas says the Mass may be offered as sacrifice.[73] At the same time, he does not identify sacrifice with offering. There is sacrifice only when something is done to the things offered, by way of either immolation, holocaust, or consecration, and it is this that makes it a priestly act.[74] In the Mass he distinguishes the sequence of offering gifts, consecrating them, and consuming them. The people offer gifts before the preface, but the priest alone consecrates them by the words of Christ, and they are then consumed in communion. Referring to the prayers of the canon of the Mass, Thomas finds there an offering of the sacrifice.[75] This offering is representative of Christ's sacrifice on the cross and is made in commemoration of it.

Because the Mass is a commemoration of the sacrifice of the cross and has its efficacy from it, and because Christ still acts as high-priest and mediator in heaven, the church may offer the Mass as sacrifice.[76] Elsewhere he says that the priest "offers prayers" in the Mass in the person of the whole church.[77] He makes a distinction between the efficacy of the Eucharist as a sacrament and the efficacy of the prayers offered in the name of the church, which is similar to the distinction between the efficacy of the Eucharist as a sacrament and its efficacy as a sacrifice, where the reference is to the prayers of the canon.[78] Does this mean that the Eucharist is a sacrifice inasmuch as the church offers prayers in commemoration of Christ's passion, which is represented in the consecration? The prayers of the church would then be joined with Christ's heavenly mediation and the representation of his sacrifice in what they represent of the church's own devotion and self-offering. This would mean that the priest consecrates Christ's body and blood and effects the representation of his sacrifice in the person of Christ, or by the power of Christ,[79] but *offers* the sacrifice in the person of the church.

Though he makes this detour, as it were, in explaining how the Eucharist is offered, it is obvious that the efficacy of Christ's passion is

---

72. See q. 79, art. 2.

73. Q. 79, art. 7, c.

74. For his definition of sacrifice, see IIa IIae, q. 85, art. 3, ad 3m.: "sacrificia proprie dicuntur quando circa res Deo oblatas aliquid fit."

75. III, Q. 83, art. 4, c.

76. See q. 79, art. 5, c. and art. 7, c.

77. See q. 82, art. 6, c.: "...oratio in Missa profertur a sacerdote in persona totius ecclesiae, cuius sacerdos est minister."

78. Q. 79, art. 7, c. Interestingly, according to q. 82, art. 7, ad 3m., an excommunicated priest can consecrate because he has the power of Christ to do this, but he cannot offer the prayers of the church, because he is separated from its unity.

79. See q. 64, art. 2, ad 3m.

exercised primarily through communion. It is in receiving Christ, in commemoration of his passion, that the faithful are healed from sin, nourished, inebriated with love, and joined with Christ in his self-offering. It is, in other words, in the consecration that makes Christ present and in the communion of the people with him in receiving him that the efficacious presence of the passion is chiefly realized. Whereas in the other sacraments the priest acts in the person of Christ[80] in mediating the grace of the sacrament, here he acts in the person of Christ in consecrating the body and blood but not in mediating grace.[81] It is Christ himself who directly mediates the grace through the sacramental gift by which he is personally united with the recipient. In receiving the mediator of grace himself, the recipient receives the grace of his passion.[82]

EUCHARIST AND CAUSALITY

There are several ways in which according to Thomas instrumental efficient causality works in the Eucharist, as there are several instrumental causes. The listing of instrumental causes is the same as for the other sacraments, namely, the sign action, the minister, and Christ himself in his humanity, as primary instrument of his divinity, and the passion of Christ. The actions in which these instrumental causes operate are the consecration of the bread and wine by which they become Christ's body and blood, the offering of the sacrifice or the representative immolation through which grace derives even for noncommunicants, and the communication of grace through communion. The intervention of these diverse causes is not however identical with regard to each of these effects.

In the other sacraments, Christ confers grace through the instrumentality of priest and sign. The priest is said to act *in persona Christi,* inasmuch as he posits the sign that signifies Christ's passion and in the power of Christ efficaciously mediates grace.[83] In the Eucharist, he acts *in persona Christi* in consecrating the bread and wine in a way that is different from his action in other sacraments. In the other sacraments, he uses a power that has been given to him by Christ and hence he uses the word *Ego* in the form. In the Eucharist his words are those of Christ, since they are intended to signify that it is Christ himself who

---

80. Q. 78, art. 4, c.

81. Since however it is he who consecrates the sacrament, he also is the one who ought to distribute communion. See q. 82, art. 3.

82. Q. 62, art. 5.

83. The best study on the role of the priest is that of B. Marliangeas, *Clés pour une théologie du ministère: In Persona Christi, in Persona Ecclesiae* (Paris: Ed. Beauchesne, 1978).

is acting in virtue of his own words and the instrumental action of the priest is simply to pronounce those words.[84] Finally, in the conferring of grace in communion it is Christ himself who acts directly through his self-gift. This of course is still mediated through the signs of bread and wine, but not through the instrumentality of the priest. The case of the grace received through the offering of the sacrifice rather than through communion does not fit so well into the schema. There it seems to be the priest who mediates this grace inasmuch as he acts in the person of Christ in making the offering, that is, in virtue of a power given to him by Christ.

The intervention of instrumental causes is thus not identical in the cases of consecration, offering, and conferral of grace through communion. In all three cases, however, the instrumental efficacy of Christ's passion is at work. Indeed, whatever other instrumentalities intervene it is always finally to the power of Christ's passion that efficacy is due.

To understand how this is so, Thomas's explanation of sacramental efficacy has to be related back to the use of this category in q. 48. art. 6. There he says that the passion was and is the instrumental cause of grace because it was the action of the person of the Word made flesh. Hence it is the Word made flesh who caused redemption through his passion and who in the church acts in the sacraments as primary instrumental cause of grace.

The Analogy of Instrument

Though in writing of sacramental efficacy Aquinas at times uses language and images that suggest the production of grace, it needs to be very clear that causality is for him an analogous category. As outlined in q. 62, art. 1, the problem to be resolved is the reduction of sacrament by some to a mere occasion on which Christ gives grace. To explain how it belongs within Christ's and the church's mediation of grace, Thomas adopts the analogy of instrumental causality. For this purpose, the concept has to be emptied of material connotations that suggest the image of God producing grace in a quasi-physical way. The three ideas best employed to understand how it fits into the economy of grace are those of interactive personal relation, intention, and exemplarity.

In using the word *cause* to speak of interaction between persons, one does not think of something flowing from one into another or of a direct physical effect of one on the other. There is rather a relation in being and presence such that what comes into being does so within the relationship and in dependence upon it. A good example of the nature of

---

84. See q. 78, art. 1, c.: " ... in perfectione huius sacramenti nihil agit nisi quod profert verba Christi."

this kind of causality is that of the relation between teacher and student.[85] One cannot say that knowledge flows from the teacher into the head of the student, nor that the teacher acts within the student's head to cause thinking therein. Thought is the student's own action from within. Of its nature, it does not require a teacher but in actual fact occurs within the contact with the teacher and would not be precisely what it is without the teacher. When the teacher teaches, the student thinks. To express the definite connection between the two activities, it can be said that the teacher causes the student to think. The relation is real but elusive and certainly not to be equated with the action of a carpenter producing an article of furniture. To speak of God as primary cause, and of Christ, Christ's passion, the minister, and the sacramental action as instrumental causes fits into this analogous use of the term *cause*.

In explaining the causality of sacrament, Aquinas does indeed give the example of using a saw in making furniture,[86] but he does this not to suggest the image of physical production but to show two other things. First, he shows that the effect is not proportionate to the instrument's own innate power. Second, he shows that the instrument leaves its own distinctive mark on the final effect, such that it would be different were it to be brought to being by the same agent but with a different instrument. God does not strictly need sacraments to give human persons grace, nor is grace proportionate to any human or material agent. Nonetheless in the economy of redemption, grace is in fact mediated through a succession of agents and actions. All of these stand in relation to each other and to grace in such a way that grace bears the mark and quality of this multiple relationship.

Another factor in Aquinas's explanation of instrumental causality is his appeal to exemplarity. For Aquinas, God's causal action is located in the divine practical intellect. In that intellect he also places the exemplarity of created and grace-filled realities. When he posits interconnected instrumental causes of sacrament, the issue is how each relates to this divine act. That is why intention and signification have such importance. Christ, church, and minister participate in the divine intention by way of their own intentional acts. The sacramental sign expresses the divine intention when it expresses the ministerial intention, and so through him the ecclesial and christic intention. In Christ's passion God's exemplary intention, or what God wills and intends for humans, is manifested in Christ's human action. In and through its formal exemplarity, it is efficacious for redemption and leaves its imprint on the human order. By the same token Christ's merit and willing self-offering is the exemplar of all

---

85. See David Burrell, *Aquinas: God and Action* (Notre Dame: Notre Dame University Press, 1979), 133, referring to the *Summa*, I, q. 117, art. 1, ad 1m.

86. Q. 62, art. 1, c.

lives lived in the grace of this redemptive economy, and it is as form or exemplar that it brings what is potential to act.

In looking back to q. 48 on the passion of Christ one notes how Aquinas first explains the sense in which Christ's suffering was an act of merit, satisfaction, and sacrifice. Only after this does he say that it is efficacious cause. It is in its exemplarity as merit, satisfaction, and sacrifice that the passion is efficient cause. The relation between the category of efficient cause and the other modes of redemption is that of efficient action to exemplar. Merit, satisfaction, and sacrifice manifest what is needed in a world that has to be liberated from sin and restored to grace. They show what a human economy of redemption is, the solidarity between Christ and redeemed sinners, and the interaction between the redeemed themselves in sharing the grace of the head. It is according to this intention, to this exemplar, that Christ wills redemption and is its principal instrument. It is by representing this exemplar in its worship that the church mediates grace, and more specifically that sacramental action draws people efficaciously into the solidarity of Christ's grace or into a share in his merit, satisfaction, and sacrifice.

In working through Aquinas's explanations of instrumental causality we find that exemplarity, intention, and relation are central realities. There is the exemplarity of a redeemed order, expressed in Christ's redemptive passion and represented in sacramental signification. The world is informed, or brought to form, by this exemplar, through the mediation of Christ's intention, the intention of the church, and the intention of the minister, with which the intention of the recipient is joined in harmony. All of these agents are bound together in the bringing into being of an order marked by the solidarity of shared merit, the restoration of justice through mercy, and the communion of loving sacrifice.

Signifying and Causing

Even though signification and causality are thus closely knit together, it appears that for Thomas signifying and causing are not totally identified. The mere act of signifying does not confer grace, though it may elicit faith as in the sacraments of the Old Law.[87] This seems odd to some contemporary theologians who would like to attribute the flow of grace to the sign *qua* sign. It makes perfect sense however within Thomistic thought.

Beyond the capacity to signify by use of the proper matter and form, to be causes of grace the sacraments of the New Law have to be endowed in act with a power that gives rise to an effect that goes beyond their na-

---

87. On sacraments of the Old Law, see q. 62, art. 1 and art. 6.

tive power to signify. Aquinas refers to this as a *virtus fluens*,[88] operative only in the moment of sacramental action and not attributable to signification as such, even though operative through it. In fact Aquinas never says of sacraments *significando causant*, that is, he does not say that they cause by signifying.[89]

This would seem to follow from Aquinas's basic understanding of the analogy of being. Every creature is by virtue of receiving from God, of being moved from potentiality to act in its being and in its every action. Only God attains to the being of things. In keeping with this is the principle that an instrumental cause is never adequate to the effect as such. It does not attain to the being of the effect but only to its being in a particular way. In the economy of grace this particular being has to do with belonging within the relationships of the economy of redemption, as ordered by God's intention and act. It is this divine intention that attains to the being of the effect. Without the divine intention, the instruments may well signify grace but grace is not caused. The idea of the *virtus fluens* is itself an analogy, one that says that the power to give grace is not totally identified with the power to signify, just as in the saw's capacity to cut a sharp edge there is no adequate proportion to what the carpenter makes.

To see that there is not perfect identity between sign and cause is better suited to understanding sacrament than an approach that relies on theories of ritual efficacy. What happens does indeed happen within an order where symbolic expression invites personal engagement and affects the nature and quality of the human person's relation with God. But it is only when we see how signs, or in more contemporary language symbols, do not of themselves explain the offer and advent of grace that we see what they truly signify of God's gracious love and of the nature of grace.

The point seems to be well respected in the shift that Edward Schillebeeckx made forty years ago from talking of efficient causality to talking of symbolic causality.[90] He keeps cause and symbolic interaction distinct though related. He can stress the interpersonal in a way in which Aquinas did not achieve through using the simple categories of sign and instrument, but he does not collapse coming to be in grace into the interpersonal of symbolic communication. Grace belongs in the interpersonal order to which symbolic interaction is vital and in which there

---

88. See q. 62, art. 4.

89. From his use of the term *significando efficitur* in posthumously transcribing Thomas's notes on 1 Corinthians 11, it would seem that not even the faithful scribe Reginald grasped the point. See *Expositio in epistolam ad Corinthios*, 1:670.

90. Edward Schillebeeckx, *De Sacramentele Heilseconomie* (Antwerp: 'T Groeit, 1952), and the short English work, *Christ the Sacrament of the Encounter with God* (London: Sheed & Ward, 1963).

is the analogy of an encounter with God. Schillebeeckx even uses the example of the music that comes from a drummer drumming to show how grace comes through symbolic action. However, ultimately he gives considerable place to the need for apophatic language in talking of God. Whatever we can explain of the order in which it occurs, being in grace, as all being, is in total dependence on God in a way that has no conceptual analogates but allows only of simple affirmation. For one who keeps that negation in mind, the analogy of symbolic interaction may indeed serve better to explain the interpersonal than the analogy of instrument, but the reason why Aquinas kept a distinction between sign and cause is satisfied. The inadequacy of the medium to the effect is as important to understanding how grace comes from God alone as the analogies of instrument or symbolic interaction are necessary to understand that it is given with an ordered and interactive relation of persons. To see that he is engaged in dialectic rather than synthesis may be the best approach to understanding Thomas.

It is in appreciation of the interpersonal character of these explanations that we may best understand the power of the distinctions made about the action of instrumental causes in the Eucharist. The action of the priest, acting in the person of Christ and in the person of the church, is needed for the consecration of the bread and wine and for the offering of the representative sacrifice. It is not however operative in sacramental communion, where Christ acts directly in giving himself and his grace to communicants through the instrumentality of the signs of bread and wine. It is this direct relationship with Christ of each person that stands at the heart of the communion of all in one body, of that holy bonding that makes Christ and his members unite together as though they were one person.

Faith and Sacrament

The intention of the subject is necessary to the reception of the sacrament. Faith is necessary to receiving its grace. Yet according to Thomas neither the intention nor the faith belong among the causes. Though in his explanation of the character, he speaks of the baptismal character as a passive potency, he does not in fact attribute a passive role to the Eucharist's participants.[91] They are to make offering, to sing praises, to make intercession, to share peace with others, and to respond in love to Christ in communion. Their intention and faith have the full nature of human acts. They embrace the relationship to Christ and to the church that is the economy of grace.

---

91. On character, see q. 63, art. 1–6.

If Aquinas does not attribute any causal efficacy to them, this is because the origin and mediation of grace are in no way in the hands of
the subject. Grace, inclusive of faith, is possessed in total dependence;
it is pure gift. Grace as a radical altering of being may not be merited
or emerge in any way from personal effort. What is thus emphasized
is the quality of faith as gift and response. Communion in grace, being alive to the memory of the passion, offering self in communion
with Christ's offering, are activities of faith and acts of worship, but
they are not in any way the source-point of sanctification. They neither constitute the sign of the passion, nor make the grace signified
present, though they are inherent to what is signified and given, that
is, the power to believe, to love, and to worship. In this sense, though
in this sense only, the power of the baptized to worship is a passive
power. That is to say, through and through it is an enabled power, a
response.

Summary

The thought of Thomas can be summarized as follows. He puts his treatment of the Eucharist in context by opening it with a question that places
it in the economy of grace and closing it with a question on the rite of
celebration. It is clearly the action of the Eucharist within the economy
of redemption that is his concern. At the same time, his theology is centered around the presence of the living Christ in the sacrament and looks
to the gift that he makes of himself to the faithful in communion. The
sacrifice or immolation of the cross is represented through the matter
and form that consecrate the elements. The faithful are brought to join
in Christ's offering through the prayers of the priest, but it is primarily
in communion that they are made beneficiaries of the fruit of the passion. There they receive the grace that nourishes them in their lives of
faith, offers a remedy for sin, uplifts them with the sweet inebriation
of Christ's love, and joins them together in the one body of Christ, in
foretaste of eternal communion with the Word. In explaining all of this,
within the orbit of faith, Aquinas draws principally on the philosophy
of Aristotle, and thus on the categories of substance, matter and form,
and efficient causality.

THOMAS IN HIS TIME

To situate Thomas fully in his own time, one has to ask how his thought
harmonized with the devotional developments noted earlier and how
it compared with other contemporary theologies.

Relation to Cultural Realities

In many respects, Thomas's theology of the Eucharist served to relate its celebration to the social needs of his time. By drawing on the idea of exemplarity, he related the sacrament to the passion of Christ and to the solidarity of Christians with him, "as though one person." Thus eucharistic commemoration could furnish in the exemplarity of Christ's immolation a model for the life of the church as a community and for life in society. Since the exemplarity in question consisted of solidarity in restoring justice through a satisfaction prompted by love, it was an apt model for responding to the disorders of society and for holding it in unity.

It is possible to appreciate this relation of theology to ritual practice, and beyond practice to ethics, by considering the horizons of the cultural world as Aquinas conceived it. It was a world of solidarity in grace, of interdependence in dependence on the one mediator, Jesus Christ. It was a world of unity, whose foil is the world of sin, united only in its malice.[92] The most central religious expression of this world is the sacrifice of Christ's death, a voluntary propulsion through death beyond death, out of a great love that enfolds all humanity and gathers all into the unity of God. In such a world, God's presence is there in the being of things at the heart of creation and emerges in gratuitous gift in the events of salvation. The world itself, humanity, history, and Christ's passion intertwine. The things of earth, the life of the body, the life of grace, the life of the interpersonal, and the celebration of worship come to be through God's act and yet truly represent a human interaction of which the Word made flesh is the center. This is indeed a world that has its social, institutional, and ritual forms, so that it is within such a socialized existence that divine mystery is expressed and humans are united through Christ with God, but the center of the world is divine love as manifested in Jesus Christ.

There is a component to this eucharistic theology that is obviously conservative, though liberal. It is conservative in the sense that it supports the given order of things and indeed aspires to its restoration according to the divine exemplar. Inasmuch as he embraced a hierarchical ordering of world and church and inasmuch as he placed the sacramental presence of Christ himself as the key point to eucharistic understanding and inasmuch as he included the analogy of sacrifice, his thought provided a model of cultural integration for developments in the Mass system and in nonliturgical eucharistic devotion. In that sense, the thought-form provided by Thomas served the societal and cultural integration of the Eucharist as public symbol.

---

92. See q. 8, arts. 7 and 8, on the members of the devil and of the antichrist.

His thought was however liberal inasmuch as it integrated new perspectives that promoted interpersonal exchange within the given system. First is the attempt to enlighten eucharistic faith by an understanding that could be grasped by people of his time and within the categories familiar at least to the learned. Second is the attention to the human subject and personal act. Third is the interpersonal character of eucharistic celebration and communion. Fourth is the distinction that is kept between sign and cause, so that the expression of mystery is never taken as adequate to the mystery itself. This dovetails with his understanding of faith as openness to divine mystery in a total receptivity to graced being and comprehensive of the desire for the blessed life. Fifth is the relation of Eucharist to the total human order into which the examples of love and justice expressed in sacrifice and satisfaction need to be integrated to bring about the reconciliation of all with each other and with God. Sixth, though he seemed reconciled to the fact of infrequent communion and though his explanation of the presence of Christ gave a foundation to eucharistic devotions, in his theology the Eucharist always remains a sacrament to be consumed, not to be looked at.

In the combination of these six factors there is the seed for eucharistic development within changing cultural and social conditions. Ironically, it is only within present-day theology that these possibilities have been exploited in rereadings of his sacramental theology.

Thomas and Bonaventure

A good foil for his thought from his own time is that of Saint Bonaventure.[93] The ideas of Aquinas may have been too erudite to have the popular influence of Bonaventure, whose work was more directly related to the devotional strands noted in the previous two chapters.[94]

In all his writings on the Eucharist, Bonaventure stressed the affective remembrance of Christ's passion and union with him in ardent love. To give the reasons, in God's wisdom, for the institution of the sacrament he constantly referred to the words of Christ in Matthew 28:20. It is in and through the Eucharist that Christ remains always in his church, in a way suited to wayfarers who live by faith and must see divine realities under the veil of the flesh. Cited first in the commentary on the sentences, the text is evoked again in the *Breviloquium*[95] and in the tract

93. For a comparison between Thomas and Bonaventure, see P.-M. Gy, "La relation au Christ dans l'Eucharistie."

94. Bonaventure treated of the Eucharist in *Commentaria in Quatuor Libros Sententiarum*, Dist. VIII–XIII, *Opera Omnia*, vol. 4 (Quaracchi: ex Typographia Collegii S. Bonaventurae, 1889); *Breviloquium*, Pars VI, Cap. IX, *Opera Omnia*, vol. 5 (Quaracchi, 1891); *Sermo III, De Sanctissimo Corpore Christi, Opera Omnia*, vol. 5; *Tractatus de Praeparatione ad Missam, Opera Omnia*, vol. 8 (Quaracchi, 1898).

95. *Breviloquium* VI, IX.

on the preparation for Mass, written for priests of the Order of Saint Francis.[96]

There is however an interesting turn in Bonaventure's theology, between the commentary on the Sentences and the later works. In the commentary, there is no treatment of the offering of the Mass as sacrifice. The reasons given for the institution of the sacrament are derived from its nature as food and from its institution at the Last Supper.[97] Above all, it is a sign and sacrament of love that unites its recipients in ardent communion with Christ and with each other. Christ gave it to his church immediately before his passion, so that he might remain always with it and so that through this sacrament his suffering and death might be held in memory. He gave it as food, so that it might sustain and refresh the life of wayfarers.

In the later works, there is the same emphasis on love and its ardor, as well as on remembering the passion, but now three reasons are given for this sacrament of Christ's real and abiding presence. They are the need for a placatory sacrifice, satisfied by the offering of Christ's very body and blood; the need for a sacrament in which the faithful could be united in a communion of the heart with Christ until the end of time; and the need for sustenance on the part of those who live by the flesh and must attain divine realities through bodily signs.[98]

Hence in the later works of Bonaventure there is an assimilation of the practice of offering sacrifice that is absent in Aquinas, who in relation to this topic continued to underline the presence of the sacrifice of the cross through figurative and efficacious representation, whatever allowance he made for an offering for people not present. Furthermore, in the use of Matthew 28:20 and in his way of accentuating the ardor of love and the condescension of the Son of God in hiding beneath the sacramental signs, Bonaventure did more than Thomas to give a place in theology for the new kinds of devotion noted in previous chapters of this book. Though of course he repeated the doctrine of substantial change, his imagery was much more corporeal and tangible than the way of negation postulated by Thomas's explanation of this truth. As already noted, Thomas saw the presence strictly in relation to communion and explained it in such a way that it promoted the contemplation of the mystery of the Word or of the risen Christ rather than a devout welcome to the presence of a humble but majestic guest. Though there was clearly room in his theology for an affective commemoration of Christ's

---

96. *De Praeparatione ad Missam,* Cap. I, 1, 4.

97. Dist. VIII, P. 1, art. 2, qq. 1 and 2.

98. *Breviloquium* VI, 9: "... necesse est, ipsum in hoc sacramento veraciter esse contentum, exigente hoc perfectione *sacrificii* placativi, *sacramenti* unitivi et *viatici* refectivi." See also *Sermo de Sanctissimo Corpore Christi,* I, 3–6. The same emphasis on love and sacrifice is found in the treatise, *De praeparatione ad Missam.*

passion, his main line of argument was that the Eucharist put us in a communion of faith with the mystery by which we had been saved and by which we were destined to the fullness of life in glory.

CONCLUSION

In short, the eucharistic theology of Aquinas fostered an intellectual understanding in line with the Aristotelian interest of the times, expressed the symbolic relation of the sacrament to the need for order and justice, enhanced the role of the individual person through its stress on faith, and fostered a contemplative participation in its celebration. On the other side, it did not capture the devotional imagination of the era in a way that allowed it to be readily accommodated to popular explanation or to a liturgical renewal that could incorporate the action and piety of the new devotion. Furthermore, because of its focus on hierarchical order it was ill-suited to the movements in the church that gave more importance to the role of the person and to the intersubjective character of a community built up by the participation of all its members.

Chapter 11

DEVELOPMENTS OF EUCHARISTIC DOCTRINES FROM THE CONDEMNATION OF BERENGAR TO THE COUNCIL OF TRENT

Catholic theology for several centuries looked to the Council of Trent for the formulation of church doctrine on the Eucharist. Today it is better appreciated how much this formulation owed to the controversies of the time and to medieval developments. The aim of this chapter then is to see what teachings were fixed as doctrines between Berengar and the Council of Trent, and why. When the purpose of doctrinal definition within its historical surroundings is understood, it is possible to see what is the true nature of its guiding force in reflection on eucharistic faith.

DOCTRINE

The broad notion of doctrine that we find in the early and late medieval church is that it is the truth of the Christian religion that needs to be thought about and explained. It is that which is communicated by God to the church, primarily through the medium of the scriptures. All reflection on the faith comes from the reading of the sacred page, for faith and its beliefs are a participation in God's own knowledge and are ordered towards the light of vision. Reason plays its role in explaining this doctrine, but it has to be careful to keep its point of departure in God's word. Thomas Aquinas speaks of doctrine, or sacred doctrine, where we might speak of theology. His choice of terms makes it clear that he does not wish to confuse a rational argumentation about God with reason's service of the faith.[1]

The study of authorities was considered essential to the formulation of doctrine. In the *Catena Aurea*, in his scriptural commentaries, and in the *Summa Theologiae* one finds how Aquinas went about settling the content of the faith on eucharistic matters. He quoted authorities, who were for the most part the great fathers of the church who had been given wide recognition over a period of centuries. Especially in the *Catena Aurea*, which he drew up at the behest of Pope Urban IV, there is a clear effort to include Eastern as well as Western writers. Popes and councils were important but not exclusive references. The tendency to associate doctrine, as distinct from theology, with magisterial teaching is not found until after the Council of Trent.

Though the role of the magisterium gained in importance in controlling faith and practice, it was only after the Council of Trent that its teaching seemed to be somewhat cut off from its starting-point in the reflection on the scriptures and from its location in that tradition that is formulated by appeal to a much wider group of authorities. In looking at the Acts of the Council of Trent itself, one notes how much the argumentation still followed the procedure of an appeal to authorities that collates magisterial statements with other sources, such as fathers of the church, liturgical texts, and even medieval theologians. All of these authorities cast mutual light on each other in laying out right doctrine.

The idea that Thomas had about the relation between scripture and tradition appears in the fact that he presented the texts from the magisterium and ecclesiastical writers in the form of a reading of the scriptures, or of a commentary on them. The desire to be faithful to the scriptures was primordial.

On the other hand, neither Thomas Aquinas nor those who preceded him went to the scripture or to authorities as though all that needed to be done was to transcribe or even expound them. Since authorities do not always seem to say the same thing, fixing doctrine required a use of dialectic, but this too was done in clear reference to scriptural texts, since it was their meaning that had to be made clear. Questions were seen to arise from the scriptural text and other questions were brought to it out of the disputes of the period. Thus the issues of presence in truth or in sign, of the sacramental and spiritual consumption of the eucharistic substance, of the ecclesial significance of the rites, of the grace received, and of the manner in which Christ's passion is represented were all looked at for what authorities might have to say

---

1. See *Summa Theologiae* I, q. 1. See the note "Sacra Doctrina" by Thomas Gilby in the Blackfriars' edition *Summa Theologiae* (New York and London: McGraw-Hill and Eyre and Spottiswoode, 1976), 1:58–66.

on them. In some sense, one could say that before offering explanation it had to be asked whether there was a doctrine on these points. The doctrine however would have to be set in terms of the questions asked and could not be formulated as though it were an ahistorical corpus of belief.

It would seem that for Aquinas some eucharistic questions were settled by this kind of authoritative teaching. These include the institution of the sacrament by Christ, the power of the ordained priesthood, the presence in truth or reality rather than in sign only, the sacramental rather than the fleshly manner of Christ's presence, the representation of Christ's passion in the rites, the ecclesial nature of the sacrament, and the gift of grace through its mediation. In regard to each of these points, however, he proffered and argued different explanations that fitted within the range of what was deemed doctrinally acceptable.

Doctrine and Practice

In examining eucharistic doctrines, it is important to see them in relation to questions of practice. These include such matters as celebration and devotion and the relation of the Eucharist to the framework of ecclesial life. The challenge to a way of expressing the faith often originated in a challenge to a practice and the defense of doctrine was also a defense of a particular practice. Doctrine, in short, always has a practical as well as an intellectual purpose.

In the eleventh century, Berengar's approach to sacramental signification had implications for eucharistic devotion, but in later eucharistic controversies the implications were even broader. Among the Cathars, Albigensians, Waldensians, and Spirituals,[2] the call to live a more authentic evangelical life was associated with a challenge to the power of priests to consecrate or the claim that the Eucharist could be celebrated without an ordained minister. The deeper issues of faith cannot be dissociated from this practical side of the controversy.

The process whereby dissenters were dealt with in the Middle Ages is an unsavory story.[3] It belongs within a world of political as well as religious strife. Gross persecution is part of the story. Fair judgment on persons and efforts at reconciliation were of scant concern when accusations were made. Berengar, many of those accused of dualism, the poor followers of the converted merchant Valdes, and John Hus were treated

---

2. On such heresies and their repression, see Gordon Leff, *Heresy in the Later Middle Ages*, 2 vols. (Manchester, 1967) and M. D. Lambert, *Medieval Heresy: Popular Movements from Bogomil to Hus* (London: Edward Arnold Publishers, 1977). The latter work is an overview of studies written in a number of languages.

3. Innocent III in face of popular movements and heresies set an example of accommodation in dealing with the Humiliati and the followers of Francis of Assisi. See Lambert, *Medieval Heresy*, 95–101. Unfortunately this did not set the tone for later actions.

ignobly. The history of the Reformation and Counter-Reformation is surely not one of the disinterested quest for truth. None of this is irrelevant to an understanding of doctrinal formulation, since it gives a better idea of what was practically involved.

On the other side, church authorities fostered eucharistic devotions of a public nature that remained juxtaposed rather than well integrated into the liturgical rhythm of celebration. The great public occasions of communion at Easter and the procession for the feast of Corpus Christi, as well as stipendiary offerings for Masses said by priests, were integral to the kind of piety thought to be in keeping with the nature of the church and conducive to salvation, as well as to the Christian ordering of society. The doctrinal quibbles of those who were in course of time condemned were deemed all the more noxious because they undermined such devotional practice.

EARLY MAGISTERIAL DECISIONS

The earliest magisterial decisions were made in opposition to the teaching of Berengar. Without having to decide on the true nature of Berengar's own positions, it may be noted that the controversy contributed to theological method in showing the need for a dialectic between authorities and a clear formulation of sacramental questions. The profession of faith imposed on him by the Council of Rome (1059 C.E.) is crudely physicist, for who today would care to state that communicants chew on the body of Christ?[4] However, what the profession answers is the suspicion that Berengar denied the identity of the sacramental body with the body that Christ took from the Virgin Mary and in which he died upon the cross. He was thought to hold for a presence only in sign, by way of opposition to presence in truth. Some of Berengar's critics cleared up the confusion by introducing the notions of substance and substantial change into the debate. However ill-defined these notions remained at the time, they made it possible to distinguish in the sacrament between real change and the appearances of change.

The next significant moment in magisterial action is the imposition by the Fourth Lateran Council (1215 C.E.) of a profession of faith on the Albigensians.[5] A number of points in this profession show the juncture between doctrine and practice both in what was condemned and in

---

4. Council of Rome, DS 690. For a good succinct presentation, see Nathan Mitchell, *Cult and Controversy: The Worship of the Eucharist Outside Mass* (New York: Pueblo Publishing Company, 1982), 137–51. For a perceptive comment on how this controversy fits into the development of eucharistic doctrine, see H. Chadwick, "Ego Berengarius," *Journal of Theological Studies* 40 (1989): 414–45.

5. Lateran IV, DS 802.

what was defended. In the positions repudiated, there was a challenge to priestly authority and power by those who looked for a relation between living the apostolic life and the celebration of the sacraments. There was the idea of a people's church in which the baptized could celebrate the Eucharist without benefit of ordained minister if a worthy one were not available. There was the dualist suspicion of sacrament, questioning the idea that the spiritual could be communicated through material means. As church authority saw it, a denial of the change of bread and wine into the body and blood of Christ and a denial of the power of the ordained to consecrate went together.

Hence the heretics were asked to profess belief in transubstantiation, that is, in the change of the substance of bread and wine into the substance of Christ's body and blood respectively, and in the power of the priest, and of the priest alone, to consecrate. In this way it was upheld that Christ is truly present in the visible sacrament of his body and blood. It was also upheld that a validly ordained priest can consecrate irrespective of his worthiness, since the power to do so comes from Christ and not from the minister. Lastly it followed from the imposed profession that for a valid consecration of the Eucharist the action of an ordained priest is necessary.

TRANSUBSTANTIATION

At this point it is useful to see what was intended by the term *transubstantiation,* since it has subsequently been the cause of so much dissent among Christians.[6] It was Lanfranc who, in his response to Berengar, gave coinage to the words *substance* and *substantial.* In his usage they were not yet technical terms but allowed him to distinguish between the appearance of reality and the reality itself. Apparently it was Roland Bandinelli, later Pope Alexander III, who first used the term *transubstantiation* along the same nontechnical lines.

Later writers gave more attention to the meaning of these terms, principally Baldwin of Forde, Alan of Lille, and Peter of Capua. Baldwin and Alan appear to have thought of no alternative to transubstantiation or the change of one substance into another, if the substantial presence of Christ in the sacrament was to be understood properly. It is likely therefore that they did not give it a highly developed philosophical meaning. Peter, however, records three opinions on the matter. One is

---

6. For this development, see John McCue, "The Doctrine of Transubstantiation from Berengar through Trent: The Point at Issue," *Harvard Theological Review* 61 (1968): 385–430; Joseph Ratzinger, "Das Problem der Transubstantiation und der Frage nach dem Sinne der Eucharistie," *Theologische Quartalschrift* 147 (1967): 129–58.

the position that the substance of bread and the substance of wine remain simultaneously with the substance of Christ's body and blood, a position that came to be dubbed *consubstantiation*. A second is that the substance of bread and wine are annihilated and then replaced by the substance of Christ's body and blood. The third position recorded is that of substantial change. Peter himself holds for the third position, but he does not think that the previous two are contrary to the doctrine of the real presence.

Since the point of the profession of faith asked of the heretics in 1215 C.E. by the Fourth Lateran Council is the real presence of Christ in the Eucharist, it is not so clear what was intended by the words "transsubstantiatis pane in corpus, et vino in sanguinem potestate divina."[7] At the time, some apparently thought that the accent was on the words "potestate divina," i.e., on the divine power operating through the priest, in opposition to Albigensian positions requiring the faith and moral standing of the priest himself. It was some decades before the conciliar decision was taken to be a definition of *transubstantiation*, but even then it was thought to be open to different explanations.

It was Thomas Aquinas who put the idea of substantial change as a sacramental explanation on a scientific footing, employing categories adopted from the philosophy of Aristotle. It is interesting that though he takes Lateran IV as a definition of faith, his argument against explanations other than his own is derived from what he sees to be their metaphysical impossibility. As explained in the previous chapter, the exclusion of the localized presence of Christ's body and blood and the affirmation of a presence in an order of being known only to faith and analogously to intelligence are twin components of Thomas's theology.

After him, positions developed, both practical and theoretical, that were not conducive to a good understanding of substantial change. William of Ockham and Duns Scotus both understood the Lateran definition to exclude *consubstantiation* as heretical. On the other hand, unlike Thomas they considered it a metaphysical possibility, indeed one more readily intelligible than substantial transmutation. If God, according to them, chose the means of transubstantiation this was a choice between different means, made by virtue of an act of divine power and divine free will. According to Ockham and to Peter d'Ailly, who was influential in the workings of the Council of Constance (1414–18 C.E.), annihilation of the substance of bread and wine with their replacement by the substance of Christ's body and blood would be in conformity with the teaching of Lateran IV, though consubstantiation would not. Without clear explanation, the risk was that substantial change could seem to be

---

7. "The bread transubstantiated into the body, the wine into the blood by divine power."

some kind of miraculous physical mutation, involving change not only in bread and wine but even in Christ's own body.

The Condemnation of Wyclifian Errors

It is in this context that one has to consider the positions of John Wyclif and the condemnation of his teachings at the Council of Constance (1415 C.E.).[8] It was this condemnation that gave a more definite place to transubstantiation within official teaching.

There is no obvious logic in the development of Wyclif's teachings, though considered in retrospect connections are apparent. In part his positions originated in his criticism of ecclesiastical abuses, especially among unreformed clergy. In that he was in continuity with the earlier challenges posed by the followers of the evangelical and apostolic way of life. In part also his ideas were opposed to the nominalism of William of Ockham, which he countered by his own brand of Platonic philosophy. In opposing Ockham, he enunciated the principle that human persons do not come to the knowledge of reality through the senses. Knowledge is rather obtained through the intellect's perception of the intelligibility of things, that intelligibility which they have by reason of their participation in divine intelligibility. For Wyclif this had particular application to the truths of salvation, which are contained in God's foreknowledge and can be learned from the scriptures by anyone who reads them properly.

As far as a theology of the church is concerned, this position led Wyclif to a predestinarian ecclesiology. The church is the body of the elect, the elect being those who lead the true evangelical life. Bishops and priests may well not be part of this church, despite their position in ecclesiastical institutions. From this there followed a practical challenge to the sacramental celebration of priests, both on the grounds of personal unworthiness and on the grounds that there is no warrant for ecclesiastical institutions in the scriptures.

It was only towards the end of his life that John Wyclif developed his thought on the Eucharist. It then became the fine point of his challenge to ecclesiastical authority. Specifically, he rejected the doctrine formulated at Lateran IV. He considered it to have no scriptural basis and to be philosophically absurd, reading as he did Ockham's explanation of

---

8. On Wyclif, see Maurice Keen, "Wyclif, the Bible and Transubstantiation," and Gordon Leff, "Wyclif and Hus: A Doctrinal Comparison," both in *Wyclif in His Times*, edited by Anthony Kenny (Oxford: Clarendon Press, 1986), 1–16 and 105–26. Both articles refer to the wider literature. See also Jeremy I. Catto, "John Wyclif and the Cult of the Eucharist," in *The Bible in the Medieval World: Essays in Memory of Beryl Smalley*, edited by Katherine Walsh and Diana Wood, Studies in Church History, Subsidia 4 (Oxford: Blackwell, 1985), 269–82.

the doctrine. He formulated his own explanation of eucharistic presence around the idea that after the consecration the bread and wine remain, not on their own account but as the sacraments of Christ's presence. He seems to have explained this latter in terms of spiritual presence, which he opposed to physical. He emphasized that this presence comes about through the power of the Word, not through the power of the priest. Since he considered that the idea of priestly power replaced the power of the Word in the church, he found the teaching of Lateran IV "a shoddy claim for sacerdotal magic."[9]

In addressing eucharistic doctrine, the immediate concern of the Council of Constance was with John Hus and the Hussites.[10] It took up the positions of John Wyclif, then dead, because they were thought to have influenced that movement. In condemning Wyclif's teachings, the Council of Constance listed five errors: (a) the substance of bread and wine remain in the sacrament of the altar; (b) the accidents of bread and wine do not remain without their proper subject; (c) Christ is not really present in the sacrament in his proper corporeal presence; (d) if bishops or priests are in mortal sin, they do not ordain, they do not consecrate, they do not confect, they do not baptize; (e) there is no foundation in the gospel to the teaching that Christ instituted the Mass.

The central point made by Constance is that the substance of bread and wine do not remain after the consecration, for this would be contrary to what is implied by the real presence of Christ's body and blood. Since Wyclif had used the philosophical term *accidentia* in formulating his own position, saying that is was impossible to have accidents without their proper substance, this word was included in the conciliar propositions. Some centuries later, the Council of Trent chose not to include the word in its definition of substantial change, since at Constance it was more associated with the condemnation of Wyclif than with a necessary explanation of true doctrine.

THE MASS BEFORE TRENT

Though nothing was magisterially defined before the Council of Trent on the sacrifice of the Mass, it is useful to see how its theology had evolved after Thomas.[11] This helps to explain the problems raised by the

---

9. Keen, "Wyclif, the Bible and Transubstantiation," 14.

10. Council of Constance, DS 1151–55. On the condemnation of Hus, see Lambert, *Medieval Heresy*, 296–307.

11. The key article is that by Erwin Iserloh, "Der Wert der Messe in der Diskussion der Theologen vom Mittelalter bis zum 16. Jahrhundert," *Zeitschrift für katholische Theologie* 83 (1961): 44–79. See the summary in David N. Power, *The Sacrifice We Offer: The Tridentine Dogma and Its Reinterpretation* (Edinburgh: T. & T. Clark; New York: Crossroad, 1987), 41–

Reformers and answered by Catholic controversialists in the sixteenth century.

Behind the theological development lies the practice of offering Mass for the living and the dead and the stipendiary system that supported this. Once this practice was accepted as legitimate and suitable, it had to be given a fitting theological explanation. The discussion of the value of the Mass as exemplified in Gabriel Biel had a strong influence in pre-Tridentine theology, but it is not to be reduced to the limits of that discussion.[12]

Following the lead of medieval theology, theologians continued to look for the essence of the sacrifice in the sacramental representation of Christ's passion and immolation. Some found this in the consecration under two kinds, some located it more particularly in the words signifying the chalice as "blood poured out," some indeed included both consecration and communion in the sign. Starting with Bonaventure and Scotus, the oblation was placed after the consecration, not before it or in it, as in Aquinas. Offering was thus seen as the offering of the body and blood that were made present through the consecration. On this basis, some writers took the actual offering of the Mass to be that of the church, not of Christ, though it was done for the application of Christ's merits. The discussion of the fruits of the Mass followed from this, often relating their quantity and application to the faith and merits of the church or of its celebrants. In other words, though the sacrifice of Christ commemorated was seen as having infinite value, the offering of his body and blood in the Mass by the church for the application of this sacrifice was given finite value. Linked with this discussion was that of the nature of sacrifice in general, and the discussion of the origins of the rites of the (Roman) Mass. Following arguments made popular by Biel, many traced these back at least in their essence to apostolic times. Biel in turn probably borrowed from Thomas Netter.[13]

---

45. See also Maurice Lepin, *L'idée du sacrifice de la Messe d'après les théologiens depuis l'origine jusqu'à nos jours* (Paris: Beauchesne, 1926).

One respondent to Wyclif in the fourteenth century whose work influenced the Catholic apologists of the sixteenth was the English Carmelite Thomas Netter. In his writing, he collected early authorities to oppose to Wyclif in his refutation both of the doctrine of transubstantiation and of the apostolic origins of the order of the Mass. This provided a ready arsenal for the controversialists who responded to Luther and the other sixteenth-century Reformers on the doctrine of the real presence and on the sacrifice of the Mass. See Thomas Netter (Waldensis), *Doctrinale antiquitatum fidei Ecclesiae Catholicae*, vol. 3. This work was originally published about 1421, but received several printings in the course of the sixteenth century.

12. Gabriel Biel, *Canonis Misse Expositio*, edited by Heiko A. Obermann and William J. Courtenay (Wiesbaden: Franz Steiner Verlag, 1963). On the value of the Mass see Lectio 27.

13. On the treatment of the Roman canon at Trent, see David N. Power, "The Priestly Prayer: The Tridentine Theologians and the Roman Canon," in *Fountain of Life*, edited by Gerard Austin (Washington, D.C.: Pastoral Press, 1991), 131–64.

At the time of the Reformation, an important issue in Catholic theology was the relation of the Mass to the sacrifice of the cross. The position of apologists such as Kaspar Schatzgeyer,[14] who explained the sacrifice of the Mass as a representation of that of the cross and not as a distinct though dependent sacrifice, exercised an important influence at the Council of Trent. The Reformers, however, seem to have been more cognizant of theories about the value of the Mass, which they linked with the way in which its offering had in practice replaced the communion of all the faithful.

REFORMATION AND THE COUNCIL OF TRENT

The two points of doctrine on which the Council of Trent made pronouncements concerned Christ's sacramental presence and the sacrifice of the Mass. To see the background to Trent's teaching, attention is given here primarily to the practical and doctrinal issues raised by Martin Luther and John Calvin.

The Reformers: The Practical Agenda

Though in time considerable differences emerged among the Reformers themselves, the eucharistic agenda was set by the early writings of Martin Luther on the Lord's Supper.[15] For him, Catholic sacramental practice was rife with a theology of works' righteousness, and it deprived people of the genuine gospel of Jesus Christ. For the testament and sacrament of God's mercy offered to the people through the death of Jesus Christ the Mass, according to Luther, substituted the offering of sacrifice, as exemplified in the offertory prayers, in the canon, and in the stipendiary system. For the proclamation and preaching of the word, it substituted the awe of priestly action. It effectively suppressed the priesthood of all believers because of the infrequent invitation to communion, the denial of the chalice, and the omission of the intercessions of the faithful. When the Eucharist was exposed for veneration or carried about in processions, Luther found that this stole attention from the real purpose of the sacrament, which is communion.

The practical response whereby he countered this corruption appeared in the various revisions of the rite of the Mass, which in time he

---

14. Kaspar Schatzgeyer, *Schriften zur Verteidigung der Messe,* published and introduced by Erwin Iserloh and Peter Fabisch, Corpus Catholicorum 37 (Münster Westfalen: Aschendorffsche Verlagsbuchhandlung, 1984).

15. See the writings of Martin Luther collected in volumes 35 and 36 of *Luther's Works,* American edition (Philadelphia: Fortress Press, 1959).

referred to primarily as the Sacrament of the Lord's Supper.[16] The central point of these reforms was to restore the Mass as a sacrament to be given to the people. To get rid of works' righteousness, Luther systematically removed all notion of offering propitiatory sacrifice. He eliminated the offertory prayers and the Roman canon and made of the service a communion rite under both kinds. The communion followed immediately after the reading of the supper narrative according to Paul's version. The ordinal left ample room for that which Luther termed the sacrifice of thanksgiving and for the people's self-offering, as well as for the offering of gifts to benefit the poor. He saw all of this as quite distinct from the offering made by a sacrificial priesthood.

The order of celebration gave an important place to the proclamation of the scriptures in the vernacular and to preaching. It also promoted the singing of hymns in the vernacular, in keeping with Luther's ideas about the educational value of music.[17]

By and large, the different Reformers made similar changes in the order of service, sharing as they did similar concerns.[18] By way of summary, these points may be noted from sixteenth-century liturgies:

(a) The primacy given to receiving the sacrament as a communion in Christ's body and blood and the connection between this and the proclamation of the gospel.

(b) The gradual introduction of the vernacular into all parts of the rite.

(c) The removal of all mention of sacrifice that smacked of propitiation.

(d) The importance given to the Lord's Prayer, as the one authentic dominical prayer.

(e) The retention of various prayers of memorial, thanksgiving and intercession, but without indication of priestly sacrifice.

(f) The role of hymnody in fostering devotion and faith.

(g) The importance given to the role of the minister as minister of word and sacrament and as leader of the congregation in prayer.

(h) The collection for the poor, to express the social and communal significance of the Supper.

---

16. See his orders for the celebration of the Lord's Supper, I. Pahl, *Coena Domini* I, Spicilegium Friburgense 29 (Fribourg: Fribourg University Press, 1983), 33–39; R. C. D. Jasper and G. J. Cuming, *Prayers of the Eucharist: Early and Reformed*, 3d ed. (New York: Pueblo Publishing Company, 1987), 189–99, give an English translation.

17. It was not his original purpose to eliminate Latin completely, since he thought that knowledge of Latin belonged in a well-rounded education, but his liturgical reforms were chiefly concerned with the general populace.

18. These are all collected in Pahl, *Coena Domini*.

The Reformers: Doctrinal Issues

As one with these practical initiatives, Luther and the other Reformers sharply attacked the Catholic doctrine of sacrifice and the value of the priest's offering for the living and the dead. Luther's personal view of the Mass, or Lord's Supper, was that is was Christ's testament, the offer of mercy to sinners who believed in God's saving word and approached the table in faith. The notion of priestly mediation seemed to him to contradict this and to smack of works' righteousness. The Eucharist is sacrament, not sacrifice, and gift, not mediation.

Luther held ardently to the real presence though, because of his opposition to the devotions centering on the reserved sacrament, he emphasized the moment of the actual rite and reception in speaking of this presence. His firm conviction about Christ's presence appeared most strongly in his virulent polemics against Ulrich Zwingli.[19]

Even while defending the doctrine of the real presence, he strongly attacked the notion of transubstantiation. He found it lacking any basis in the scriptures and metaphysically absurd. Of Thomas Aquinas, he said that he knew neither his scriptures nor his Aristotle when he proposed this explanation.[20] He saw it as nothing more than a sophistry that would hold that the material things of bread and wine could change into the body and blood of Christ. Rather than espouse either this theory or the annihilation of the substance of bread and wine, he at times spoke of the permanence of bread and wine as signs of Christ's gift. He used the expression that Christ is present "in, with, and under" the elements of bread and wine.

As a result, it is often said that Luther used the notions of consubstantiation and divine ubiquity to explain Christ's presence in the sacrament. His position is more complex than that. He had resort to the analogy of the union of two natures in the incarnation, and on this he was simply pursuing a thought that he found in early Christian writing. In a more theoretical way, he related sacramental presence to Christ's Lordship, which gave him power over all things and gave his humanity some share in the qualities of the divinity. Among these is ubiquity, and it is by reason of this quality that Christ can be present wherever the sacrament is celebrated, offering his grace and his mercy through the gift of his body and blood. Clearly this is no simplistic teaching of the concomitance of two subjects under the same appearances, but an effort to

---

19. See "That These Words of Christ, 'This Is My Body,' etc., Still Stand Firm against the Fanatics," Luther's Works 37:4–150.

20. "The Babylonian Captivity of the Church," Luther's Works 36:29. It appears to have been principally through the writings of Ockham that Luther learned of transubstantiation.

explain a truth by way of what he found to be some better proposition than transubstantiation, as he understood it.

In the past, Catholic manuals of theology dismissed the explanation of sacramental presence in John Calvin as a reduction to presence in power only, not in substance. Calvin however also wanted to account for the traditional eucharistic faith while avoiding the notion of transubstantiation.[21] He wanted to find a way that would accentuate the sacramental rather than physical or material manner of this presence. Though he refused to speak of a physical, local, or substantial presence of the body and blood, he did say that Christ himself is the substance of the sacrament. To make his point, he appealed to the works of Augustine, especially his commentary on John 6, and wrote of Christ's presence in the power of the Spirit, explaining communion as a reception in the Spirit and in faith. In appealing to the operation of the Spirit of Christ, he was able to stress the personal and relational aspect of the sacramental presence. Not only is the Spirit the agent of the presence, but it is the bond that exists between Christ and the believer who receives in faith.

There was a Platonic coloring to Calvin's adherence to Augustine, affecting his sense of the relation between reality and sign. For him, though the sign is essentially distinct from the thing signified it conveys that reality to those who perceive the sign. The bread and wine are not mere tokens, for in the words of Christ there comes about a genuine change of names and a metonymy that allows one to refer to them in truth as the body and blood of Christ. John Calvin's eucharistic teaching, like that of Luther, is not a denial of the traditional doctrine but a search for an explanation that would seem more satisfactory than transubstantiation and that would foster sacramental communion rather than the offering of sacrifice or devotions that centered on the reserved sacrament.

The Council of Trent

A number of Catholic theologians were quick to enter the field of controversy against Luther and then against the other Reformers, enunciating Catholic doctrine and listing the scriptural and ecclesiastical authorities on whose credit this doctrine was built.[22] When bishops and theologians convened for the Council of Trent, they were directly concerned with formulating right doctrine. There was indeed a growing awareness

---

21. See Kilian McDonnell, *John Calvin, the Church and the Eucharist* (Princeton: Princeton University Press, 1967).

22. For an account of early controversialists, see *Die Confutatio der Confessio Augustana vom 3. August 1530*, edited by Herbert Immenkötter (Münster Westfalen: Aschendorffsche Verlagsbuchhandlung, 1979).

of the need to initiate some practical change, especially by way of correcting clerical abuses in the celebration of Mass and the administration of the sacraments and by way of instructing the faithful. Reform decrees addressed these issues, but both these and the doctrinal decrees show fundamental support for the prevailing economy of Mass offering and eucharistic devotion. The errors extracted from the writings of the Reformers and submitted to debate show the desire to maintain a Catholic piety built on these practical foundations. The eventual conciliar refusal to extend the chalice to the baptized and to consider the use of the vernacular in the Mass, though not intended as definitive solutions to these problems, were in keeping with the fundamental intent of fostering Catholic as against Reformation piety.[23]

The doctrine of the real presence and the doctrine of the sacrifice of the Mass were taken up in separate sessions and elaborated in separate decrees.[24] This was largely due to the nature of the council's concerns, but the separation had long-term ill effects on Catholic teaching, theology, and religious education. A further problem arose from the fact that in the aftermath of the council most attention was given to the anathemas in the canons. The expository matter of the chapters of the decree was often neglected. In theological interpretation the procedure was often to see the exact opposite of what was anathematized as doctrinal definition, but studies of the conciliar acts show that this is too simplistic an approach.[25] Had the teaching in the chapters on the nature of memorial and representation been given as much attention as the anathema against those denying the propitiatory character of the eucharistic sacrifice, theology and catechesis might have taken a different turn.

Substantial Presence and Change

The sense in which the Reformers opposed transubstantiation and the meaning of the Tridentine definition have become clearer today in the light of historical studies. To the Reformers the doctrine of transubstantiation seemed to justify devotions centered on the reserved sacrament, so they spoke preferably of a presence of Christ in the use of the sacrament, that is, in the communion rite. They suspected Catholics of defending a physical presence of Christ and thought that transubstantiation meant some kind of physical transmutation. It was in the light of this opposition and this preference that the Tridentine theologians summed up Luther's position as consubstantiation and took exception

23. John Huels, "The Cup of Blessing," in *One Table, Many Laws: Essays on Catholic Eucharistic Practice* (Collegeville, Minn.: Liturgical Press, 1986), 37–53.

24. DS 1635–61 (C.E. 1551); DS 1738–59 (C.E. 1562).

25. See J. Wohlmuth, *Realpräsenz und Transsubstantiation im Konzil von Trient* (Bern and Frankfurt, 1975).

to the idea of presence only in the moment of use. Other positions, such as those of Calvin or Zwingli, were summed up as theologies of presence in sign only, or only in the power to offer the fruits of the passion to communicants.

In canons 1–4 of the decree on the sacrament of the Eucharist, the council anathematized positions that could be summarized in these ways.[26] As its key point, the council taught and defined the substantial presence of Christ in the sacrament, in either kind, body and blood, soul and divinity. Positively, this upheld the doctrine of substantial presence. Negatively, it excluded the idea of presence only in sign or only in effective power, or the idea of a presence that would be restricted to the moment of communion.

Because it seemed integral to the idea of substantial presence, the council also taught that Christ became present through substantial change, that is, through the change of the whole being of bread into the body of Christ and of the whole being of the wine into the blood of Christ, only the species or appearances of bread and wine remaining after the consecration. It deliberately excluded the term *accidents* to describe what remained and of the word *transubstantiation* said that it was an apt term whereby to describe the substantial change effected.[27]

In recent Catholic theology[28] and in ecumenical dialogue,[29] the exact meaning of these teachings has been much discussed. In this discussion attention is given to the points of agreement on the Eucharist that exist between churches, as well as to the exact point of disagreement between the Reformers and the Catholic position as defined at Trent.

The points made by Karl Rahner may be summarized here to clarify the sense given by the council to substantial change.[30] As he presents it, the doctrine is offered as an explanation of the eucharistic gift that is based on a reading of the words of Jesus at the Last Supper, reported in the Synoptics and in St. Paul. Furthermore, what is present in the sacrament results from that action of the Mass, which the council calls *benedictio* or *consecratio*. Hence the reference designating what is present is to an act or event or happening that occurs within the celebration of the Eucharist. In distinguishing between *substance* and *species*, by the

---

26. DS 1651–54.

27. DS 1642.

28. Most important in Catholic theology is the work of Edward Schillebeeckx, *The Eucharist* (London: Sheed & Ward, 1968), and the essay by Karl Rahner, "The Presence of Christ in the Sacrament of the Lord's Supper," in *Theological Investigations* (New York: Crossroad, 1982), 4:287–311.

29. Most notable are the statements of the Roman Catholic/Evangelical Lutheran German dialogue. See the recent publication *The Condemnations of the Reformation Era: Do They Still Divide?* edited by Karl Lehmann and Wolfhart Pannenberg, translated by Margaret Kohl (Minneapolis: Fortress Press, 1990).

30. "The Presence of Christ in the Sacrament of the Lord's Supper."

former the council wants to designate that which is the proper and definitive reality of what results from this act. *Species* means the way in which the reality presents itself, that is, in the form or under the appearance of bread and wine. To reduce this to spiritual symbolism or to state that bread and body, wine and blood, are *both* present would be a contradiction of what is said in Jesus' words and of the intended sense of the Tridentine dogma.

The council therefore speaks of the wonderful transformation that takes place, which it calls substantial change, that is, a change in the definitive reality of what is present and presented in the sacrament. It also gives legitimacy to the use of *transubstantiation* to refer to this transformation. Rahner then makes the point that this is a logical rather than ontic explanation of what has taken place in the blessing. By this he means that it has to be understood by way of reference back to the action and by way of reference to the New Testament words. There is no particular philosophical or metaphysical explanation espoused, a matter borne out by the decision not to use the word *accidentia* to refer to what remains of the bread and wine. The doctrine of Trent simply says that something happens that involves a change in the definitive reality of what is present as a result of the liturgical or sacramental action. It does not intend to offer any philosophical explanation as to *how* this takes place.

In recent ecumenical dialogue in Germany, it has been suggested that the teachings of Luther, Calvin, and Trent were all different ways of attempting to state and to explain the same fundamental truth.[31] All referred on the one hand to the words of Jesus in the New Testament and on the other to the nature of the sacramental or eucharistic action. All wished to explain the nature and change in the definitive reality resulting from the sacramental action. In that sense, Trent's teaching on substantial change, Luther's analogy with the doctrine of the incarnation, his appeal to Christ's Lordship that led him to compare Christ's sacramental presence with God's ubiquity, and Calvin's teaching on a presence of Christ through the power of the Spirit are three different ways of trying to explain the one mystery in which fundamentally all professed faith and belief. According to this statement,

> These different theories were deliberately defined over against one another, and under the conditions of the sixteenth century they were apparently irreconcilable. But they lose their antithetical (and mutually exclusive) character inasmuch as it has to be admitted that each of them has its obvious strengths and weaknesses, and

---

31. See *The Condemnations of the Reformation Era: Do They Still Divide?*, the section on the Eucharist, 84–117.

that none of them can claim exclusive validity of such a kind that in each given case the other form of doctrine would have to be judged heretical.[32]

Against this background, the partners in the Roman Catholic/ Lutheran dialogue listed the points of common faith in churches looking back to any one of these forebears:

> The exalted Lord is present in the Lord's Supper,
> in the body and blood he gave
> with his divinity and his humanity
> through the word of promise
> in the meal gifts of bread and wine
> in the power of the Holy Spirit
> for reception through the congregation.[33]

If these points are held in common between churches, even with the divergence in explanation of the mystery that remains, the participants did not see a reason for holding out on reciprocal anathematizations over eucharistic beliefs.

The Sacrifice of the Mass[34]

It was opposition to the offering of the Mass for the living and the dead, together with all that was entailed in this, that stirred up the controversy over the sacrifice of the Mass. There is a definite divergence between an understanding of the Eucharist that places the accent on sacrament and gift and one that places it on offering and sacrifice. Unfortunately, at Trent the doctrine on the sacrament and the doctrine on the sacrifice were separated and expressed in two distinct decrees.

In the words of Trent itself, the key point was the nature of the Mass as a sacrifice of propitiation, to be offered for the living and the dead, for the remission of sins, and for other necessities. Rather than being clearly defined, *propitiation* in the decree is a descriptive word, whose reference is twofold. First, there is reference back to the meaning of scriptural words, particularly those of Christ's memorial command (Luke 22:19; 1 Cor. 11:24).[35] Second, there is reference to the action of the

---

32. Ibid., 115.

33. Ibid.

34. DS 1738–59. See Hubert Jedin, *Geschichte des Konzils von Trient*, 3:338–58; 4/1:174– 209 (Freiburg im Breisgau: Herder, 1970/75); David N. Power, *The Sacrifice We Offer: The Tridentine Dogma and Its Reinterpretation* (Edinburgh: T. & T. Clark; New York: Crossroad, 1987).

35. In the conciliar sessions, there was considerable debate as to whether Christ had actually offered a sacrifice at the Last Supper or whether simply in anticipation of the cross

ordained priest in the celebration, when he acts in virtue of this memorial command. What is intended in the decree is the action of the priest
in offering as distinct from the act of taking communion by the faithful.
As a description of what he does in virtue of the memorial command,
to offer propitiation in the sense that Trent gives it is to perform an act
that obtains some remission of sin for either living or dead, distinct from
the grace obtained through the reception of communion.[36] With this
understanding, Trent took it that sacrifice of propitiation means something different from sacrifice of thanksgiving, where what is intended in
prayer is to give grace for benefits received, as it is also something different from the faithful's self-offering that may accompany the prayer
or communion. It is quite clear, however, that in the mind of Trent the
effect of propitiatory offering does not come about without faith and repentance on the part of beneficiaries. It is also clear that in the course of
the council, the conciliar members made progress in encouraging more
frequent communion by the faithful.

The Reformers totally opposed attributing special value to the action of the priest in applying the merits of Christ to the church, as they
opposed the whole stipendiary system. They were ready to speak of the
eucharistic rite in its totality as a sacrifice of thanksgiving or to see a place
in it for the self-offering of the faithful, but for them these did not pertain
to the essence of the sacrament that is pure gift. They also remained firm
in their conviction that Catholics took from the adequacy of the sacrifice
of the cross in attributing salvific value to the priestly action.

In fact, the decree of the Council of Trent in its chapters explained
the sacrifice of the Mass completely in terms of its reference to the cross.
Of this, the Mass is a memorial and a representation. It draws its value
totally from the cross and it is intended to apply the merits of this sacrifice. In the Mass, the church through its ordained priests is able to
continue the offering of Christ under the visible signs of bread and wine
in memorial of the cross. In the final analysis, though it is done through
the instrumentality of ordained ministers, the priest offering and the
one offered, on the cross and in the Mass, are the same Christ, only the
manner of offering being different.

Theoretically, it was easy enough for Catholic apologists to answer
the Protestant objections that the Mass was magic or an offering of
works, or that it bypassed the faith of the beneficiaries of grace. The conciliar debates at the session held in Bologna also put an effective end to
any theory that would see in the Mass a sacrifice that is distinct from,

---

he had instituted the rite for a memorial sacrifice. The council did not find it necessary to
decide on this point in order to define the relation of the Mass to the sacrifice of the cross
or to find in Christ's words the institution of the memorial sacrifice.

36. The council refrained from deciding whether this is by way of suffrage or through
an *ex opere operato* efficacy akin to that of the sacraments.

though dependent on, the cross, since this would effectively constitute an offering by the church, rather than of Christ through the church.

In the context of the time, it was impossible to resolve the opposition between the notions of sacrifice of thanksgiving and sacrifice of propitiation. First, it was evident that in using these terms Reformers and Catholics were not referring to the same thing. The former meant the prayers that accompany the sacrament, the latter the distinct and proper words and action of the priest. Second, with the knowledge that they had of liturgical history, none of the participants in the controversy could see the connection between the total memorial prayer and sacramental commemoration, nor did they have a clear sense of the relation of the prayer to the rite of communion.

In fact, both parties fractured the canon of the Mass and effectively isolated the words of Christ from the context of the prayer. In discussing sacrifice, Catholic expositors gave complete attention to the words following the *Sanctus,* taking the thanksgiving portion of the prayer as mere preliminary. The communion services of the Reformers gave primacy to the words of Jesus, which they connected immediately with the act of communion. They eliminated offering prayers and explained thanksgiving and self-offering as adjunct to the sacrament, not as essential to it. In such a context, it was impossible to accurately retrieve the sense of memorial found in biblical and liturgical sources.

The various chapters and canons of the Tridentine decree show the intensely practical nature of the issue of propitiatory sacrifice, even if it is spelled out in doctrinal terms.[37] They defend the offering of Mass in honor of the saints and the orthodoxy of the Roman canon.[38] They also defend ceremonial rites that do not have direct scriptural warrants. Masses in which the priest alone received communion (Masses that, however large or small the attendance of the faithful, the Reformers called "private") were declared a legitimate way for the priest to exercise his role as the church's public minister.[39] There is some encouragement of more frequent communion and a stress on the pastoral duty to explain the Mass and to unfold the scriptures. However, these matters are given a secondary place, the defense of the Mass as known at the time being that which was deemed most important.

The positions taken by the Council of Trent, combining doctrine and practice, may be summarized in this way:

---

37. DS 1744–50; 1754–59.

38. Tridentine debates show how important the idea of the apostolic origin of this prayer was to Catholic apologists and how much they relied on this supposed origin in defending the sacrifice of the Mass.

39. For Trent, the priest both makes application of Christ's merits and, when celebrating in public, affords the faithful the opportunity to unite themselves spiritually with Christ's offering.

(a) In fostering a sacramental memorial and representation of Christ's sacrifice on the cross, it intended to exclude: a purely subjective remembrance; a simple pleading of Christ's blood; or the sufficiency of thanksgiving, intercession, and self-offering that would but accompany the sacrament of communion.

(b) It specifically located this sacramental memorial and its efficacy in the act of the priest. This is performed in virtue of the power and ordinance of Jesus Christ.

(c) Practically, this meant that a benefit accrues from the priestly action that is distinct from the grace of eucharistic communion.

(d) In the offering of the sacrifice for the living and the dead and in the celebration of Masses in honor of the saints, the council found an important expression of the communion of the church on earth and of the communion between the living and the dead.

In present ecumenical dialogue the notion of memorial has been better examined, especially in relation to its biblical foundations. It has thus served to overcome some of the differences between churches on the eucharistic sacrifice. There has also been considerable retrieval, in theory and liturgical practice, of the role of the eucharistic prayer in keeping memorial. Given the comprehensive nature of this prayer and its relation to the work of Christ, its better understanding helps churches to set aside the opposition between objective and subjective commemoration, and that between sacrifice of thanksgiving and sacrifice of propitiation. It also clarifies the relation between prayer and communion rite and between word and sacrament. The inclusion of the epiclesis of the Spirit brings the role of the Spirit back into the theology of the Eucharist.

Of the controversies over the sacrifice of the Mass, the above mentioned German report has this to say:

It has been found possible to state in common our believing conviction about the uniqueness and full sufficiency of Jesus Christ's sacrifice on the cross, as well as the bearing and scope of the *anamnesis* in the eucharistic celebration of the church.[40]

The same report makes the point that the node of the problem in the sixteenth century was the separation of sacrifice and sacrament.[41] On the Catholic side, that the Mass was so often offered without its use as sacrament obscured the original intent and nature of the Lord's Supper, or Eucharist. On the Reformation side, stress on the gift of the

---

40. *The Condemnations of the Reformation Era,* 114.
41. Ibid., 87.

Lord's body and blood meant that not enough attention was given to the anamnetic or sacramental representation of the sacrifice of the cross.

Though a better understanding of the original controversy is now attained, a number of nerve points still remain sensitive:

(a) There are different attitudes to the language of offering and sacrifice. This is evident even in a comparison between the new eucharistic prayers of the Roman rite and those introduced into the liturgical books of other churches.[42] How the self-offering of the faithful and the sacrifice of thanksgiving relate to the efficacious representation of the cross appears to be seen in different ways.

(b) The precise role of the ordained minister in relation to Christ and to the church remains unresolved. Current Catholic magisterial teaching clearly attributes particular efficacy to his representation of Christ.[43] Protestant churches relate this role more directly to the proclamation of the word and in the minister's prayer find an expression of the congregation's prayer.

(c) The connection between proclaiming the words of institution from the supper narrative and the invocation of the Holy Spirit has been given no common explanation.

(d) It is commonly recognized that a commemoration of the dead was part of the Christian tradition from early times and that it ought to have some part in the rite. However, the Catholic position on the efficacy of the priest's offering in the power of Christ is not accepted by other churches. On the awkward question of Masses for the dead, the German report on Roman Catholic and Evangelical Lutheran dialogue appeals to the notion of intercessory remembrance.[44] This is similar to the approach taken to propitiatory sacrifice by the Faith and Order Commission of the World Council of Churches when it relates this notion to union with the heavenly intercession of Christ.[45] While this resolution makes place for the remembrance of the dead in the Eucharist by all, it does not answer the question of the value of the priest's sacramental action at the core of the liturgy.

(e) Many points of practice are still a source of tension. Such are the stipendiary system, the frequency of celebration, and the private offering of Mass by priests. It is unclear whether these reflect seri-

---

42. See David N. Power, "Anamnesis: Remembering, We Offer," in *Eucharistic Prayers: An Ecumenical Study of their Development and Structure*, edited by Frank C. Senn (New York: Paulist Press, 1987), 146–68.

43. See Power, *The Sacrifice We Offer*, 21–26.

44. *The Condemnations of the Reformation Era*, 113.

45. *On Baptism, Eucharist and Ministry*, section on Eucharist, Commentary (8): "It is in the light of the significance of the Eucharist as intercession that references to the Eucharist in Catholic theology as 'propitiatory sacrifice' may be understood. The understanding is that there is only one expiation, that of the unique sacrifice of the cross, made actual in the Eucharist and presented before the Father in the intercession of Christ for all humanity."

ous doctrinal divergence or whether they belong within the area of legitimate divergence.

The point that seems to be still most at issue is the mediating role of the ordained ministry. Is there a fundamental contradiction between the Reformation view of ministry and sacrament as the proclamation of the forgiveness of sins in Jesus Christ and the Catholic position that the priest mediates a sacramental participation in the sacrifice of Christ and brings the merits of Christ to bear upon human life for those who have faith? The Congregation for the Doctrine of the Faith seems to find that there is a difference that hinders communion between churches,[46] but perhaps if the matter is clarified this will appear as legitimate pluralism.

Two points in Protestant theology could serve as a bridge with Catholic theology. First, the Reformers readily made reference not only to Christ's heavenly self-offering but also to his heavenly and priestly intercession, in which he pleaded his own blood. Secondly, for the Reformers, in the liturgy of the Lord's Supper as well as proclaiming and distributing the sacrament, the minister led the people in a prayer that is taken up by Christ and joined with his own.[47] This latter role however was not taken to be integral to the sacrament, though it did follow from it. Can it be said that in Catholic practice there is more room within an understanding *of the sacrament itself* for the inclusion of the distinct roles of the priest in offering the sacrament and his role in pressing the intercession of the blood of Christ?[48] In other words, Catholic doctrine allows for a sacramental expression both of the offer of the gift of grace in the body and blood of Christ and of Christ's heavenly intercession.

In neither case is there merit on the part of minister or church. The mediation attributed to the priest is not his own, but that of Christ's action through him. This is true whether it be the transformation of the bread and wine in blessing, the proclamation of the sacramental gift in the words of covenant, or the intercession made for the living and the dead. In these essential liturgical acts, Catholic doctrine attributes nothing whatsoever to the merits or personal mediation of the priest. His

46. See Congregation for the Doctrine of the Faith, "Response to ARCIC I's Final Report," *Origins* 21 (1991/92): 441ff.

47. See John M. Barkley, "Pleading His Eternal Sacrifice in the Reformed Liturgy," in *The Sacrifice of Praise: Studies on the Themes of Thanksgiving and Redemption in the Central Prayers of the Eucharistic and Baptismal Liturgies,* edited by Bryan D. Spinks (Rome: C.L.V., 1981), 123–40.

48. A perfectly legitimate way of explaining the application of the fruits of the Mass for the living and the dead, as taught by Trent. When the so-called 'propitiatory' efficacy of the priest's act is understood as efficacious intercession rather than as an act of application that is efficacious *ex opere operato*, reconciliation between Protestant and Catholic positions is more readily attainable.

words and action are through and through the sacramental expression of Christ's mediation, in offering himself to God, in offering God's gift to the people in the reality of his own body and blood, and in making intercession. If Catholic theology (as distinct from magisterial teaching) can place these actions in the context of the memorial remembrance and prayer, it is even clearer how the pasch of Christ operates through the action of the priest.[49] When this is met by a Protestant theology and practice that takes up again the import of the commemorative prayer, the differences need not be seen as in opposition to each other in a radical way.

CONTEMPORARY MAGISTERIUM[50]

The Constitution on the Liturgy of the Second Vatican Council, while defining the Eucharist as the sacrifice of Christ's body and blood, gave firm importance to the centrality of the notion of memorial in its doctrine and practice. It also highlighted the communal nature of the sacrament and the invitation to communion given to all the faithful, with due attention to the symbolism of meal or table.[51] It placed the Tridentine emphasis on Christ's presence in the eucharistic species in the context of his presence in the assembly, in the Word, and in the minister.[52] At the same time, even while teaching the communal nature of Christian liturgy it retained the teaching on its hierarchical character.

Subsequent magisterial teaching, whether of Paul VI[53] or of John Paul II,[54] has endeavoured to harmonize new approaches with what had become the traditional Roman Catholic emphasis on sacrifice, presence, transubstantiation, and priesthood. The General Instruction of the Roman Missal[55] showed a clear concern to underline these past doctrinal positions, even while allowing that renewal of rites which encourages

---

49. See David N. Power, "Representing Christ in Community and Sacrament," in *Being a Priest Today*, edited by Donald J. Goergen (Collegeville, Minn.: Liturgical Press, 1992), 97–123.

50. A compendium of documents in English translation, covering the crucial period 1963–79 is found in *Documents on the Liturgy 1963–1979: Conciliar, Papal and Curial Texts*, translated and edited by the International Commission on English in the Liturgy (Collegeville: Liturgical Press, 1982).

51. Second Vatican Council, *Constitution on the Liturgy*, art. 47. In *Documents on the Liturgy* 14.

52. *Constitution on the Liturgy*, art. 7. In *Documents on the Liturgy*, 6.

53. Most noteworthy for its concern to relate new to old on the presence of Christ in the sacrament is the encyclical letter *Mysterium Fidei* of September 3, 1965. In *Documents on the Liturgy*, 378–92.

54. Important is his letter of Holy Thursday 1980, *Dominicae Cenae*. In *Origins* 9, no. 41 (1980): 653–65.

55. See the *editio typica* of 1975, translated in *Documents on the Liturgy*, 465–553.

the congregation's participation and accentuates the reality of the assembly. After its initial publication, it was modified to respond to the problems raised by traditionalists with the revised Order of Mass. While treating of the Eucharist as an action of the church and of the assembly, it is very careful to always describe the Mass as first and foremost the action of Christ through the ministry of the priest, even though Christ is present not only in him but also in the assembly and in the word.[56]

In current theology, it has to be asked whether the categories of memorial, sacramental representation, and table communion can integrate the more particular emphasis of the Tridentine teaching on sacrifice, priesthood, and substantial change, without doing violence either to the longer tradition, to defined dogmas, or to the necessary differentiation of roles in the assembly. It is this tension I hope to resolve in following chapters, integrating various doctrinal developments, even while opening up new horizons of thought and practice.

CONCLUSION

Doctrines proposed by the magisterium fit into the larger complexity of tradition, comprehensive of teaching and practice. The church as a living organism is ever in the process of developing and reexamining the origins and emergence of its faith. Its principal points of reference are scriptural origins and whatever are the current problems and questions. Within this process, questions about orthodox belief and about orthodox practice are ever mingled.

Particular formulations of doctrine, whether coming from magisterial teaching or from church confessions, usually emerged in times of controversy. The unfortunate fate of Catholic eucharistic theology was that for too long the doctrines and practices approved at Trent were given a Counter-Reformation status and set the stage for several centuries. Today, their contribution can be better appreciated within the larger context of tradition, where the point of the Reformation challenge is better understood.

In ecumenical dialogue today, there is generally an effort to list themes that allow for common understanding and mutual respect. For example, the BEM document of the Faith and Order Commission of the World Council of Churches reflects the common effort to retrieve a theology and a form of celebration that precede doctrinal separation.[57] It

---

56. See Chapter II, no. 7, of the General Instruction, *Documents on the Liturgy*, 471.

57. *Baptism, Eucharist and Ministry*, Faith and Order Paper No. 111 (Geneva: World Council of Churches, 1982).

gives these headings to its presentation of the Eucharist: thanksgiving to the Father, anamnesis or memorial of Christ, invocation of the Spirit, communion of the faithful, and meal of the kingdom. At the same time, for the promotion of sincere dialogue, it is recognized that it is necessary to see how and why specific doctrines were formulated. This is the right context in which to seek a revitalization of eucharistic thought and practice through an appropriation of tradition.

Part V

REVITALIZING
THE EUCHARISTIC
TRADITION TODAY

Chapter 12

CONTEMPORARY READINGS OF THOMAS AQUINAS ON THE EUCHARIST

Some major periods of eucharistic development have been given scrutiny in preceding chapters of this book, and this has been completed by a more general survey of other centuries. It is now time to consider more specifically what this conversation with tradition means for the present and its revitalization of eucharistic thought and celebration.

As already indicated in the first chapter of the book, there are some major problems and possibilities in retrieving tradition arising from the current context. These have to do with the ways in which memorial is related to prevailing notions of history and divine action, with the appreciation of the power of language, with the relation of eucharistic remembrance to human suffering, and with the need to integrate new currents and realities more successfully than was done in the past. Paradoxically, Eucharist can be renewed as a living and vital tradition when it pays fuller attention to the discontinuities of history, to those who are outside the mainstream, to the victims of evil, and to the suffering that is caused in the crumbling of civilization and culture.

Contemporary retrievals and critiques of the theology of Aquinas are a good place to start the conversation with tradition. These have in fact played a large part in the renewal of eucharistic thought and give the major lines along which to pursue further considerations.

OF SIGNS AND SYMBOLS

Significando Causant

In the early part of the twentieth century, some neo-Thomists made the role of sign and signification in the sacramental theology of Aquinas the focal point of their writing. In particular, Louis Billot[1] and Anscar Vonier[2] promoted the adage that the sacraments cause *by* signifying, not simply *what* they signify. In other words, they wished to include the activity of sign as sign in the causal operation of sacraments. This theoretical emphasis on the nature of the sacrament as sign coordinated well with the pastoral interest in promoting liturgical comprehension and fuller liturgical participation.

Later in the century, some, notably William Van Roo, located the *virtus fluens*, or transient power of the sacrament, in the effective signification of the ritual.[3] To explain this efficacy, Van Roo took examples from the legal order, such as the drawing up of a legal document that has effect when it is composed according to required forms and duly signed. In this way he coordinated the ideas of sign and of cause and avoided the physical connotations that some associated with analogies such as the instrumentality of a saw or of a fire that burns. This emphasis on sign activity also related sacraments more effectively to the order of human communication.

The drawback of this new emphasis on sign was that it associated sign with cause more closely than did Thomas himself. When some writers began to appeal to the human sciences and especially to studies on rite and symbol to explain the role of sacraments in the church, nothing seemed to be left that could not be given a humanistic or empirical explanation. In eucharistic theology, this meant that the terms *transignification* and *transfinalization* were preferred to the word *transubstantiation,* often leaving ontological questions unheeded.[4]

Symbolic Causality

The term *symbolic causality*, instead of simply *efficient instrumental causality*, was used by Karl Rahner and Edward Schillebeeckx. Both wanted to remove any idea of material production from the operation of sacrament, to take fuller account of the interpersonal, and at the same time keep ontological considerations in mind. It was through the understanding of symbol that they developed and expanded on the definition of sacrament as sign in Thomistic theology and related it to the reality and activity of the assembly of faithful, in distinction from Thomas's emphasis on the role of the priest.

---

1. Louis Billot, *De Ecclesiae Sacramentis* (Rome: Gregorian University Press, 1932).

2. Anscar Vonier, *A Key to the Doctrine of the Eucharist* (New York: Benziger Brothers, 1927).

3. William Van Roo, *De Sacramentis in genere*, 2d ed. (Rome: Gregorian University Press, 1960).

4. For a summary of this debate, see Joseph Powers, *Eucharistic Theology* (New York: Seabury Press, 1967).

Karl Rahner

Karl Rahner wanted to present a sacramental theology that would re-main in continuity with that of Thomas Aquinas and yet enlarge upon it, especially in view of a different conception of grace. In an essay on the sacramental theology of Aquinas he pointed out that, while pursuing the insight that the nature of sacraments as signs is at the heart of sacramental theology, several drawbacks in this theology needed to be addressed today.[5] First, the theology of the *Summa* suggests the idea that grace is produced, despite the analogous concept of cause that it employs. Second, the relation between sign and cause is too thinly explained. Third, the connection between word and sacrament requires exploration, since Aquinas narrows it to the relation of the form to the matter. Fourth, Thomas still holds to a ahistorical and juridical notion of the institution of the sacraments by Christ.

In writing on the role of the person in the sacramental event, Rahner stressed the relation between God's presence in the world and the event of God through the grace given expression in sacraments.[6] If the theology of Aquinas suggests that grace is a product of sacraments, this is because it was customary to think of sacraments as bringing the gift of grace where it was not present. This meant a strong contrast between grace and its absence, or between a situation of grace and one of non-grace. Rahner found the embryo of a richer explanation of sacramental grace in Thomas's theorem that when grace is given outside the conferring of sacraments (as he deemed it to happen quite often) it includes a desire for sacraments, and in a special way for the Eucharist, even if this is only implicit. For Rahner this showed that Thomas did not tie grace to its "production" in sacraments, and he pursued an inquiry that would show the relation between the grace that is already offered in human life and sacramental celebration. Thus he described the sacramental event as a bringing to expression of a grace which is pervasive in the world. Grace is present in the world by reason of God's self-communication in the very act of creation, when human beings were already called to that fullness of divine communion that theology has called supernatural because it is totally gratuitous and beyond humanity's natural capacities. The sacramental event is therefore a coming forth of that grace into symbolic expression, so that reality may be seen and personally lived in the explicit faith of divine gift and presence. It is the power of the sacraments, and particularly of the Eucharist, to relate this pervading divine

---

5. "Introductory Observations on Thomas Aquinas's Theology of the Sacraments in General," *Theological Investigations* (New York: Crossroad, 1982), 14:149–85.

6. "Considerations on the Active Role of the Person in the Sacramental Event," *Theological Investigations* (New York: Crossroad, 1982), 14:161–82.

presence to the sacrifice of Christ in its eschatological significance for humanity and for cosmic reality.

Put in other terms, whereas Aquinas related the need for sacrament to a concept of human nature, Rahner related it to history and world. He saw the gift of grace as the history of God's presence to the world. Sacramental celebration belongs within this history, revealing the presence of God at the heart of the world in its different historical moments as these relate to God's manifestation in the pasch of Jesus Christ, which belongs within human history.

Rahner used the term *event* of sacrament because of sacrament's relation to human life and history. Through symbol, and in the anamnesis of the passion, the Word comes with the gift of the Spirit to human persons in their oneness with the universe and in the surrender of all reality to the Father in sacrifice. In return those who participate in the Mass come to be consciously and more fully a part of the mystery of the Word and Spirit in the world, embracing all cosmic and human reality. In sacrament, they bring human and earthly realities beyond their suffering into a communion of joy and hope with Christ. Hence in the Eucharist, the presence of grace in the world, the proclamation of this grace in the Word, the Word's climax in the gift of the body and blood, and the symbolic self-expression of the church in blessing and in meal come together within the same celebration of the pervasive divine grace that is manifested in this way. What is realized in the community or in the person in the Eucharist is the actualization *for them* of the grace woven into the history of the world and opening up to the mystery of divine self-communication.

Rahner spoke of putting the sacrament in relation to the presence of grace in the world as a Copernican revolution in sacramental theology.[7] To find a way in which to express the causality of sacrament that fits this turn and to make a better link between sign and cause, he thought it possible to take a new point of departure in Thomas's attention in his theology of grace to the human subject and its free activity. For Rahner, this activity can be best appreciated by using the idea of symbolic causality. Symbolic interaction is the key to human becoming, as it is key to the presence of one to another. Indeed the two converge, for one becomes present to another in the very process of appropriating the self through the symbol. By analogy, God can be said to be present to the world through the Word Incarnate and through the symbols that commemorate the mysteries of his flesh. By responding to these symbols,

---

7. Karl Rahner, "Considerations on the Active Role of the Person in the Sacramental Event," 161–74. Later in his life, Rahner confessed that the phrase may have been an exaggeration, though he still saw the point as important: "On the Theology of Worship," *Theological Investigations* (New York: Crossroad, 1983), 19:149.

which are the free and committed offer of the gift of the divine self, the faithful become present to God, to each other, and to the world.

Rahner thought that Aquinas might have related sacrament to the presence of God in the world had he taken fuller account of the matter used in sacrament to create the sign. He found that Thomas at times seemed to force the matter's natural properties into a preconceived conformity to word. If, however, water, bread, and wine were taken for what they say about humanity's place in the world they could provide a starting-point for considering how grace touches this being in the world. This would also make it possible to see the relation between God's presence in creation and God's presence in sacramental grace, God's coming to be in the other of creation and of graced humanity.

In considering sacramental symbols, the relation of word to matter is more fully developed in Rahner than in Aquinas. The word of the sacrament embraces the proclamation of the gospel, the offer of grace that is expressed in scripture and preaching. It is this that is connected with the sacramental elements and rites to constitute the reality of symbolic communication. To attend only to the sacramental form, as Aquinas did, does not bring out what is in fact signified in the sacraments. The word already has a sacramental character when it is proclaimed as God's offer of grace within the church. When united with the elements and ritual actions, it constitutes these as offer and communication to those who are thus ritually touched.

This symbolic self-expression of the church as communion in grace and bearer of grace to human persons is realized in all the sacraments.[8] In the Eucharist it reaches its climax. In the Eucharist Rahner relates the proclamation of Christ to the presence of Christ in the prayer of the church and at the sacramental table. Where the word of God

> attains its absolute climax, as the incarnational and eschatological word of God, and absolute self-expression of the church as a whole and as directed to the individual, the word of the Eucharist is heard.[9]

In keeping with this notion of coming to be through symbolic self-expression and communication, Rahner's focus on the ecclesial aspect of sacrament and Eucharist differs from the dominantly institutional categories of Aquinas. He takes sacramental celebration as the core expression of the nature of the church community. In this action it both expresses its worship of God as a communion in the grace of the paschal mystery and its mission as the bearer of the offer of God's grace to

---

8. See the two articles "The Theology of the Symbol" and "The Word and the Eucharist," in *Theological Investigations* (New York: Crossroad, 1982), 4:221–86.

9. Rahner, "The Word and the Eucharist," 286.

its members. In the sacramental celebration this offer of grace is given through word and rite. Aquinas favored strict institutional origins for each of the sacraments, whereas Rahner chose to stress the evolution in time necessary to the process of arriving at an adequate ecclesial self-expression. Not simply Christ's determination but the church's reception of his word and memory of his deeds go into forging the sacramental symbol. This leads to a better appreciation of the historical emergence of sacramental rites over a period of time, since it took several centuries before reconciliation, anointing, and marriage were fully and properly appreciated and celebrated in sacramental form. The Eucharist, however, for its part is the dominical sacrament. From the beginning of the church and to this day it is the fundamental and central expression of the nature of the church as a communion in Christ's mystery and as the bearer in word and rite of the offer of grace to those who respond to the invitation to partake of his sacrifice.

While this theology richly explores the nature of sacraments as signs and sign's relation to grace, there is some problem with Rahner's continued use of the category of cause. When Rahner says that it is in signifying that the sacraments can be said to cause, this depends on Rahner's understanding that the sign activity of the sacrament is symbolic. That is to say, it is the expression and manifestation of the grace offered and of the human person's coming to be. When the meaning of terms is so changed, what is left of the categories of causality? In fact what Rahner does is to propose an ontological theory that says that persons come in communion with another/others through symbolic expression. He then grafts the traditional category of cause on to this theory, in order to remain in continuity with theological discourse.

Edward Schillebeeckx

As the English title of his book suggests, personal encounter is a key expression for Edward Schillebeeckx's sacramental theology.[10] With this at the center he brought attention to event and symbolic interaction into the Thomistic synthesis, in a way similar to that followed by Rahner.

There is however a different nuance to his position. While in his early work on sacrament he spoke of symbolic causality, to a number of readers it was not clear how fully Schillebeeckx related symbol and cause. It was in his small work *The Eucharist* that his differentiation between the symbolic and the ontological became clear.[11] In addressing the dispute over the merits of the words *transignification* and *transubstantiation*

---

10. *Christ the Sacrament of the Encounter with God* (Kansas City: Sheed Andrews and McMeel, A Sheed & Ward Classic, 1963).

11. Edward Schillebeeckx, *The Eucharist* (London: Sheed & Ward, 1968).

in eucharistic theology he emphasized the importance of the former in bringing the notion of shared meaning into focus. At the same time, he did not find it an adequate substitute for the traditional language about substantial change and substantial presence. The meaning expressed and appropriated by the church is not identical with the reality present, though it is an important way of grasping it and appropriating its gift into life. The meaning that humans can appropriate through faith in God's saving activity or in Christ's presence is but a partial attainment of the reality signified. Ontological language is necessary to express that which is beyond the power of signification.

This was in keeping with Schillebeeckx's general thought on analogy. The images and ideas that humans have of God and of God's presence are indeed integrated into communion with the divine but because of God's transcendence they give no conceptual knowledge that can be predicated of God's nature.[12] In a similar way, while we can affirm the presence of Christ in the Eucharist and find a meaning to that presence in the remembrance of event and in symbol, we have no adequate idea of what the reality is in itself.

Schillebeeckx saw the language of substance and species at Trent or substance and accident in Thomas as a rather historically conditioned language that nonetheless conveys something unassailable. It was used to affirm the real nature of Christ's own presence in the Eucharist as something distinct from all the externals of the sign, whether the material or even the verbal. Since it was used analogously and together with necessary negations, it always indicated that the truth of the presence is irreducible to human concepts. The modern emphasis on sign and symbol and encounter helps us to see the part that the Eucharist has in human living but it does not sufficiently account for the transcendent aspect of the reality present and given in sacrament.

In early works, Schillebeeckx gave a markedly transhistorical quality to the passion and resurrection of Christ, taking this as a condition for the pasch's symbolic continuation in the liturgy of the church. He located the essence of the passion in an act of Christ's will that transcends time and is still operative in the sacrament that represents the historical event of the pasch. This explanation risked placing both mystery and the life of grace on a plane quite distinct from the flow of human event in its temporal setting. In the work that he has since done on soteriology and ecclesiology, the historical reality of Christ's passion and the historical realization of grace are to the fore. Concentrating on the Abba experience of Jesus and the Spirit experience of the church, he points in the midst of human history to a filial and even mystical relationship to

---

12. See *Revelation and Theology* (New York: Herder & Herder, 1967), 1:84–95.

God to which liturgy and the ethics of the gospel give expression.[13] As the ultimate meaning of Jesus' earthly activity there is his surrender to God in death, in solidarity with human suffering.

As the death of Jesus needs to be located in its social and religious context, so the memory of that death needs to be expressed in symbols and forms of prayer that are pertinent to the total historical situation of those who live in the faith of Christ, especially as this touches human suffering. At the heart of liturgical memorial there is the church's experience of Christ's Spirit that allows it to affirm the resurrection. The authenticity of liturgical memorial is, as it were, born from its immediacy to current historical reality and is verified in the ethical and liberating action of the community that keeps memory. Most of all, memorial cannot remain alien to human suffering but has to be a voice of hope spoken in the midst of suffering, not only for oneself but for others. The hope that is celebrated in liturgy must have its proper political dimensions, that is, a this-worldly and not simply an other-worldly quality.

Though Schillebeeckx has not done much to develop the implications of this for eucharistic theology,[14] he has made room for two developments. First, in his book on ministry, *The Church with a Human Face,* he offered a critique of ideological patterns in the church that has its implications for the celebration of the Eucharist. Sacramental commemoration in the church has over the course of time been accommodated to social and political patterns. Though such a relation is necessary, it can impede the movement of liberating grace if the interests of structure prevail over the word, prayer, and ritual. Second, his work opens the way to a fuller consideration of what it means to represent the passion of Christ through an active memory that draws the complexities of human life and the realities of human suffering into the remembrance of the Savior. His homily in *Christ* exemplifies a memory that is no mere recital but takes on the task of interpreting Christ's passion in relation to human suffering and current realities.

Summary

What these retrievals of Thomistic sacramental and eucharistic theology did was to give greater value to Thomas's basic definition of sacrament as a sign and to the relation between this and effect. Early retrievals risked too close a link between sign and cause. Later writers put this retrieval into the context of the interpersonal in a way that gave promi-

---

13. Much of his thought is summarized in the book *Church: The Human Story of God* (New York: Crossroad, 1990). On liturgy and memory of Christ, see *Christ: The Experience of Jesus as Lord* (New York: Crossroad, 1980), 814–17.

14. Though see the homily and eucharistic prayer with which he concludes *Christ,* 840–51.

nence and elaboration to something latent in Aquinas's explanation of multiple instrumental causes, starting with the passion of Christ. Instead of using the terms of instrumental causality, they highlighted what symbol and symbolic exchange express beyond the simpler notion of sign as conveyor of knowledge. Along these lines they were also able to give greater value to the full range of word and rite used in the Eucharist rather than relying so heavily on the "matter and form" of the consecration. Once the symbolic exchange is seen to include the entire celebration it is another step to a critique of the way in which language and ritual use may limit the possibilities of meaning and communication.

If one is as careful as Schillebeeckx to keep the distinction between signified and signification, though the signification is realized to be deficient the referent beyond the range of signification holds. Whatever communion in meaning comes about in sacrament, it does not mean the fullness of communion with the reality signified. Within the context of personal encounter, the limits of sacramental meaning are placed within the limits of present reality and at the same time are seen to express the desire for communion with Christ in eschatological fullness.

CRITICAL APPROACH TO THOMAS: METAPHYSICS PUT IN QUESTION

Rather than reappropriating key aspects of Thomas's thought, the recent sacramental theology of Louis-Marie Chauvet constitutes a radical critique of the Thomistic approach to worship, as indeed more fundamentally of its way of conceiving God's relation to the world and to human existence.[15] Chauvet believes that a rethinking of these issues is necessary in face of Martin Heidegger's critique of Western metaphysics. Theology has to take on the task of thinking the Christian mystery from its origins and of rethinking various formulations of faith.

Heidegger was convinced that a universal concept of Being inherited from Western philosophy prevents us from seeing things as they are or as they come into being. The conceptualization of being led to the forgetting of Being and the inability to see the advent of Being in its surprising manifestations. Because of the value attached to the universal idea of Being humanity had become, as seen by Heidegger, insensitive to its own mortality, to the death that all living things must face without illusion.

To understand the development of the universal concept of Being

---

15. Louis-Marie Chauvet, *Symbole et sacrement: Une relecture sacramentelle de l'existence chrétienne* (Paris: Ed. du Cerf, 1987).

one has to retrieve the issues that its formulation addressed. One finds that it is the reality of human being's presence in and to the world that was at stake, as well as its being in time and thus being towards death. The universal concept of being expresses the communion of humanity's being in the world with the world, beneath an experience that is often sensed as alienation or imprisonment. It is by reason of participation in earthly and cosmic reality that humanity's own destiny has to be understood, not in divorce from it. As the concept came to be used, however, it ignored differences, especially the difference between Being and beings. It helped to stifle experience and the question's raised by experience. Since it provided an answer and a meaning to reality before events occurred, it suppressed whatever new events could reveal about being in the world and in time, and about Being's own manifestation.

Language too fell victim to this reduction of reality and experience to the universal. Words are deprived of their power to reveal when they are used to classify. In the naming of things by the use of simple and daily words such as *jug* and *bread*, there is a power to call to a communion with the world that is lost when there is no more attention to the naming and only the object is held in view. The process of naming things has to be recaptured, for it is in this way that it is discovered what the name calls into communion and how things are related to a greater horizon. To rediscover this power of naming and gathering together Heidegger pursued thought about poetic language. However, the power to reveal as well as conceal at root belongs to ordinary language. Poetry serves to bring us back again to the power of words to bring things and worlds into vision, to offer meanings even while expressing ultimate mystery. A simple word like *bread* may be used only to classify edible items, or it may continue to ring with its power to evoke humanity's presence in and to a vaster world.

After Heidegger the manipulation of language by what is deemed right-thinking has been even more acutely observed. Critics point to a centering of reality in the self, in ego-consciousness, that impedes attention to the fullness of reality and to language alike. One might say that persons and societies are so centered on their own minds that they neither see nor hear any more. Derrida's play with script that teases the reader into looking for new meanings in texts is well-known. While some are baffled by this, there is no denying that we do tend to take it for granted that we know the meaning of words and texts, until startled into realizing that we may not after all have grasped what they project.

Other criticisms have drawn attention to the uses of power in determining the standard meanings of written and ritual texts. There is here a double risk. First, insistence on maintaining a sense of order suppresses and camouflages the absence of meaning in life, and indeed the absence of the human itself in acts that are nonetheless recorded on the pages of history. Second, authoritative interpretation that allows only for canonical meanings of texts and rites suppresses alternative meanings that they may at least potentially project.

The only way of overcoming tradition's sterility is to be attentive to the issues that were at stake in the significant moments of tradition's development and to see them again in the light of contemporary questions. This pertains both to the origin of ideas or concepts and to the use of language. Questions have to be raised again, the process of thinking and naming reconsidered. One is not faithful to a tradition if one only looks for traditional answers.

All of this has repercussions on theology. It affects the ways in which we think about and name God or explain the reality of Jesus Christ. In proposing a sacramental reading of Christian existence, rather than simply a theology of sacraments, Chauvet has drawn attention to several problem areas in the Thomistic approach to sacrament. It assumes specific concepts of grace, cause, God, Christ, and history, which are problematic and too limited. Chauvet endeavors to rethink these realities together on the basis of a nonmetaphysical but symbolic thinking of God's presence to the church in Christ.

The defect in using metaphysics to explain sacraments comes from the use of the concepts of efficient and exemplarity causality to express God's action in the world, for grace is thus turned into an object that resembles objects purchased in markets or produced in factories. Along with this way of conceptualizing grace as spiritual entity, there is a manipulation of language that is particularly harmful to the celebration of sacrament. In fact, a particular idea of the relation between thought and language is the radical problem in Western metaphysics. Language is not allowed to shape being in the world and to open up thought but is turned into an instrument for expressing what is considered as right-thinking. It is supposed that speakers or writers are in such possession of their thought that they can give it clear expression and that they can judge the adequacy of the thought to its object.

To respond to this problem, Chauvet wants to rethink the language of the paschal mystery from within language itself and in its nature as event. He is persuaded that attention to the language of sacramental tradition, rather than to metaphysical theories about sacrament, makes it possible to attend anew to what is said about God's advent in Christ, about the divine presence in the world, and about God's sacramental gift. To see how this approach affects the eucharistic theology found in Aquinas, attention is given first to Chauvet's critique of causality and then to his critique of the manipulation of language.[16]

---

16. For Chauvet's specific critique of Thomism, see *Symbole et sacrement*, 51–80 and 463–84.

Critique of Causality

A key problem with sacramental theology is that it has become partner to a broader metaphysical tradition. Chauvet dubs metaphysics instrumentalist thinking, which cannot allow for the event of beings except in terms of production. Everything is thought of as having its origin in something else and is never respected in the sheer gratuity of its being there. Moreover, because of a universal notion of being underlying all beings, the singularity of what events or is disclosed is neglected, all things being reduced to particular realizations of what is the general.

Chauvet contrasts two kinds of coming to be in order to make his point that certain realities have to be thought of in terms other than those of productive action. He compares the relation of a boat to a boat-builder with that of a beloved to a lover. While the boat-builder actually produces the boat by things done with its materials, the lover cannot be said to produce the love of the beloved. The lover simply stands in a relation to the loved one that allows the latter to respond. The response arises from the heart of the loved one, not from the action of the lover. Chauvet contends that in this latter case one cannot talk of causality but only of coming to be in response to another. The truly human, which is found in such realities as love, pleasure, and joy, cannot be seen as caused, for cause in Chauvet's eyes necessarily implies producing by reason of the action of one upon the other. This kind of human coming to be can only be represented symbolically in its gratuitous emergence, within the world of meaning expressed in language, symbol, and rite.

This is what Chauvet takes as a paradigm for the order of grace and hence also for sacramental action. To use the logic of causality in speaking of grace devalues it in his eyes and runs contrary to the reality of the interpersonal and gratuitous order where grace belongs.

The revision of thought and language that this entails has to extend to talk about God. Not only must sacramental theology rid itself of the conception of producing grace, it must be freed likewise of the concept of God as self-cause and first cause of all things. Using this language of God is essentially to think of the divinity within an order of beings and to risk taking a univocal understanding of being as the ground for thinking about God. For Chauvet, the concept of God as first and universal cause contradicts the biblical origins of Christian God-language. In the scriptures, God is shown to enter history in the gratuitous manifestation of the cross. This divine epiphany defies a causal and providential explanation of event and history. It symbolically represents the advent of God in the midst of human suffering, simply as the presence of one who offers love as gift and invites response.

Chauvet finds that the symbolism of the exchange of gifts fits better into an understanding of the Eucharist than that of sacrifice, when it is understood as immolative cultic activity, which is in fact done away with through the death of Jesus.[17] His concern is to express the relation between humans and God in gratuitous terms and in terms that respect the human person's free response, rather than in terms of causality or through the image of sacrificial immolation. As God is present in the free gift of Christ's pasch and of the Spirit, so the church responds freely with its own gift. The initiative of God is affirmed, but there is no constraint on the believer.

Chauvet is aware of the distinction that Aquinas makes between the judgment or affirmation of being's dependency and the conceptualization of God based on the relation of effect to cause. Nonetheless, whatever circumspection he shows in the use of the analogy of efficient cause to explain sacramental action and efficacy, Chauvet thinks that Thomas passes too readily from the analogy of being to conceptual analogies in explaining the divine nature and in explaining God's relation to the world.

Critique of Thomas's Approach to Language

Chauvet suggests that it is the approach to language that is at the root of the instrumentalist and productive thinking that he associates with causality. This deserves consideration.[18]

Since the entire sacramental theology of Aquinas is organized around the notion of sign, which is explained by the way in which words complete matter, any retrieval or critique of Thomistic sacramental theology must therefore address the question of how he sees the functioning of language. Following Aristotle, Thomas thought of language as something produced by thought, and ultimately by things. The thing produces the phantasm and the phantasm the *species impressa*. From the *species impressa* the intellect produces in itself the *species expressa*, or intelligible species. From this it produces a word that is either a concept or a judgment. Outward language follows on thought and is an instrument of thought and is used for communicating thought to others. This concept of language is built into the understanding of instrumental sacramental causality, for the effect is produced when words complement the matter, establishing the threefold signification of Christ's passion, grace, and future glory.

In Thomistic ideas about language there is the supposition that the speaker/writer has possession of thought, or is present to the self in

---

17. Chauvet actually thinks that symbolic exchange is truer to an original anthropological understanding of sacrifice, and on this point he appeals to the theory of Hubert Mauss. What he specifically wants to be rid of is the idea of sacrifice as immolation.

18. On the emergence of the concept of language in the history of Western thought, see Hans-Georg Gadamer, *Truth and Method* (New York: Crossroad, 1988), 366–97.

thought, and on this condition is ready to move to speech. This is what Chauvet criticizes. He finds that no attention is paid to the fact that the world is constituted by language and that it is in language that one is brought to dwell in the world. Language precedes thought, not only for individuals but for whole cultures. Language precedes thought and cannot simply be looked upon as a code ready at hand to express meanings. It is through language that signification is constituted, even beyond the speaker's actual grasp of what is signified. This is not simply because the ideas are too deep to grasp at once, but because they are imbedded in the language world to which people belong. Reflection on language therefore is needed in order to think about the reality to which one belongs, and even about one's own self.

Chauvet's reading of Aquinas certainly points to some aspects of his thought on language that are problematic for eucharistic theology. The most problematic of all is the way in which the human relation between thought and word served as an analogue for divine exemplary causality in the theory of sacramental causality. This only seems to bolster the image of production, as though God produced grace according to a plan. As a result, it takes away from the interpersonal character of the economy of grace, otherwise important to Thomistic theology.

Apart from this fundamental problem, Thomas's way of dealing with diverse forms of discourse limits the power of sacramental symbolism. He distinguishes sharply between conceptual discourse and metaphorical discourse.[19] The latter belongs to rhetoric and is an ornament that makes ideas more persuasive and appealing to the heart.

The analogical predication of concepts is his way of dealing with plurivocity and with similarity in difference. This leaves little room for the power of metaphor or of the imagination to reconstrue or disclose reality, especially in the area of the interpersonal. In eucharistic theology, therefore, the retrieval of such Old Testament images as the paschal lamb or the manna serves only to illustrate the conceptual theology of substance, grace, and causality.

The general distinction that Thomas makes between the literal and the spiritual sense of the scriptures is applied to the Eucharist in his way of relating the spiritual effects to the fundamental questions of presence and sacrifice. On the one hand, his insistence that the spiritual meaning has to be related to the literal controlled allegorical fantasy both in the interpretation of the scripture and in the explanation of eucharistic rites. On the other hand, however, the theory of Christ's substantial presence dominated eucharistic theology. This was the literal sense of the sacrament expressed in the words of consecration, to which all spiritual meaning needed to be related. In the long run, this minimized the

---

19. On language, see the *Summa Theologiae* I, q. 1, art. 9 and 10.

more personal reality of the sacrament as the sacrament of the body of Christ uniting the redeemed in the communion of the grace of the head.

Chauvet rightly alerts his readers to the broad world of language to which sacraments belong. This world is set by the scriptural tradition within which Christ is proclaimed and made known and which constitutes the original canon of meaning for the life of the church. To see how it belongs in sacramental memorial, it is necessary to go beyond the words of consecration to the words of the blessing, and beyond the words of the blessing to the total narrative and ritual context. Handed down and modified across the centuries and in different cultures, sacramental expression has known embellishments and restraints. At times it has been broadened in its power to include reality and unfold meaning, at times, however, limited by the restraints of both culture and institution. All of this is pertinent to eucharistic theology, which cannot be developed in isolation from thought about liturgical expression.

Chauvet and Stanislas Breton

In several places in his book Chauvet mentions Stanislas Breton.[20] To find language appropriate to express God's presence in sacrament he appeals to Breton's idea of *meontology*. On this ground he thinks that it is possible to use apophatic and metaphorical language to name God's eucharistic presence in Christ without resorting to metaphysical terms. Some consideration of Breton's work will help us to understand Chauvet's critique of Thomism more fully and to see an approach that is offered as an alternative.

For Breton, philosophical thought retains a function, even if a limited one, in theology. It can reveal the structure of human being and even make its contribution to theology by doing this. Breton takes this fundamental structure of human being to be relation to the other, its *esse ad* without which it has no *esse in se*. The ultimate referent of this relationship is however unattainable to human thought. Its ineffability is betrayed by any use of the analogy of names, which allows known qualities to be predicated in an eminent way, with all restrictions removed, to the ultimate other. Even though the analogy of being as employed by Aquinas refers strictly to the act of being and not to any concept of being, Breton finds that it too readily opens the way to other analogies that trespass on the ineffable. Hence he finds that even the language of being confuses when employed of the divine.

Breton thinks that it would be equally misplaced to take analogies from philosophical or theological anthropology to name God or to ex-

---

20. Stanislas Breton is a philosopher turned theologian. His major theological works are *Ecriture et Révélation* (Paris: Desclée, 1978), *Le Verbe et la Croix* (Paris: Desclée, 1981), and *Unicité et monothéisme* (Paris: Desclée, 1983).

plain Christ's suffering as God's suffering. To go beyond the dilemma of God-language therefore Breton takes the notion of meontology from the philosophies of Plotinus and Proclus. Consequently he likes to use the term *the ONE* to refer to that which is at the origin and which is the ultimate referent of human being. To talk of meontology is first to deny of the One any ontological concept, whether founded in an analogy of being or in an understanding of the human person. The One is nothing of that which proceeds from it, or which has its being in dependency on it. That is, the created shares no qualities with the One, no analogical predications are possible that include the created and its origin. Besides then being a denial of such ontological predication, meontology can also be said to refer to that which is beyond ontology, beyond even analogical human thought, beyond any possibility of comparison, even by way of eminence.

The language used of the One is metaphorical, and to the word *metaphorical* Breton attaches the power to carry the speaker to a communion beyond language and thought.[21] Thus metaphorical language and apophatic language converge in referring to the ineffable. Metaphor is born out of event, out of a situation in which something hidden is sensed to make itself present, to come to be among us while remaining in its nature concealed. As a beneficent presence it is gift and invitation, gift of a power of action freed from limits, invitation to pass in responsive self-gift to communion with the one whose presence is believed. Names given to God out of this event are metaphoric. As metaphors they offer unlikely conjugates for predication, so that the unlike is necessary to the likeness suggested. By their power to create modes of *being towards*, they carry those who use them forward towards the ineffable.

The relation of the world to the One who thus events can be expressed in the Neoplatonist language, also adopted by Thomas Aquinas, of *exitus/reditus*, and of the Many and the One. The many who come forth from the One seek to be reintegrated into it. This return is possible only to those who refuse the illusions of divine representation, who do not attach themselves to any structural or conceptual representation of the divine in the world. Such representation in fact exalts not the infinite, but the finite that pretends to a similarity to the infinite. Hence the language of representation in naming the One is totally the language of event and of apophatic naming. The One comes in the event and though named from/for the event remains essentially unnamed.

For Breton this understanding of the relation of the many to the One is a suitable language in which to speak of the mystery of the cross. In the cross of Christ the One advents in the world and out of this event

---

21. For a brief presentation of his idea of metaphor, see the article "Faut-il parler des anges?," *Revue des Sciences Philosophiques et Théologiques* 64 (1980): 225–40.

takes the name of Father. The proclamation of Christ on the cross is the Word that speaks this event. Inasmuch as the eventing is spoken and commemorated in the church, God is present as Spirit in the hearts of the faithful. Relying heavily on 1 Corinthians 1, Breton points out that the language of the cross, the language that represents God's advent through the cross, cannot imbibe any human wisdom. Whether the wisdom be that of philosophy or of religious institution it is refuted by the wisdom of the cross. The cross tells us that *God* cannot be represented in human concept or in institution, though the *event of the cross* to become a power in human lives needs to be represented. It is in effect represented in words, rites, and institutions, as well as in a more concrete way in ethical behavior. Even on this representation however there is a limit for no representation is ever adequate to the event represented, let alone to the One who advents in the event. It is never, that is to say, God who is being represented but the event of God's coming. Faithful representation of this event includes the negation of the possibility of representing God. The divine names taken from the event include this negation, as well as negation of its own adequacy to the event itself.

Like any other event in this world, the cross takes on the full character as event only when brought to language. Indeed for Breton, this means essentially being brought to written form, since it is written form that makes it available outside contracted space and time. Things of course happen but their place in history depends on being brought to language. Why then is the language of representation never adequate to the event? Because the language used to make the event come to be as communicable event by its very nature shows that there is more projected in the expression than is actually apprehended. In this sense the representation and commemoration of the cross is inexhaustible, even though it is in the course of time expressed in acknowledged doctrinal, sacramental, and ethical traditions whose fidelity to the originating event is affirmed. Since therefore the cross of Christ is also opening the way to new expression, the cross is ever eventing in the church, and God is ever eventing through the cross. Though this occurs in many forms of language, at the heart of the life of the church and of its representation of the cross or the pasch there is always the eucharistic commemoration. It is this representation of the cross that Chauvet incorporates into eucharistic theology, as a way of avoiding metaphysics.

THE PLEA FOR ONTOLOGY

Not all who attend to the Heideggerian critique are satisfied that it is adequately answered outside the metaphysical tradition itself. It is on the basis of a reading of Aquinas himself and an attempt to rethink the questions that he raised that some contemporary writers have responded to the critique. William Hill took up the issue some time ago.[22] Yves Labbé[23] and Ghislain Lafont[24] have offered appreciative but critical responses to Chauvet in the context of their own larger corpus of writing, which continue to bear a relation to Thomism.

William Hill

Hill has in a special way responded to the Heideggerian accusation that Western metaphysics leads to the forgetfulness of being. Hill pointed out that production is not an integral part of Thomas's causal analogy in explaining creation and sacrament. It is the analogy of being, not the analogy of action upon another, that governs his thought. In fact, he employed this Aristotelian category of efficient cause in order to accentuate the distance between God and creatures. In Neoplatonism, participating being could too easily be seen as an emanation from God, glossing the difference between God and beings. The analogy of being avoids this. It may be best seen from the side of the finite thing. Thomas pointed to the ontological structure of created being rather than to an image of God acting. Created being exists in dependence on, or beholden to, the one who is totally Act.

If one were to apply Hill's ideas to eucharistic theology, to insist that God is first and principal cause of grace is to underline the gratuity of grace and the relation of total dependence on God at the core of one's being and of being saved. Furthermore, as already pointed out, to speak of Christ, church, and minister as instrumental causes is to accentuate the order of relations within which one comes to be in grace. Finding in the sacrifice of Christ not only an instrumental cause but also an exemplar of the life of grace enhances this sense of relation and communion. Causal language for Aquinas was only analogous. What he intended was to express a relationship in those celebrating sacraments to God as Savior, through communion with Christ and the church, in the memory of Christ's passion. All stand in relation to God within the memory of Christ's passion and by way of sharing in the relation to which he gave expression in his loving obedience. This said, the dependency on God

---

22. William Hill, "Rescuing Theism: A Bridge between Aquinas and Heidegger," *Heythrop Journal* 27 (1987): 377–93.

23. Yves Labbé, "Réceptions théologiques de la 'Postmodernité': A propos de deux livres récents de G. Lafont et L.-M. Chauvet," *Revue des Sciences Philosophiques et Théologiques* 72 (1988): 397–426. See also his work *Essai sur le Monothéisme Trinitaire* (Paris: Ed. du Cerf, 1987).

24. See his review of *Symbole et sacrement* in *Ecclesia Orans* 5 (1988): 231–35. See also Ghislain Lafont, *Dieu, le temps et l'être* (Paris: Ed. du Cerf, 1986).

which is expressed in causal language is a dependency in the act of being. There is no intention of saying that God acts on persons in some physical way.

If the analogy of being is to be kept, it can respond to the issues raised by Aquinas without developing it along the lines in which he wrote of causality. What it fundamentally affirms is that in created reality there is a real relationality to God in the very fact of being. As William Hill states the matter, this analogy enables us to keep the "insistence upon the ultimacy of the Giver behind not only the Gift but the Giving."[25] As Lafont states it, holding on to the analogy of being shows how the human person is constituted in the very act of being, as well as in openness to the infinite, by a creative word of God.[26]

Pursuing this trend of thought, it can be said that in the reality of Christ and in the gift of the Spirit there is a genuine divine self-communication that could not be thought of without the event of revelation but that, once given, can be understood by way of analogy with the relation of being to its origin. As he is professed in faith as Incarnate Word, there is in Christ's humanity a relation to the life of God that allows us to see in him a divine presence that involves God's self. Veiled though the revelation be, and under the conditions of the wisdom of the cross, the passover of Christ as a person is not a coming to be of God, but God coming to be among us in the invitation to communion with God the Giver. The gift of the Spirit, which is God's presence in the communion of the church and in the heart of the sanctified, engenders in the receiver the capacity of a free response to God's coming and revealing. Some language however other than that of efficient causality is needed to express the interpersonal or intersubjective communion resulting from the divine presence in the economy of grace.

Christ is present in the church in and through the memorial of his passion. He is present in the sacrament precisely inasmuch as it is a memorial of the passion. Even Thomas touched on this in relating the presence to the signs that signify the passion or immolation. It is not possible to be in communion with Christ in the sacrament without being in communion with his passion. One cannot receive Christ's self-gift without committing oneself to live by the truth of the passion. When one relates the sacramental signs to Christ, it is to his advent as God's offer

---

25. William Hill, "Rescuing Theism," 388. He continues: "In the end, the primordial Giver is revealed as God, who is ultimate in an unqualified sense and the origin of the becoming which characterizes the universe of finite persons."

26. G. Lafont, *Dieu, le temps et l'être*, 330: "La parole de Dieu *créatrice* constituerait l'étant dans son acte d'être, sa spécificité, sa dynamique, mais aussi, dans le cas de l'étant libre, son ouverture infinie; la parole de Dieu *adressée* proposerait une *rupture symbolique* dans la dynamique liée à la création, à seule fin de permettre à l'ouverture de s'élargir jusqu'à la communion divine et par suite à la transfiguration d'un monde."

in the suffering of the cross that one must needs relate them. The referent of the sacrament, whether it be to its godly origin or to its finality, to
the Christ present or to his suffering, is to ultimate transcendence. The
giftedness of grace and life of the Spirit that comes through the sacrament is the gift of being related to God in communion with the passion
of Christ.

Being and Narrative: Labbé and Lafont

For Labbé and Lafont, the way to capture this sense of communion in
and with Christ is to relate the analogy of being to the power of narrative. For a world that is totally dependent for its being on God, God
comes through the events of the Old Testament pasch and especially in
the event of Christ's death and resurrection. It is by tracing the origin
of grace to these events and to their remembrance in narrative that we
learn what grace is, and who God is.

This narrative remembrance effects a rupture with mythical and
metaphysical thinking,[27] captured best perhaps in the symbols of the
burning bush and the cross[28] as they represent the implications of God's
manifestation to Moses and in Christ. The name that Yahweh manifests to Moses and the name which Christ gives to God from the cross
both indicate the difference between God as revealed and the image or
thought of God represented in myth, in religious institution, in ritual,
and in philosophy. It is from this starting-point of negation that Christian theology strives to understand God's presence and action in the
world.

Here it should be noted that when it comes to the revelation of God's
own being, for Labbé and Lafont it is not necessary to go the way of
meontology to avoid metaphysical theories of causality. If Thomas or
Thomism made a mistake, it was to allow philosophically conceived notions about God and creatures dictate the terms of theological thinking.
It may be possible to think from the language of revelation and of event,
and then by an analogy of faith use philosophical notions to elucidate
the mystery, always testing theological explanation against its fidelity to
the biblical narrative.

Our concern here, however, is not directly with the theology of God
but rather with what questions and avenues of thought are offered to
eucharistic theology. A possible line of exploration seems to be opened
up by putting the analogy of being and narrative into critical conjunc-

---

27. See ibid.
28. Breton also makes a strong appeal to these symbols as negation of the power
of religious system and philosophical thought to provide an understanding of God's
revelation.

tion. Further consideration of this may be deferred to the next chapter, where it will be linked with a theology of memorial.

CONCLUSION

These contemporary conversations with the sacramental thought of Thomas Aquinas alert us to several things that must put twists on any contemporary retrieval of his place in the eucharistic tradition.

What has been more fully appreciated of late is the personalism of his thought on the Eucharist. The theology of sacramental grace in the *Summa* is one of communion in the passion of Christ and in the hope of glory. Sacraments are interpersonal in their nature and celebration and though Aquinas was most intent on the role of ordained ministry, his eucharistic theology has an underlying ecclesiology of some importance. What emerges however from the discussions reviewed is that the theory of efficient causality is not adequate to the interpersonal character of eucharistic communion. On the other hand, the theorem that a *votum* for the Eucharist is inherent to every gift of grace appears on examination to show both an appreciation of a pervasive presence of grace in the lives of human persons and an insight into how sacramental celebration expresses the fuller reality of the grace of Christ.

Another point that emerges from contemporary discussions of his sacramental theology is the way in which it upholds the apophatic nature of sacramental signification and Christ's eucharistic presence. Though the sacrament clearly affirms Christ's presence and the gift of grace, reality is not reducible to perceived meaning and communion in grace is more deeply rooted than in shared meaning.

The full import of classifying sacraments as signs has come to light by enlarging this to include a deeper grasp of symbolic expression and exchange. This however points to the limits of Thomas's idea of sign and signification and of his understanding of the relation between language and thought. With a fuller appreciation of language, the latent possibilities of symbol, narrative, blessing, and ritual in expressing communion in grace and the naming of the God revealed in Christ can be retrieved.

From the conversations with Thomas, it emerges that three kinds of discourse are needed in eucharistic theology. The basic form of discourse is that of memorial, where narrative, blessing, and poetic imagery dominate. Ontological discourse is also necessary in order to express the structure of created being and its relation to the transcendent, as well as to differentiate between reality and the meaning that is expressed and communicated. Institutional discourse expresses how members of a community interrelate, how they relate to a tradition, and how power is exercised and distributed within it. This last needs a more critical basis than what is found in the theology of Thomas Aquinas, just as the first has to show a greater sense of the adequacy of linguistic expression than he does.

How these orientations that emerge from conversations with Aquinas can be incorporated into an ongoing revision of eucharistic thought and practice will be considered next.

Chapter 13

SACRAMENT
OF THE CHURCH

The image of conversation has been used to express the way in which the church appropriates its many-faceted eucharistic tradition. How some of this conversation has begun to take shape was seen in the previous chapter in the ways in which theologians now approach a reading of Thomas Aquinas. If the conversation is broadened to take the full tradition and the contemporary situation into account, what kind of theology develops?

The theology offered has to be one that accommodates multiple cultural expression and allows for exchange and communion within diversity. It must also be attentive to the ruins in the midst of which Christ's memorial is celebrated, to the victims of human history, and to the sufferings that result when the edifice of the human collapses.

In looking to the past, it has been seen how in some respects the *lex orandi* was always more central to a community of faith than the precisely formulated *lex credendi*, contained in creeds, doctrinal teaching, and theologies. It is not, however, possible to give either the rule of belief or the rule of prayer logical or chronological priority over the other. They work themselves out in close interaction, in every age.

Especially in ritual performance one can see the influence of ideas or theologies on liturgical meaning and participation. In the early church eucharistic celebration was regulated by a sense of looking backward to the redemptive pasch of Christ and forward to eschatological fulfilment. In Eastern churches of the post-Constantinian era the prevailing perspective was that of typological representation of Christ's mysteries, with resultant effects on the form of the anaphora and on liturgical rites such as the Great Entrance. From the origins of the Latin tradition, sacrifice and offering provided the primary motif, which led eventually to the complex medieval hierarchical celebration and daily Mass system. For the sixteenth-century Reformers the theology of justification by faith, in response to God's Word and proclamation of forgiveness in Christ, dictated liturgical change.

Even while noting the limitations that these overarching perspectives sometimes put on participation in the liturgy, due attention was given to approaches to the sacrament that were never well integrated into liturgical understanding and piety. These experiences and expressions that contrast with accepted modes of thought and practice offer alternative sources for a revitalization of tradition. These often have to do with persons, groups, and pieties that were in their time marginal to central trends. As far as we are concerned, they too belong to the tradition and may offer inspiration and challenges to contemporary developments.

Looking at today's reality, it is clear that there is as yet no dominant theological or cultural perspective at work in eucharistic practice. There are also different trends, not always well acknowledged by church authority but important in themselves. A theology or theological reflection is needed that can integrate this diversity, as well as show what eucharistic memorial means in a time when people have to be more sensitive to human failure and suffering. The framework for such reflection is that of eucharistic celebration and the key heuristic is that of understanding memorial in light of the power that language expression has to bring past event into present time. In this the appreciation of the emergence and role of language that is found in contemporary thought is helpful.

Three chapters are devoted to this theological reflection, which is as much a method as it is a ready-made system. A liturgical celebration that makes the communion rite the climax of the celebration of an ecclesial sacrament is the key to the first. An understanding of the relation between memorial and language is key to the second. In the third, some practical consequences are suggested, affecting the canon of remembrance, ritual performance, and Christian ethics.

In this chapter, the three points considered within the framework of liturgical celebration are the centrality of the communion table, the nature of the Eucharist as sacrament of the church, and the communion in the Spirit that is both ground and fruit of such celebration.

THE COMMUNION TABLE

Of primary importance in the *lex orandi* of the Eucharist is the centrality of *the communion table*. This must also be central to the *lex credendi*. Any adequate Catholic theology takes the communion table as the central act of the liturgy.[1] In the gift given at the table, the self-gift of Christ on the cross is mediated and the life of the Spirit is shared in communion with the risen Lord. It is by way of the quadruple reference to supper, cross, resurrection, and eschatological hope that the meaning of eucharistic communion is expressed.

The fundamental appeal here is to the New Testament traditions. The Pauline texts on the Lord's Supper identify the reality of the church with the communion in the one loaf and the one covenant cup. It is because all eat and drink of the Lord's body and blood that they are themselves one body and one covenant people, and it is from within this communion that they proclaim his death in word and in witness. The testamentary tradition of the Johannine Gospel highlights the communion of love within which the gift is given, as well as the character of loving service inherent to the gift of Christ's body and blood. Taking these texts along with what was seen about the breaking of the bread in the Acts of the Apostles, one recognizes the larger context of service, communion, prayer, and ritual, to which the communion table belongs and from which it derives its full significance.

All the discussions on the presence of Christ in the Eucharist and on communion in his sacrifice through the eucharistic memorial need to be interpreted in relation to what is given in communion. It is not the reality of Christ present in the host as a thing that is the point of discussion, but the reality of what the Lord gives to the faithful in this symbolic action of the bread and the wine. Similarly the principal sacramental representation of Christ's paschal mystery is located in the communion action, not in the prayer of blessing, nor in any repetition of Christ's own words. Of course it cannot be *this* type of ritual eating and drinking without the proclamatory word and the memorial blessing, but the symbolism at the center of the entire action is the communion gift and its reception. As the climax of the liturgical action, it is theologically the point around which words, rites, and symbols converge.

From earliest times, Christian writers have stressed that the gifts offered are the body and blood of Christ. Many explanations of this have been offered, including the Tridentine definition that the substance of bread and wine are changed into the body and blood of Christ. As presented by Thomas Aquinas, the theory of substantial presence and substantial change explained the sacramental reality of communion with the risen Christ within the unity of the church, a communion that meant participation in his life and contemplation of his mystery. In other words, the speculative theory of substantial presence was ordered

---

1. See Hans Urs von Balthasar, *The Glory of the Lord: A Theological Aesthetics* (New York: Crossroad, 1982), 1:573: "The accent must fall on the encounter of Christ and the Church in the act of the meal: this is where the center of gravity lies. . . . The true sacramental sign in the Eucharist is the event of eating and drinking."

to an appreciation of Christ's personal self-gift. In recent decades, explanations of symbolic expression and symbolic exchange showed how communion in Christ changes the meaning of human lives. By explaining that the sacramental reality of Christ's pasch must relate to the divine self-communication operative in the act of creation, Karl Rahner showed how the Eucharist takes up and transforms human life within the total reality of the world.

What needs to be brought to the fore today is that it is by communion in the flesh and blood of Christ that the faithful come to share in the hope of his resurrection and in the gift of eternal life, for it is this that most tellingly transforms human life and gives hope in times of stress. A deep union with Christ himself in the eschatological gift of the Spirit is what is offered and promised, but it has to be guaranteed by a communion with him in his suffering through the way of discipleship on this earth. The full import of this is expressed in the symbolic promise of the second coming, the meaning and truth of which it is impossible for us to express in conceptual terms.

The notions of substantial presence and substantial change serve as limit concepts to express the truth and reality of the gift given in communion and so of the communion with Christ in the mysteries of his flesh mediated by the sacrament. They mean that Christ's presence can be reduced neither to physical presence, subjective memory, symbolic exchange, nor shared meaning. Humans are limited in their grasp of reality. The church can never claim to fully grasp the meaning or signification of sharing in the reality of Christ's pasch or in his gift of self. In the power of the blessing, the symbols of bread and wine signify the meaning of Christ's gift and pasch, but they offer a reality beyond what can be signified in sign or in human language or grasped by earthly intelligence.

Symbolism of the Bread and Wine

The memory of Christ is appropriated by a community that is brought together around the table on which it has set bread and wine. The symbolism of eating and drinking, or of nourishment, has always served to express the intimacy of communion with Christ that the sacrament offers. What needs stronger elaboration is how the bread and wine in their own selves express human existence, how their change represents the transformation of this existence, and how communion in the blessed flesh and blood of Christ is thus a communion that reaches to the depths of human reality and of Christ's part in it.

The meaning of the symbolic act can be considered on four levels of significance. First one can see how a community expresses its desires and aspirations in gathering at table to share food and drink. Second one can see how this relates to the social and institutional factors of human living. Third there is the significance of sharing this rite in a community of mutual service and nondiscrimination. Fourth, in virtue of the blessing the gathering at the table becomes the action by which the death and resurrection of Jesus Christ are proclaimed and he himself is present among them as servant and as Lord, transforming the manner of their presence in the world in which they live and to which they give shape and offering his own self as life's nourishment.

At the first level of meaning there is the common significance of bread and wine, expressing the essential urges of hunger and thirst. They offer nourishment and refreshment but cannot satiate. Produced from the grain sown in the field and from the grapes of the vine pressed and crushed, they recall the unending struggle between life and death. Signifying nourishment and refreshment, they also call to mind their opposites of famine and drought. Their dependence on seasonal cycles brings humanity into the larger cosmic reality. It is because of this that in religious history they are often allied with the representations of cosmic deities and sacrificial rituals, for in this way humanity's oneness with the universe is affirmed.

At a second level of signification, which follows on the first, bread and wine relate to social, economic, and cultural realities. Their production belongs to an intersubjective and organized human society. The needs of the many are met only if there is social cohesion. In traditional biblical and rabbinic blessings while God is thanked for what the earth produces, blessing is asked for the land. This is the recognition of a covenant that includes social and political factors.

Furthermore, bread blessed at table necessarily puts all present in mind of the abundance or want experienced by those who gather. The affinity between the domestic church and family ritual is worth considering. If fathers and mothers invoke a blessing over the family table they do not in so doing empty their minds of all thought of what it took to place the food on the table. If provisions are meagre and the next meal unpredictable they think of this as they pray. In their blessing, they are often wont to mention others who are in want. So it is that church gatherings are faced by their ritual with issues of human need and human justice. The eschatological promise of the rule of God, though it transcends our concepts of time, is tied to the hope of a covenant justice here on earth.

Coming to the significance drawn from the nature of the community that gathers, the sharing of bread and wine takes on the characteristics of Christian assembly. It belongs to the bonding of believers in common identity, in mutual service, in charity, and in hope. The sharing in a mutual service that overcomes social distinction is brought out strongly in the testamentary tradition of the Last Supper. Those united in this way cannot approach the ordinary affairs of life expressed in the bread and wine as though they were not bonded in service and eschatological expectation.

Finally, all of this is related to the representation of Christ's suffering and death for the many and to the gift of his life. It is in the body of the Spirit-filled community as it breaks bread and pours out wine to drink that Christ and his death are represented. It is precisely as actions of the common table, shared in memorial thanksgiving, that these signify Christ's saving death and abiding presence. Nothing of the innate meaning of food and drink is abolished in order to accommodate this representation. All is taken up into the eschatological promise of the passion narrative, the images of the table playing with the remembrance of the passion.

Centered on the cross, the passion narrative employs various images of exile and return, election and abandonment, judgment and counter-judgment, descent and ascent, redemption and expiation, priestliness and sacrifice. In the light of this richly told story the human reality of sharing food and drink taken from the earth becomes one with communion in the passion. Around that table, the community is itself a living testimony to the truth and the promise of what was done on the cross. Being one with the earth, being in the world, being together as a community that hopes, are affirmed but transformed by the memory of Christ and the blessing that it evokes. This does not mean that all is now comprehended. The vision of reality may remain disjunctive, but a new sense of being in the world and of being in communion is projected that changes the horizon and the hope within which people live.

SACRAMENT OF THE CHURCH

Consideration of the Eucharist as sacrament of the church naturally follows on this reflection on the communion table. In the course of this work, it has been seen how the Eucharist functioned in various ways and in different ages as the *public symbol* in which the very identity of the church was expressed and appropriated. Hence when theology designates the Eucharist as the sacrament of the church, this is no mere abstract ecclesiology. It refers to the ways in which through eucharistic rite and devotion communities develop a sense of inner coherence and of public identity. The cultural aspect of this practical theology is important.

In early centuries, the eucharistic action was celebrated in its fullness as Christ's mystery, and in its particularity as the gathering of the local church. This was spelled out in the imagery of the one assembly or in the idea of recapitulation in the Word. It was also expressed in the symbolism of the one bread, shared in the communion of the one Spirit, and of the one sacrifice in which access is had to the Father.[2]

In early medieval theology the ecclesial meaning of the Mass was often located in the fraction of the bread, theologians and commentators using the term the *mystical body* to include communion with the saints and all the departed. The symbolism of the fraction, and eventually the unity of all in the devout gaze, or the gathering of all into the sacrificial prayer of the priest largely replaced the symbolism and reality of the communion rite. Though the communion table had receded in importance, the communal signification of the Eucharist remained.[3]

The Lord's Supper of the Reformation on the other hand gathered the church around the Word of God and the table, accepting through word and sacrament the forgiveness of sin. This was a celebration that gave more coherent attention to the individual person and the person's personal consciousness of sin and faith in Christ. The church's role in public life changed accordingly. There was some movement back to the ideal of the church as the domestic eucharistic community, in which the participation of each member was guaranteed by sincere personal faith. However, the celebration of the Lord's Supper supplied no symbol of common and public unity that could vie with Mass-offerings and with the public reverence of the host on occasions such as the festivities of Corpus Christi.[4]

The secularization of the Western world has made it difficult for both Catholic church and Reformation churches to find ways in which the common celebration of the Eucharist can express the church's identity within society and the relation that their members have to the public domain. On other continents, where the hegemony of Western culture has been broken, the struggle is to embody eucharistic faith in cultural idiom, even while cultures are in a state of flux due to global communications.

A certain nostalgia for times past leads some Catholics back to Counter-Reformation Catholicism. Through Mass and eucharistic adoration people may be encouraged to develop a life of piety that creates of church membership a preserve of holiness and faith, with a priesthood and an authority that give voice to a divine presence and a divine teaching that counteract the secularist trends of modern society. One should never ignore the power that this has as a countercultural symbol. It offers a sense of special identity in a world to which people do not know

---

2. In evoking these images from earlier chapters, the names of Ignatius, Irenaeus, and Augustine come to mind.

3. See chapters 8 and 9 of this work, 163–207.

4. John Bossy illustrates the "migrations of the holy" to the state, music and words, once the centrality of the Mass was lost. See *Christianity in the West 1400–1700* (Oxford and New York: Oxford University Press, 1987), 153–71.

how to relate as believers. Because it is not countercultural from within but separates itself from the culture, it cannot succeed. A Catholicism that is more sensitive to its own presence in society and to its mission to contribute in faith to the realities of human community needs to find a different kind of eucharistic celebration.

The images used to express the reality of the people who gather for the Eucharist are vital to the self-realization of the church in the Eucharist. To call the gathering a priestly people connotes something quite different from calling it a hierarchical assembly, and the two suggest quite different modes of participation in the liturgy. To call the people a living sacrifice in Christ because they join in a sacerdotal and sacrificial act is quite different from saying that they become a living sacrifice through the sacraments of baptism and eucharistic reception.

There is a need to retrieve from tradition images that can express a strong sense of the church as a local community, receiving salvation and giving witness in its own time and place within a diversity of cultures. Attending to the imagery of the parables and sayings of Jesus may serve this purpose, since many of them are of a homely and domestic turn. Not only in John, but in the Synoptics as well Jesus speaks of his followers as people bound to each other in the power of service and in a bonding of loyalty that is akin to family bonding. He offers the model of the child to express the reality of the reign to which his disciples are subject in two senses. First, the child, who represents the weak and expropriated of this world, must be always welcome to the table. Second, none can eat and drink of the table unless they come as little children, totally open to and totally dependent on what they are to be given. It is in such sayings that Sophia, godly wisdom, takes incarnation in Christ and it is through the gift of this wisdom that the church becomes a wisdom community.

As seen in an early chapter of the book, John Reumann has suggested that recapturing the notion of covenant is important to a proper understanding of memorial. As a covenant people, the church lives under the pledge of God's fidelity and in the remembrance of its vow to give God praise in word and deed. This vow includes the commitment to recall the story of the passion and its promise even in times of desperation. As a covenant community the church lives out the witness to God required of it, and with the hope that the remembrance of Christ's saving passion inspires. Through drinking of the cup of which Christ drank, through sharing together in the cup of the blood poured out, the church expresses and appropriates its reality as a covenant people. Covenant as a covenant founded in the two commandments of love of God and neighbor, as an eschatological wisdom that is an alternative wisdom to wisdoms of the world, shapes the community of those who take part in the sacrament.

The reality of the church as an eschatological people, living in the hope of Christ's promises, is brought out in the very nature of the sacramental action. Receiving in communion the eschatological gift of the Spirit, the church does not confound present reality with the gift given and promised. Though the self-gift of Christ is total, it is mediated through limiting symbols and rites that cannot capture the totality of the gift. It is not only the devotion of the faithful that limits the measure of the gift, but it is the mode of giving. What is revealed is simultaneously veiled, what is present is at the same time absent, and this is how the gift comes to the faithful. The fullness of the reality is as yet only promised, and the church can never adequately capture the meaning of what it shares in sacrament and in its own giving of witness, where it imitates what it has offered and imbibed. The event of sacrament is always the event of Christ's pasch coming again to event, but always limited in its expression by time and place. Like the event that it commemorates, the Eucharist shows the traces of God's presence and love, while never showing the fullness of truth in which *all and everything* is embraced in this love. As an eschatological people offered reality in the truth and the limit of symbolic exchange, each local church lives in the embrace and promise of the event of sacrament, but always in the darkness of a faith that relies on what it trusts more than on what it sees. The trust is invited by the cross, the promise of the resurrection, and the gift of the Spirit. This trust remains alive at the very point where the church must abjure other wisdoms.

In this eschatological humility, the church community learns to embrace the suffering of others, even the suffering of the dead and the suffering of the earth. It embraces this suffering in the confidence of the love offered and shown and in the hope that the event of God's servant among the suffering offers, not because it makes everything clear but rather because it draws wayfarers to itself and in itself gives a glimpse of God.

Multicultural Orthodoxy

The church's realization of its sacramentally centered and public self is historically and culturally conditioned. While the tradition shows what were the universal factors in eucharistic practice and belief, it also makes it clear that there is no rigid uniformity to the sacramental imagery and to the metaphors of redemption that have been employed. The rediscovery of the local church and of Catholicity as a communion of diverse churches can be helped by a richer mining of the images and symbols found in diverse eucharistic traditions.

Examples of cultural and ritual diversity have been seen in the course of this work. It was seen how in one liturgy Christ was remembered as the manifestation of divine knowledge, in another as the Word whose advent restored immortality to humankind with the forgiveness of sins, in another as the Word in whose death the work of creation is re-capitulated, and in still another as the high-priest who entered into the exercise of an eternal priesthood through the offering of the cross. In ritual expression, the sense of participation in the heavenly liturgy of the Byzantine tradition differs from the ideal of a host of cultic offerings rendered by the people found in the Roman and Alexandrian traditions.

In opening their hearts to Christ, young churches today are looking in their liturgies for an expression that will allow him to find a dwelling place within their cultures and in the midst of their redemptive needs. To associate Christ's memory with the memory of their ancestors and to find in his gift of salvation a healing power is important to the churches of Africa. To look to Christ as the embodiment of the holy lends vitality to the celebration of the Eucharist in India. To proclaim how through the pasch he brought redemption to peoples enslaved by economic, re-ligious, and cultural ideologies is the way in which churches in Latin America open their congregations to receive the gifts of his body and blood. In many non-Western cultures there is still a bonding of kin-ship and family that has largely disappeared in the West. Though these cultures are themselves in the midst of change, it is still possible for non-Western churches to find creative ways to draw on the domestic and kinship imagery that is inherent to their lives and to their living memory.[5]

Within the Western world, congregational differences may appear within the one local church, especially as those who remained marginal for a long time find that Christ's word invites them to a fuller humanity in the realization of their own power. For women, to hear Jesus an-nounced as Sophia, to know the church as a people gathered in the discipleship of this wisdom, to remember the women in the story of Christ's coming and Christ's pasch is the road on which to find their proper place within the people made holy by the gift of the eschato-logical Spirit. For different ethnic and social groups, a new sense of belonging in the eucharistic community emerges in the diversity of ways in which they celebrate.

A new eucharistic realization of this multicultural orthodoxy comes about by being open to the sense of the preposition *to*. When Jesus at the Last Supper pronounced his body given *for* the world, and his blood shed *for* sinners, he gave it *to* all at table, saying: Take and eat, take and

---

5. Since the production and sharing of food and drink is so central to cultural identity, it is sad to note that the use of elements for the Eucharist other than wheaten bread and grape wine is seen as a problem. The problem arises because of institutional and sacral approaches to sacraments. The advent of Christ through symbol into the lives and cul-tures of peoples is however impeded by the enforced use of materials alien to climate, soil, economy, and culture.

drink. The gospel is not to be identified with a deposit of faith, nor is the Eucharist to be seen simply as a presence before the people brought about by a priestly act. The gospel is proclaimed *to* the people, the body and blood offered *to* them. It is in their own faith that the gift of word and table is received, by that faith and through mutual service that these gifts are shared and an apostolic community engendered. Ministerial action in the community is intended to ensure that the offer comes across to the people as an offer of Christ's love and service, directed to them and not enclosed within priestly power.[6]

There is no threat to the unity of communion in this multicultural orthodoxy, though of course it is not without its tensions. Each church, in its own time and culture, receives and appropriates the memory of Christ's pasch. It configures itself through this memory. Each configuration is eschatological, not only in the sense that it looks to a future but also in the sense that it anticipates the final judgment upon itself, attending to its own inadequacy to the mystery of Christ's fullness. Within the particularity of liturgical expression there is the openness to the other and the desire for a transcending communion, inherent to eucharistic praise and to the communion in Christ's body and blood. It is not a desire for a communion in which all particular churches or congregations, with their cultural and liturgical differences, will be simply obliterated. It is rather a desire for a communion in which each becomes its full self through communion with the other, realizing itself in symbolic exchange between churches and in the hope of Christ's fullness. There is in other words a mutual communion and enrichment between eucharistic communities that take form in specific cultures. Each finds itself in its relation to others within the mystery of Christ. It finds its own faith in the mystery of Christ's advent, its own efforts to give expression to paschal memory and to live the testament of service, both mirrored and completed in its communion with other churches.

In this sense, whatever potential divisiveness there may be in multicultural orthodoxy is offset by a communion that has to be given its own symbolic expression. How eucharistic communities that relate to cultural diversity are to symbolically express their communion in Christ with other churches and see this as necessary to their own becoming in Christ has to be kept in view in the process of liturgical creativity.

COMMUNION IN THE SPIRIT

In the eucharistic tradition of Eastern churches, the epiclesis or prayer for the gift of the Spirit was deemed essential to the memorial action. In

---

6. See Hans Urs von Balthasar, *The Glory of the Lord,* 1:573.

Western tradition, Augustine and John Calvin are the primary witnesses to the truth that communion with Christ in the sacrament is realized in the Spirit, and only in the Spirit.

The Spirit is God's eschatological gift. Its sending is the realization of covenant promise and its presence keeps promise and hope alive. The coming together of the believing community in proclamation, prayer, symbol, and covenant commitment occurs within the communion of the Spirit, and it is in the life of the Spirit that Jesus is recognized in his suffering as the one who brings the promise of God's freedom to those who suffer.

It is in this appreciation of the role of the Spirit in the liturgy that we can see Eucharist's relation to ethics or to praxis. The Spirit is freedom. It is freedom from sin and death. It is a freedom to remember, to invoke God's name, and to hope with a love from which nothing can separate us. It is the freedom to reconstrue the story and to capture in it the suffering and the hope of human beings, even of earth itself, in new situations in which release from evil is petitioned. The action of the Spirit comes to expression in the different forms of liberating discourse that belong to keeping memory of Christ. Narrative, prophetic discourse, eschatological sayings, hymns of anamnetic praise and lament reconstrue the vision of reality and connect it with the event and expectation of Christ's pasch.

Praxis is the criterion for authentic and life-giving memorial. Where a community in virtue of its remembrance of Jesus Christ engages in freeing and life-giving practice and service, this can only be in the power of the Spirit. There is the inner testimony of freedom to listen, to hear, to accept challenge, to live within a new horizon. There is the outer testimony of service in a love modelled on the foot-washing of Christ. These together are the guarantees of Christ's event in the memorial action of the church. God's redemptive power works in human lives and in human history through the convergence of the work of the Spirit at work in the heart with that which in the flawed forms of human speech unveils in the language of the cross the love of God at work in human events.[7]

The gift of the Spirit is God's own self-communication to those who are in communion with Christ. Even when language addressed to God is apophatic, to affirm the gift of the Spirit in the human community and in creation is to affirm the reality of the gift, of the divine self-communication. It is to affirm it with the metaphors taken from the scriptures, where this gift is called wind and fire, creative brooding and the vital principle of human living.

It is because of the reality of the gift of the Spirit, mediated through

---

7. David Power, "The Holy Spirit: Scripture, Tradition, and Interpretation," in *Keeping the Faith: Essays to Mark the Centenary of Lux Mundi,* edited by Geoffrey Wainwright (Philadelphia: Fortress Press, 1988), 152–78.

Christ's self-gift, that it is possible to retain modernity's turn to the subject within theological perspective, despite the critique of its excessive rationality. Belief in the gift of the Spirit for the freedom of the person and for communion between persons allows us to look to the praxis of freedom and reciprocity as a criterion of truth. To uphold the possibility of communion and common pursuit in face of the questions put to traditional eucharistic theology and to religious institutions, it is not necessary to fall back on the unquestioned authority of the institution or of the word. The gift of the Spirit allows for the testing of spirits within the communion of believers, in the shared interest of being open to the memory of Christ, the power of his cross, and the eschatological hope of judgment given in the resurrection.

It is in the power of this Spirit that the Christian people keep memorial of Christ's pasch and find it represented in their midst. It is to these notions of memorial and representation that we now turn.

Chapter 14

MEMORIAL AND REPRESENTATION

Pursuing the thought of the previous chapter, the principal points to be considered here are memorial and representation. Sacrifice and the uses of ontology in eucharistic theology will be considered in the light of these concerns.

MEMORIAL

It is in the community of the church and at the communion table that memorial is kept of Christ's pasch. Much has been done with the notion of memorial to put a balance back into eucharistic celebration and to overcome animosities between churches and confessions.[1] In the course of retrieving a biblical understanding of memorial, a ritual structure of narrative, blessing, and sacramental action has been made clearer.[2] Keeping this functional within eucharistic celebration is the fundamental way of retrieving good memorial practice. Developing a theory of memorial is, however, another thing.

Remembered, Represented, Imitated

The first thing to consider is how the event of Christ's cross, or of his pasch, is remembered, represented, and imitated. The object of memorial has been differently named down through the centuries. Sometimes it is named as the death of Christ, sometimes as his cross or as his sacrifice, sometimes as his pasch. In the *anamnesis* of eucharistic prayers, the tendency is to name the passion, the death, the burial, the resurrection, the ascension, and the seating at God's right hand, as well as the expectation of Christ's second coming.[3] However named, it has always been

---

1. See above, p. 260.
2. See above, pp. 50f.
3. On this, see above p. 137.

part of the church's grasp of memorial that the mystery remembered becomes a living reality in the lives of those who celebrated it liturgically. For early writers, this was implied in the very idea of symbolic or sacramental representation. Medieval monastic theology included it in the notion of presence in mystery and thus spoke of the faithful imitating Christ's immolation and pasch. Thomas Aquinas spelt it out in Aristotelian terms through the category of exemplary and efficient causality. It would help us today to relate our understanding of memorial more precisely to the memorial acts of narrative, blessing, and ritual. This can be done through a better grasp of language's role in making past events a living reality in a community or society.

Memorial and History

The relation of the remembered event to the present and its continued influence on history is the crux of a current eucharistic theology. Central to the understanding of memorial presented here is the idea that a remembered event becomes a force in history, or is integrated into time and history, by being narrated. It is by the power of language that events are represented and transform reality.

In discussing the critique of Western metaphysics' neglect of the real power of language, it has been seen how some theologians wanted to ally the analogy of being with narrative, and with an appeal to ethical orientations.[4] It is this alliance that serves to explain the world's relation to God and God's advent in history. The analogy of being is needed to affirm the reality of language's reference outside a closed system of never-ending play with words. It is also needed to affirm God's abiding presence to the world and to human beings, so that creation is not reduced to some past and once-for-all act, and revelation and grace cannot be reduced to an idealist fiction.

Given the profound but restrained ontological basis expressed in the analogy of being, it is through narrative that we can express how a remembered event relates to time and to historical contingency.[5] The power of language in bringing reality to being is affirmed, so that thought must take its point of departure in the narrative. Past events are not treated as though they had to be, or even could be, reenacted, in order to have affected history and being in this world. It is their recounting that gives them the power to change the horizon of existence and offer future generations new possibilities of being.

---

4. See the works of Yves Labbé and Ghislain Lafont cited in chapter 11. See the recent article by Yves Labbé, "La théologie et la philosophie entrecroisées," *Revue des Sciences Philosophiques et Théologiques* 75 (1991): 185–210.

5. See Hayden White, *The Content of the Form: Narrative Discourse and Historical Representation* (Baltimore and London: Johns Hopkins University Press, 1987).

Event becomes event, that is a reality that belongs in a human world, through language. It would be wrong to think of an event that affects life for others in itself and is then brought to language. Whatever is liberating and influential in an action or event is presented to others through language. In this sense, one can say that it events through language.

The power of the narrative comes from the way in which it expresses the contours of being in time and relates remembered events to these contours. It portrays the necessary immersion in the contingent, while also expressing the desire to live meaningfully in terms of some reality not confined within the contingent. By its construal of events, it shows how all efforts to be and to become are related to the future, seeking to achieve a way of measuring being and act that transcends the present confinement within time. The promise of freedom from the constraints of confined existence offered by memory of significant events is placed by narrative at the very heart of the event of being. By its very stress on time, however, narrative allows for the absence of what it represents. It does not convey the illusion that the person or event remembered is present as though enfleshed in the here and now. The presence evoked is more illusive; it is both a revealing and a veiling of the reality or person represented.

The appropriation is prompted and promoted through other forms of discourse that complement narrative. Such are poetry, lament, laud, proclamation, and prescription. When the story and other forms of discourse are fitted into ritual observance, they are more immediately related to the bonding, structure, and value-expression of the society or community that keeps remembrance. Remembered event, ethical horizon, and community reality thus converge in the ritual act of appropriation that prompts an ongoing discursive and ethical appropriation.

Foundational Narrative

Among peoples and traditions, there are such things as foundational narratives. It is from these that communities draw their vigor, in reference to them that they express the horizon within which they live. As the life of a community develops over time, new events are illumined by their relation to the foundational narrative.

When an event takes on a central role in a culture or in forging a people's historical identity, the original narrative account continues to be repeated in succeeding generations. However, one finds that with the progress of time, or in face of new events that seem unconnected with this identity, the original event is retold in a new construal. It is by creative representation in fresh narrative that a past event reconfirms its presence in time and history. The promise of the original narration is such that it needs fresh poetic exploration, even while this exploration keeps its connection with the originating event that is looked to as the moment of promise. In other words, a simple recital of an original narrative is not sufficient to keep the living presence of a past event. It needs to be completed by a creative reconstrual that relates its promise to other times.

History and Narrative

The aim of narrative is to bring past, present, and future together in a consistent world of meaning. It aspires to show how persons, communities, and events belong in a time greater than their own time. It is in this regard, however, that some of the ambiguities inherent to narrative arise, not uninfluenced by metaphysical concepts. Is it actually possible to have the comprehensive vision of time toward which narrative of its nature seems to aspire? Or must narratives be more particular, accounting only for limited stretches of time and event, marked only by the traces of the desire for totality rather than the capacity to embrace it? Is it the desire for a unifying force that transcends it that makes a narrative significant beyond the particular event that it narrates, rather than its capacity to include a vision of the whole and an answer to everything?

Mythic narrative attempts to encompass everything and to set universal patterns, to offer a story into which all persons, times, and places may fit. Historical narrative may imitate the mythic if backed by concepts of totality. Any metaphysics that contends that the whole may be thought, albeit analogously, whether in terms of providence or of world-spirit, supports comprehensive historical narrative.

There is however another kind of historical narrative that in remaining more immediate to the conditions of human life recognizes that it is not possible to comprehend everything in one story or history or to offer consistent patterns of being and action in time. Ontologically, the claim of this kind of narrative is supported by an outlook that eschews causal categories and while affirming the gratuity of being does not attempt to explain its relation to the infinite in analogous terms.

There is thus a conflict between a narrative of history that includes everything and orders all events into a meaningful pattern and the narrative of events that allows for the inexplicability of the whole. It aspires to complete comprehension of the whole of time, but remains caught in humanity's inevitable particularities and time's unfathomable discontinuities. In the narrative that bears the imprint of myth there is the attempt to show how and why one thing followed another, so that if one looks hard enough cause and effect emerge. It can even go to the extreme of presenting a universal ordered intelligibility, ascribing it to some transcendent intellect that can encompass the whole span of humanity's existence on earth.

The second type of narrative is both more and less ambitious. It is less ambitious because it lays no claim to ideal patterns, even though it expresses the quest and desire for wholeness in a world that lacks even its clear ideal. It can take up the factuality and contingency of single events or brief periods and place one narrative after another in the sequence of time in which events occurred without pretending to show that one of necessity followed the other, nor even by what reasons and motivations it departed from what went before. It accepts the agony of human and historical unconnectedness, but bursts with the desire for connection and the effort to seek it out beyond the contingency of past and present, even while it avoids the vanity of suppressing what does not fit, in order to present an ordered pattern. It is however more ambitious because it claims a hearing everywhere by reason of its very challenge to claims to see things whole, presenting instead the invitation to live in contingency with the hope of being given the gift to transcend it.

Biblical and Eucharistic Narrative

To tackle the issue of memorial and representation in the Eucharist, we need to draw on the power of narrative thus described and pay greater attention to the power of language to both reveal and transform. Instead of thinking of language as the way of expressing the thought, it has to be heard as the medium through which God advents. The cross of Christ is proclaimed as the originating event of salvation in its being expressed in preaching and canonical writing. The suffering of Christ and the love of Christ do not transform the world by the mere fact of having occurred. They are salvific in being brought to expression within an already existing narrative tradition, changing this tradition from within. While the model for retelling this narrative in the life of the church has often been that of a Word that comprehends and speaks all things, the biblical narrative seems more modest. It recounts the story of the just one who in face of the contingency of his own love and the darkness of facing death keeps trust in God.

In the second chapter devoted to reflections on New Testament texts in this work, attention was drawn to a prophetic mode of keeping memorial through narrative and blessing. It was there suggested that in this mode it was the shattering experience of calamity that invited the commemoration of salvific origins, while at the same time making the recasting of the narrative essential. Far from taking the historical event of God's covenant with Israel as a once and for all action whose meaning and form of remembrance were forever clear, the prophetic tradition had to ask what meaning it could have in the light of what had more recently come to pass. Prophetic tradition and songs of lament keep to the vow of praise rendered by the people's ancestors, in response to God's own pledge of fidelity. They have, however, to keep the memory from new points of departure that often make the remembrance difficult.

The appropriation of the remembered event into the living community is a central concern of prophetic remembrance. This is why it has to be reconstrued through new configurations of the tradition. In drawing attention therefore to this kind of commemoration, it was thought that the best way of understanding a past event's relation to the present is not by starting from the side of that event itself. The starting-point is rather what is asked of it by current reality and what future it can promise to a devastated people who see their world in ruins about them.

Placing Christ's central act of self-surrender on the transtemporal plane does not adequately explain the enduring worth and meaning of his death. Instead of considering the origin of salvific events and sacramental act in the eternal Logos, we can consider the Logos coming into human contingency as contingent word. It is through the testimony of believers, beginning with the first disciples and the word whereby they pass on their testimony, that the cross and resurrection enter into human history. Celebrated at the communion table, the word transforms that which congregants themselves are in this symbolic rite.

Starting always with the profession that salvation is given to us in Jesus Christ, the narrative over the course of twenty centuries has taken on an extraordinary variety of configurations. It may be only today that we claim the *seconde naiveté* that allows us to see inside our storytelling, but in any case even in the past the narrative was reconstrued to take in the contingent facts and shapes of given times and places so that the remembrance of Christ could carry believers through such contingencies. Christ on his cross thus appears as the wisdom of those who find no part in worldly wisdom, as the victor in a struggle with death and sin for those who are the primary victims of earthly powers, as the one whose love is the supreme justice in a society set apart by the rivalry of particular interests, or as the dead Christ of people who find God closer in death than in a life where they themselves are valued less than dead things.

As in the recollection of all events, however, in the church we have also seen the tension between the narrative that attempts a totally intelligible history and the narrative that expresses hope beyond the discontinuities that it cannot tame. Alongside the continuing appearance of liturgical, poetic, iconic, and popular narratives that are fitted to the particularities of time and situation, there have been the mythic and erudite presentations of the pasch of Christ that offer it as the order of things that God wills for the world. This is the issue of logocentrism imported into belief, the persuasion that it is possible to link all times and events and seasons together into one whole narrative that reflects the mind of God. The typological explanation of the scriptures, the linking of secular events to God's way of preparing people for the gospel, the making of secular history the stage on which saints live the *exempla* of the virtues of Christ, and the reduction of suffering and catastrophe to events allowed by divine providence for humanity's greater good are all part of this logocentrism.

A less integral way of remembering the passion of Christ makes God's presence more powerful because it is less ambitious and nonlogocentric. It says that God's advent is as love and promise in the suffering and struggle of Jesus Christ, but not in a way that bypasses the discontinuities and contingencies of human history. It is a presence in the midst of such restrictions that gives hope beyond them, though it does not reveal what the origin or eventuality of historical events may be. The very contingency of Jesus' life and ministry and death, the result of a gratuitous evil, humanly speaking leading to nothing for the people whose lives he sought to improve, is the condition of God's event in the world. There is no discernible pattern that makes either it or its outcome predictable. It happens. The Christian community may then link it with a tradition of past and future by a creative use of root metaphors and stories taken from the original covenant. However, in showing how generations are linked in hope across time it need not pretend to find an ordered vision of providence that incorporates the concepts of divine causality and exemplarity.

God events in human history in places and times that are unpredicted and afford no explanation of why it should be this place and this time. Creative narrative can indeed wed the event with advents of other places and times that also show an unpredictable presence among the disadvantaged of the earth and a hope of carrying suffering itself into the bringing forth of being. It belies itself however if it goes beyond that to try to show a planned sequence of some perceived providential disposition. The interlocking of narratives around the paschal narrative reveals a deep structure of being in history that is the event of paschal faith and the event of God's love. This deep structure is however a way to be that in the midst of the discontinuous, the illogical, the repressive, the claims of other wisdoms, and out of the suffering that this brings, finds the possibilities of being and communion. The God who thus events, events in contingency, not in the manifestation of providential design, remaining ineffable but close and tangible as Christ's flesh in the covenant security of presence among the suffering.

To retain the word *event* to express the reality of God's revelation is to say that it is not related to the intelligibility of a large picture of history orderly conceived. Instead it belongs in the midst of events of suffering, hope, and loving triumph that are marked by their contingency, their discontinuity with patterns, their simplicity, and their worldly weakness; this eventing occurs when least expected, is in a mere human way without issue, and yet is irrepressible in its vitality for the addressees of the beatitudes. Rather than a providential pattern of meaning, what is affirmed is a divine presence that gives the power of self-affirmation and freedom to the disinherited and the victim.

Sacramental Memorial

The importance of the eucharistic prayer or blessing does not lie in the fact that it is itself narrative. It is rather the appropriation of narrative through the forms of discourse that shape relationships within belief. During the centuries in which diverse eucharistic families developed, the language of prayer was largely that of thanksgiving and intercession, with a gradual assimilation of the language of offering. Today, in the light of what is known about Hebrew blessing it seems suitable to take in confession of sin and lamentation, since these are forms of discourse that enable us to find the presence of the suffering and loving Christ in the midst of turmoil and even disillusionment. As with a ritual sharing of the body and blood or a ritual washing of feet, so with such prayer the church's ethical vision and horizon are formed.

Sacramental memorial that is the completion of narrative in blessing and ritual may be best understood if seen itself as an event. By all means it has its institutional components and belongs within a tradition of prayer and rite, but it is a creative and eventful moment in that tradition. Through the narrative Christ events again in the community, within the aspirations of its ritual expression, transforming them into new being. The community itself events within its time and society, as a proclamation and witness of this way of God's being among humans and on the earth. In its narrative and in its ethics of compassion, the Christian community finds the presence of Christ in suffering. It reflects his love, appearing as varyingly as are the sufferings to which word is addressed. It does not however presume to offer a reason for suffering. It says in simplicity, in celebration, and in action that God is there present, both revealed and concealed, and that those who suffer belong in the body of Christ, at the table of his body and blood. There God events anew in Christ and in his members. The eventful character of the eucharistic action has to do with the suffering remembered and the sufferings that it draws into the story and to the table, offering them as it were to Christ for his eventing. The sacramental celebration is not faithful to the event of the pasch that it represents unless it remains faithful to its own eventful character.

In light of the relation between event and language, Christ may be said to be present to the church in the word that brings the event of his pasch to word, that word in which his self-gift is renewed. His resurrection from the dead signifies the limitless capacity to take form in those who become his body on earth. As far as his body on earth is concerned, the eucharistic memorial is a power to be and to become, to event again in sacrament in new places, incorporating persons and things into the communion of God's love.

The proclamation of the cross at the heart of the narrative, or the symbol of the cross, limits the resort to metaphysical or mythic thinking to explain Christ's salvific work. Though the ontological basis for a theology of redemption is kept through the analogy of being, the cross limits the capacity of metaphysical speculation to offer analogies. As expressed by Saint Paul, the wisdom of the cross runs counter to the wisdom of the Jews and the wisdom of the Greeks. That is to say, it proclaims that the love of God shown in the cross cannot be represented in religious cultic systems or in philosophical concepts. No image of God grounded either in myth or in metaphysics can be employed to explain how redemption comes through the cross. This has to be thought from the symbol of the cross itself, as it relates to the narrative of Jesus' ministry, trial, judgment, and death. It is there that God's wisdom and judgment on the world are made known, precisely as a counterwisdom to human wisdoms.

The power of the language in which the memory of the cross is kept invites surrender to the God whose trace is found in the love of Christ in the midst of suffering, and who is named from within this story and its appropriation to new situations of suffering. The ultimacy of this surrender is a contemplation that occurs beyond the language and celebration of sacrament. In the practical order, it is compassion and action that emerge out of the faith in God's loving presence in the here and the now, without the need for the consolation of the knowledge of a providential order or without the presumption of entering the mind of God as a condition for believing in love. This love events in the community of faith and in the presence of this community in time and place, even in the midst of discontinuities and ambiguities to which there is no intelligible pattern.

Remembering Suffering

Relating the suffering of humanity to the remembrance of Christ is a matter of critical importance for eucharistic celebration. In modern concepts of history or in traditional Christian concepts of providence, there is an optimism that stands up with difficulty in face of the cultural ruins of history and of humankind's awesome capacity to cause mass death. In the Nazi camp or in the killing fields of Cambodia or in the corridor of death across Kuwait, the life-world itself is first destroyed and all connection with an intelligible course of events disappears. It offers little hope to say that in an action of memorial, it is possible in the midst of this to contemplate a Word, or see an intelligible law of the cross at work in reordering human events.

As already remarked, the cross disrupts mythic and metaphysical thinking. It does so not only as a critique of concepts and representations of God, but even more poignantly because it locates God's advent in suffering itself. With the event of the pasch, it is impossible to know and love God except from within the divine embrace of humanity's suffering. It is impossible to speak of God except from this starting-point. This is not a matter of saying that God allows suffering so that we may be awakened to contingency and a knowledge of the divine. It is rather to admit the inadequacy of any metaphysical or mythic explanation of suffering, and yet to say that the God who withdraws from the world in suffering is truly present within it. In the immersion in suffering of Christ and in the protest against suffering of this very immersion and in the eschatological hope of the resurrection and judgment that deny the finality of suffering and death, God is present in the affairs of earth.

When Christ events anew in eucharistic memorial it is not only to affirm the eschatological hope of the pasch, but to become present anew to suffering and among sufferers. The weak, the suffering, the underprivileged, the children, are always the privileged to whom Christ wants to be particularly present in the liturgy of the table ritual and of the ethics of foot-washing. What the church tends to overlook, or to struggle against the grain to realize in its rites, is this presence *to*, relying so readily as it does on a sense of the presence *of* Christ. The affective knowledge of God is tied to this presence of Christ in sacramental memorial and service among the suffering.

The question to be faced then is how a salvific event of the past may be represented in such a shattered present as ours, how God may still be said to come among us in a world that knows such reality. It is not a matter of explaining how we are enabled to rise above the ephemeral and the sinful to be one with Christ, but of retaining the faith that Christ is present as God's advocate in such a world. How may a promise for the future be maintained in a present that so totally negates human life, both in those to whom evil is done and in the perpetrator? Suffering patiently borne and senseless suffering are not at all on the same level of understanding and reality. It is the possibility of Christ's presence to senseless suffering that is the issue for today's eucharistic celebration. Can the memory of those who died senselessly, in an age or situation when any comprehensible or structured life-world had been shattered, be caught up in the memory of Christ? Can the dead even now be given life among the living through this memory? Can they be guaranteed a future though seemingly deprived of its possibilities in their suffering?

Remembrance of the Dead

Within this understanding of memorial action as both earthly and eschatological hope, the remembrance of the dead takes on new significance. This is particularly important for an age of absurd death.[6] If the Eucharist as memorial is truly a proclamation of eschatological hope, what are we to say of it as the place for the remembrance of the dead? It was the persuasion that the living and the dead are united in the hope of the final resurrection that first led to the commemoration of the dead in the Eucharist. In the Middle Ages, with the conviction that many of the dead still stood in need of the forgiveness of sins, offering the memorial sacrifice for them was a bond of communion between the living and the dead.

In this age when many die so senselessly, how are the dead to be remembered? What hope is held out for those whose individuality is lost in the midst of mass death. Even death by natural calamity seems quite different when it occurs as another instance of mass death, too often associated with the poor living conditions of those so vulnerable to this kind of destruction. In the commemoration of Christ, hope for the future is held out even for those who died such absurd deaths. Their inclusion in Christ's death may restore them an individuality within a common hope that death denied them. In a communion with them through remembrance, the church embraces a hope for a future within this world when the meek inherit the earth, when swords are beat into ploughshares. To associate the victims of absurd death with this hope is to embrace them in a communion of life and expectation, where death is overcome by communion with Christ's death and by the hope of the eschatological expectation awakened by his rising from the dead.

Remembering Creation

Peculiar to our time is a fresh appreciation of what the letter to the Romans means about the travail of creation. If we include the enigma of suffering in the remembrance of Christ, it has to include the suffering of all creation, not only human suffering.

When Christ was professed as the Logos, or eternal Word, in whom both redemption and creation have their origin, creation could be read-

---

6. Philip Aries in his work *The Hour of Our Death* (New York: Knopf, 1981) suggests that historical epochs may be classified by reason of the prevailing cultural attitudes to death. Thus he speaks of an age of tamed death, of an age of the death of the self, of an age of the death of the other. Of recent time, he says that it is the age of hidden death, of the denial of death. With recent calamities, such as the Nazi Holocaust, Hiroshima, the killing fields of Cambodia, the Vietnam War, the war in the Persian Gulf, and the AIDS epidemic, death has again forced itself into view, with powerful impact on the imagination. It is, however, as absurd death that it has made its appearance.

ily enough included as the remembrance of a salvific event. Some of the ancient eucharistic prayers already included the work of creation in their commemoration. Creation and the story of Adam's sin fitted into prayer, on such occasions as the paschal vigil, and into the theology of Christian writers, as though they belonged to a sequential historical development. We are more aware today that creation and the story of sin cannot be placed on the same historical footing as the redemptive acts of Christ.

There are two important supports in biblical tradition to the inclusion of the world's suffering in Christian memorial. First, as Cesare Giraudo has pointed out, the story of Adam's creation, sin, and promised reconciliation is background to the Christ story and the paschal/eucharistic ritual.[7] Second, the creation story with which Genesis opens makes us mindful of the material world and cosmos as God's creation and as humankind's dwelling place. This addresses the disharmony with the world that is a feature of modern human existence.

The creation story and the story of redemption cannot be given a similar historical footing. The prayer has to recognize the mythic nature of the creation narratives. As myth they say something about humankind's relation to the material world and about the reality of sin that is disruptive of human solidarity with the earth and with the creator of the universe. The story is expressive of a lived condition and has nothing to do with any historical moment. Included in the eucharistic prayer, the imagery taken from Genesis reflects disharmony and the need for reconciliation between humankind and earth so that it may be included in the hope awakened by Christ's redemptive work.

Anticipative Memory

The language that is spoken in eucharistic memory is the language of anticipative memory. It is the language of *kairos*. This is not quite historical time, if by that we mean an overarching vision of all times from beginning to end, rendered intelligible in a theology of origins. It is rather the sense of an event that occurs even now, with a promise whose fulfilment can be anticipated. This sense of a gracious presence in the midst of what cannot be reduced to the intelligible does not offer time-plans for the kingdom as future, as past, or as present. It bestows on us a present time in which God graciously events, in the anticipation of the fullness of a reign in which love and divine justice prevail. The discontinuity that marks the flow of human history comes not simply from

---

7. Cesare Giraudo, *Eucaristia per la Chiesa: Prospettive teologiche sull'eucaristia a partire dalla "lex orandi"* (Brescia: Morcelliana Editrice; Rome: Editrice Pontificia Università Gregoriana, 1989), 36–76.

evil but from the manner of God's gracious intervention in reversing evil. Eschatological images, arising from the memory of Christ's voluntary suffering and death, include judgment, reversal, life prevailing over death, community reconciliation, and freedom. The Eucharist engages the hope that by living in the expectation of the utopian fulfilment of these promises, the continued guarantee of God's love brings some measured realization to those who live their part in the covenant.

REPRESENTATION

It is against the background of what has been said about memorial that we can address the various issues of representation classically raised by eucharistic doctrine.

For Saint Thomas Aquinas the presence of Christ in the sacrament and the representation of his passion could be explained by two related sets of categories. It was his merit to have applied the philosophical thought of Aristotle to both questions, by using two different analogies. To explain Christ's own presence he used the analogy of substantial change; to explain the efficacious representation of the passion that of efficient causality. These different analogies were unified by relating the exemplary causality of the sacraments to a theology of the Word Incarnate. In the eternal Word of God lies the exemplar of creation and redemption. When the Word took flesh, the voluntary sacrifice rendered in his humanity expressed the conformity of his mind and will to the eternal Word and was both exemplar and efficient cause for human redemption. It is the Word who in the flesh made satisfaction for sin who is present in the sacrament and it is the exemplarity of his death that gives its signification to eucharistic memorial.

After Aquinas, the two points of doctrine were separated, even to the point that there were two distinct decrees promulgated at the Council of Trent. The separation was in part the result of controversy and in part the result of highlighting the consecratory and sacrificial act of the priest.

In early Christian centuries, there was no such split in thought about the eucharistic mystery. The Eucharist was seen and celebrated as the mystery of the church, made one in the Spirit of the risen Lord, whose death continued to be proclaimed and whose flesh and blood nourished believers who came to the table. It was in the gathering of the faithful as his body, in the proclamation of his passion in gospel and blessing prayer and in the gift of his body and blood, that the Lord who had given his life for the world's salvation continued to be present in sacrament and in the community of love and service. Irenaeus explained the unity between Christ's self-gift, presence, and remembrance of his passion in the notion that redemption is recapitulation into the eternal

Word. When the Word became flesh, his presence in the world found form in the lineage of the just who suffered in innocence and whose first exemplar was Abel. The eternal Word remains present in the suffering of the just, in the free offering of the redeemed, in the church's recall of his own death as the death of the just one, and in the gift of the food and drink that bring forgiveness of sin and immortality, even to the human body. In this as in all early Christian thought, the relation of present to past was expressed primarily in terms of the salvation that it won and the hope and the future that it guaranteed.[8]

However, from the mystagogical catechesis of the fourth century forward, the church seems to have looked for other theories of representation that express its awe before the mystery of the Eucharist and that at least offer grounds for the idea of a reenactment of past events in ritual representation. In a special way, John Chrysostom began to look for signs that signified Christ's active sacrifice or offering within the eucharistic ritual or for links with a present heavenly offering. One of the effects of this was to center less attention on the communion table where all gather as one and more on the liturgical actions of the bishop or priest and other clergy. Simultaneously, in both East and West, but especially in the West, the presence of Christ himself was related to the species in a way that risked separating this presence from the community action of eating and drinking.

Contemporary theologies have tried to develop a theology of the Eucharist that unifies these different points of doctrine. One of the favored procedures, which has had a significant place in ecumenical conversations, is to speak of reenactment or re-presentation, so that the Lord is believed to be present in the church in the re-presentation of his paschal mystery. There has been some influence of fifth-century theology at work in this, as well as an appeal to biblical concepts of memorial.[9] To explain the idea further, Catholic theologians often look to the mind of Christ in his once-and-for-all, and now abiding, self-surrender to the Father as that which relates the doctrine of sacramental sacrifice to the doctrine of eucharistic presence. Unfortunately, this suggests that it is in moving to a transcendental plane outside of time that Christians find communion with Christ. As a result the relation of eucharistic representation to earthly and historical reality may have been weakened.

The fundamental problem with theories of representation, past and current, has to do with the relation of language to thought. It is assumed that in speech or writing one is expressing a clearly possessed thought. The self-presence in thought that is believed to be possible to

---

8. See above, p. 98.
9. As explained on pp. 42–51, this appeal does not seem to be justified.

the human person is then predicated of God, in an eminent way. It is claimed that it is possible to think of God's eternal Word made manifest in the word proclaimed according to this analogy and with the use of analogous concepts. Language's preshaping of the world in which we live is largely ignored. The need to dwell in language, even to play within it, to discover its ideologies and its creative power is passed over.

A new point of departure from which to understand representation can be found in what has been said of event's coming to be event through language. The Christ who consummated his presence on earth in the passion is present to time and place in the gift of the word proclaimed, brought to blessing, and sealed in table-fellowship. In the representation of person and event, however, there is a continued absence that qualifies the presence. Thomas Aquinas himself was not insensitive to this when he stressed the difference between sacramental and physical presence, or the difference between the presence of Jesus Christ among his disciples and his sacramental presence in the church.

As a presence of one to another, representation occurs within a space, where being present means also keeping distant. Any attempt to suppress the otherness of the represented, to realize a kind of symbiosis, is a failure in communication. One does not see oneself whole physically except reflected in a mirror. One cannot know one's own thoughts and sentiments unless they are distanced from the mind and heart in expression. One does not enter directly into the mind and heart of another but relies for communication on what is placed between that one and oneself. This image of a space within which one is represented to another while keeping distant is applicable also to representation across time. One does not relive a past event with immediacy to it, but enters into it slowly and ambiguously by deciphering the words of the story and the monuments left behind. There is indeed so much space between the present and past events that this has been filled in by much retelling and comment that cast both light and shadow on their meaning and make of any return to a distant past a meandering down through the ages.

When it is affirmed that God and Christ are present in the eucharistic action or that they are represented in it, this means that they are present subject to all the modalities of symbolic expression and communication. This implies distance within the being present. Some attempt has been made to get over this by affirming that God is more intimate to us than we are to our own being. However, it is impossible to ignore the icon or mirror in which this has to be manifested for conscious communion. Such representation is inevitably determined by historical particularities. Very specifically, the historical particularities of the bread and wine to be blessed are necessary to the sacramental presence. When they are obscured within the appeal to a transcendent moment in the passion, the presence in the here and the now of actual reality is unfortunately obscured.

As said above, the presence of Christ is given to the church through the medium of narrative, blessing, bread and wine, eating and drinking, within a community of service. These are representations that at first seem to be forms alien to the event remembered. Certainly they are not figurative imitations of it, despite what has often been claimed in various types of allegorical comment. It is in the very alien quality of their form that they are most apt to represent. They point to what life becomes when Christ's death is remembered in communion and hope. In an age of disillusioned grandeur, what a humble yet powerful beginning it is to think of God's presence and being among us from images of self-emptying, suffering service, and crucial countertestimony. Footwashing and a welcoming table bespeak Christ's presence, not some exercise of domination. In the middle of the celebration is the cross, symbol of contradiction, a new wisdom, neither of the Jews nor of the Greeks, neither of classical philosophies nor of contemporary ones, neither of Nordic nor of Southern cultures, and yet seeking to find voice within all of these. Even within the debris of all these wisdoms, the Christian people know God's love for humanity and for the world through the remembrance of the cross. The representation embraces the forms of human reality, yet in its inadequacy looks to an eschatological point that is ever beyond us. Always known as in a glass darkly, the love that is manifested is yet full of promised effulgence.

Communion in the mystery cannot be translated into the apparent immediacy of the intersubjective, once the distance in such communication has been appreciated. There has to be due regard for the otherness of communion, for the absence in the presence. At the same time, in the use of representative forms, the institutional cannot be privileged as it was privileged for example by Thomas Aquinas. He brought a concept of hierarchical ordering in the universe to bear on his theology and related priestly power to an institution of the priesthood and sacraments by Christ, as well as to an ideal of superiority in leadership. Within the longer tradition, it is clear that the transforming power of Eucharist resides in the liturgical action itself. Representation comes about through the act of remembrance, as the event remembered passes into language anew, by a retrieval of forms and images and a weaving into the circle of gathering through the renewal of forms. The role of the presider has to be conceived in terms of how it serves the prayer of the community, its unity, its coherent ritual action, its relation to other communities, and its openness to the word that is proclaimed, gathers, invites, and promises.

In summary, one may say that, as for memorial, representation is best understood in terms of presence *to,* or being present to another, *through* intermediary expression. God is present to the church in Christ, and

Christ is present through the mediation of language and ritual. The past event through which God was present in history is present to a gathered community, and the gathered community is present to it, through language and ritual.

Retaining the ontological foundation to this mediation offered by the analogy of being,[10] we affirm the reality of the one who is present and of the presence, as well as the reality of life's transformation through the appropriation of the commemorated event. At the same time, the need for mediated representation postulates the distance, the inadequacy of the mediated presence to the reality represented.[11]

SACRIFICE: THE LANGUAGE OF METAPHOR

What is perhaps most lacking in an appreciation of eucharistic language is attention to the creative and transformative power of metaphor. This shows up in a particularly poignant way in regard to the image of sacrifice. Much of the acrimony surrounding the nature of the Eucharist as sacrifice might have been avoided had the metaphorical nature of Christian sacrificial language been noted. To remark on this is not to reduce the term to literary ornamentation or to bypass the doctrinal questions involved, especially that of the relation of the Mass to the mystery of the cross. It is rather to reconsider these in the light of the power of language.

Though it is not the first context in which the word *sacrifice* is used, it is the reference to the prayer of memorial thanksgiving as sacrifice that draws its meaning most sharply to attention.[12] In early Christian times there is note of a dominant cultural viewpoint that either God or intermediaries had to be approached through the rites of sacrifice. Even a philosopher like Porphry believed this, as Augustine attested in *The City of God*.[13] When Justin Martyr said that Christians did indeed have a sacrifice but that it was no other than the thanks rendered for redemption in the death of Christ, his words recast religious reality in a new mould. They said something startling about the way to God that eliminated cultic sacrifice from the picture and placed the grateful memory of the cross in its stead and replaced the rites of sacrifice with the table of Christ's body and blood.

---

10. See above, pp. 286–289.

11. See the discussion in chapter 10 (pp. 233–235) on Thomas's retention of a distinction between the sign-value of sacraments and their causal efficacy. What is said here is in continuity with that distinction.

12. See the articles by L.-M. Chauvet, "Le sacrifice de la messe: Représentation et expiation," *Lumière et Vie* 29 (1980): 69–83; "Un statut chrétien du sacrifice," *Lumière et Vie* 29 (1980): 85–106.

13. Augustine, *The City of God*, Book X, 21–31.

Later theology pointed to the death of Christ as the highest sacrifice in which all other sacrifices are fulfilled and for that reason rendered obsolete. That was not the meaning of the word as it was applied to the Eucharist and to the death of Christ in early writers, nor the meaning of taking the language of offering into the thanksgiving prayer itself. All ritual offerings ceased because of the way in which the Word Incarnate had wrestled with humankind's alienation from God in death and sin. Christ's pasch and its Eucharist were not one, albeit the highest form, in a series. They were outside the series, a totally different kind of reality. One could call them sacrifices because they realized superabundantly the end and purpose of sacrifice. To do this is to take sacrifice apart and to point to a different reality as the way to God, which the elite of society, such as Porphry, ought to have recognized because of the witness of the martyrs.[14] The religious awe and power associated with cultic sacrifice was transferred to the memorial Eucharist, to the death remembered, to lives lived in obedience to this gospel, and to the witness of the martyrs.

As is well known, in earliest times no cultic vocabulary was attached to presiding at the Eucharist. The one pronouncing the prayer and blessing the table was given only a functional designation. Words like *presider, supervisor,* or *bishop* were enough to designate the officiant, just as they designated the ministerial role of leadership in the church. When the presider was in time called a priest, at first this meant nothing more than what was meant by designating the prayer or the blessed gifts a sacrifice. It was strictly in association with his role of eucharistic and community presidency that the term was applied to him. When, following a Latin translation of some words in Paul, the term *ex persona Christi* was employed, this was to show that whatever was done by way of sanctification and blessing in sacrament was done in the power of Christ.[15] This is nothing other than to associate the power of Christ with the church's liturgical actions, but it opened the way to extending the metaphorical usage of sacrificial and priestly language to the minister.

Already in John Chrysostom's relation of the action of the bishop to Christ's heavenly liturgy there is a tendency to employ the words *sacrifice* and *priest* in a more mythical than metaphorical sense. This is linked with a change in the understanding of memorial. From finding in the memorial the present's relation to past and future, the church had come to find in it a representation of a heavenly or transcendent reality. In this context, the language of sacrifice assumed anew something of its cultic and mythic character. The sacrificial act of Eucharist was again given propitiatory and cultic power. It appealed anew to the cultic shed-

---

14. Ibid., 32
15. B. Marliangeas, *Clés pour une théologie du ministère: In Persona Christi, In Persona Ecclesiae* (Paris: Ed. Beauchesne, 1978).

ding of blood and the offering of victims as a way of escaping evil and making retribution for sin.

As things stand at present, the language of priesthood and sacrifice needs to be once more demythologized. We have to understand first why Christians, as all other humans, resort so readily to this cultic and mythic world. It is one thing to repudiate the cultic sense and the need for victims that it seems to sanction. It is another to understand what it is in human life that seems to cry out for this mode of commerce with the divine. Only when we understand that can we understand how the memorial of the cross truly reverses human expectations.

The life-world of rural peoples, which prevails even today outside technologically ordered societies, was that of the seasonal cycle and the life cycle. This world came alive for them through its population by spirits and intermediaries. If the spirits were propitious, the cycles themselves were benevolent. Angering spirits or showing them neglect was hazardous to the life-world. When peoples were Christianized, the saints or the dead took over the role of the spirits. Hence it happened often that Mass was offered in honor of saints or of the Virgin or in remembrance of the dead. These became mediators with the mediator Christ. Remembrance of Christ himself and of his passion and suffering was often combined with the persuasion that his suffering appeased God and so rendered the surrounding world benevolent.

In urban and technological society, though the life-world is not close to natural rhythms the language of sacrifice retains its appeal. Even there it seems to impose a sense of order, to offer a means of overcoming the disorder caused by injustice and division and offense against rule. In a more obscure way sacrifice can even be seen as a guarantee against the unexpected, which is readily confused with evil.

In this context, it is the power of the Christian use of the language of sacrifice as a language of reversal that has to be brought again to the fore.[16] It reverses the quest to restore order by preparing victims and appeasing a threatening anger, whether that of God or that of spirits that abide in the universe. Instead it points to a communion of solidarity in love in God's Spirit that withstands human judgment and prevails in the midst of suffering. It reverses the need to renounce a right to fruits of the earth so that they may be sacred to God, by acknowledging in the name of Christ and with thanksgiving that even our daily bread and wine is a gift of God and a communion in godly love when it is eaten in faith. It reverses the attempt to set aside special times and acts of worship by revealing that the people freed in Christ are themselves "sacrifice," that

---

16. This is not said by way of comparison with Old Testament worship, which in its own way is a story of reversal, but by way of contrast with what appears to be a rather universal human instinct to want to "make sacrifice."

true worship is a life lived in faith and according to the gospel and in Eucharist celebrated as such. In the cross of Christ believers have been freed once and for all from evil powers, sin, and death. Anxieties and fears are still to be named, but in a context wherein eschatological hope promises a divine expiation and liberation. Faith in God's mercy as offered in Christ takes over from the urge to propitiate divine anger or to seek other intermediaries.

It is the demythologization of sacrifice, the predication that relates it to Christ's love, to thanksgiving, to a life of obedience to the gospel, that offers a new paradigm for justice. Redemption is not wrought by violent action that invites violent retribution, but by nonviolent justice that witnesses in face of rejection to the power of communion. It is not by victimizing oneself heroically, but by an unflinching stand for truth, even if it involves martyrdom, that one witnesses to God's justice. It is not by a self-oblation of mortified desire, but by a giving of self for others in truth and justice that the reign of God is promoted. It is not by a mythic reenactment of a primordial sacred event, but by a retrieval of the eschaton into the story. In the story, the image of Christ's return figures as judgment upon malevolence and as a reversal of values. It promises that evil can be overcome and the power of life restored.

It is then as the language of reversal, a reversal brought about by remembrance of the blood of Christ, that the essential aspect of the doctrine of sacrifice has to be recaptured. The power of the storied language by which his death is remembered continues to reverse the order of things in which sin, death, and the powers of evil prevail, so that where these abound love, life, and good may more abound. His love proclaimed reverses the order of religion in which the judgment of God demands satisfaction to one in which a communion with a forgiving and loving God is possible. To celebrate this reversal, recourse can be had to some of the images other than sacrifice that tradition supplies. Such are the conflict between light and darkness, the divine reversal of the judgment passed against the just by the wicked, or the descent into hell to bring the news of release to those held in bondage.[17]

By failing to renew itself, the language of liturgy may fail to convey the power of Christ's death to liberate people from the harm and the sorrow that jeopardize their existence. It may fail more drastically in inviting people to that communion in life and in hope that is nourished at the table of the body and blood of the Savior. As early eucharistic tradition celebrated it, this is the table at which freedom is bestowed, sins forgiven, and immortality already conferred.[18]

---

17. These were found in the prayer and theology of the pre-Nicene church, recalled in the early chapters of this work.

18. Every time in history that attention moved from the communion table to the rit-

It is hardly however in the symbolism of the exchange of gifts that the language of sacrifice is reversed.[19] The acknowledgment of a gracious and gratuitous presence in the midst of the people is what is expressed in thanksgiving and ritual sharing. Such acknowledgment is meant to find its focal point in the bread and wine set on the table in the middle of the assembly. In the bread and wine of the people there is the presence of a God who is revealed by being veiled under these symbols, just as the divine love continues to be revealed under the veil of Christ's suffering. The gratuity of God's presence at the heart of creation, the gratuity of God's advent in Jesus Christ, and the gratuity of the Spirit dwelling in the hearts of the people who convene as one are expressed in thanksgiving over these realities of daily life and in the communion of a common table that knows of no discrimination. All this is summed up in the symbolic reality of their transformation into the gift of Christ's body and blood.

THE APPEAL TO ONTOLOGY

Something more needs to be said about the recourse to ontology in eucharistic theology, putting in more summary form a number of points that have already been made. While the limits of ontology in grounding good eucharistic discourse and action have been noted, there are two fundamental principles that still orient celebration if well understood. The first affirms the total gratuity of finite being. The second speaks of humanity's inner orientation to seek the principle of all things, to find the source of life and being outside itself and its own making. Despite the limits on thought about the One, we know that all things find their being eventually by way of return to the One who is the principle of all that is. This includes the notion that the One remains intimately present to things and to humans in the act of their self-creation. This quest however has to be pursued only with the utmost rigor of the use of the *via negativa* in the use of concepts in naming God.

Ontology serves not as an onto-theology to conceptualize God's action, but as insight into the mode of God's coming to us through the cross and the mode of the human response in faith to this event. It assures us of a real participation in God through the reality of God's self-gift and unveils the bound conditions under which that gift comes.

---

ual actions of ministers, this seemed to go with renewed images of a God who demands victims, even if it is God who supplies the supreme Victim. The ordering of society and church then also reflected a justice that prevailed over charity, whatever the efforts of such as Thomas Aquinas to show the primacy of love and mercy.

19. This is the theory of Louis-Marie Chauvet, *Symbole et sacrement: Une relecture sacramentelle de l'existence chrétienne* (Paris: Ed. du Cerf, 1988), 273–323.

To ground the belief in the mystery of the Eucharist in the analogy of being as expression of the beholdedness of created existence is to affirm the reality of the gift given, of the giving, and of the giver. It affirms that the God who events in cross and sacrament is not enclosed in the world of language and temporality. To relate this to narrativity is to reckon with the temporality of the giving, to respond to God's being in the world and in human history under the conditions of temporal being. At the same time, the narrative form discloses the effort to fullness of being, to communion with the other, to a participation in life beyond the constrictions of time. It locates the identity of any human life or any society within the urge to a fullness of communion that can only be bestowed upon it. Such conceptualizations belong to an ontology that is wedded to the power of language to shepherd being. If the One and the presence of the One is ineffable, the narrative of revelation surprises us with the story of its gratuitous advent. To complement the ontological foundation therefore, the linguistic foundation for eucharistic theology lies in that appreciation of poetic and metaphoric language, which makes it possible to reach out beyond the capacities of philosophical language.

Holding the symbolism of the cross at the center of commemorative narrative and prayer is to accept a rupture with mythic or metaphysical thinking. This is so because the God who is acknowledged in the belief in the cross is present to the suffering of the world in a nonexplicative but compassionate way. The history of onto-theology shows us what efforts have been made to explain the existence of evil within the belief in a God of goodness. They are in the end rather desolate. The cross does not presume such explanation but is a promise of liberation through and by means of a presence effected in and through suffering.

The kind of ontology here espoused does not try to conceptualize history in its totality, because this would be to resort to causal thinking that presumes an ontology of the divine nature. Narrative itself reveals the impossibility of conceiving a duration that enfolds all times as one and total. Within the narrative form, there is a tension between the time of event narrated and a time that is not narrated except in mythic narrative. Being conscious of humanity's ruptures with the world that it inhabits and of the discontinuities of history, it is not possible to allow the mythic to absorb all narratives of event in time. It is at the point of tension that we live today, and at the point of tension that we know the gift of Christ.

The image of eternity itself is negation. It expresses the inability to conceptualize a reality that is not encompassed within the boundaries of timeliness. In naming God, addressing God out of Christ's commemoration, meontology has more to say to us than ontology. The language about God is apophatic through and through. It says that the triune relation that we have to God in naming the origin as Father, the being in history as Word, and the freedom to respond in hope as Spirit is a real participation in divine life, but it does not presume to take philosophical concepts to theologize the inner life of God. In living life as we celebrate it in Eucharist, we see only as in a glass darkly. We are however overwhelmed by a love that events where death seems to most abound. The Eucharist, Christ's memorial and table of his gifts, invites us to a communion with the God thus gratuitously revealed, in a hope that transforms being in this world by reason of the power of such love's promise.

In short, an ontology that retains modernity's unbending concern with the human subject, while stressing the negation and self-surrender of faith, is vital. The risk of postmodernism is that of enclosure in text, without reference to the unenclosed truth or to the ineffable of the subject, as it were both beneath and beyond language. Some theologians who accept the critique of modernity and of Western metaphysics seem to fall back on some kind of hypostatized textuality or institutionality, granting an authoritative status to scripture or to church institution that modernity has happily relativized by relating them to experience and praxis. Belief in the reality of the gift of the Spirit enables us to retain the importance of the intersubjective as testing ground of a truth and a love that frees. It incorporates the constitutive relation of the subject to the other, and of the human community to other, and of the need to test the communion in the Spirit generated in keeping memorial of Jesus Christ.

CONCLUSION

The presentation of eucharistic theology offered in these two chapters was prefaced by considering the relation between the *lex orandi* and the *lex credendi*, noting how an operative theology influences the rite and practice of celebration. The points considered in turn were the communion table, the nature of the Eucharist as ecclesial sacrament and communion in the Spirit, memorial, representation, sacrifice, and the appeal to ontology.

It is wagered that this theology may serve the purpose of mediating the eucharistic tradition to a multicultural church and a communion of diverse eucharistic communities because of a twofold stress. This is first the stress on the intersubjective nature of Eucharist, as it is centered on the communion table and celebrated in historically realized communities. Second it is the stress on the role of language in mediating the paschal event and in shaping the life-world of eucharistic churches. It is also wagered that this theology can allow for a narrative and a blessing that integrate the suffering and hope of people disoriented by tragedy and cultural loss, because of how it allows memorial to be reconstrued. Within this framework of thought and practice there is room for a varied integration of the tradition without breaking conversation between communities that can be quite diverse as they nurture faith in Christ within a disoriented world.

Chapter 15

REVITALIZING EUCHARISTIC PRAYER AND PRACTICE

This final chapter offers some suggestions for eucharistic practice by way of reflection on these three points: canon of remembrance, ritual performance, and relation to ethics. They flow from the systematic considerations of the previous two chapters. In these suggestions, the integration of persons, human realities, and forms of prayer that are to date marginal is deemed of great importance.

CANON OF REMEMBRANCE

Some diversity in the canon of remembrance from one age to another or within any particular age has been noted throughout this study. To place present directions within the larger tradition, five points will be taken up under this heading. These have to do with the narrative basis of remembrance, the inclusion first of the Jewish people and then of feminist concerns in eucharistic memorial, the role of lament in the eucharistic prayer, and adherence to the matrix of culture in the Eucharists of non-Western churches.

Word and Ritual Flow

The narrative basis of liturgical memorial has been stressed in this study. On the other hand, the place of scriptural readings within the eucharistic service throughout the ages is not reducible to any one precise purpose.[1] The earliest homilies for the paschal vigil suggest that at least on that occasion they provided the narrative foundation for the Easter

---

1. For a brief historical overview, see Paul F. Bradshaw, "The Use of the Bible in Liturgy: Some Historical Perspectives," *Studia Liturgica* 22 (1992): 1–16.

proclamation and Eucharist, incorporating the typological understanding of Old Testament scriptures into the interpretation of the historical reality of Christ's pasch. The few words we owe to Justin about the Sunday liturgy indicate a more didactic or catechetical purpose, in which case the connection between scripture readings and prayer formulas would have been less direct. Apart from this didactic purpose, where there was a more or less set thanksgiving formula for each Sunday, as Justin also indicates, the prayer would hardly have taken up the stories and images of the day's readings.

By way of contrast, the early Latin form of the Roman liturgy, with its variable prefaces, provides an instance when scriptural reading and thanksgiving prayer were interwoven. The sermons of Leo the Great, in particular for Easter and Ascension, show how various purposes could be combined.[2] Taking the passion narrative, the resurrection appearances, or ascension stories as his basis, Leo proclaimed the historical reality commemorated, worked some of the other readings into didactic instruction on the nature of the Christian life, and ended with a peroration that already anticipated the thanksgiving prayer. This instance of ritual flow shows how the event remembered is proclaimed in a narrative, interpreted in instruction, carries over into blessing, and gathers the people at the table of Christ's body and blood.

This is a schema that could be profitably drawn upon today and that is within the range of current understanding of how the scriptures use various forms of discourse to open up the meaning and appropriation of the Christ event. When, for example, it is understood that a parable serves not only to give a moral lesson but to present the eschatological horizon of Christ's preaching and death, then it is possible to take imagery from the parable into the eucharistic prayer. This then serves to recall Christ's mystery in an interpretative way, to show how it is related to human life, and to invite a thanksgiving that is anticipatory of what the mystery promises. In short, the more we know of language forms in both scriptures and prayer the greater are the possibilities of connecting narrative commemoration, ethical horizon, and commemorative oration.

Hence within the tradition of prayers that vary with the season or the feast, the scriptural word of any Sunday or feast could serve as the basis for the memorial prayer. Without being able to go into all the issues that arise from the need for lectionary revision, an example can be taken from the current Roman lectionary to show how a better ritual flow is possible.

The example given here is of a prayer composed for the twenty-fifth

---

2. See the English translation of his sermons in *Nicene and Post-Nicene Fathers*, series 2, vol. 12, sermons LXXI–LXXIV.

Sunday of the year, Cycle B, when the readings are: Wisdom 2:12, 17–20 (with response from Psalm 54:3–4, 5, 6–8); James 3:16–4:3; Mark 9:30–37:[3]

In the peace of the Spirit, O God, we are bidden by your grace to come to the table set by Christ and to give you praise and thanksgiving for the work which you have wrought in him for the world.

We come to find a wisdom which reveals your presence even in the midst of a time troubled by discrimination, jealousy, and strife, of a time wherein death knows no bounds, and we thank you for the just one in whose shameful death your love prevailed.

R/. We thank you, O God, proclaiming the harvest of your justice.

We thank you for the welcome which Jesus extended to children, receiving into his arms and touching with his healing hand all those whom the world rejects and demeans. He who was savior of all became servant of all, so that the world may aspire to a new justice.

We thank you that by the Spirit the little ones still receive Christ's welcome among those whom he did not disdain to call sisters and brothers.

We proclaim with hope that in the revilement of the just one, your wisdom prevailed over the wisdoms of the world.

R/. We thank you, O God, proclaiming the harvest of your justice.

Therefore with all those who have lived and died in the cross of Christ and have gone forward to the blessed light, we sing your praise:

Holy, holy, holy, etc.

In proclaiming this holiness that is revealed to children, we recall Christ's desire to remain in a communion of love with his own and to leave the memory of his passion as a judgment of the evil-doer and a hope for the suffering.

For on the night on which he was delivered into the power of those who would put him to death, he took bread in his hands, said the blessing over it, and gave it to his disciples, saying:

Take and eat, this is my body delivered over for you.

When the supper was finished, he took a cup into his hands, said the blessing over it, and gave it to his disciples, saying:

Take and drink, this is the cup of the covenant in my blood poured out for you.

Do this in memory of me.

---

3. The composition is the author's own.

Wherefore, O God, we recall his coming among us, his deliverance to death, his descending to the abode of the dead, his resurrection from the tomb, his ascending to your right hand, and the pouring out of his Spirit, thanking you and keeping memory of the covenant sealed in his blood at the table of the meek of the earth as he commanded.

R/. We thank you, O God, proclaiming the harvest of your justice.

We ask you to send your Spirit upon these gifts and upon the gathering of those whom Christ welcomes and who welcome others in his name. Gather them through this blessed bread and wine into the communion of one body and one covenant, where peace is cultivated and the harvest of justice shared.

R/. We ask you, O God, in the eager hope of your welcome.

Look with kindly countenance on the children who need help, on the afflicted and the outcast.

Look with kindly countenance on your church that it may keep your testament at this table and in its service of the world.

Look on those who minister in this church, and in the churches with which it is united in peace.

R/. We ask you, O God, in the eager hope of your welcome.

Look upon those who have departed our midst and who have left this life, trusting in your mercy and your justice.

R/. We ask you, O God, in the eager hope of your welcome.

May all those who have professed Christ's name be gathered at the final resurrection into the unending welcome of your love and vision,

All/. For through him and with him and in him, in the unity of the Spirit, all praise and honor is yours for ever and ever. Amen.

Explanation of the Text. The text was written in the conviction that the scriptures of many Sundays lend themselves to a commemorative prayer that builds up from the memory evoked in the liturgy of the word, remaining essentially a memorial of God's action and revelation in Christ. The metaphors and concepts that express the memory of Christ have differed from age to age. This prayer is meant to use language that speaks more to the power of this memory in our time. The episode in the gospel is taken as a metaphorical proclamation of the mystery of Christ in its totality. The commemoration based on this episode incorporates the ethical orientation found in the readings from Wisdom, the day's psalm, and James. Thus the scriptures of the day offer images of a justice and peace that derive from the suffering of the just one and of a kingdom in which children are the foremost. The proclamation offers a new wisdom. These images and hopes are taken up in the prayer in a way that seems to recognize the troubled mind of this age, as well as the eschatological aspirations of believers.

The structure of the prayer is quite traditional, though it allows for some freedom in the placement of thanksgiving, proclamation, and intercession and opens with something like a vow to give praise, even in the midst of affliction and doubt. The nature of the prayer as a table blessing is highlighted, as is the nature of the community that gathers there in the hope of God's kingdom. The allusion to offering is quite reduced. Thus proclamation, thanksgiving, and intercession[4] prevail, in keeping with early tradition.

Two refrains are inserted for the congregation. This style seems to be necessary today to engage a congregation in the prayer with the presider and to ensure that it really is the prayer of the church. Since the refrains are simple and may be simply set to music, the need to have books in hand is avoided.

The naming of God and the address to God are done from within the experience of salvation and the experience of need. The God acclaimed is the one whose name is given in the preferential love for the children and the weak. If this identification of divine love with the love of children and the childlike, with the love that remains with the just in their trial, challenges assumptions about the divinity, this negation has to be part of the naming. It is God's gracious presence that is acknowledged, and it is from this presence that the prayer lifts up its participants to communion with the one from whom come gift, the yearning for justice, and the promise of the harvest of justice.

Christian Remembrance and the Jewish People

In most striking ways it was the Holocaust of the Jewish people under the Nazi regime that brought home the failure of enlightened Western civilization. After a period of much vaunted progress, this happened. It is a zero point in history.[5] For Christian liturgy, the Holocaust serves as a reminder of how much its own history has fostered animosity against the Jewish people, or at best treated them as but forerunners to the church. Within many liturgical and spiritual traditions, their history provides allegory, little more. In other cases, Jews are reviled in liturgy. As he gives thought to the centuries of anti-Semitism, inclusive of these liturgical factors, David Tracy says: "Every trace of that tradition should not

---

4. There is room within the text for some elaboration of the intercessions for the living and the dead.

5. See Emilio Baccarini, "The Holocaust Forces us to Think...," *SIDIC* 22, no. 3 (1989): 20–24.

only be removed but repented for."[6] Repentance, lament, and respectful remembrance of God's covenant with Israel have to become part of the canon of the church's eucharistic memorial.

Repentance is never simply regret. It has to be conversion of heart, attitude, and behavior. At the same time that the sin against the Jewish people that has marred Christian worship is recognized, the religious factor blocked out by sin needs to be retrieved. It is not enough to be enlightened in our study of the origins of Christian Eucharist by comparative studies with Jewish prayer. The faith content of this prayer has to be brought to the fore. Jesus is incomprehensible except as a Jew, a fact too simply obliterated by the high christology of the Divine Word. His address to God as *Abba* is an address to the God of Abraham, Isaac, and Jacob, to the God of the covenant with Israel. If with Jesus we invoke the God of the covenant, of the living and not of the dead, we need to recognize this as a living faith of the people who to this day live by it.

Acknowledging this puts a challenge to Christian worship that is quite new, namely, the call to give recognition to the place that the Jewish people still hold in testifying to God's presence in the world and in the life of humanity. This is something that we ought to have known before, but that the Holocaust has brought starkly before our eyes. Ironically so, since it happens in the midst of an event that raises fundamental questions for the Jewish people themselves about their covenant with Yahweh. In the past, even Jewish communities have been inclined to look on pogroms and other calamities as God's punishment and have emerged from such realities with a fidelity renewed by repentance. With the Holocaust, this is an inadequate response, for it is an event that raises questions about Yahweh's fidelity. In line with the tradition of prophetic remembrance, the story of Exodus and covenant has to be given fundamental reconsideration and given a new formulation within worship.

As Lawrence Hoffman has pointed out in writing of Jewish worship, every significant change in its form and content has taken place in face of some event or set of events that are not accommodated within established patterns.[7] In similar vein, Irving Greenberg talks of the Holocaust as orienting event.[8] God cannot be invoked as before, and things may

---

6. David Tracy, "Religious Values after the Holocaust: A Catholic View," in *Jews and Christians after the Holocaust*, edited by Abraham J. Peck (Philadelphia: Fortress Press, 1982), 94. For some important orientations, see Bishops' Committee on the Liturgy, National Conference of Catholic Bishops, *God's Mercy Endures Forever: Guidelines on the Presentation of Jews and Judaism in Catholic Preaching* (Washington, D.C.: USCC Office of Publishing and Promotion Service, 1988).

7. Lawrence A. Hoffman, *Beyond the Text: A Holistic Approach to Liturgy* (Bloomington and Indianapolis: Indiana University Press, 1987), 116–44.

8. Irving Greenberg, "Religious Values after the Holocaust: A Jewish View," in *Jews and Christians After the Holocaust*, 63–86.

not proceed as before, as though it had never occurred. It is a radical disruption of history, secular and religious.

Christian remembrance of Christ might perhaps begin to embrace the remembrance of the Holocaust when Christians face the reality of historical discontinuity. It is discontinuity that puts sharp questions to beliefs in a divine providence and in the eschatological fulfillment that Christians believe was given in Jesus Christ. The Holocaust can only be thought of as a threat to a divine promise made to the Jewish people. Does the remembrance of Christ not have to include this threat and elicit a hope that stands up in front of it? For Christians, it is not permissible to record the violence against the Jewish people as one more instance of outrage of human against human. It has its own peculiar religious and historical significance. It strikes against the Christian tendency to take Jewish history as mere preparation, or the Hebrew scriptures as foils to the gospel. God is still implicated in the fate of the Jewish people, and the divine gift given in ritual celebration and remembrance can be received only by those whose faith stands up against the disruption of history with its apocalyptic sting.

It would of course be wrong to consider that matters have to be resolved theologically before they can be prayed over. Confession of faith "against the grain" has its constant role in the life of faith and provides a foundation for more theoretical reflection. To be a free and faithful confession, indeed, it has to be freed from some of the theoretical constraints put upon it by past ages. It would be presumptuous to offer a theological explanation of the Holocaust if it were not grounded in the confessional and disconcerting remembrance of a salvation and a Savior who is not alien to these victims, whose fate does not leave his memory untouched.

Women's Remembrance

To enlarge the canon in a way that responds to discrimination against women is no easy task. The starting-point has to be an honest recognition of what has come to pass. As Mary Collins states it,

> The Sunday eucharistic assembly has for centuries provided the ritual setting in which all lay Catholics learned that they were not clerics, learned the consequences of their lesser status, and learned about women's special deficiencies based on their sexual identity. Ritual learning is preconscious, not conscious, learning. The overt content the Eucharist celebrates is the mystery of Christ. Yet through the centuries the whole church learned through the restrictions placed on women's liturgical participation that baptized women were still unfit for singing at worship, for reading the scrip-

tures, for preaching the word, for approaching the altar, for leading public prayer.[9]

In the need for women's liberation from patriarchy, within society and within the church, the remembrance of the pasch has to be recast in order to ground a renewed communion in thanksgiving and at the table of Christ's body and blood. What feminist theology and liturgy are now exploring has to be incorporated into the common Eucharist, though that needless to say takes time. It is obvious that the structures of rite and ministry and the words and images used have to be more inclusive.

Inclusiveness does not simply mean including the faces of both genders but an inclusion of women's concerns and distinctive contributions. In remembering the story of Christ, the imagery of feminist insight projects a different image of the Christ and of church. Sophia or wisdom expresses the truth both of Jesus' ministry and death and of the community of discipleship. The place of women has to be larger in the narrative, taking in the remembrance of Mary as daughter of Israel, of the Mary who washed Jesus' feet, of the Samaritan woman who proclaimed him as the Christ, and of Martha who in face of death's devastation professed the resurrection. Such an inclusion brings us closer to the reality of the church as a community of equals within the richness of diversity.

In short, in enlarging the canon of remembrance much has to be noted from the past and evoked from the past that has been forgotten. Beginning with the New Testament itself, it has to be noted that ecclesial and sacramental structures did not evolve fully from the memory of Christ or from a participation of all. The contribution of women was made but it was not properly incorporated because of the adoption of prevailing social paradigms. When women play a larger role in the church, they do not simply fit into the structures but they change them. To ground this participation, the narrative remembrance has to be broadened and has to become the common action. The initiative, however, is at present with women who are exploring their own modes of expression. Their rites, their forms of remembrance, their prayer, as these are shaped in a variety of circumstances, have to become integral to eucharistic development.

Lamentation

In discussing the Jewish background to the origin and development of the Christian *eucharistia*, recent studies have looked at *todah* prayers in general, rather than staying with an earlier concentration on the *birkat*

---

9. Mary Collins, "The Refusal of Women in Clerical Circles," in *Women in the Church*, I, edited by Madonna Kolbenschlag (Washington, D.C.: Pastoral Press, 1987), 60.

ha-mazon. While this is essentially a genre of commemorative blessing, in which thanksgiving and intercession predominate, it allows for the insertion of other prayer forms, such as the confession of sins. Moreover, some of the psalms in the Hebrew psalter that hark back to the days of covenant with Yahweh turn to lament in face of the current situation of the people.

Since we celebrate amid the ruins of culture and human community, it would seem that within the prayer it is time for Christians to include lament. Lament is a form of reversal. It points to that within a people's lives and history which betrays the hope of the promises. Israel lamented not only the invasion of foreign powers. It lamented also the religious and political ideologies that prevented the people as such from living in complete fidelity to the covenant or that oppressed some within the people. Lamentation before God and in the community of faith energizes. It dares to name the suffering, the oppression, the ideology, the wrestling with faith. In naming these, it also brings to name fresh sources of life and hope.[10]

Within the Western world and within the global human community there are ideologies that are oppressive of human life and of nature. They are the systemic sin that stand in the way of God's rule. To allow room for open and faithful covenant remembrance, they have to be named and lamented. There are also systemic discriminations within the church itself, such as that against women already mentioned. All of these have to be named in sorrow or bewailed in order to open the way to the event of God in eucharistic remembrance. Such eucharistic lamentation, to allow a verbal paradox, belongs within the genre of prophetic remembrance.

Again it is good to make the point by way of example. Herewith is a type of commemorative blessing that admits lamentation into the text:[11]

> Blessed are you, Lord God, because when we fear to speak words of foolishness or falsehood, you gather us here to confess your name.
>
> When justice seems to have fled from the earth, you gather us in the promise of a rule where justice and peace shall kiss.
>
> How long, O God, shall you allow death and evil to prevail over your people? [Here there is room to indicate specific trials, sorrows, or injustices]. Our voices are stilled by the pain that we behold on the faces of those so doomed.
>
> Be comforted, you say, but where is comfort?

---

10. See this author's reflections on lamentation in worship, "When to Worship Is to Lament," in *Worship: Culture and Theology* (Washington, D.C.: Pastoral Press, 1990), 155–73.

11. This is the author's own composition. For a lengthier version, see *Worship* 59 (1985): 452–55.

Peace, you proclaim, but where is peace?

Receive my truth, you ask, but where is truth?

Open then our ears, O God, to hear the stories in which you still dare to speak, so that we may acclaim your holy name.

R/. The peace of God shall be revealed, for the mouth of God has spoken.

We thank you, O God, whatever our trembling, because when we are laid low, we find you in our midst, in the one on whom the Spirit has descended, on whom your strong right hand has rested.

We praise you for Jesus Christ, for he is the one in whose suffering your judgment speaks and in whose fire we are baptized.

In him we have been promised another rule, a compassionate presence, even amid strife and suffering and in hours of darkness.

Joining then with the abandoned of the earth, with the poor who are the blessed of your reign, and with the peacemakers who are your children of predilection, we raise up our voices in a hymn of yearning and awe that has never ceased to give you praise:

Congregation/. Holy, etc.

In wonder before this holiness now so starkly clothed, we ask you, merciful and compassionate one, to bless your people here assembled, and to bless the bread and wine of tears that they bring to this table.

Let them, even in doubt, give witness to your name.

Unite us in the power of the Spirit as we recall that night on which your beloved child Jesus, already consumed in the fire of his passion, took bread in his hands, lifted up his eyes to you, his Father, gave thanks, and blessed the bread, and gave it to those assembled with him, saying: Take and eat, this is my body, given for you.

Likewise after supper, with fear already in his heart, he took the cup of wine, raised his eyes to you, gave thanks, and blessed the cup, passing it to his disciples saying: Take and drink from this, all of you, for this is the cup of my blood, the new and everlasting covenant, shed for you and for many that sins may be forgiven.

In this remembrance, O God, we proclaim your truth.

R/. The peace of God shall be revealed, for the mouth of God has spoken.

In keeping with our Savior's command, O God from whom all life comes, we hold in memory the advent of your comfort among us in the flesh of the daughter of Sion.

We remember the voice of the Baptist announcing his coming in judgment.

We hold dear the passion in which this judgment and your justice cried out.

We acclaim the resurrection in which we hope to find the glory of all flesh.

R/. The peace of God shall be revealed, for the mouth of God has spoken.

Grant, O God, that we may in the life of the Spirit eat and drink together at this table, unto the hope of your everlasting peace and the blessed resurrection of the dead.

Do not withdraw from us the light that will illumine the darkness of our times.

R/. Remember, O God, lest we perish.

Remember the goodness of your created work and do not abandon it to pilfering and destructive hands.

Remember your own word of covenant to those who suffer injustice and destruction, for if you forget, how shall we remember?

R/. Remember, O God, lest we perish.

[The intercessions could be extended at this point according to circumstances and need].

Remember those who are with us only in memory, having passed from our midst in death. Remember especially those whose lives were cruelly or wantonly destroyed, or those whose names even have perished from the earth. Grant to them rest and peace, and grant us to share with them the hope of a new heaven and a new earth, where there is no need for sun or moon for the Lamb of the Covenant is the light.

R/. Remember, O God, lest we forget.

Vouchsafe, O God, that heaven and earth, living and dead, the remembered and the forgotten, we may be gathered into the one offering of glory and praise that is raised up before your face, in the hope of everlasting peace.

R/. For through Christ, and in Christ, and with Christ, all glory and honor is yours, almighty Father, in the unity of the Holy Spirit, through all ages of ages. Amen.

Explanation of the Text. The text is written as one that can be prayed in remembrance of Jesus Christ in a time of calamity. While the format is one of thanksgiving and intercession, it starts with a lamentation that recognizes the difficulty of giving thanks. The lamentation is however introduced by something resembling the vow to praise God, for the church wishes to keep its covenant to acknowledge God's advent in Christ, even when its faith is darkened.

When the lament is admitted, thanksgiving for Christ has to be made precisely from the point of distress, however challenging this be to faith. It is then that a soteriology that looks to the coming of God in the sufferings of Jesus comes into play. In those sufferings, the prayer invites us to see God's loving compassion with humankind's sorrow. In them and in the remembrance of the resurrection a covenant promise of greater justice and peace is held out to the afflicted. God and Christ are named by those to whom is revealed the divine compassion that stands firm in the midst of suffering, oppression, and calamity.

In the intercessions, the format is that of a plea to God to remember, both Christ and all those with whom covenant has been made. The hope however is expressed in terms of a corporate hope for humankind, shared still by the living and the dead.

In short, this prayer is intended as an example of two possibilities within the tradition of eucharistic prayer. The first is freedom in the format, when the greater prayer tradition of complex forms is allowed to complement the simple format of thanksgiving and intercession. The second is the power to include remembrance and hope amid the ruins that lament dares to bring forward, even when it means searching anew for the divine name.

The Matrix of Culture

Among many peoples and cultures evangelized from Europe, it is time to recognize the matrix of their own culture in the telling of the Christ story, the celebration of rites, the use of symbols, and the composition of prayers. Though there has been some adaptation, as with the rite approved for Zaire, the stage of creativity where the culture is truly matrix has scarcely begun. The insistence is still that the Roman Mass is the matrix and all cultural adaptation has to be done within it. Some inroads are made on this, as with the model of village gathering or the commemoration of the ancestors introduced into the "Rite Zairois." However, this is a timid enough beginning, especially when one sees how the commemoration of the ancestors is paralleled with the naming of Abraham, Abel, and Melchizedech within the Roman canon.

The cultural matrix is still not respected when nothing more is done than to adopt images from a people's story or use their musical forms and bodily ritual. The process of contextualization that allows for remembrance and ritual expression from within the culture is more complex and without some experimentation can hardly even be understood.[12] Naturally, this author cannot compose a prayer from within a non-Nordic culture. He can only dialogue, say, with a member of the Ilocano people from the northern island of the Philippines, Luzon, or

---

12. For the model of contextualization in bringing the gospel to a people, see Robert J. Schreiter, *Constructing Local Theologies* (Maryknoll, N.Y.: Orbis Books, 1986).

with a member of the Igbo people of Nigeria to gather some sense of what this might be like.[13]

The Ilocanos are an example of what is still a largely rural people, who live from the soil and wrestle with nature in providing for their needs, including the needs of education for their children. Retaining much from the religiosity of their pre-Christian history and much influenced by Spanish culture through the process of colonial evangelization, lately they are subject for a variety of reasons to larger influence from North America. This is quite an amalgam of cultural forces, but the matrix is still the culture of a people who live close to the land. Harmony with the land and with nature is vital to them. This and any great degree of prosperity is made difficult by reason of socioeconomic structures, imposed on them by the wider world community of trade and production. Their religiosity peoples their life-world with spirits, with their ancestors, and with the souls of the dead. They have a strong sense of extended family and kinship across generations, so that ancestors and the dead are still very much a part of a living community. Their acceptance of the gospel led them to give a part in their lives to the Virgin and to the saints, which largely corresponds to the role of spirits or of the dead. When they remember Christ, as in the Good Friday *Pasión*, it is his suffering that they remember. In weeping over his torments and over the sorrow of his mother, they weep over all the afflictions that beset human life as they know it and over all the just and innocent who suffer senselessly.

The Igbo people for their part are also caught in the flux of cultures through global associations. They have a lively sense of communion with nature and of communion with their ancestors. The movement of body and oral expression are their language tradition in which communion in life is expressed. Subject to much suffering and a precarious hold on life, ritual healing is very important to them and redemption of any sort cannot be conceived without reference to this.

Peoples such as the Ilocano and the Igbo need a redemptive power to give them a living hope that can be passed on to their children, without passing them to the fortune of emigration and eventual alienation from their native soil and culture. Since their life-world is one of dependency on nature and of frequent calamity, both natural and human made, their religious instinct tends to adopt two strategies quite common among such people down through the ages. The first is to appease the life-world through the patronage of the saints and of the dead, in whom nature is often by proxy appeased and pleased. The second is to adopt an attitude of patient resignation in face of

---

13. In fact, these two cultures are represented among the students with whom the author has worked in recent years. Hence their choice as examples of a larger dialogue.

distress, a resignation fostered by a certain kind of devotion to the suffering Christ and to his sorrowing mother and even bordering on fatalism.

If there is a negative side to these strategies, one must also look to them for their liberative power. A sense of communion with nature and of communion with the dead gives a depth to the lives of these people that has largely disappeared from Western society, where some actually have to make a crusade of ecological concern because of the general tenor of the culture. A union between body and spirit is also inherent to these non-Western peoples, in ways often lost in the northern continents. Is it possible for eucharistic narrative and prayer to offer some liberation within these memories and devotions? Can the Ilocanos make of the saints companions who give them inner strength? Can they allow themselves to hope with their dead for a future of greater justice, finding in the remembrance of Christ's suffering the motif of compassion and of struggle against death and the forces of destruction? Their sense of communion with nature, one with their sense of communion with the dead, may be kept alive in eucharistic memorial. In their remembrance of Christ's suffering they may find a liberating compassion that encompasses the dead, living humanity, and the earth itself.

In similar vein, one may ask whether rituals of healing can become a part of African celebrations of reconciliation and eucharistic communion. Can the memory of ancestors and communion with them be more vividly expressed than in the approved Roman rite for use in the church of Zaire?

One necessary preliminary to the association of Eucharist with cultural models would be to allow the people to bring their own lives and life struggle to the table in the food and drink that their earth and their hands provide. In this way, they would be blessed in Christ's memory in their own lives and commune with his body and blood in the transformation of the symbols of their own existence and life-world. It is over this reality that the words are again spoken: this is my body, this is the covenant in my blood. It seems to be a matter of institutional ideology that there is still insistence on the use of wheaten bread and grape wine. The provision can hardly be based on a plea for historical continuity with what Jesus blessed at the Last Supper. If what he used was leavened bread, this has already been broken in Western churches. If what he used was unleavened bread, it has been broken in Eastern churches. In other words, adaptation of the matter of the sacrament is not a novelty in the tradition. On the other hand, it is vital to the memory of Christ from within a culture.

In developing prayers of anticipative memory from within these cultures there must always be conversation with the prayer forms of the

Judeo-Christian tradition. However, that tradition is itself open enough in structure to allow peoples to explore the way of expressing memory from within the forms of their own prayer traditions. One ought not start with set ideas about the structure of the eucharistic prayer, incorporating cultural elements into it. It is more appropriate to start with the prayer forms of the people, asking how within these the historical and eschatological memory of Christ may be expressed in an address to God. The prayer forms may then develop through an internal dynamism, receiving into themselves the life-giving Spirit of paschal memory and anticipation.

The contrast experiences that are found among such peoples are an integral part of liturgical contextualization. For example, a eucharistic service celebrated among them without a priest cannot be simply set over against a priest-presided assembly as a communion service compared with a Mass or as a word service compared with a sacrament. The sacramental takes shape among the people, as an act of a believing community, whenever they congregate to hear the word, express their unity in Christ in ritual form, and keep memory of him in culturally rooted prayer forms. Within the gatherings of basic Christian communities, the relation to people's struggle and hope, cultural rites and prayers, often finds more freedom of expression than in the priest-presided liturgy. The sacramentality of Christ's presence in such gatherings has first to be acknowledged and then affirmed in a renewal of official liturgy and in a rethinking of the appropriate ordination procedures. Ecclesial life and development is poorly grasped if its sacramental features are reduced to the formally approved actions of priest or assembly. On the other hand, these contrast sacramental expressions cannot come to the full level of public symbol if not assumed into socially and institutionally integrated forms of church life.

Sometimes, in perhaps unexpected ways, the contrast experience may be associated with what appear to be rather traditional devotions. Women mystics in the Middle Ages developed a new and distinctive sensitivity to the humanity and suffering of Christ through the devout look. Within the cultures mentioned, women religious and lay groups may find that they give better expression to their memory of Christ and its association with liberative praxis in eucharistic adoration. This is a devotion that they have made their own over centuries and wherein they have a freedom of expression not so easily gained where clergy dominate. One can never assess a devotion only by its externals. It is always necessary to ask what it represents in the life of a people or a community, and what relation to the cultural milieu and to ethical practice it engenders.

RITUAL PERFORMANCE

From these considerations[14] on the canon of remembrance, one may pass to some thoughts on ritual performance. This has already been touched on in what has been said about enlarging the canon and about the ritual flow. The general principles are twofold. First, the Eucharist is a congregation of the baptized and is built up in its communion in Christ through a variety of ministries that express the work of the Spirit in bonding the congregation. Second, each community in its eucharistic celebration is in communion with other congregations, within the unity of the apostolic tradition. Its rites and ministries need to reflect this wider belonging and communion.

Communion Table

Starting with the primacy of the communion table, one has to think more about its provision and about its ritual. If the food and drink do not come from the people who gather, if they do not represent their lives, then the meaning of their transformation into the body and blood of Christ is lessened. The tradition of remembrance, invitation, transformation, and promise is large enough to include different kinds of food and drink, provided the ritual captures the meaning of Christ's table blessing and invitation to keep memorial.

In the rites of the communion table, while ministering to another and receiving from another have considerable significance, the distinction between clerical access and lay access is misrepresentative of the nature of the community of disciples. In 1972, Paul VI restored the ministries of acolyte and reader as ministries of the baptized, though unfortunately placing gender restrictions on them. Since then there have been murmurings that say that the baptized should distribute communion only if there are not enough clergy present. This of course contradicts the principle that in the assembly the baptized properly give communion to each other, with due attention to the order that is needed for good ritual. If the sick are included in the celebration by the sending of ministers, these same ministers ought to be able to minister within the assembly itself.

Visual Representation[14].

The history of eucharistic practice shows that there has ever been some tension between an appeal to visual representation and participation in

---

14. See David N. Power, "Eucharistic Celebration: Action, Word, Sight," *Liturgical Ministry* 1 (Summer 1992): 78–84

liturgical action. In Eastern traditions, it took on significant proportions in the figurative interpretations given to the actions of the ministers, when the priest is taken to represent Christ the High Priest and certain movements of the deacons are seen to recall moments of the three days of the passion, death, burial, and raising up of Christ. All of this had an influence on the developments of ritual action. In the West, allegorical explanations of the Mass accommodated the role of the people as spectators and consolidated the taking of attention away from the table to other parts of the ritual. The high point of visual representation occurred of course in the devotion to the host and its elevation during the liturgy. It went well with the strong appeal to the harmony of sight and sound that marked the cathedral liturgies of the Romanesque and Gothic periods of architecture. As has been seen, the problem with this was not that the eucharistic bread was treated as a thing, for the devotion to Christ thus expressed was intensely personal. The problem was rather that it seemed to distance the people from the liturgical action and placed too many intermediaries between them and Christ.

While recent liturgical renewal has brought people back to a more frequent access to the communion table, it has lost much in good visual representation. This actually redounds on the rites and on participation in them. Without adequate attention to the aesthetics of space and things and without due reverence for the visual appearance of harmony in action, bodily participation can degenerate to a rough and tumble or to a slouch towards the table. The place of gathering may of necessity be very humble, as when communities in some southern countries come together on a hillside, under a tree, or in a roughly made hut. It can in other places be kept quite deliberately simple, so as to accentuate the domestic character of the church and its assembly. None of this excludes care for the visual aspects of place and rite.

The visual representation of the holy that seems most desirable has to do with the community and with the gifts placed on the communion table. On the first score, one recalls that in Christian perspective the divine mystery dwells in the community itself. The space in which they gather and the actions that they perform ought to reflect the sense of this mystery. On the second score, the appearance of the elements, the table on which they are set, and the ritual approach to the table, should all suggest the holiness of the gift and the awesome nature of the communion to which the Christian people are invited. In such ways, attention to the visual may draw participants more fully into the action rather than away from it, as was the danger in other periods of eucharistic history.

Rites of Gathering

Appropriate rites of gathering became a focal point of inculturation in revising the rite of the Eucharist for use in the church of Zaire. At first the focus was quite clerical. It was thought that instead of following the Roman model where the people come to the church where the priest awaits them, it would be fitting to have the priest summons the people as a village chief summons a tribal gathering. Later however it became clearer that within the culture itself assembly starts among the people, that song and ritual dance constitute their coming together. This then provided another model for gathering rites, brought to the fore more in practice than in approved texts.

By way of contrast, in the Indian liturgy, the gathering rite centers around the welcome given in the congregation to the minister, who is welcomed as messenger and representative of the holy. In sign of their own harmony with the holy, the congregation seat themselves upon the ground as they come together.

In gathering rites, there needs to be sensitivity to a variety of types of assembling in any local church. There are domestic gatherings in which because of the ambience and the nature of the community it is inappropriate to try to reproduce solemn assembly. We are reminded of how the communion table in early Christian decades belonged within the fuller context signified by the term *the breaking of the bread*. This fuller context may well be retrieved within communities of a more domestic type. Since the domestic assembly is strongly reminiscent of the supper room and of the testamentary tradition of the Last Supper, rites of welcome to those who come might be modelled on the washing of the feet. Special welcome to the child and to the stranger might well suit some occasions.

The purpose of the gathering can also be signalled by gestures of welcome given to the prophetic word that is to be read and meditated. On the other hand, placing the bread and wine on the table at the beginning of the action the community might start by letting the bread and wine speak to them, open up to them the manner and reality of their being in the world, map out the space within which they are to hear the word of God and invoke a eucharistic blessing.

It would be naive to revert to domestic models in all eucharistic gatherings. Some assemblies are more like the gathering of the popular church, where at a time of fiesta the memory of the Virgin, the saints, the ancestors, and the living dead has to have a part. The gathering that starts from the point of departure of the people may well include symbols that represent this total congregation. Litanies that call together this wonderful assembly constitute a good invitation to hear with them the liberating message of the gospel. It is better heard when addressed to the people in the familiarity of their own devotion and holy companions. The remembrance of Christ's sufferings and the promise of his resurrection can touch them in those places of their lives in which they have recourse to the saints and to the dead. The invitation to the eucharistic table cannot be such as to invite them to leave their lives and needs behind in order to have access to it.

Presiding

The role of the priest has too often been spoken of as a power received. It is properly understood in what it says of the reality of church communion. Ordination to ministry in fact expresses the ecclesial reality of inner unity, Catholic communion, and apostolic foundation. The role of the presider is to let speak and work those realities that presidency serves. First is the power of the word, which is spoken in the assembly through proclamation and charismatic interpretation. Much is at times made of the role of the homily in liturgy, even though it is often found sadly lacking in practice. The most effective approach to the homily is to see it as a community action, the result of a common reflection on the word of God within the context of human life. Too much discussion of the homily sees it as the presider's personal responsibility, even as the witness of his personal faith. It is more to the point to see that his role is to allow the community to have a voice, to be the channel through which the response to faith that comes out of a communion in hearing the word and living in the Spirit is given expression. Finding the practical dynamics by which this is effected is itself a challenge.

Second, and much related to this, is the place to be given to the testimony of a community's apostolic witness. The image of the bishop yielding his chair to the beggar found in the *Didascalia* can surely charge the imagination with other possibilities. The third and most powerful reality that presidency serves is the invitation to the communion table to receive Christ's own offer of his body and blood. When the ritual performance of the communion rite is such as to express the bonding in Christ of members with each other in the sharing of Christ's own gift, the nature of the presider's role is more accurately expressed in its character as a service.

RELATION OF EUCHARIST TO ETHICS

The Two New Testament Traditions

The existence together of the cultic and testamentary supper traditions is the key to the relation between Eucharist and Christian ethics.

As is clear from previous discussions, the testamentary tradition complements the cultic in two ways. It exemplifies how Jesus Christ is to be remembered as servant. It shows how those who gather at the table together are to act towards each other in fulfilling the commandment of love heard at the communion table. Today we are compelled to ask in what measure the foundation in these two traditions allows Eucharist to include concerns for justice and the reconciliation of peoples.

The Liberating Power of Memory: Hope amid the Ruins

The church is called to serve the justice of God's rule. This is a justice always in the future, always in tension with the present realities, yet to be anticipated in some form of realization even now. The church as a community of believers is held back from serving this rule because of its own prejudices and discriminations. Often the believers find themselves caught in a web of injustice and strife that destroys the capacity for a full human life among the believers themselves or among fellow beings.

It is proclaimed in the story of the death and resurrection of Jesus Christ that even in suffering the power of God prevails in the history of the world. In his death, Jesus is presented as eschatological judge in whom the triumph of God's power will prevail. The suffering servant, who serves with and for the people and against whom judgment is pronounced in human courts, is himself the judge in whose resurrection and future coming the judgment of God supersedes all human judgment.

In the paschal narrative, the hearers of the word hear of their own future hope and expectation. The force of God's love prevails amid all the discontinuities of history and keeps hope alive. The memory of all who suffered is taken into the memory of Christ. This dangerous memory stands as judgment on human injustice and as promise of freedom. It liberates from prejudice and fear. It offers a critique of human ideologies and institutions, political and religious. In faith and anticipative memory, Christian peoples can always give testimony to an alternative world, in which love and justice prevail.

Verification through Praxis[15]

Liturgy finally leads to doxology and contemplation, in the communion with Christ at his table. As participation in his mystery it must be authen-

---

15. Compare with the author's work, *Unsearchable Riches: The Symbolic Nature of Liturgy* (New York: Pueblo Publishing Company, 1984), 213–16. Compare also what has been said on the ontology of intersubjectivity in the preceding chapter.

ticated by the community's testimony. In that sense, liturgy is never its own justification. It does not establish its own truth. It is verified by the practice of the beatitudes and the solidarity with the suffering of those who proclaim Jesus as Lord. In this age of liturgical crisis, it is important for the church to look to the contrast experiences and the contrast liturgical models provided by those communities that live the struggle for freedom in faith, love, and hope. The orthodoxy of the eucharistic canon is verified by the orthopraxis of solidarity with victims and with those who hope and serve the fullness of human life, even in the midst of suffering and injustice.

CONCLUSION

The conversation with eucharistic tradition has shown how the liturgy of the mystery has always been served by the adoption of available thought-forms from culture. While serving in one or several respects to nurture faith and devotion, any thought-form invariably carries inner limitations. In time thought-forms may have a restrictive influence on eucharistic practice, so that appeal is then made to other available modes of construing reality. It is awareness of the thought-forms of the past, plus the incorporation of more culturally adequate thought-forms for the present, that allows us to address the practical issues of remembrance, ritual, and ethics from with the Eucharist.

Eucharistic memorial both obliges us and permits us to live the given moment in eschatological hope. This is not to be translated into a time-plan for the future but it allows us to keep hope alive in the expectation of the unexpected intervention of divine love. Where sin abounds, grace does more abound. Which is to say that in the midst of absurdity we are to look for a saving love. To receive this hope, the common order of the Eucharist yields often before the characteristic expression of different communities, caught in different situations and faced by different tragedies.

Even today, there are theologians and scientists who would like to revive the argument from order. They need to look at human experience and see how affected it is by disorder. In disorder there is an inexplicability that cannot be exorcised by the theorems of sin's disruption or God's permissive will. Experienced as surd, sin will have nothing of logical explanations. The defeat of sin and death requires a faith that likewise gets the believer beyond intelligible explanations of love's work. Looking to the cross and the symbols of the body and the blood within which the symbols of human living are encased, we can indeed see the presence of God's love. We ought not however presume to explain the order behind the event in any myth of origins or any theodicy. Love's gratuity is accepted, with the hope that it gives. To be accepted, it does not need this kind of explanation.

In what has been said about the canon of remembrance and ritual performance, it is clear that in celebrating the mystery of the Eucharist as a commemorative event of the salvific event of the cross, language is given a primary role. Language mediates the advent of God and brings the church to being within a world shaped by language.

Modernity's interest in the subject still serves in directing the intersubjective character of communion in memory and Spirit. It compels us to draw all persons into the communion, allowing each to communicate and enhance freedom within communion. It makes us cognizant of some of the forms of authentic interaction. It alerts us to the relation to other that is integral to the constitution of the human person and of any human community. It invites to the verification in experience of the truth proclaimed.

All the words and the rites of celebration lead however to the still moment of communion, when at last in the gift of Christ's body and blood the invitation into contemplation is heard and accepted. The words and the rites gather into one a diversity of persons and cultures, the living and the dead, human events past and present, lives rich and impoverished, earth and its cycles and its inner yearnings. All these are gathered into the pasch of Christ and into the promise that it offers. In the hope of that promise, the church receives the covenant of an abiding being in God that eye has not seen and ear has not heard. Groping for a name, it can only proclaim the hope of glory. Even amid the ruins.

EPILOGUE

This book has been about mediating eucharistic worship to culture. It has looked at various ways in which that was done in the past. To foster eucharistic renewal in our own time, a theological reflection has been offered (a) that places the meaning of the Eucharist in relation to the framework of liturgical celebration and (b) that within an approach to the place of memorial in history and human life seeks to accommodate a variety of cultural expressions. It may be summarized in five points:

1. Liturgical structure, where the communion table is central but some flexibility is possible in rites and forms, provides the framework for a culturally aware theological reflection.

2. The liturgical structure of memorial can be considered in light of its ritual flow: gathering in covenant and mutual service, the recall of the narrative of Christ's pasch completed by the other forms of biblical discourse that express its meaning, the narrative's evocation in a blessing prayer that acknowledges God's loving work and presence, and communion at the table of ecclesial gathering in the gifts that have been blessed in blessing God.

3. In relating memorial or liturgical remembrance to human history orientation is taken from its nature as a language event. The event of Christ's pasch is brought into the present as a divine action of grace through the proper use of forms of language that capture the eschatological horizon of the foundational narrative and the commitment of the community to live by that hope.

4. Remembered within suffering, Christ brings the hope that in his death and resurrection and in its commemoration there is a reversal of the dominion of sin and death in human life and history that opens up to the eschatological future of final communion with God in Christ and in the Spirit.

5. Liturgical memorial must be constantly renewed by the integration of new historical and cultural realities, new memories, new directions in narrative, prayer, and ritual, and by the inclusion of the marginal.

Selected Bibliography
of Works in English

[References to works in other languages are found in the notes to each chapter.]

1. Historical Overview

Cabié, Robert. *The Eucharist.* Vol. 2 of *The Church at Prayer*, edited by Aimé G. Martimort, translated by Matthew J. O'Connell. Collegeville, Minn.: Liturgical Press, 1986. This is an overview of the development of the rites of the Eucharist, with bibliography at the beginning of each chapter.

Dix, Gregory. *The Shape of the Liturgy.* Additional notes by Paul V. Marshall. New York: Seabury Press, 1982. This is a classic work, originally published in 1945, on the development of the eucharistic liturgy and eucharistic practice, relating these to developments in eucharistic thought. So that it may continue to serve its purpose, it has been brought up to date on some questions in the notes by Paul Marshall for the 1982 edition.

Stone, Darwell. *A History of the Doctrine of the Holy Eucharist.* 2 vols. London: Longmans, Green & Co., 1909. Though dated, this is still one of the best works on the history of eucharistic doctrine and theology, surveying early, medieval, and modern thought, with ample quotations from pertinent documents and writers.

2. Scriptural Studies

The New Testament in General

Jeremias, Joachim. *The Eucharistic Words of Jesus.* Translated from the 3d German edition by Norman Perrin. London: SCM Press, 1966; Philadelphia: Fortress Press, 1977. A work that has assumed the status of a classic in the field and to which all refer, either to agree or disagree with the author's positions.

Kodell, Jerome. *The Eucharist in the New Testament.* Wilmington, Del.: Michael Glazier, 1988. This is a very simple but clear presentation of recent approaches to a study of the Eucharist in the New Testament.

Léon-Dufour, Xavier. *Sharing the Eucharistic Bread: The Witness of the New Testament.* Translated by Matthew J. O'Connell. New York: Paulist Press, 1982.

353

A comprehensive survey of pertinent New Testament texts, enriched by the author's theological insights. Clearly Roman Catholic in perspective, it is open to ecumenical dialogue and a contemporary appreciation of the symbolic.

Marshall, I. Howard. *Last Supper and Lord's Supper.* Grand Rapids: William B. Eerdmans Publishing Company, 1980. A solid and smooth survey of studies, showing particular familiarity with works in German. Clearly Evangelical in perspective and at times polemical in style, but of help to any discerning reader.

Reumann, John. *The Supper of the Lord: The New Testament, Ecumenical Dialogues, and Faith and Order on Eucharist.* Philadelphia: Fortress Press, 1985. Though only the first fifty pages are on the New Testament, the material is presented in a way that takes all recent studies into account. It is of particular help in understanding the ecumenical dialogue on the Eucharist of recent decades and does much to foster its continued pursuit.

Studies on Memorial

Chenderlin, Fritz. *"Do This as My Memorial:" The Semantic and Conceptual Background and Value of Anamnesis in 1 Corinthians 11:24–25.* Analecta Biblica 99. Rome: Biblical Institute Press, 1982. Though addressed to the study of one specific text, this work surveys the range of literature on memorial. Useful, despite its cumbersome form of presentation.

Childs, Brevard S. *Memory and Tradition in Israel.* Studies in Biblical Theology 37. London: SCM Press, 1962. A standard work on memory, not confined to cult, but basic to an understanding of liturgical memorial.

Thurian, Max. *The Eucharistic Memorial.* 2 vols. Translated from the French. London: Lutterworth Press, 1961. One of the earliest works to present memorial as a key to both eucharistic theology and ecumenical reconciliation.

Westermann, Claus. *Praise and Lament in the Psalms.* Translated by Keith R. Crim and Richard N. Soulen. Atlanta: John Knox Press, 1981. Though not addressed to the Eucharist, this work is very helpful for insight into the prayer of memory. Its discussion of the relation between keeping memory and historical event is particularly important.

3. *The Eucharistic Prayer*

Bouley, Alan. *From Freedom to Formula: The Evolution of the Eucharistic Prayer from Oral Improvisation to Written Texts.* Washington, D.C.: Catholic University of America Press, 1981. Useful for insight into the development of the prayer before texts were fixed.

Bouyer, Louis. *Eucharist: Theology and Spirituality of the Eucharistic Prayer.* Translated by Charles Underhill Quinn. Notre Dame: Notre Dame University Press, 1968. Despite many studies on particular texts and on the Jewish background to the prayer, this work has not been superseded as a basic history and study of eucharistic texts.

Jasper, R. C. D., and G. J. Cuming. *Prayers of the Eucharist: Early and Reformed.* Texts translated and edited with commentary. 3d ed., revised and enlarged. New York: Pueblo Publishing Company, 1987. Exactly what the title says. A very useful instrument for study for those not familiar with the original languages of the prayers. Gives bibliographies for each prayer. Unfortunately, for the early church it takes no notice of the prayers in the apocryphal writings. It does however include texts from the Reformation era.

Ligier, Louis. "The Origins of the Eucharistic Prayer: From the Last Supper to the Eucharist." *Studia Liturgica* 9 (1973): 161–85. One of the contributions that has left its mark on the study of the prayer, adding particularly to an understanding of its relation to Jewish origins and of the place and purpose of the supper narrative.

Mazza, Enrico. *The Eucharistic Prayers of the Roman Rite.* Translated by Matthew J. O'Connell. New York: Pueblo Publishing Company, 1986. This study of the current texts of the Roman Rite is done in the light of history and with a theological interest. Very helpful not only on the traditional canon of the Mass, but also on the new prayers of the Roman Rite.

Senn, Frank, ed. *New Eucharistic Prayers: An Ecumenical Study of Their Development and Structure.* New York: Paulist Press, 1987. A study on prayers used in churches on the North American continent, it contains valuable historical and theological insights.

Talley, Thomas. "The Eucharistic Prayer of the Ancient Church According to Recent Research: Results and Reflections." *Studia Liturgica* 11 (1976): 138–58.

———. "From *Berakah* to *Eucharistia*: A Reopening Question." *Worship* 50 (1976): 115–37.

———. "The Literary Structure of the Eucharistic Prayer." *Worship* 58 (1984): 404–20. Together Talley's articles constitute a useful survey of literature in various languages, with the author's own judgment on disputed factors.

4. The Eucharistic Theology of Early Christian Centuries

Chapters in Darwell Stone, *A History of the Doctrine of the Holy Eucharist.*

Rordorf, Willy, et al. *The Eucharist of the Early Christians.* Translated by Matthew J. O'Connell. New York: Pueblo Publishing Company, 1978. Essays by various authors on writers of the first three centuries.

Schultz, Hans-Joachim. *The Byzantine Liturgy: Symbolic Structure and Faith Expression.* Translated by Matthew J. O'Connell. English edition introduced and reviewed by Robert J. Taft. New York: Pueblo Publishing Company, 1986. Useful for an understanding of the development of the Byzantine liturgy and for an introduction to Eastern writers on liturgy and Eucharist up to Nicholas Cabasilas.

Sheerin, Daniel J. *The Eucharist*. Message of the Fathers of the Church, vol. 7. Wilmington, Del.: Michael Glazier, 1986. This is a cornucopia of texts in English translation from writers, liturgical works, and hymn collections up to the eighth century (though most are from the first five centuries). The editor adds some bibliographical suggestions for further reading. Since the work is systematically arranged under headings that correspond more to current interest than to early Christianity, it has to be used with care. Its principal advantage is that it makes a selection of texts readily available and may lead a reader to look into some writers more fully.

5. The Eucharistic Theology and Practice of the Western Medieval Church

Chapters in Darwell Stone, *A History of the Doctrine of the Holy Eucharist*.

Bossy, John. "The Mass as a Social Institution, 1200–1700." *Past and Present* 100 (1983): 29–61. Written from the perspective of a sociology of culture, this essay helps to make the late medieval ritual of the Mass comprehensible by placing it in its cultural setting. The article could be read in conjunction with the author's *Christianity in the West 1400–1700* (New York and Oxford: Oxford University Press, 1987).

Macy, Gary. *The Theologies of the Eucharist in the Early Scholastic Period*. Oxford: Clarendon Press, 1984. A helpful survey of early monastic and scholastic theology prior to Thomas Aquinas and Bonaventure. There is no adequate study of the eucharistic theology of these two authors in English.

Mitchell, Nathan. *Cult and Controversy: The Worship of the Eucharist outside Mass*. New York: Pueblo Publishing Company, 1982. The first half of this book is historical. Its focus is on the debates of the eighth and eleventh centuries on eucharistic presence, but it is very helpful in relating theology to practice and devotion. The second half looks at recent official documentation on the cult of the Eucharist outside Mass.

Rubin, Miri. *Corpus Christi. The Eucharist in Late Medieval Culture*. Cambridge and New York: Cambridge University Press, 1991. A study of the development of the feast of Corpus Christi, this work relates it to the range of eucharistic devotion and practice within the cultural setting. Theories of culture are brought to bear upon the topic.

6. The Eucharistic Doctrine of the Council of Trent in Its Relation to the Questions of the Reformation

Lehmann, Karl, and Wolfhart Pannenberg, eds. *The Condemnations of the Reformation Era: Do They Still Divide?* Translated by Margaret Kohl. Minneapolis: Fortress Press, 1990. The essays in this volume, which results from the dialogue between the Roman Catholic Church and the Evangelical Lutheran Church in Germany, give a clear comprehension of the theologies of Calvin,

Luther, and Trent in their historical setting and relate controverted points to current ecumenical convergence.

McCue, James F. "The Doctrine of Transubstantiation from Berengar through Trent: The Point at Issue." *Harvard Theological Review* 61 (1968): 385–430. This article places the position of Trent on transubstantiation within its setting of pre-Reformation theology and Reformation controversy.

Power, David N., *The Sacrifice We Offer: The Tridentine Dogma and Its Reinterpretation*. Edinburgh: T. & T. Clark; New York: Crossroad Publishing Company, 1987. A study of the discussions on sacrifice at the Council of Trent and an interpretation of the doctrine that emerged, putting it in relation to contemporary ecumenical dialogue.

Rahner, Karl. "The Presence of Christ in the Sacrament of the Lord's Supper." *Theological Investigations,* vol. 4. Translated by Kevin Smyth. London: Darton, Longman & Todd Ltd, 1974; New York: Crossroad Publishing Company, 1982, 287–311. A helpful discussion of the doctrine of Trent on the real presence, showing the exact purpose and boundaries of this doctrine.

Schillebeeckx, Edward. *The Eucharist.* Translated by N. D. Smith. New York: Sheed & Ward, 1968. In light of current approaches to real presence and transubstantiation, this work gives a clear presentation of the teaching of the Council of Trent and relates it to scholastic theologies.

7. Contemporary Magisterial Teaching

Congregation of Rites, Instruction *Eucharisticum Mysterium* on worship of the Eucharist, May 25, 1967. Included in *Documents on the Liturgy 1963–1979,* cited below, 395–420. This is the 1967 instruction of the congregation, giving doctrinal and practical directives for the worship of the Eucharist in line with the documents of the Second Vatican Council.

Congregation for Divine Worship, General Instruction of the Roman Missal, *editio typica altera,* March 27, 1975. Included in *Documents on the Liturgy 1963–1979,* cited below, 465–533. As well as practical directives for the celebration of the Eucharist, this gives the doctrinal rationale for the changes in the order of celebration and relates new orientations to traditional Catholic categories.

Documents on the Liturgy 1963–1979: Conciliar, Papal and Curial Texts. Translated and edited by the International Commission on English in the Liturgy. Collegeville, Minn.: Liturgical Press, 1982, 375–707. All the Roman documents on the Eucharist for a vital period of eucharistic development gathered together in English translation.

John Paul II. Apostolic Letter *Dominicae Cenae* about the mystery and worship of the Eucharist, February 1980. *Origins* 9, no. 41 (1980): 653–65. Treats of the Eucharist as mystery, memorial, sacrifice, and sacrament of ecclesial communion and of the roles of the ordained minister and faithful.

Paul VI. Encyclical Letter *Mysterium Fidei* on the doctrine and worship of the Eucharist, September 3, 1965. Included in *Documents on the Liturgy 1963–1979*, cited above, 378–92. The pope takes up the question of Christ's eucharistic presence and of transubstantiation, in light of theological discussions and suggested conceptual alternatives such as transignification.

8. Some Contemporary Theologies

Collins, Mary, and David N. Power, eds. *Can We Always Celebrate the Eucharist? Concilium* 152. Edinburgh: T. & T. Clark, 1982. This issue of the international theological review *Concilium* addresses the question of the frequency of eucharistic celebration, considering it from the points of view of doctrine, history, spirituality, and ritual performance.

Crockett, William R. *Eucharist: Symbol of Transformation.* New York: Pueblo Publishing Company, 1989. An ecumenically oriented Anglican theology, with appeal to what the author sees as key moments in the history of theology.

Heron, Alasdair I. C. *Table and Tradition: Toward an Ecumenical Understanding of the Eucharist.* Philadelphia: Westminster Press, 1983. An ecumenically oriented Calvinist theology, with appeal to what the author sees as key moments in the history of theology.

Powers, Joseph M. *Eucharistic Theology.* New York: Seabury Press, 1967. A survey and assessment of Roman Catholic discussions of the real presence in the 1950s and 1960s.

Rahner, Karl. *Theological Investigations.* Vol. 4, Part Five. Translated by Kevin Smyth. London: Darton, Longman & Todd Ltd., 1974; New York: Crossroad Publishing Company, 1982, 221–320. Containing Rahner's well-known "Theology of the Symbol" and essays on Word and Eucharist and on presence, this is a eucharistic theology done within Rahner's own methodology.

Schillebeeckx, Edward. *The Eucharist.* Translated by N. D. Smith. New York: Sheed & Ward, 1968. An important study of the classical theology of transubstantiation and of the doctrine of the Council of Trent in relation to the issues raised about contemporary theology in the 1965 encyclical of Paul VI *Mysterium Fidei.*

Schmemann, Alexander. *The Eucharist: Sacrament of the Kingdom.* New York: St. Vladimir's Seminary Press, 1988. Posthumously published, this is a rich presentation of Eastern thought on the Eucharist in its relation to church and kingdom.

Seasoltz, Kevin, ed. *Living Bread, Saving Cup.* Collegeville, Minn.: Liturgical Press, 1987. This is a collection of articles on the Eucharist that first appeared in the review *Worship.* They address a number of practical current or controverted issues, such as Mass stipends, concelebration, and celebrations without a priest, as well as doctrinal issues such as transubstantiation/ transignification and sacrifice.

Stevenson, Kenneth. *Eucharist and Offering.* New York: Pueblo Publishing Company, 1986. A valiant effort to resolve the problems inherent in the tradition on eucharistic sacrifice by a historical study of texts, principally liturgical, and the application of some contemporary hermeneutical categories.

9. Ecumenical Conversations

Baptism, Eucharist and Ministry. Faith and Order Paper No. 111. Geneva: WCC, 1982. This has become the major point of reference in continuing ecumenical discussions on the Eucharist and has received many official and unofficial responses from the churches.

Baptism, Eucharist and Ministry 1982–1990. Report on the Process and Responses. Faith and Order Paper No. 149. Geneva: WCC, 1990. This volume summarizes responses to the above document.

Growth in Agreement: Reports and Agreed Statements of Ecumenical Conversations on a World Level. Edited by Harding Meyer and Lukas Vischer. New York: Paulist Press; Geneva: WCC, 1984. This volume contains the major ecumenical statements on the Eucharist after the Second Vatican Council.

Reumann, John. *The Supper of the Lord: The New Testament, Ecumenical Dialogues, and Faith and Order on Eucharist.* Philadelphia: Fortress Press, 1985. This is an excellent discussion of the points of convergence and divergence and of the unresolved issues in current ecumenical conversations on the Eucharist.

Index of Subjects

Index of Names

Note: page references in italics refer to the footnotes.